BEAUTEOUS TRUTH

BEAUTEOUS TRUTH

Faith, Reason, Literature and Culture

By
JOSEPH PEARCE

Foreword by
CARDINAL RAYMOND BURKE

ST. AUGUSTINE'S PRESS
South Bend, Indiana

Manufactured in the United States of America

1 2 3 4 5 6   20 19 18 17 16 15 14

Library of Congress Cataloging in Publication Data
Pearce, Joseph, 1961–
Beauteous Truth: Faith, Reason, Literature and Culture /
By Joseph Pearce; Foreword by Cardinal Raymond Burke.
pages   cm
Includes index.
ISBN 978-1-58731-067-6 (alk. paper)
1. Religion and literature. 2. Religion and culture.
3. Civilization, Western. 4. Faith and reason.
5. Truth in literature. I. Title.
PN49.P38 2013
809'.93382 – dc23   2012039815

∞ The paper used in this publication meets the minimum requirements of the
American National Standard for Information Sciences Permanence of Paper
for Printed Materials, ANSI Z39.481984.

ST. AUGUSTINE'S PRESS
www.staugustine.net

For Leo Patrick and Evangeline Marie

CONTENTS

ACKNOWLEDGMENTS

Many of the essays in this volume were originally published in the *Saint Austin Review*, the Catholic cultural journal of which I am co-editor. The remaining essays were first published in a variety of venues, many of which have long since slipped my memory. These include the *American Spectator*, the *American Conservative*, *First Things*, *Dappled Things*, *Chronicles*, *Our Sunday Visitor*, the *Chesterton Review*, *Catholic World Report*, *This Rock*, *Gilbert* Magazine, and *Red Cultural* (Chile).

FOREWORD

For those, like myself, who have enjoyed and greatly benefitted from reading the essays of Joseph Pearce, published in a variety of venues, especially as editorials in the *Saint Austin Review*, but who have not practically been able to save them in an effective way for future consultation and reflection, the present volume is indeed a great gift. For those who are not familiar with the essays of Joseph Pearce, the volume represents a treasure of the most solid Catholic thought on important aspects of culture, both historical and contemporary, especially as it expresses itself through literature. Joseph Pearce has a remarkable gift of writing about history, literature, and culture in general. His writing is objective and accessible, that is, it shows his steadfast attention to the truth and to language which manifests the same truth in its inherent beauty or natural attractiveness. The fifth essay in this collection, "History Revisited," for instance, is a sterling example of his gift for such writing.

The essays of Joseph Pearce reveal his profound understanding of reason and faith, of classical realist philosophy and Catholic doctrine, which permits him to write about history, literature, and culture in general with an unfailing attention to the objective reality of God and of His earthly creation, that is, of man and of the world. I refer, for instance, to the fourth essay in the collection, "Fides et Ratio: Faith and Philosophy." As Pearce learned from his mentor, G. K. Chesterton, Catholic doctrine is not some confessional or sectarian ideology but an unbroken enunciation of unchanging truth in every time, even as Catholic worship, God's most wonderful gift to man and the highest and most perfect expression of religion, reflects the incomparable beauty of the truth. In the same way, Catholic moral teaching and discipline safeguards and fosters the living of the truth in every attitude, word and action. Pearce's frequent references to Catholic faith, worship and practice give testimony, in a remarkable way, to the freedom and peace which knowing and living the Catholic faith bring even in the most difficult and challenging times of life. I think, for example, of his essay on J. R. R. Tolkien, "The Catholic Genius of J. R. R. Tolkien."

The title of this collection of his essays is most apt, for each of the sev-enty-seven essays contained in the collection, as well as the collection as a whole, seeks to express the truth in a way which reflects at the same time its connatural beauty and goodness. What is manifest in the essays collect-ed herein is clearly also manifest in the numerous biographies and literary studies written by Pearce, and in his recent autobiographical volume, *Race with the Devil: My Journey from Racial Hatred to Rational Love*.[1] Thus, the present volume is an important complement of Pearce's already impres-sive literary corpus. In that sense, I hope that, in time, his future essays will also be collected in such a volume.

In the present collection, Pearce not only makes easily accessible a good number of his essays, but he has carefully ordered their presentation to help the reader to enter as deeply as possible into the subjects he treats and to understand as much as possible the essential relationship of the var-ious subjects to one another. Part One, "Defining Our Terms," contains the essays which treat directly the philosophical and theological principles which are the key to the understanding of Pearce's presentation of the his-tory of literature (Part Two, "Celebrating Our Heritage"), of various forms of literature (Part Three, "Literary Landscapes"), of individual authors (Part Four, "Literary Portraits"), and of his own life as an author (Part Five, "Self-Portraits"). In short, his essays in Parts Two, Three, Four, and Five provide rich examples of the convergence of truth with goodness and beau-ty, which he illustrates by means of his essays in Part One. In fact, as he sagely observes, in a world which has turned its back on objective truth and no longer knows the difference between what is good and what is evil, it is often beauty with its ineluctable attractiveness which reaches the most hardened heart, inspiring the humble gratitude which slowly opens the heart to know truth and to pursue goodness. I refer especially to the first essay of the collection, "Beauty is Truth: Faith and Aesthetics."

As one enters into the subjects presented by Pearce, he becomes aware not only that Pearce knows well the works of great writers but that his imagination and even his writing style have been influenced by them. One notes frequent references to the modern world in terms of images and char-acters in Dante's *Divine Comedy* or in Tolkien's *Lord of the Rings*. Pearce has also imbibed something of G. K. Chesterton's playful way of using paradoxes to present familiar realities in a new light. His own writing thus

1   Cf. Joseph Pearce, *Race with the Devil: My Journey from Racial Hatred to Rational Love* (Charlotte, NC: Saint Benedict Press, 2013).

conveys in a vivid way the truths which he illuminates in the authors whom he studies.

Ultimately, the essays of Pearce reflect the profound conversion of mind and heart which he underwent in his youth and which has become for him, as it must for every Christian, his way of life. It is the daily carrying of the cross with Christ which leads the Christian ever more into the truth and prepares him for the contemplation of the fullness of the truth in the Kingdom of Heaven, which is aptly called the Beatific Vision.[2] It is the conversion of the mind and heart from a self-centered, empty and violent life to a life centered upon God and neighbor, and, therefore, always richer in appreciation of the mystery of human life made in God's own image and likeness for the sake of sharing in God's faithful, enduring, and life-giving love. It is the daily turning to Christ Who alone is man's salvation, Who alone gives to man the grace to live the truth in love. I refer, in particular, to essay 76, "Race with the Devil: A Journey from the Hell of Hatred to the Well of Mercy," and essay 77, "Hope is the Sweetness of Our Life."

The human conscience, the faculty of the soul upon which God has written His life-giving and love-giving law, inspires this conversion and sustains it daily, for it is indeed the intimate voice of God leading us in the way of lasting freedom and peace for which He has created us. From the moment of the Creation, God the Creator has written His law upon every human heart, and by the Redemptive Incarnation, by taking for Himself a human heart and filling it with His divine love, God the Redeemer has illumined the law in the most wonderful manner possible. Thus, every human heart finds its rest solely in the Heart of Jesus, God the Son made man, as Saint Augustine declared in his *Confessions*: "When spirits slide away from you they are stripped of their vesture of light and exposed in their native darkness, and then their unhappy restlessness amply proves to us how noble is each rational creature you have made, for nothing less than yourself can suffice to give it any measure of blessed rest, nor indeed can it be its own satisfaction."[3]

Saint Paul teaches us in the Letter to the Romans that God speaks the truth to us by means of our conscience. He speaks to us the truth which alone produces the goodness of pure and selfless love in our lives, the

2   Cf. Mt 10:37–39 and 16:24–25; Mk 8:34–35; Lk 9:23–24 and 14:27.
3   Saint Augustine of Hippo, *The Confessions*, tr. Maria Boulding, O.S.B. (Hyde Park, NY: New City Press, 1997), XIII, 9.

goodness which is the most beautiful reality in the world, the goodness which all of culture, including literature, seeks to ponder and reflect. Reflecting upon the fact that even those who have not yet received the gift of faith know what is right and what is wrong, Saint Paul declared: "They show that what the law requires is written on their hearts, while their conscience also bears witness and their conflicting thoughts accuse or perhaps excuse them on that day when, according to my gospel, God judges the secrets of men by Christ Jesus."[4]

Sadly, in our day, many have lost the sense of the objectivity of conscience, that ultimate objectivity which has its font in the Lord of Heaven and Earth. As a context in which to appreciate more deeply the truth and beauty of the philosophical and theological riches contained in the essays of Joseph Pearce, I propose a brief reflection on the notion of conscience, inspired by Pope Benedict XVI's 2010 Christmas Address to the Roman Curia. A significant part of this Christmas Address is devoted to a reflection upon the three conversions of the saintly countryman of Joseph Pearce, Blessed John Henry Cardinal Newman, whom Benedict XVI had declared blessed during his Apostolic visit to Great Britain in September of 2010. In an interview given at the time, "Newman's Beatification" (essay 39), Pearce reflects on the influence of Blessed Cardinal Newman in his life. Reflections on Blessed Cardinal Newman are also found in essay 25, "The Victorian Age," and essay 38, "Newman, Manning, and Their Age."

In the 2010 Christmas Address, Pope Benedict XVI concentrated his attention on the first conversion, the conversion "to faith in the living God."[5] Until his first conversion, Newman shared the thinking "of the average men of his time and indeed of the average men of today."[6] According to this way of thinking, men consider the existence of God "as something uncertain, something with no essential role to play in their lives."[7] Regarding Newman before his first conversion, Benedict XVI

4   Rm 2:15–16.
5   ". . . alla fede nel Dio vivente." Benedictus PP. XVI, Allocutio "Omina Nativitatis novique Anni Curiae Romanae significantur," 20 Decembris 2010, *Acta Apostolicae Sedis* 103 (2011), 39. [Hereafter, Alloc2010] English translation: *L'Osservatore Romano*, weekly edition in English, 22–29 December, 14. [Hereafter, Alloc2010Eng]
6   ". . . la media degli uomini del suo tempo e come la media degli uomini anche di oggi, . . ." Alloc2010, 39. English translation: Alloc2010Eng, 14.
7   ". . . come qualcosa di insicuro, che non ha nessun ruolo essenziale nella propria vita." Alloc2010, 39. English translation: Alloc2010Eng, 14.

observed: "What appeared genuinely real to him, as to the men of his and our day, is the empirical, matter that can be grasped."[8] By means of his conversion, "Newman recognized that it is exactly the other way round: that God and the soul, man's spiritual identity, constitute what is genuinely real, what counts."[9]

But how did Newman receive the grace of conversion? As Benedict XVI explained: "The driving force that impelled Newman along the path of conversion was conscience."[10] Benedict XVI, profoundly aware of the contemporary confusion about conscience, which has its roots in the so-called Enlightenment and the contemporary Nihilism and Deconstructionism which are its ultimate fruit, rightly asked the further question about the meaning of conscience. To answer this question, he first described the contemporary confusion regarding conscience:

In modern thinking, the word "conscience" signifies that for moral and religious questions, it is the subjective dimension, the individual, that constitutes the final authority for decision. The world is divided into the realms of the objective and the subjective. To the objective realm belong things that can be calculated and verified by experiment. Religion and morals fall outside the scope of these methods and are therefore considered to lie within the subjective realm. Here, it is said, there are in the final analysis no objective criteria. The ultimate instance that can decide here is therefore the subject alone and precisely this is what the word "conscience" expresses: in this realm only the individual, with his intuitions and experiences, can decide.[11]

8   "Veramente reale appariva a lui, come agli uomini del suo e del nostro tempo, l'empirico, ciò che è materialmente afferrabile." Alloc2010, 39. English translation: Alloc2010Eng, 14.
9   ". . . Newman riconosce che le cose stanno proprio al contrario: che Dio e l'anima, l'essere se stesso dell'uomo a livello spirituale, costituiscono ciò che è veramente reale, ciò che conta." Alloc2010, 39. English translation: Alloc2010Eng, 14.
10 "La forza motrice che spingeva sul cammino della conversione era in Newman la coscienza." Alloc2010, 39. English translation: Alloc2010Eng, 14.
11 "Nel pensiero moderno, la parola «coscienza» significa che in materia di morale e di religione, la dimensione soggettiva, l'individuo, costituisce l'ultima istanza della decisione. Il mondo viene diviso negli ambiti dell'oggettivo e del soggettivo. All'oggettivo appartengono le cose che si possono calcolare e verificare mediante l'esperimento. La religione e la morale sono sottratte a questi metodi e perciò sono

The Pope's description uncovers the total contradiction between the reality of conscience as the voice of God and the modern concept of conscience. Practically, living in a culture profoundly confused about conscience, we recognize how the modern notion of conscience, instead of leading one into truth revealed by reason and faith, and into the incomparable beauty of pure and selfless love, leads man into a self-centered isolation by which he justifies attitudes, words and actions which violate his own nature and the inviolable dignity of the other.

Benedict XVI then described Blessed Newman's understanding of conscience, in accord with the unbroken tradition of Catholic thinking. He declared:

> Newman's understanding of conscience is diametrically opposed to this [modern thinking]. For him, "conscience" means man's capacity for truth: the capacity to recognize precisely in the decision-making areas of his life — religions and morals — a truth, *the* truth. At the same time, conscience is both capacity for truth and obedience to the truth which manifests itself to anyone who seeks it with an open heart. The path of Newman's conversions is a path of conscience — not a path of self-asserting subjectivity but, on the contrary, a path of obedience to the truth that was gradually opening up to him.[12]

Benedict XVI then confronts a contradictory situation regarding Newman and conscience, namely, the claim of some that in fact Newman held a

considerate come ambito del soggettivo. Qui non esisterebbero, in ultima analisi, dei criteri oggettivi. L'ultima istanza che qui può decidere sarebbe pertanto solo il soggetto, e con la parola «coscienza» si esprime, appunto, questo: in questo ambito può decidere solo il singolo, l'individuo con le sue intuizioni ed esperienze." Alloc2010, 39–40. English translation: Alloc2010, 14.

12 "La concezione che Newman ha della coscienza è diametralmente opposta. Per lui «coscienza» significa la capacità di verità dell'uomo: la capacità di riconoscere proprio negli ambiti decisivi della sua esistenza – religione e morale – una verità, *la* verità. La coscienza, la capacità dell'uomo di riconoscere la verità, gli impone con ciò, al tempo stesso, il dovere di incamminarsi verso la verità, di cercarla e di sottomettersi ad essa laddove la incontra. Coscienza è capacità di verità e obbedienza nei confronti della verità, che si mostra all'uomo che cerca col cuore aperto. Il cammino delle conversioni di Newman è un cammino della coscienza – un cammino non della soggettività che si afferma, ma, proprio al contrario, dell'obbedienza verso la verità che passo passo si apriva a lui." Alloc2010, 40. English translation: Alloc2010Eng, 14.

completely subjective notion of conscience, quoting his statement in the Letter to the Duke of Norfolk "in which he said — should he have to propose a toast — that he would drink first to conscience and then to the Pope."[13]

In truth, however, for Newman, as Benedict XVI pointed out, the primacy of conscience is not based upon "the binding quality of some subjective intuition"[14] but on "the accessibility and the binding force of truth."[15] It is the conscience, the voice of God speaking to our souls, which is, in Newman's words, "the aboriginal Vicar of Christ."[16] As such, the conscience is ever attuned to Christ Himself Who instructs and informs it through His Vicar, the Roman Pontiff, and the Bishops in communion with him. The Blessed Cardinal Newman observed that conscience "is a messenger of Him, who, both in nature and in grace, speaks to us behind a veil, and teaches and rules us by His representatives."[17] Thus Benedict XVI concludes his brief reflection on conscience in the thought of Blessed Cardinal Newman:

> It is an expression of the accessibility and the binding force of truth: on this its primacy is based. The second toast then can be dedicated to the Pope because it is his task to demand obedience to the truth.[18]

One sees how conscience, informed by the truth revealed by reason and faith, enables the individual to see and respond to himself, to others, and to the world, in accord with the mind and heart of Christ, God Incarnate.

---

13 ". . . alla sua parola secondo cui egli – nel caso avesse dovuto fare un brindisi – avrebbe brindato prima alla coscienza e poi al Papa." Alloc2010, 40. English translation, Alloc2010Eng, 14.

14 ". . . l'ultima obbligatorietà dell'intuizione soggettiva." Alloc2010, 40. English translation: Alloc2010Eng, 14.

15 ". . . dell'accessibilità e della forza vincolante della verità . . ." Alloc2010, 40. English translation: Alloc2010Eng, 14.

16 John Henry Cardinal Newman, "A Letter Addressed to His Grace the Duke of Norfolk on Occasion of Mr. Gladstone's Recent Expostulation," 27 December 1874, in *Certain Difficulties Felt by Anglicans in Catholic Teaching II* (London: Longmans, Green, and Co., 1900), p. 248.

17 *Ibid.*, p. 248.

18 "È espressione dell'accessibilità e della forza vincolante della verità: in ciò si fonda il suo primato. Al Papa può essere dedicato il secondo brindisi, perché è compito suo esigere l'obbedienza nei confronti della verità." Alloc2010, 40–41. English translation: Alloc2010Eng, 14.

The irreplaceable service of conscience in the daily conversion of mind and heart to Christ is essentially related to the transformation of society. Pope Benedict XVI provided an extraordinary reflection on the place of reason and faith in the transformation of society in his address at Westminster Hall in London on September 17, 2010, during his Apostolic Visit to the United Kingdom,[19] and in his address at the Bundestag in Berlin on September 22, 2011, during his Apostolic Visit to Germany.[20] In the latter, having reflected upon the meaning of conscience as a "listening heart," the gift which King Solomon requested from God at the beginning of his reign, Benedict XVI urged us to practice "an ecology of man," declaring:

> Man too has a nature that he must respect and that he cannot manipulate at will. Man is not merely self-creating freedom. Man does not create himself. He is intellect and will, but he is also nature, and his will is rightly ordered if he respects his nature, listens to it and accepts himself for who he is, as one who did not create himself. In this way, and in no other, is true human freedom fulfilled.[21]

Only by the cultivation of a rightly-formed conscience can a society serve the common good and develop in the way of freedom and peace.

Several of Pearce's essays reflect upon the state of society in England and in the United States. I think of "What is England" (essay 10), "American Faith and Culture" (essay 12), "Catholic Social Thought and

19 Cf. Benedictus PP. XVI, Allocutio, "Iter Apostolicum Summi Pontificis in Regnum Unitum: Londinii in Aula Vestmonasteriensi colloquium Benedicti XVI cum primoribus Societatis Civilis; cum doctis viris culturae, scientiis et operum conductioni deditis; cum Corpore Legatorum et Religiosis Auctoritatibus," 17 Septembris 2010, *Acta Apostolicae Sedis* 102 (2010), 635–639, especially 636–638.

20 Cf. Benedictus PP. XVI, Allocutio, "Iter Apostolicum in Germaniam: ad Berolinensem foederatum coetum oratorum," 22 Septembris 2011, *Acta Apostolicae Sedis* 103 (2011) 663–669, especially 667–669.

21 "Auch der Mensch hat eine Natur, die er achten muß und die er nicht beliebig manipulieren kann. Der Mensch ist nicht nur sich selbst machende Freiheit. Der Mensch macht sich nicht selbst. Er is Geist und Wille, aber er ist auch Natur, und sein Wille ist dann recht, wenn er auf die Natur achtet, sie hört und sich annimmt als der, der er ist und der sich nicht selbst gemacht hat. Gerade so und nur so vollzieht sich wahre menschliche Freiheit." Ibid., 668. English translation: *L'Osservatore Romano*, weekly edition in English, 28 September 2011, p. 7.

Literature" (essay 28), "English Roads to Rome" (essay 29), and "Home Thoughts from Abroad" (essay 75). Pearce expresses in a clear and attractive way the need of what Benedict XVI called "an ecology of man," the fundamental need of respect for the order which God has placed in Creation and restored by the Redemptive Incarnation.

It is my hope that setting the whole of Joseph Pearce's essays within the context of this reflection on conscience helps to open up to the reader the clear and rich philosophical and theological thought articulated in them. In reading the essays, the reader will be led to reflect with Pearce on so many important aspects of life and faith, of history and culture, which I have not been able to note. I think, for instance, of Pearce's treatment of the ordained priesthood in essay 19, "The Priest's Hole," in essay 30, "Literary Priests," and in essay 31, "*In Persona Christi*: The Priest in Modern Fiction," and of the Blessed Virgin Mary, Mother of Divine Grace, in essay 77, "Hope Is the Sweetness of Our Life." Pearce's essays remain a treasure of philosophical and theological reflections to be mined by the thoughtful reader.

In closing, I express deepest gratitude to Joseph Pearce for bringing together and ordering his essays, in order that they may be easily accessible both to those of us who are already familiar with them and to those who have not yet come to know them. Most of all, I express the gratitude of his readers for his highly-qualified and tireless pursuit of the truth revealed to the heart of man by reason and by faith as it is manifest in the beautiful and the good. It is my hope that his pursuit may inspire the same pursuit in the reader, who, attracted by the beauty of the truth, will be ever more disposed to follow the truth by what is most beautiful of all, a good and holy life.

Raymond Leo Cardinal BURKE
Prefect of the Supreme Tribunal of the Apostolic Signatura
7 October 2013 – Memorial of Our Lady of the Rosary

PART ONE
DEFINING OUR TERMS

1. BEAUTY IS TRUTH: FAITH AND AESTHETICS

"Beauty is truth, truth beauty,— that is all
Ye know on earth, and all ye need to know . . ."
— John Keats (Ode on a Grecian Urn)

John Keats's pithy praise of beauty is both beautiful and elusive. It beguiles us; it seduces us; but does it satisfy us? Is it a satisfactory explanation of the relationship between the beautiful and the true? Doesn't it beg more questions than it answers? If beauty is truth, what is truth; if truth is beautiful, what is beauty? These are questions that have animated the greatest philosophers since the time of Plato and Aristotle.

For the Greeks, and for Augustine and Thomas Aquinas, the good, the true, and the beautiful are inextricably entwined. And, for the Christian, they are not only entwined but ultimately are one and the same thing: they are the Thing that is Christ.

Jesus Christ is the answer to Pilate's perennial question: *quid est veritas?* It is Christ Himself who is truth. And it is Christ who is also beauty and goodness. Christ is the very incarnation of the good, the true and the beautiful. He is these three things rolled into one. Truth is, therefore, trinitarian. It is one with the good and the beautiful.

Since, properly understood, they are synonymous with Christ, it can be seen that the good, the true and the beautiful are the ends for which we strive. They are, however, also the means by which we attain the end. Christ is not merely the truth and the life, he is the way. He is not only the end, He is the means. All that is good, all that is true and all that is beautiful have their source in Christ and lead us to Him. This is true beauty, but it is a beauty and truth that is unseen by the scribes, pharisees and hypocrites who have always sought to crucify the beautiful and the true on the altar of self-idolatry. For such as these, the purpose of the cross is to highlight cross-purposes, in the sense that those blinded by pride can see only the meaningless contradiction and not the meaningful paradox. They ask Pilate's question not for the purposes of finding an answer, nor in the Socratic sense of seeking to prompt further questions, but merely as a means of affirming that there is no answer. For deconstructed man, Pilate's question is purely rhetorical because there is nothing but rhetoric. Words are toys with which we persuade ourselves that nothing is persuasive.

Deconstructed man is also disintegrated man. He fails to see the integration of goodness, truth and beauty, and thereby condemns himself to a segregated cosmos in which sin is good, ugliness is beautiful, and truth is a lie. This is the fragmentation that leads to madness. It is literally the explosion of truth into disintegrating pieces.

The challenge of integrating our segregated culture has been central to the mission of the Church down the centuries. From the early heresies and the early modern monstrosities of Machiavelli, to the more modern errors of Marx and Mammon, the Catholic Church has been combating error from her very beginning. For two thousand years, she has continued to speak universally and univocally against the self-deification that leads to self-destruction. With her infallible wisdom she uses the dynamism of orthodoxy to defuse the truth-exploding dynamite of heresy.

This ancient and venerable office of the Church was evident in November 2008 in a public event sponsored by the Pontifical Academy of Fine Arts and Literature on the theme, "the universality of beauty: a comparison between aesthetics and ethics." Pope Benedict, in a message to those gathering at this convocation, stressed the "urgent need for a renewed dialogue between aesthetics and ethics, between beauty, truth and goodness." The Holy Father lamented the "dramatically-evident split" between the pursuit of the external trappings of beauty and the idea of a beauty rooted in truth and goodness: "Indeed, searching for a beauty that is foreign to or separate from the human search for truth and goodness would become (as unfortunately happens) mere aestheticism and, especially for the very young, a path leading to ephemeral values and to banal and superficial appearances, even a flight into an artificial paradise that masks inner emptiness."

Reiterating the necessity of contemporary culture to rediscover the integration of beauty, truth and goodness, the Pope stressed that the commitment to recover and rediscover this philosophical integrity was even more important for Christians: "And if such a commitment applies to everyone, it applies even more to believers, to the disciples of Christ, who are called by the Lord to 'give reasons' for all the beauty and truth of their faith."

Invoking the wisdom of his predecessor, the Holy Father referred to John Paul II's *Letter to Artists*, "which invites us to reflect upon . . . the fruitful dialogue between Holy Scripture and various forms of art, whence countless masterpieces have emerged." When Christians create works that "render glory unto the Father," Pope Benedict asserted, they speak of the "goodness and profound truth" that they are portraying, as well as the integrity and sanctity of the artist or author. Knowing how to "read and scrutinize the beauty of works of art inspired by the faith" can lead Christians to a "unique path that brings us close to God and His Word." This path was itself a means to evangelize the wider culture through the power of beauty and, as such, the Pope urged believers to learn how to "communicate with the language of images and symbols . . . in order effectively to reach our contemporaries."

With his customary eloquence and sagacity, the Holy Father has provided the truth that elevates Keats's poetic epigram to a level beyond mere banality. In an age of rational illiteracy, in which deconstructed man has turned his back contemptuously on truth, the power of beauty still speaks in colours beyond words and thoughts. In an age in which love and goodness have been narcissistically inverted so that all love and goodness are about "me" and not the "other"; an age in which the self-sacrificial heart of true love has been removed and replaced by egocentric counterfeit "loves"; in such an age, beauty still pulsates with healthier passions and nobler desires.

Even an age that can't think or love, can still be touched by beauty. A sunrise still speaks to the most hardened hearts and arouses feelings of inarticulate gratitude. And gratitude is full of grace, arousing the desire to say "thank you" to someone. Such gratitude is the birth of humility in proud hearts, the birth-pangs of which will break the heart itself.

The proud heart must be broken in order that it might be healed. For, as Oscar Wilde knew all too well, it is only through a broken heart that Lord Christ may enter in. Oh, may His beauty break our hearts, so that we may know Him truly and so that we may taste and see that He is good. In the name of the Good, the True and the Beautiful. Amen.

2. TOWARDS A DEFINITION OF CULTURE

In my confused, impetuous and misspent youth I believed, with the arrogance of ignorance, that I knew the answers to all the most important questions in life. The world's problems could be solved politically and economically. All that was needed were the right policies, and the right government to put the policies into practice. It was all so simple. All so easy. The biggest problem was convincing the older people how simple it all was. It was a pity, in fact, that old people were so stupid. Such were the thoughts of my thoughtless youth.

And as for culture, who cared about culture anyway? At best it was fun, like listening to the latest rock band, or watching one's favourite football team; at worst it was a needless distraction from the real issues, which were political and economic. And religion? What a waste of time that was. Religion was utterly irrelevant. It had no connection to the real world or the real issues.

How wrong I was. How wrong and how lost.

There was one older person in my youth whom I took seriously, largely, I'm sure, because his prejudices reflected mine. He was not, in fact, very old. He was in his thirties. But as a teenager "old" begins at twenty-five! He was something of a mentor and I remember that he would often begin a discussion with an insistence that we "define our terms." If we were discussing capitalism, or communism, or free trade, or the free market, or private property, he would always begin by asking me to define what I meant by these things. He would also ask probing questions such as whether private enterprise and free enterprise were the same thing. Although I was sometimes irritated by this somewhat stolid approach to debate, I realize now that he was teaching me how to think. He was taking me, slowly but surely, from mere derivatives, such as politics and economics, to an appreciation of the important things, such as philosophy and, eventually, theology. As such, I remain very much in his debt, intellectually speaking.

I would like to take my former mentor's approach to our discussion of culture. What *is* culture? What *isn't* culture? As a word it is too lightly used and too often abused. As a living thing it is too often taken for granted and all too often not fully appreciated for what it is. It is, therefore, time that we looked at culture with a clarity of vision that is often absent. In short, it is time to define our terms.

First, we can say that culture is *human* (and ultimately divine). It does not belong to, or come forth from, other animate creatures. There is no canine culture; no civilization of chimpanzees; no planet of the apes. Only people make music, write poetry, build cathedrals or paint pictures. For a Christian, the fact that something is peculiarly human marks it as a sign that man, unlike the animals, is made in the image of God. Culture is, therefore, a mark of God's image in us. But what sort of mark is it? It is a *creative* mark. Culture is *creative*. It is the art of *making*. It is the image of the Creator's creativity in his creatures. Our imagination is the image of God's Imagination in us. There is, therefore, something both human and divine in the creativity that creates culture. It is the gift of the Giver finding creative expression in the personhood of the gifted. On a mystical level one can see an image of both the Trinity and the Incarnation in this primal truth of culture. The Trinity is the eternal expression of Divine Vitality, the source of all Creativity, and the Incarnation is the eternal and temporal giving of this Divine Vitality, this Primal Gift, in the Created humanity of Christ, to mankind. On the deepest level, the Trinity and the Incarnation are the Archetypes of all culture. They are the source from which all culture springs, and they are the end which all properly ordered culture serves.

This is so essentially true that it has been recognized implicitly by the pagans of antiquity and even by the atheists of modernity, by those who believed in many gods and by those who believed in no God at all. Homer and Virgil began their epics by invoking their Muse, the goddess of creativity, to pour forth her gifts into them so that they might tell their tales with truth and beauty. Even Shelley, the avowed atheist, is forced to speak of the creative gift in mystical language. In *A Defense of Poetry* he writes:

> Poetry is not like reasoning, a power to be exerted according to the determination of the will. A man cannot say, "I will compose poetry." The greatest poet even cannot say it; for the mind in creation is as a fading coal which some invisible influence, like an inconstant wind, awakens to transitory brightness; this power arises from within, like the color of a flower which fades and changes as it is developed, and the conscious portions of our natures are unprophetic either of its approach or its

departure. Could this influence be durable in its original purity and force, it is impossible to predict the greatness of the results; but when composition begins, inspiration is already on the decline, and the most glorious poetry that has ever been communicated to the world is probably a feeble shadow of the original conceptions of the poet.

The remarkable thing about these words of Shelley, an atheist musing about his Muse, is the fact that, in the final sentence quoted above, he agrees with the memorable lines of T. S. Eliot, in "The Hollow Men," that "between the potency and the existence falls the shadow." For Eliot, a Christian, the falling of the shadow is itself the Shadow of the Fall; but even for Shelley, who seems to have disbelieved in the Fall and who sympathized with Milton's Satan, the shadow still exists. There is, therefore, an amazing, and ironically amusing, convergence between the pagans, the Christians and the atheists over the mystical nature of the creative gift. The gift itself is pure and spiritual, not merely for the pagan and the Christian but for the atheist also. Shelley calls the creative Muse or gift a "spirit of good" of which (or to whom) the poet is a mere minister.

At this point one can see the emergence of obvious objections spawning awkward questions. If creativity is a gift from God why does He permit atheists such as Shelley, or willful liars like Dan Brown, to abuse the gift? Worse, why does He permit awful manifestations of low culture, such as the gyrating inanities posing as music on MTV, or the obscenities and blasphemies of much modern art, or all the other manifestations of our pornocratic zeitgeist? Furthermore, can this effluent from the spiritual sewage of man's blackened soul be called "culture"? And, if so, does culture *per se* have any meaningful value? In response, we should point out that God does not remove a gift the moment it is abused. Take the gift of life, for instance. If He removed the gift of life the moment we sinned none of us would have reached puberty! As with life, so with love. The gift of love is not removed merely because many of us abuse it selfishly or lasciviously. Indeed, if the gift of love were removed the moment it was abused our first loves would have been our last! As with life and love, so with freedom. God gave us our freedom and He doesn't remove it the moment we abuse it. He even leaves us free to go to Hell, should we wish. And as with life, love and freedom, so with creativity. He gives us our talents, leaving us free to use them, abuse them or bury them as we will. He gives us our creative pearls and He lets us keep them, even if we cast them before swine.

But what of the meaning of culture? Is bad art still culture? If so, what's so special about culture? These are good questions and they are best answered with other questions. What is the meaning of man? Is a sinner still a man? If so, what's so special about man? Man is special because he's made in the image of God. A bad man is still made in the image of God, though the image is broken. Similarly creativity is special because it is a mark of the image of God in man, and culture is special because it is the mark of God's creative image in human society or, at its highest, in Christian civilisation. Bad culture still bears the mark of God's image, though it is an image distorted and broken by abuse or sin. Good culture, like a good man, must truly reflect the goodness of its Creator. Men are called to be saints and culture is called to be saintly. We need to convert the culture in the same way that we need to convert the man. Culture, like man, must repent. It must be reoriented. It must be turned again towards its source, the Giver of light and life, and the fountainhead of all Beauty.

3. FAITH AND POPULAR CULTURE

A barrel-organ in the street suddenly sprang with a jerk into a jovial tune.
Syme stood up taut, as if it had been a bugle before the battle. He found him-
self filled with a supernatural courage that came from nowhere. The jingling
music seemed full of the vivacity, the vulgarity, and the irrational valour of
the poor, who in all those unclean streets were all clinging to the decencies
and the charities of Christendom.
— G. K. Chesterton (The Man Who Was Thursday)

Chesterton is seldom wrong. In fact, he is so seldom wrong that it is normally the height of folly to even contemplate contradicting him. And yet his
ceaseless championing of the healthy "vulgarity" of the poor is sometimes
hard to swallow. Although such praise of the "vulgar" was due in part to a
healthy Dickensian (and Christian) love for the common man, it was also
due to a less than healthy attachment to the cause of the French Revolution.
This naïveté found expression in another Chestertonian aphorism in which
he tells us that evolution is what happens when everyone is asleep but revolution is what happens when everyone is awake. One wonders in what way
the mindless mobs of Paris or Moscow can be said to have been "awake,"
unless wakefulness is seen as being synonymous with madness.

Pace Chesterton, it is clearly necessary to draw a distinction between
the healthy "popular culture" of the *rooted* common man, and the inane
"pop culture" of the *rootless* masses. Those with roots *evolve*; those without roots *revolve* or *revolt*. Chesterton understood this, of course, though
he sometimes seems to have forgotten it in his haste to champion the poor
against the rich. It was, after all, Chesterton who warned that the "coming
peril" was not "bolshevism" but was "standardization by a low standard,"
or, to use our ugly modern vernacular, the coming peril is the "dumbing
down" of culture. And let's not forget that the "vulgarity" of which
Chesterton (or Syme) was speaking in *The Man Who Was Thursday* was
"clinging to the decencies and the charities of Christendom."

It can be seen, therefore, that healthy popular culture is *rooted*, it *clings*. It is rooted in the decencies and charities of Christendom. This fundamental truth was grasped with refreshing gusto in the recently released song, "Roots," by the Devonshire folk group, Show of Hands:

> *A minister said his vision of hell*
> *Was three folk singers in a pub near Wells;*
> *Well, I've got a vision of urban sprawl,*
> *It's pubs where no-one ever sings at all,*
> *And everyone stares at a great big screen,*
> *Overpaid soccer stars, prancing teens,*
> *Australian soaps, American rap,*
> *Estuary English, baseball caps . . .*
> *Without our stories or our songs,*
> *How will we know where we've come from?*
> *I've lost St George in the Union Jack,*
> *It's my flag too and I want it back.*
> *Seed, bud, flower, fruit,*
> *Never gonna grow without their roots,*
> *Branch, stem, shoots— We need roots.*

This is true popular culture at its best. It is reminiscent of the rootedness of Tolkien's Treebeard, a courageous and indomitable rootedness which curses the vulgarity of the rootless orcs and the evil powers that they serve. It is the folk culture of the Shire, not the "pop culture" of Isengard or Mordor.

It is appropriate that this short perambulation on the subject of faith and popular culture should have wended its way to Tolkien. *The Lord of the Rings* is the apotheosis of literary folk culture. It unites high and popular culture, fusing the loftiest heights of literary achievement with the lowly accessibility of the popular novel. Furthermore, and if the aforementioned were not enough, the fusion of high and popular culture is achieved through the infusion of faith. *The Lord of the Rings* is the very incarnation of faith and popular culture!

Let's conclude, therefore, by judging popular culture from the loftily low vantage point of the Shire. If it fits in the Shire it passes the culture test; if it doesn't fit in the Shire it fails the test and is consequently consigned to the anti-cultural wastelands of pop vulgarity.

Folk music fits in the Shire, as does folk dancing. Morris dancers are honorary hobbits, break dancers are not! Some country music fits comfortably in the Shire, offering its homegrown morality expressed with

Chestertonian wordplay and paradox, whereas other modern manifestations of country music are fit only for Isengard! Real ale, brewed by micro-breweries, is fit for hobbits to imbibe to their hearts' content; Bud-Lite and other mass-produced examples of chemical fizz posing as beer are fit for nothing but orc-swill. And, needless to say, there is no room in the Shire for MTV, so-called "reality" TV, pornography, gadget-worship and other products of the maggot-folk of Mordor.

And as for the place of faith in the Shire, Tolkien knew that those with roots will cling to the faith of their fathers. Orcs, on the other hand, are faithless because they are fatherless. Branch, stem, shoots—we need roots!

4. *FIDES ET RATIO:*
FAITH AND PHILOSOPHY

One of modernity's many misperceptions is that Christianity is irrational. It is somehow assumed by moderns that the beliefs of Christians, or even the more generic belief in God, are somehow superstitious and that such beliefs fly in the face of "reason." This prejudiced presumption, rooted in ignorance, enables the moderns to avoid thinking about questions of faith. It also allows the moderns to presume that Christians and their beliefs can be safely ignored and marginalized. This is decidedly odd for, as Chesterton reminds us, the Catholic Church is the "one continuous intelligent institution that has been thinking about thinking for two thousand years."

Let's pause for a moment so that we can fully appreciate the enormity of Chesterton's statement. The Catholic Church has been thinking about thinking for two thousand years. Shouldn't this cause the modern to at least pause for thought?

The problem is that the modern seldom pauses and hardly ever thinks. He's too busy and too thoughtless to concern himself with such things. Needless to say, however, that his thoughtlessness will not deter him from reiterating his judgment. He can still say, in passing, and in haste, that he doesn't have time for "religion" or "Christianity" because such irrational nonsense is, well, a waste of time.

It would be a waste of time asking the modern to explain himself because he would no doubt feel that he had said nothing requiring an explanation. Let's insist nonetheless on some clarification. What, for example, does he mean by something being "irrational"? What exactly does he mean by "reason"? And while we're trying to get him to define his terms we might also ask him what he means by time. Does he know what he's wasting? He might be intrigued to learn that time is much more than something that merely passes, whether we waste it or not. It is not merely a matter of history but mystery. He might also be surprised to discover that "reason," like time, is also a mysterious matter, in the sense that reason leads us to the unavoidable acceptance of mystery. In short, and to paraphrase Hamlet, there are more things in heaven and earth than are dreamt of in the modern's philosophy—in so far as the modern can be said to possess a philosophy.

And, of course, our juxtaposition of time and reason takes us back to the "one continuous intelligent institution that has been thinking about thinking for two thousand years." The Catholic Church has not only been thinking about thinking for two millennia, it has been thinking about those who were thinking about thinking in the preceding millennium also. It was Augustine who synthesized the thought of Plato with Christian doctrine; it was Aquinas who baptised the philosophy of Aristotle. Nor should it be forgotten that the Church was a defender of *realism* as distinct from the nominalism and *de facto* relativism of William of Ockham and his followers. Little does the modern know that he has abandoned realism in favour of nominalism, or that his much touted "realism" is in fact only nominal, as is everything else he believes! The tragedy, or comedy, of the modern mind is that it has gone far beyond the errors of Ockham or even the reductionism of Descartes. Beginning with the Cartesian "I think, therefore I am," modern man has descended to the ultimate *reductio ad absurdum*: "I don't think, therefore am I?"

It would be easy to laugh at the modern. He is, after all, pitifully funny, not least of all when he is laughing at us. Yet we should try to make him break the habit of a lifetime by inducing him to think a little. We should begin by insisting that he ceases to follow the disastrous advice of Polonius that we must be true to ourselves above all else, and begin instead to see that we must be true to the truth that is beyond ourselves. In order to do so, we might like to ponder Hamlet's immortal question: "To be, or not to be." This is indeed the question, and to find the answer we have to think about what it is to *be* and what it is *not to be*. We have to ponder the question of *being* itself. A human being who fails to ponder *being* is scarcely being human at all. And once we ponder *being* we make the ontological leap from physics to metaphysics, a leap that enables the mind to enter the magical-rational realm in which reason meets mystery in a nuptial embrace from which the fruits of philosophy flow.

Let's leave our modern with a few parting questions, each of which should help him understand the essential connection between faith and reason. What is time? How did time begin? Is the absence of time, timelessness? What *is* timelessness? How does Nothing become Something? What is "nothing"? What is "something"? Having given him something to think about, we might remind him that he might find it helpful to listen to the "one continuous intelligent institution that has been thinking about thinking for two thousand years."

5. HISTORY REVISITED

It is always prudent to know what we are talking about before we begin to say anything. It is, therefore, important to know what history is before we talk about it, or before we consider visiting or revisiting it. The problem is that history has more than one generally accepted definition, and, confusingly, those definitions could be said to contradict each other. History can be defined as the "aggregate of past events" but also as a "continuous methodical record of past events." These definitions are so different that they constitute two entirely different things. The first is all that has *happened* in the past, the second is all that has been *recorded* in or about the past.[1] The first is entirely *independent* of man's record of it. It is an objective reality; it simply *is*. The second, by contrast, is entirely *dependent* upon man's record of it.

It is absolutely crucial that we are aware of these two definitions of history and that we avoid conflating them when we think or talk about the past. The first definition considers history as synonymous with the past itself, with those things that *really* happened, so it is *real* regardless of the imperfect perception of it. A thing that truly *is* does not owe its existence to the way that it is perceived or misperceived by those experiencing or recording it. It simply is. It is *real*. This understanding of history might be called historical realism.

The second definition, taken to its logical conclusion, assumes that something that really happened in the past does not qualify as "history" if no record of it remains. All that is unknown or undocumented is "unhistorical." The logical conclusion of this subjective view of history is that history itself is not true, in any objective sense, but is merely as true or false as the surviving records. It is only *relatively* true. It is a human construct and is therefore as false and fallible as the humans who constructed it. This understanding might be called historical relativism.

It must be stressed, however, that historical relativism is not synonymous with philosophical relativism. On the contrary, it is simply applying to the past the same criteria for understanding reality that we apply in the present. Since none of us is omniscient, we go through our everyday lives making judgments based upon our own limited knowledge of the people and events that we meet and experience. Although we have limited knowledge we use our wisdom and understanding to make judgments. The greater our wisdom and understanding, the better our judgment will be, i.e., the closer that our *relative* judgment will conform to *objective* reality. And what is true of our engagement with the present is true of our engagement with the past. Although our knowledge of the past is limited by the "continuous methodical record of past events," we need to use our wisdom and understanding to make judgments about the past. The greater our wisdom and understanding, the better our judgment will be, i.e., the closer that our *relative* judgment of the "record of past events" will conform with the "aggregate of past events," which is *objective* historical reality. It can be seen, therefore, that historical relativism is the raw data whereas our philosophical and theological assumptions are the means by which the data is processed. As such, it is philosophy and theology[2] that determine the extent to which our understanding conforms to reality, whether we are speaking of the past or the present. A false philosophy or theology will lead to a false understanding of the facts and therefore a false reading of reality.

If, therefore, Christianity is true, i.e., if it conforms to reality, it follows that only the wisdom and understanding of orthodox Christian scholars will interpret the knowledge of the past correctly, or as near to correctly as is humanly possible. If Christianity is true, this statement is true, even if it makes secularist historians apoplectic. Nonetheless, it is necessary for Christian scholars to engage with the wider secular academy, even if the wider academy is actually narrower in its breadth of understanding. As such, a modus operandi should prevail in which scholars of differing philosophies can agree to differ while working together. This modus operandi must be based upon practical objectivity, i.e., by the necessity of seeing history though the eyes and minds of its protagonists. Historians must desist from judging the past from the perspective of the present until they have shown that they understand the past on its own terms. In other words, historians should refrain from passing judgment until they can show that they know and understand the thing being judged. In practice, this means that historians must learn about the major ideas that have animated the past. They must know and understand Christian philosophy and theology, the dominant force in history for almost 1500 years, and they must know it and understand it as well as the people they are studying understood it. In short, no historian should be taken seriously unless he is also a theologian and philosopher.

The problem is that philosophical relativism does not believe in objective truth and is therefore unlikely to see the point of studying history objectively. If there's no such thing as objective truth, why try to record it? All that's left is the pursuit of the individual historian's agenda, which is the reduction of history to the level of propaganda. Thus, for instance, we see the rewriting of history from a feminist perspective, a Marxist perspective, a "queer" perspective, a post-modern perspective, et cetera, ad nauseam. Thus our culture's understanding of its past has been poisoned by the bitter fruit of relativism.

Relativism makes no effort to see history through the eyes of the protagonists; it makes no effort to get inside the heads and hearts of the people it studies; it does not seek to understand the times in which the protagonists lived. It does not try to see history as it *really was*, which, from the perspective of truth, is what it *really is*, but judges history from its own relativist perspective. It does not look at history through the eyes of history, i.e., looking at the past through the eyes of the past, but through the eyes of the historian's own prejudices. The historian no longer tries to understand the past and learn from it. On the contrary, he judges the past from the perspective of the fads and fashions of his own zeitgeist and not the zeitgeist of the time being studied, condemning or condoning the latter according to the moral presumptions of the former. This, to put the matter bluntly, is historical ignorance; it is, to put the matter more bluntly still, historical bigotry. Thus, for instance, we see how secular historians refuse to use the terms BC (Before Christ) and AD (Anno Domini, i.e., the Year of Our Lord) and insist upon CE and BCE (Common Era and Before the Common Era). This is not only the pursuit of a secular fundamentalist agenda, inspired by a hatred of Christianity and by implication a contempt for the past, it is patently dishonest. The historical fact is that the year zero marks the year in which Christ is believed to have been born, and yet the birth of Christ has been banned by historians in the sense that it must not be acknowledged, on pains of academic excommunication. It is no longer permitted for any historian to commit the "heresy" of employing the terms BC and AD in an academic paper, and failure to conform invariably means a refusal to publish the paper in question. In similar fashion, these secular fundamentalists force their students to conform to the ban on BC and AD, extending their intellectual intolerance to the classroom.

Compare this secular fundamentalist intolerance towards Christianity with the tolerance of Christianity towards paganism with regard to the naming of the months of the year or the days of the week. Even to this day, we use the pagan names for the months of the year (Janus, Mars, etc.) and the days of the week: Sun-day, Moon-day, Tiw's-day, Woden's-day, Thor's-day, Frigg's-day, Saturn's-day. If the age of Christendom had been as intolerant as the age of secular fundamentalism, we would surely be referring to Christ-Day, Mary-Day, Peter-Day, etc. All of this should be obvious to anyone who truly understands history. It is, after all, not Christianity but secularism that is responsible for the greatest crimes of history, from the secular ambition of the Roman Emperors to the secular designs of Henry VIII, and from the mass homicide of the French and Russian Revolutions to the genocide of the Third Reich. The lessons of history are clear enough for those with eyes to see. Secularism is intolerant, bigoted and ultimately deadly. It kills everything it touches, including the study of history itself. Such lessons are always worth remembering; indeed, we forget them at our peril.

6. SCIENCE VERSUS SCIENTISM

The understanding of science has changed considerably in the past few hundred years. It used to embrace all aspects of the art of knowing or seeing the truth, including philosophy and theology. Since the misnamed "Enlightenment," however, this understanding of science has been narrowed so that it is now restricted to a knowledge of those things that can be known from the observation of purely physical phenomena. Whereas the ancient world differentiated between a knowledge of natural philosophy and a knowledge of other areas of philosophy, between physics and metaphysics, the modern world has granted a monopoly to the former and has sought to put the latter out of business. Such philosophical materialism leads to the idolization or worship of science, in its narrower sense, considering it the only oracle that speaks with authority and infallibility. It is, however, necessary to distance *science*, the "god" being worshipped, from the *scientism* of those who worship it. Science is, and has always been, a noble art. It is good whereas scientism is evil. The former shows us an aspect of reality, the latter distorts what has been shown so that reality is obscured or hidden.

In its narrower sense, science (natural philosophy) leads to a greater understanding of that part of the truth with which it is concerned, i.e., the physical cosmos. It does not and cannot enlighten us about anything but these things. It is concerned solely with the physical *facts*, and does not tell us anything about those parts of the truth which, being metaphysical, are beyond its scope of vision. Once we understand this fact, we see that science is an authentic path of knowledge, which, as a rational art, harmonises with the truths of authentic philosophy. Science is, for instance, intrinsically and implicitly anti-relativist in its essence and in its modus operandi. It concerns itself with objectivity, with objectively verifiable data, with the facts, and the facts alone. It spurns all prejudice and opinion that flies in the face of the observable objectivity of the data. It is also intrinsically traditionalist in the sense that it is always building on the discoveries of the past. Such traditionalism was epitomized by the great physicist, Sir Isaac

Newton, when he stated that, if he had "seen a little further it is by standing on the shoulders of Giants."

Today's scientists are always building on the foundations laid by their illustrious forebears, thereby enshrining tradition at the heart of true science. It is no surprise, however, that Sir Isaac Newton was not merely standing on the shoulders of the giants of science but on the shoulders of the giants of philosophy and theology also. It is significant, for instance, that the aforementioned phrase for which Newton is famous was borrowed from Bernard of Chartres, who coined the phrase in Latin (*nanos gigantium humeris insidentes*). According to John of Salisbury, writing in 1159, "Bernard of Chartres used to say that we are like dwarfs on the shoulders of giants, so that we can see more than they, and things at a greater distance, not by virtue of any sharpness of sight on our part, or any physical distinction, but because we are carried high and raised up by their giant size." According to the mediaeval historian, Richard Southern, Bernard was comparing the modern scholar of his own time, i.e., the twelfth century, with the giant philosophers of ancient Greece and Rome. In such a statement he was no doubt alluding to the influence of Plato on St. Augustine but was also unwittingly prophesying the influence of Aristotle on St. Thomas Aquinas in the following century.

Yet it would seem that Bernard also had theology as well as philosophy in mind when he uttered his timeless metaphor. This is suggested by the stained glass windows in the south transept of Chartres Cathedral, which depict the four Evangelists (Matthew, Mark, Luke, and John) sitting on the shoulders of the four major prophets of the Old Testament (Isaiah, Jeremiah, Ezekiel, and Daniel), the latter of whom are shown as giants in stature compared to the relatively diminutive stature of the authors of the Gospels. The truth is that the Evangelists see further than the Old Testament prophets because they have witnessed the coming of the Messiah of whom the prophets had spoken. Thus we see that Newton's use of the metaphor to signify the traditionalist nature of physics dovetails with its usage by Bernard of Chartres to signify the traditionalism of philosophy and theology, thereby suggesting the transcendent unity of the three sciences as servants of the all-encompassing unity of faith and reason. It is also worthy of note that Newton may have borrowed the phrase from his near contemporary, George Herbert, who, in *Jacula Prudentum* (1651), wrote "A dwarf on a giant's shoulders sees farther of the two." In any event, Herbert's use of the phrase illustrates the role of literature as an agent of the same unifying principle of *fides et ratio* of which physics, philosophy and theology are servants.

Considering the unity of faith and reason, it should come as no surprise that the Church has been a major contributor to the progress of the physical sciences throughout the centuries. Nicolaus Copernicus, the founder of modern astronomy, was a Third Order Dominican; Basil Valentine, one of the founding fathers of modern chemistry, was a Benedictine monk; Thomas Linacre, founder of the Royal College of Physicians, was a priest; Athanasius Kircher, a pioneer in diverse scientific disciplines including microbiology, astronomy, and physics, was a Jesuit; Nicolas Steno, a pioneering anatomist and the father of geology and stratigraphy, was a convert to Catholicism who became a priest and, as a bishop, a leading figure in the Counter-Reformation; René Just Haüy, the pioneering mineralogist and father of crystallography, was a Premonstratensian and honorary canon of Notre Dame Cathedral; and Gregor Mendel, the father of genetics, was an Augustinian monk. Such a procession of scientists, all of whom were priests or in holy orders, constitutes a veritable scientific *eminenti* and *illustrissimi*. It also nails the lie that the Church has been an enemy of scientific progress.

If the foregoing demonstrates that science is good, there is no escaping the fact that scientism is not only bad but is guilty of giving true science a bad name. True science has a noble tradition, interwoven with that of the Church in the shared desire to discover the truth; scientism, in contrast, has its ignoble roots in the sordid profession of alchemy, seeking to turn base metal into worldly riches or seeking in vain for the elixir of life. Science seeks the truth and nothing but the truth; scientism seeks the power that scientific discoveries can wield. Science, like its older sisters, philosophy and theology, seeks to unravel the mystery of God's Creation; scientism makes its Faustian pact with the Devil. From the scientific racism of the Nazis, who mixed Nietzschean pride with the so-called "science" of phrenology and racial anthropology, to the madness of Marx, an advocate of scientism whose so-called "scientific materialism" led to the murder of millions of people in the name of "scientific progress," to the advocates of infanticide who justify abortion through the pseudo-scientific denial that life begins at conception, the crimes of scientism in the name of bogus "science" are both manifold and deadly. It is clear that science needs to shake off the shackles of scientism, thereby freeing itself from the superstitious and supercilious superficiality of its untrustworthy disciple.

Scientism, to misquote Oscar Wilde, is science's own Judas. It betrays its master, its god, with a kiss. Having been complicit in the treacherous crucifixion of its master, we can safely prophesy that it will now go and hang itself!

7. SEX AND CULTURE

Oh what a tangled web we weave,
When first we practise to deceive!
— Sir Walter Scott, *Marmion, Canto vi. Stanza 17*,
first published in 1808

I can't get no satisfaction . . .
— The Rolling Stones (1965)

The world has come a long way in the two hundred years since Sir Walter Scott's *Marmion* was first published. Some, no doubt, would call the distance traveled over those two centuries a mark of the world's "progress" but, if so, it has been an agonizing and tortuous progression in the wrong direction. More specifically it has been an arduous journey downwards, a descent into an abyss more deadly than Jules Verne's voyage via the heart of a volcano to the earth's centre; a descent more akin, in fact, to Dante's journey into an inferno infinitely and eternally more perilous than any volcano. Jules Verne, besotted with scientism, sought his inspiration and his answers in geology; Dante, immersed in scholasticism, found his inspiration and his answers in theology. Verne's *Voyage au centre de la Terre*, written in the 1860s, is already dated, a fossilized remnant of extinct scientific theories; Dante's *Divina Commedia*, written more than five hundred years earlier, is as relevant today as it was when it was first published. Put simply, and bluntly, geology is built on rock that ages whereas theology is built on the Rock that never ages.

Dante's mid-life crisis, in which he finds himself wandering aimlessly in the dark wood of sin, lost and disoriented, and in need of guidance, serves as a metaphor and a warning to each of us. If we lose sight of the permanent things we will lose sight of the meaning of life itself. We will not know the way out of the mess in which we find ourselves; we might even be in such a mess that we begin to believe that there is no way out. We might begin to believe that the dark wood is all that there is, and that there is no world beyond it. If so, we will ignore the guide who offers to show us the way out of the wood, believing that he is mistaken, or a liar. If the path doesn't exist, only a fool would look for it. Dismissing the guide as a fool we will continue our aimless wandering. At this point we are as lost as it is possible to be. Nobody is more lost than the person who doesn't even know that he's lost.

This is the situation in which the modern world finds itself. It is lost in the dark wood of sin and doesn't even know that it is lost. It has woven the tangled web so tightly about itself that it has deceived itself with its own deceit. Oh what a tangled web we weave . . .

Dante differs from the hopelessly lost souls of modernity because he knew he was lost. And he knew he was lost because he knew he was a sinner. He faces his sin, and the infernal consequences of not doing so, and is purged by the experience. Following reliable guides he finds his way Home. Unlike today's lost souls, Dante could trust his guides because he lived in a culture which believed in the existence of an infallible Guide. Following the servants of this trustworthy Guide, the Mystical Body of Christ, he escaped the wood and found the true path.

Humanity had come a long way from those days of Christian unity to the days of materialistic presumption in which Jules Verne was writing his scientific fantasy. The individualism of the Reformation and the anthropocentricity of the Enlightenment has filled the world with what Chesterton called "tangled things and texts and aching eyes." Tangled things and tangled texts, all woven together into a tangled web of self-deceit. No wonder we strain our aching eyes for a glimpse of genuine light amid the darkness.

Humanity had also come a long way from the unsatisfying science of the 1860s to the unsatisfying sex of the 1960s; from rock that ages to a rock that merely rolls. The Rolling Stones were providing a mantra for the so-called swinging sixties when they claimed that they could get no satisfaction. Rolling stones may gather no moss but they gather no satisfactory relationships either. In this context we should remind ourselves that the very word "satisfaction" comes from the Latin word *satis*, meaning "enough." One who can never get enough and always wants more is never satisfied. On the contrary he is addicted. He is enslaved by his habit. It is for this reason that the world is enslaved by its so-called "freedom." It is living a lie, deceiving itself with the self-seductive nonsense of Orwellian doublethink. Thus fornication is repackaged as sexual "liberation," which is akin to saying that hallucinogenic drugs are perceptually "liberating." Indeed the parallel is singularly apt. Sex is a drug to which the world has become addicted, and, however much it might deceive itself, an addict is not "liberated" . Forever fixated on its next fix, the world finds that it can get no satisfaction. It is, therefore, no surprise that the lack of satisfaction leads to discontentment, and to anger. And let's not forget that the sixties, for all its cant about "love," was a very angry time. In the absence of a sense of having enough we find instead a sense of outrage. Put simply, one who loses his temperance loses his temper.

J. R. R. Tolkien discussed the connection between temperance and sexual satisfaction with customary eloquence in a letter to C. S. Lewis:

> Christian marriage is not a prohibition of sexual intercourse, but the correct way of sexual temperance—in fact probably the best way of getting the most satisfying *sexual pleasure*, as alcoholic temperance is the best way of enjoying beer and wine.[3]

And so we discover the most shocking truth of all, that the most satisfying sex is likely to be found in a healthy marriage! The essence of such a marriage is the *self-giving* of both spouses, body and soul, to the other. It's not about meeting each other half way, the sort of half-hearted marriage that begins with a pre-nuptial agreement and ends in divorce, but in each giving themselves fully and completely to the other so that the two become one flesh. This is the highest meaning of marriage, as it is the highest meaning of the marital act, and it gives complete satisfaction. This good news is unheeded by the hedonistic culture, which sees only itself in narcissistic self-absorption.

Humanity has come a long way from the unsatisfying sixties and its summer of lust to the cold winter of today's loveless culture. In a world which sees sex as merely a product of human appetite, children are ignored, abused or destroyed. If sex is only a product, children are merely a byproduct to be disposed of and discarded at will. Apart from the fifty million or so unborn children who have been killed since abortion was legalized in the United States, to say nothing of the millions killed in other "enlightened" countries, broken families cause unmitigated misery even to those children who are not exterminated in the womb. The survivors of the abortion holocaust find themselves in fragmented families in which fatherless children are abused by their mothers' "partners."

And it's not only children who are the victims of a society that sees sex as merely a product of the passions. Women are also treated as a byproduct to be disposed of and discarded at will. Since their so-called "liberation," women have become sex objects in a far nastier way than was ever the case in the days before they were "liberated." In the past, men respected a woman's honour and certainly didn't expect her to gratify their every lustful desire. Today women are expected to spread themselves as a supine sacrifice to the god of instant gratification. Feminists insisted on being taken down from the pedestal of idealized femininity on which gentlemen had placed them and became in consequence mere pedals to be trodden under foot by the cads of a post-gentlemanly age. In shunning chivalry they courted chicanery.

Nor are women and children the only victims of a sex-addicted culture. Confused by their role and purpose in a world that sneers at masculine virtue and the heroism of fatherhood, lonely men pawn their souls for pornography, divorced from real life and real love, or succumb to the sodomy of Gomorrah.

In truth, Paolo and Francesca, in the second circle of Dante's hell, are not as grotesque as the denizens of today's particularly gross inferno. Stunned, stoned, and rolling from one fruitless relationship to another, today's "liberated" populace discovers the old truth that Satan offers no satisfaction to those who fall into his web of deceit. And indeed this "old truth" is as old as it is true. It is as old as Satan himself. It is nothing new, and nothing less, and nothing other than the original truth of original sin. The tangled web we weave was first woven by Adam and Eve. This is the sad truth at the darkened heart of humanity. But the good news is that the web was unwoven by the New Adam and the New Eve. The astonishing news is that the deception of the devil is always defeated by the reception of Christ.

We have come a long way from the Garden of Eden to the hell on earth in which we find ourselves and its sympathy for the devil. There is, however, a path out of the abyss. It is a purgatorial path, paved with penance and crowned with thorns. It is the path taken by Dante, the road less traveled that leads to the narrow gate of paradise.

8. SATAN AND THE ART OF DARKNESS

As soon as we begin to ponder the relationship between evil and the arts we find ourselves in the realm of paradox. If God is the Creator, and if all human creativity is an outpouring of God's creative gift in Man, how can Satan, the Destroyer, have any role to play in art? Isn't art, the expression of creativity, a gift from God, and isn't evil merely a privation of the good? If human imagination is the image of God's creativity in Man, how can Satan have any part in it? Satan is infertile. He can create nothing. He *is* Nothing. He is the Real Absence. What does this Thing, this No Thing, this Negation, have to do with the fertile expression of creativity? It would appear that he has nothing to do with it; and yet, if this is so, why is there so much evil art? This is the very heart of the paradox.

In order to unlock the priceless pearl of truth at the centre of this paradox we need to understand the nature and supernature of the creative act. The creative gift, the Muse, is the grace of inspiration that comes from God. It is pure and perfect, and untouched and untainted by evil. It is the pure potency and potential of God's very presence in the talent of the artist and in the moment of inspiration that engenders all creative work. But, as T. S. Eliot reminds us, between the potency and the existence falls the Shadow.[4] The falling of the Shadow is the Shadow of the Fall. Satan is the Shadow that falls over all acts of creativity. He is not to be found in the purity of the gift, any more than he is to be found in the purity of the Giver; he is to be found lurking in the shadows of the fallen personhood of the one who receives the gift. It is in the darkened heart of Man that the art of darkness emerges.

All art is the incarnation of the fertile relationship between grace and the sinner. The grace is pure, the sinner is not. The more the sinner acknowledges the grace, the more *graceful* his art will be. The more he is grateful for the gift, the more *grateful* will be his art, the more it will be filled with the gratitude and humility that breathes the life of wisdom into creativity. If he seeks to use the gift to give a gift back to the Giver of the gift, he will be using his talents wisely and in the manner in which they are meant to be used. If, on the other hand, the sinner fails to acknowledge the grace, the more graceless his art will be. If he is ungrateful for the gift, believing that it is not a gift at all but his own property, the more ungrateful his art will be. If he chooses to take the priceless pearl of divine inspiration and cast it before swine, he will be squandering his talent in the squalor of the gutter in which his art belongs.

To answer the riddle with which we began, we can conclude that there is so much evil art because there are so many evil artists. It's as simple as that! But why does God cast His own priceless pearls before such swine, seemingly squandering His own creative gifts on those who will only abuse the gifts and use them against Him? The answer, of course, is to be found in Christ's parable of the talents. God bestows His talents as He sees fit, giving more to some than to others. Great things are expected of those with great talents, and there will be a great price to pay for those who fail to use their talents wisely. In the interim, we are free to use or abuse our talents at will. God does not prevent those with great artistic talents from abusing those gifts abominably. They are free to do with their gifts as they will, while time is theirs, and will face the consequences of their choices when time is no longer theirs. The gift of creativity, like the gift of time or the gift of life, is not removed as soon as we use the gift sinfully. Deo gratias!

Our discussion of Satan and the art of darkness must now proceed to further paradoxical questions. Is there a difference between *evil art* and *evil in art*? Or, to put the matter differently, is there a difference between the dark arts and the art of darkness? The question is crucial because the answer is the very crux, the very cross, on which the artist hangs himself. All artists have their crosses to bear and all artists must carry them to their own Golgotha, their own Mount Doom. This is the mystery of suffering, the art of darkness, at the heart of reality. The only question is whether we will suffer our crucifixion in the manner of the Good Thief or in the manner of the Bad Thief. The good artist, like the Good Thief, knows that he is a miserable sinner and that he lives in a world of darkness. He understands the reason for the darkness and confesses his responsibility for making it even darker. The bad artist, on the other hand, like the Bad Thief, does not acknowledge that he is a sinner, and yet he can hardly deny, from the vision afforded him from his cross, that he lives in a world of darkness. In fact, he blames the darkness and not his own sin for his desperate suffering. He does not know the reason for the darkness because he does not know the reason for anything. He believes that there is no reason, affirming that everything including the darkness is meaningless. And since everything is meaningless, everything is darkness. Nothing means anything. "Nothing, again nothing," complains Eliot of these denizens of darkness. "Do you know nothing? Do you see nothing? Do you remember nothing? Are you alive, or not? Is there nothing in your head?"[5]

In this difference between the Good Thief and the Bad Thief, transposed as metaphors onto the two types of artists, we can see the crux of the difference between the dark arts and the art of darkness. Evil art makes sin attractive, denying its sinfulness and seducing us with the lie that it is only a pleasure to be grasped when the opportunity presents itself. Such art reduces all morality to mere ambivalence and ambiguity, and replaces the truths of religion with the mere opinions of the relativist. The art of darkness, on the other hand, shows the ugliness of sin and illustrates its destructive consequences. It is not *evil art* but the realistic portrayal of *evil in art*. It is not sinful but is full of sin. Thus, for instance, Byron's poetry beguiles us with the seductive pleasures of sin whereas Baudelaire revolts us with its ugliness. Baudelaire is paradoxically darker than Byron but he is much less sinful. Similarly Emily Brontë's *Wuthering Heights* is much darker in its depiction of impassioned and illicit love than the literary legion of titillating pulp fiction that glamourises adultery. Brontë's novel horrifies us with the destructive consequences of selfish obsession masquerading as love; modern novels treat the same phenomenon as attractive and harmless pleasure-seeking. The former shames the devil, warning the reader of the dangers of selfishness, the latter does the devil's dirty work, serenading us with the sensuality of lust. The former shows us Catherine and Heathcliff in their self-made hell, the latter places Paolo and Francesca in an adulterous heaven. The former uses the art of darkness to show us the truth, the latter the dark arts to weave a seductive lie. Ultimately the chasm that separates the virtue of the former with the vice of the latter is as wide as the unbridgeable abyss between hell and purgatory.

9. ETHNO-MASOCHISM
AND THE CULTURE OF DEATH

Imagine there's no heaven,
It's easy if you try,
No hell below us,
Above us only sky,
Imagine all the people
living for today . . .

These words, written by John Lennon, a man who once claimed to be more popular than Christ, are the opening lines of *Imagine*, a song which could be considered the anthem of the Culture of Death. Lennon goes on to ask us to "imagine there's no countries" and "no religion too," promising that if we have the courage to imagine these things, and to want them, there will be "nothing to kill or die for" and that "all the people" will be "living life in peace."

This peculiar cocktail of half-digested Buddhism and regurgitated Marxism is, in its essence, iconoclastic. It seeks to dismantle or deconstruct the culture of Christendom and the Faith which is its foundation. It seeks to do so because, at root, it loathes the roots from which it sprang. It is the product of what may be termed "ethno-masochism," the self-loathing which leads to a hatred of one's own heritage, one's own culture, one's own religion, one's own inner-self, one's own ethnic identity. It is masochistic because it gains a perverse pleasure in the self-degradation that goes hand in glove with the destruction of one's own cultural heritage. It is the self-gratification of self-hatred.

Ethno-masochistic iconoclasm rejects and seeks to destroy the entire canon of Christian culture purely because it is the product of a despised race of people who have committed the heinous crime of being our ancestors. As Chesterton quipped, the type of person who succumbs to this perverse rootlessness is a chronological snob who has contemptuously kicked down the ladder by which he's climbed. This supercilious arrogance is akin to racism, a psychological attitude to others based upon a presumed superiority over presumed "inferior" types. Ethno-masochists are racial inverts who hate their own kind with a vituperative vengeance. They even have their own terms of racial abuse, contemptuously dismissing the giants of the past as "dwems." Those deemed to be "dwems" are marginalized and can be abused with abandon. For those who are blissfully ignorant of such pseudo-racist labels, "dwem" is an acrimonious acronym for "dead white European males."

As with other forms of racism, the victim is blamed for characteristics for which he is not to blame. A person cannot help being black, brown or white but this lack of culpability does not prevent their being despised. Similarly dwems are despised for four different characteristics, none of which is their fault. They are hated for being dead, for being white, for being European, and for being male. Put bluntly, the dwem-hater is guilty of a four-fold hatred for those who cannot help being what they are. They not only discriminate on grounds of race, but on grounds of place; they are not merely racist but sexist; and they have an irrational contempt for the dead.

As with more publicized forms of racism, dwemism leads to injustice and, ultimately, to self-evident absurdity. Bach's B-minor Mass is dismissed because the composer is a dwem; Dante's *Divine Comedy* is derided because the poet is a dwem; Raphael's paintings are of strictly limited value because the artist is a dwem; Mozart is a dwem, Shakespeare is a dwem, Fra Angelico is a dwem; Donizetti, Dostoyevsky, Donatello, dwems. Et cetera ad nauseam ad absurdum. Admittedly only the most extreme dwemists would make these sweeping assessments. Yet, as with other forms of racism, dwemism is at its most perniciously powerful in its more subtle and diluted forms. It is the implicit dwemist downgrading of the importance of these masterworks of the cultural canon in favour of modern manifestations of ethno-masochism which represents one of the greatest challenges to Christian culture in today's culture of death.

The other dwemist approach to culture which represents a challenge to the heritage and destiny of Christendom is the assault by dwemist "critics" on the culture itself. Jacques Derrida, the recently deceased founder of the deconstructionist school of philosophy and literary criticism, spearheaded the modern, or "post-modern," assault on the great books of the western canon. At the callous hands of the deconstructionists the works of Shakespeare, Dante, Homer, Virgil and other literary giants have been vandalized, vivisected and pulled to pieces. Ignoring the fact that great literature provides a prism through which the Permanent Things can be glimpsed, and dismissive of the fact that it is this prism that gives perennial relevance to the literature itself, the deconstructionists tear the works apart with relativistic abandon and ethno-masochistic zeal. Perhaps the pithiest and best riposte to deconstructionist philosophy is given by Gandalf in *The Lord of the Rings* when he reminds Saruman that "he that breaks a thing to find out what it is has left the path of wisdom." And descending from the realm of myth to the kingdom of nursery rhyme, it might be added that deconstructionism is the triumph of humpty-dumpty-dom, the breaking of things that can't be put back together again in any meaningful sense. In this sense, deconstruction is exposed anagrammatically as the "destruction con." It is a destruction of the text under the pretext of understanding it better. The joke, however, is that the deconstructionists are actually the victims of their own confidence trick. The texts of the great books are not defeated by deconstructionism, deconstructionism is defeated by the texts. The works, as objective realities with real meaning, exist in glorious independence of those who seek to explain them or explain them away. Works such as Dante's *Divine Comedy* or the plays of Shakespeare are edifices that the deconstructionists are unable to scale. Their prejudice precludes the empathy needed for true critical judgement. As such, the great books are not edifices that the post-moderns deconstruct but are precipices from which they fall.

An edifice edifies, or at least it has the power to do so. Those who refuse to be edified through their adherence to a nihilism rooted in ethno-masochism see only an edifice to be subdued by subjectivism. Since, however, the objective reality of the work transcends all such efforts at subjection the effort is futile and self-defeating. The fool who defies, defiles and defaces the edifice only succeeds in defiling and defacing himself. The fool falls; the edifice remains.

Dante is not destroyed by deconstructionism; the *Divine Comedy* will be what it has always been long after deconstruction has decomposed. The Great Books and great masterpieces of art and music are an edifice built upon the Rock of Christian civilization and, as the Irish proverb reminds us, the one who bites the Rock loses his teeth. Truth prevails. It has nothing to fear from the toothlessness of truthlessness. Truth succours but truthlessness sucks!

Having descended to the woeful level of the modern American vernacular, we'll get in the vallecula by returning to the "groovy" excesses of the

1960s. John Lennon was unwittingly correct, perhaps, when he asked us to imagine that there was "no hell below us." Hell might not be below us but it is certainly within us and is plainly all around us. The whole of post-"Enlightenment" history, of which Lennon's *Imagine* is a product, has led inexorably to the culture of death which is a hell on earth.

"You may say I'm a dreamer, but I'm not the only one. . . ." So says Lennon. His dream is a nightmare which has come true. And, alas, he is not the only one. There are many; their name is Legion.

10. WHAT IS ENGLAND?

I recently finished reading A. N. Wilson's mostly delightful anthology of poetry, *England: A Collection of the Poetry of Place* (London: Eland Publishing, 2008). It was the first book of Wilson's that I had read since his return to Christian faith after a decade or two in the atheistic doldrums. As a longtime admirer of his work, I had prayed for such a return (though I am not claiming that my prayers were the cause of the miracle!). Nonetheless, his return to what appears to be an Anglican form of Christianity is indicative of his inability to grasp the nettle. To return to the Church of England after floundering in the desperate waters of unbelief is akin to being rescued from drowning by clambering onto a sinking ship. It is neither a satisfactory nor permanent solution to the problem.

Much of the conflicting and contradictory conundrum that lies at the heart of ANW's inability to embrace orthodoxy is to be found in his anthology of poems about England. There is, however, much that is truly excellent and inspiring in Wilson's selection and I'd like to acknowledge that which is praiseworthy before proceeding to that which is problematic.

The inclusion of Belloc's "Ha'nacker Mill" and Chesterton's "Secret People" was heartwarming, though not altogether surprising. Wilson, as the author of a mostly commendable biography of Belloc, is well-versed in the work and collective persona of the Chesterbelloc and I would have been frankly shocked had both halves of Shaw's fantastic chimaera not been represented. If only one poem from each was to be permitted, I think there are no better representations of the gist of England in Belloc's and Chesterton's poetic corpus than the solitary selection from each that Wilson has included. I was also pleased with Wilson's selection from Shakespeare. John of Gaunt's speech from *Richard II* and Henry V's speech before the battle of Harfleur are obvious choices, perhaps, but entirely justified. I would have liked to have seen Henry's other famous speech, before the battle of Agincourt, which my father used to recite to me, but this sin of omission is certainly ameliorated by the inclusion of the other two Shakespearean elegies to England.

Although many excellent poems and poets are represented, the biggest and most pleasant surprise was the sheer brilliance of the extract from Swinburne's "Winter in Northumberland." This poem is astonishingly good and reminds me of the poetry of Hopkins in its awe-struck reverence for beauty and, particularly, of Francis Thompson's "To a Snowflake" in the way it connects nature's beauty to the beauty of its Creator.

Having acknowledged that which is good in Wilson's selection, its chief weakness is Wilson's reduction of Platonism to relativism; his apparent belief that "Platonic England" is merely an England of the mind, i.e., a figment of the individual's imagination. If this is all that England is, why lament its passing with such intensity? The real tragedy of England's passing, so much a running theme through ANW's selection and commentary, is not that the England we love is a figment of the imagination but that it is *real*, in the sense that Platonic forms are real. This *real* England is present in Old English and Middle English; in Chaucer and Chesterton; in Shakespeare, Austen, and Dickens. The England to be found in these places is more real than present-day Birmingham or Leicester, which are only English in a superficial and fading sense. Nor does the England to be found in these places depend on our ability to see it. If England continues to sink into the primeval soup of "post-Christian" barbarism, it is possible that nobody will read Shakespeare a century from now. They will not want to read it, and will probably be unable to read it even if they want to. Yet the goodness, truth and beauty to be found in Shakespeare, Chaucer et al will not be in the least diminished by the inability of future generations to see it. A tree does not cease to exist because a blind man cannot see it. England will not cease to exist because the "post-English" barbarians residing in England fail to understand that which is beyond their ken.

If A. N. Wilson could acquire the philosophical realism that would unite him with Plato and Aristotle, and with the *fides et ratio* of Augustine and Aquinas, he would understand the immutability of that which is truly England. Indeed, if he acquired such wisdom, he would not have ended his anthology with a comment that eulogizes the so-called "Glorious" Revolution that exiled England's last true King and which condemned England to the sordid secularism that followed in the Revolution's wake. If he possessed such wisdom, he would have ended the anthology with Chesterton's "Secret People" instead of Hawker's "Song of the Western Men," the latter being a triumphalist anti-Catholic hymn, which, as the anthem of Cornish separatism, is about as English as "Flower of Scotland."

Perhaps we should end with a simple prayer for A. N. Wilson's conversion: *St. Thomas More, St. John Fisher, and all ye English Martyrs, the crowning pinnacle of True England, who laid down your lives to keep England in communion with the Faith of her fathers, please pray for the wandering soul of A. N. Wilson that he may be led to the One True Church founded by Our Lord Jesus Christ. Amen.*

11. WHO ARE THE CELTS?

For the great Gaels of Ireland
Are the men that God made mad,
For all their wars are merry,
And all their songs are sad.

G. K. Chesterton's lines about the Irish, from his epic poem, *The Ballad of the White Horse*, encapsulate one of the many paradoxes at the heart of the Celtic conundrum. Yet Chesterton's paradox barely scratches the surface of the enigma that the Celts present to a puzzled world. At the heart of the Celtic conundrum is a contradiction. Indeed, at the many hearts of the conundrum there are many contradictions. Let's begin by enumerating a few of them.

Ireland's heroic history of suffering is inseparable from its historic and heroic faith; yet modern Ireland, the so-called Celtic Tiger, is kept afloat by hand-outs from the old enemy, Britain, via payments from the European Union, and has turned its face contemptuously on the heroism and history of its Catholic faith. If Ireland is defined by its historic struggle against persecution, how Irish is the modern Ireland that has sold its soul and its faith for thirty pieces of silver Euros? If Ireland is defined by her faith, the Celtic Tiger is about as Celtic as, well, a tiger.

And if Ireland is defined by her Catholic faith, what about the Protestant North? Are the Ulster Loyalists Irish? What defines an Irishman? His faith; his place of birth? What of the Irish-Americans? Are they Irish? Who is more Irish, a Catholic Irishman such as James Joyce who is trying to escape from his Catholicism and from his Irishness, or a Protestant Irishman like Oscar Wilde who eventually becomes a Catholic? Who is more Irish, someone like Joyce who is walking away from the Catholic faith, or someone like C. S. Lewis, an Ulster Protestant, who is walking towards it, even though he never ultimately crosses the threshold?

Faced with such questions, one is reminded of Chesterton's discussion of the Irishness of George Bernard Shaw:

Bernard Shaw is not merely an Irishman; he is not even a typical one. He is a certain separated and peculiar kind of Irishman, which is not easy to describe. Some Nationalist Irishmen have referred to him contemptuously as a "West Briton." But this is really unfair; for whatever Mr. Shaw's mental faults may be, the easy adoption of an unmeaning phrase like "Briton" is certainly not one of them. It would be much nearer the truth to put the thing in the bold and bald terms of the old Irish song, and to call him "The anti-Irish Irishman". . . .

And since Chesterton has raised the thorny subject of the "Britons," what about Britain itself? Isn't it Celtic? Isn't that why the Celtic part of France is called Brittany and its inhabitants, Bretons? Britain, historically, was the Celtic nation invaded by the Romans and later by the various Germanic tribes. Britain is Celtic, only England is English! Historically speaking, the Celts are Brits, and the Brits Celts! The modern understanding of the word "British" is, ironically, a construct of *English* imperialism, which arose after the Reformation and became very popular in the reign of Queen Elizabeth to justify the annexation of the rest of the British Isles. Thus, "Britain" can mean, at one and the same time, the name of the land of the Celts and the name of those who invaded the land of the Celts! No wonder Chesterton referred to the word 'Briton' as "unmeaning."

But what of the word "Celt"? Is it not as meaningless? After all, we have only scratched the surface of all that is Celtic. We haven't even mentioned the Scots yet. They are certainly Celtic, whatever that means, but hardly Irish. And what does it mean to be Scottish? Does it mean being a Jacobite, a Catholic rebel? Does it mean following Bonnie Prince Charlie? Yet for every heroic Macdonald in Scottish history there is a treacherous Campbell. And isn't the Calvinism of John Knox as Celtic as the Catholicism of Bonnie Prince Charlie?

And then there's the Welsh. The Welsh seem to have lost touch with the richness of their centuries of Catholic history, ignoring it completely and forging a Celtic identity that combines the Protestant non-conformism of its recent history to the druidic mists of its ancient past. And we have hardly mentioned, though we mustn't forget, the Cornish and the Bretons, and the Celts of Iberia (and beyond).

And what of the new age hijacking and perverting of all things Celtic, from half-baked concepts of druidic paganism to even less-baked concepts of so-called Celtic Christianity?

On a more positive note, we must remember the Celtic dimension to the Catholic cultural revival in the last century: George Mackay Brown (an Orcadian Celt, as distinct from a Scottish Celt), Saunders Lewis, R. S. Thomas, George Scott-Moncrieff, David Jones (a cockney-Celt), Shane Leslie (an Anglo-Irish Celt), Compton Mackenzie, and, stretching the Celtic connection to its breaking point, Flannery O'Connor (a Georgian Celt!).

Faced with such an array of non-coalescent, conflicting Celts we are tempted to tamper with Chesterton's famous lines about the Gaels of Ireland:

> Are the great Gaels of Ireland
> Really meant to make men mad?
> For howe'er we pursue them
> There's no answer to be had!

Let's conclude, however, with an insistence that the Celts represent a real and vibrant part of our living western culture. And, in doing so, let's not fall into the post-modernist trap of believing that if something is difficult to pin down it doesn't have any meaningful existence. For the materialist, if something can't be pinned down it is nebulous; for the rest of us it is merely mysterious. We don't make the mistake that if something can't be understood it means that there is nothing to understand; this is the folly of the nihilist. The logical truth is simply that if something can't be understood it is because we can't understand it!

We might not be able to understand the Celts. They are an enigma. They slip through our fingers. Yet though they are slippery, they are real. Whether the Celts are a mystical coat of many colours, or whether they are many coats of a somewhat similar mystical colour, they are real. Long live the Celts (whoever they are), and may God bless them!

12. AMERICAN FAITH AND CULTURE

One of the mistakes of nationalism is the belief that nationhood takes precedence over God. We think of Henry VIII's establishment of a national church and the spilling of the blood of the martyrs on its altars. We are reminded, in this context, of St. Thomas More's insistence that he was the king's good servant but God's first. The saint had his priorities right and paid for it with his blood; the king had his priorities wrong and paid for it with his (eternal) life. The saint is in heaven; the king is heaven knows where!

Continuing our examination of nationalism's war on faith, we think of the secular fundamentalism of the French Revolution and its idolization of the nation and desecration of the nation's churches. We recall the nationalism of the Nazis and the patriotism of the Soviet Union. It is easy to see what happens when men worship the tribe and not the god of the tribe; and although it is true that many tribes have worshipped false gods, it is equally true that even false gods tend to be less destructive than man's idolization of himself or his own people. More people have been killed by the guillotines and gas chambers of secular fundamentalism than by all the so-called wars of religion, the latter of which were usually motivated by secular ambition masquerading as faith.

These cautionary truths need to be remembered in any consideration of American faith and culture. The United States defines itself in its pledge of allegiance as one nation *under* God. As such, all Americans must put their nation *under* God in their list of priorities. Echoing the saintly Englishman, all good Americans must be Uncle Sam's good servant but God's first. Anyone who suggests otherwise, anyone who suggests that America must come first, above all else, is not merely wrong—he is quite literally an infidel. He has abandoned faith at the altar of his American idol. Not only will such an infidel commit horrific crimes in the nation's name, if called to do so as part of his "patriotic duty," he will be betraying his nation even in the act of serving it. He will be helping to transform his nation into something unworthy of his or anyone's respect.

G. K. Chesterton summed up this patriotic problem when he quipped that saying "my country, right or wrong" is like saying "my mother, drunk or sober." Of course we should continue to love our country, even when she's drunk, but we are not truly loving her if we encourage her drunkenness by becoming drunk with her. If we find our nation intoxicated with bad ideas, or addicted to bad habits, it is our duty to sober her up!

Today's America is drunk with the intoxicating effects of materialism, worshipping Mammon as a god that gives her what she thinks she wants. In her addiction to consumerism and her idolization of gadgets, she is forgetting her duty to God. Indeed, she has forgotten the true God she is called to serve in favour of mere "godgets," the trinket deities of trivia and trash.

In order to truly serve their nation, true Americans must fearlessly criticize her for her waywardness. More importantly, we must evangelize her, bringing her to the fullness of faith in the God under Whom she owes her existence. Only when America kneels before her true God will she become truly civilized; only when she kneels will she become the land of the free and the home of the brave; only when she kneels will American faith and culture become part of the faith and culture of Christendom; only when she kneels, will she rise.

13. UNLESS YOU BECOME LIKE LITTLE CHILDREN . . .

"Unless you be converted and become as little children, you shall not enter into the kingdom of heaven." So says Christ in St. Matthew's Gospel. Yet St. Paul, seeming to contradict Christ, tells us that when he was a child he behaved like a child but now that he is old he has "put away childish things." Is this not an example of the Gospel "truth" contradicting itself? If we listen to Christ must we assume that St. Paul is in error? Indeed, if we listen to St. Paul do we assume that he is not fit for the kingdom of heaven? Has he disqualified himself, damning himself with his own words? Surely not; but, if not, how can these apparent contradictions be reconciled?

Taken together, the words of Christ and those of St. Paul constitute a paradox, which is to say that the apparent contradictions point to a profound truth.

Christ is speaking of the necessity of being "like little children," of being *child-like*. St. Paul is speaking of the necessity of growing up, of ceasing to be *childish*. The difference between being *child-like* and being *childish* is so great that never the twain shall meet. If the child-like are fit for heaven, the childish are in danger of going to hell.

Let's begin by looking at childishness, the infantile and infernal perversion of the child-like.

Dorian Gray is childish. He never wants to grow up. He wants his portrait to grow old while he stays young. The four subjects of Dr. Heidegger's Experiment, in Nathaniel Hawthorne's short story, are childish. Having ruined their lives through the follies of their youth, they repeat the errors all over again when their youth is temporarily restored to them. Given the choice to repent of their follies or to repeat them, they choose the latter. This is childish. They have learned nothing from life. They have not grown up. They have not put away childish things. The paradoxical irony is that the childish do not want to become like children, they want to remain adolescent. They don't desire the innocence of a child but the sinful freshness and fleshness of pubescent folly.

Consider the difference between the attitude of the child-like and that of the childish. The child-like grow up gracefully, the childish grow old disgracefully. The child-like mature, the childish merely wither. The childish wish to stay young; they desire eternal youth; they are tempted to lie about their age. The child-like are happy to grow old; they desire the settled tranquility of the sagacious fruits of experience. In this sense, children are not childish but child-like. They want to grow up, and the sooner the better. A five-year-old is never five years old, she's always five and a quarter, or five and a half, or nearly six!

The poet Roy Campbell described the childish fear of growing old or growing up as the Peter Panic. Peter Panic creates Peter Pandemonium. Childish parents are not able to bring up children. Unwilling to grow up themselves, how can they teach their children to do so? How many millions of children in our Peter Panic-stricken age have been condemned to a childhood in which they are brought up by aging adolescents? How much child-like innocence has been sacrificed on the altar of childish ignorance?

Remaining with Peter Pan for the moment, this is how the child-like genius, G. K. Chesterton, criticised the childish climax of J. M. Barrie's children's classic:

A very fine problem of poetic philosophy might be presented as the problem of Peter Pan. He is represented as a sort of everlasting elf, a child who never changes age after age, but who in this story falls in love with a little girl who is a normal person. He is given his choice between becoming normal with her or remaining immortal without her; and either choice might have been made a fine and effective thing. He might have said that he was a god, that he loved all but could not live for any; that he belonged not to them but to multitudes of unborn children. Or he might have chosen love, with the inevitable result of love, which is incarnation; and the inevitable result of incarnation, which is crucifixion; yes, if it were only crucifixion by becoming a clerk in a bank and growing old. But it was the fork in the road; and even in fairyland you cannot walk down two roads at once. The one real fault of sentimentalism in this fairy play is the compromise that is ultimately made; whereby he shall go free for ever but meet his human friend once a year. Like most practical compromises, it is the most unpractical of all possible courses of action. Even the baby in the nursery could have seen that Wendy would be ninety in no time, after what would appear to her immortal lover a mere idle half-hour.

The introduction of Chesterton enables us to make the transition from the childish to the child-like. Few people have castigated the former whilst encapsulating the latter more than Chesterton, whose whole life seemed to have been devoted to defending the childlike from the childish.

Chesterton's appraisal of Barrie's *Peter Pan* puts us in mind of Tolkien's Middle-earth, in which the dynamic between mortality and immortality, or between growing old and staying young, is axiomatic. Tolkien succeeds as dramatically as Barrie fails in addressing the issues raised in Chesterton's criticism of *Peter Pan*. Apart from the poignant presence of the elves who are exiled in the sorrows of the "long defeat" of Time by their immortality, the whole of *The Lord of the Rings* is about growing up, in the sense of growing wise, through self-sacrifice and the struggles of living virtuously in a world riddled with evil. It is only through the child-like innocence of Frodo and Sam that the quest is fulfilled; if they had been childish they would have refused the "burden" of the Ring and would have stayed at home in the Shire, "having fun."

Like Chesterton, Tolkien understood the childlike wisdom inherent in fairy-tales. Having been influenced greatly by Chesterton's essay "The Ethics of Elfland," Tolkien explained how fairy-tales were a window of wonder through which we see the deepest truths:

> The peculiar quality of the "joy" in successful Fantasy can thus be explained as a sudden glimpse of the underlying reality or truth. It is not only a "consolation" for the sorrow of this world, but a satisfaction, and an answer to that question, "Is it true?" . . . in the "eucatastrophe" we see a brief vision . . . a far-off gleam of *evangelium* in the real world.

It is no surprise that the greatest children's literature is written by the child-like as opposed to the childish. Whereas the child-like remain open to the sense of wonder that animates the classics of children's literature, the childish sink into the sin of cynicism that blinds them to the love and beauty of reality. Oscar Wilde described a cynic as one who knows the price of everything and the value of nothing. He also wrote that "we are all in the gutter but some of us are looking at the stars." Blinded by the plank in his own eye, the childish cynic can only see the motes in the eyes of others, not the twinkle of the reflected stars. Such as these cannot unlock the imaginative doors of fairyland.

Ultimately, as those who have spent time in fairyland know, entering faery is easier by far than it is for a camel to pass through the eye of a needle. It is as simple as an adult seeing through the eye of a child. Of course one must become small in order to see through the eye of a child; and one must become humble in order to become small; and one must ask for grace in order to become humble. It's "magic," to be sure, but the magic is easy if one makes friends with the Magician.

All of this was put far more sublimely by William Wordsworth in "Intimations of Immortality from Recollections of Early Childhood" and far more succinctly by the same poet in three lines of his sonnet, "The Rainbow":

> The Child is father of the Man;
> And I could wish myself to be
> Bound each to each by natural piety.

Chesterton was not as great a poet as Wordsworth but he was certainly as great a child. Chesterton became Christ-like by remaining child-like. In "A Second Childhood" he shows us the wisdom of wonderland:

> When all my days are ending
> And I have no song to sing,
> I think I shall not be too old
> To stare at everything;
> As I stared once at a nursery door
> Or a tall tree and a swing.

PART II
CELEBRATING OUR HERITAGE

14. THE CLASSICAL MUSE

The classical muse is much more than it seems. It is responsible for the works of Homer, Sophocles, Aeschylus *et al.* But it is much more than this. It is responsible for the philosophical musings of Socrates, Plato and Aristotle. It inspired the mind of Virgil and its Virgilian spark alighted on Dante. It can be seen wending its way to Canterbury with Chaucer's pilgrims. It flits through the plays of Shakespeare. It transformed the humanism of the Renaissance, for better or worse, from its Catholic genesis to its pseudo-pagan exodus. It descended in the likeness of a dove on the artist's vision of the Virgin and turned her into a voluptuous Venus. It oversaw the loss of art's virginity and some have accused it of turning art into the whore of post-modernity. Its august presence presided over the neo-classicism of Dryden and Pope, and precipitated, in France, the first homicidal revolution of secular fundamentalism. It reemerged, uglier than ever, in the Caesarian sickness of Hitler and Mussolini.

It is much more than it seems.

At its best it leads us to the Good, the True and the Beautiful, and to the God who is the source of all goodness, truth and beauty. But it also inspires the Good, the Bad and the Ugly, serving gods of various shapes and hues. It is to be respected, even revered, but never fully trusted. Above all, it can't be ignored.

And yet the classical muse is not only much more than it seems, it is also, at the same time, much less than it seems. Isn't this a contradiction? Is such a statement indicative of the present writer's descent from the zenith of Zeus to the nadir of nebulous nonsense? Has the muse deserted me? Have I lost my wits? Is it time for the reader to turn the page in pursuit of something and someone who makes sense? Bear with me. In defiance of any appearance to the contrary, my muse and my reason have not deserted me. On the contrary, they have simply led me through the domain of arrant and apparent nonsense in order to arrive at the gracious realm of emergent paradox, a realm in which we discover that *apparent* contradictions point to a deeper truth. It is a realm in which Chesterton is king and in which Wilde is the mischievous jester, and in which I am a loyal subject.

What, then, is the mysterious paradox to which I refer? How can the apparent contradiction be made to make sense? The answer is to be found in the fact that the classical muse is not what it seems, not merely in the sense that it is more than it seems, but in the sense that much that claims to be inspired by the classical muse is less than it seems, in the sense that it is not truly classical. The muse that inspired Chaucer's *Knight's Tale* or Shakespeare's *Pericles* was not truly classical; it was truly Christian. The truly classical muse is only to be found in antiquity. It has its fulfillment and consummation in Christ and ceases to exist following the Incarnation. It is consumed by its consummation. In the words of C. S. Lewis, speaking through the medium of Father History in *The Pilgrim's Regress*, the pagan myths were *pictures* sent by God to the pagans because in their pre-Christian ignorance they couldn't know the fullness of the truth. These pictures were mere shadows, or foreshadowings, of the True Picture who is Christ, God Incarnate.

Through His Incarnation, and His Death and Resurrection, Christ consummates his love for humanity, impregnating culture with His Presence. He is the fulfillment of the Old Law of the Jews, but He is also the fulfillment of the twilit gropings of the gentiles. He is the consummation of the inarticulate, pre-Christian musings of Homer, Aeschylus, Sophocles and Virgil, and is the fulfillment of their honest, artistic articulation of moral truths and precepts; He is the consummation of the rationally articulate but visually impaired philosophical musings of Socrates, Plato and Aristotle. He baptizes their desire and pours forth the fullness of the Truth that was beyond their grasp. He is the Way, the Truth and the Life for which they were seeking. He is also the End of their search, in both senses of the word, and is, therefore, the end of them. Henceforth the virgin musings of the pagans are no longer possible because the pagan imagination has lost its virginity. Impregnated by Christ in His Mystical Marriage with His Bride, the Church, the Muse becomes graceful, that is filled with grace. In this sense, the so-called classicism of the Renaissance or of the Augustan Age is not classical at all, nor is its muse. Neo-classicism is not classicism but is the child of Christendom. It is the fruit of Christ's marriage to the Church and is the product of a baptized imagination.

This can be seen to be true of the neo-classical musings of Dante, Chaucer or Shakespeare, or of the neo-platonic and neo-Aristotelian philosophizing of St. Augustine and St. Thomas Aquinas. But what of those manifestations of neo-classicism that are avowedly anti-Christian? What of the superciliously self-named Enlightenment or Age of Reason? What of the rationalist butchery of the French Revolution and the Third Reich, those bloodthirsty heirs of the Enlightenment's "Reason"? Even if these are not truly "classical" surely they cannot be described as Christian? Perhaps not, but they are certainly more Christian than they are classically pagan. They are not pagan because paganism is no more; it has ceased to be. They can be said to be Christian in the sense that they have grown out of the baptized culture of Christendom, even if they have grown out of it only in order to grow away from it or to spurn it. In this sense the anti-Christian manifestations of neo-classicism and other forms of so-called "post-Christianity" can be likened to prodigal sons who have strayed away from home in order to cavort with swine. Some may return, in which case there will be much rejoicing; others may simply wallow in the trough until they find their way to the inferno. Either way, they are children of Christendom.

There is another metaphor that fits the neo-classicists and "post-Christians" even more aptly than that of the parable of the prodigal son. It is that of the wife who has divorced her husband. If we see the true classicism of the pagans as man's virginity, and Christendom as man's happy marriage with Christ, we can see the "post-Christians" as a disgruntled and disillusioned divorcée. If this metaphor is employed we can see that it is possible for the bride to return to her husband but it is not possible for her to return to her virginity.[6] Regaining the true classical muse is impossible because the classical "thing" was consummated and consumed by Christ; regaining the Christian Muse is not only possible, it is necessary, because Christ *is* whereas paganism is not. The choice for (post)modern man is to return to her Husband, who is the Light of the world, or to perish. There is no other option because outside of the marriage is the Night, and not only the Night but strange things in the Night.[7]

Divorced and devoid of hope, man, as the estranged bride of Christ, finds herself in the inferno of her own deviant devising. There's no escape and no hope except for her purgatorial return to the faith of her fathers. And in this purgatorial time the classical muse, as an invaluable part of her dowry, will act as a guide leading her Home. For Homer points the way Home, as do Plato and Aristotle. The classical muse and the Christian muse are in harmony; it is only poor (post)modern man, cut off from his inheritance, who lives in discord.

15. MYTH AND THOUGHT AMONG THE GREEKS

Vernant, Jean-Pierre. *Myth and Thought among the Greeks*. Translated by Janet Lloyd and Jeff Fort. New York: Zone Books, 2006.

The prejudice and superciliousness of Vernant's approach to Greek myth and classical culture is evident in the author's introduction. We are informed from the outset of the "progress in intellectual matters or techniques of reasoning [f]rom the *homo religiosus* of the archaic cultures to [the] political, reasoning individual" of later Greek civilization (p. 15). Thus we are affronted with the unquestioned presumption that *homo religiosus* is a primitive creature who concocts myths as a product of his ignorance. Similarly we are informed blithely about "the progression from mythical to rational thought and the gradual development of the idea of the individual person" (p. 15). In making these presumptions Vernant is guilty of sundering *fides* from *ratio* and, in so doing, has created a schism between himself and the men of whom he writes. There was no schism between *fides et ratio*, or between myth and reason, in the eyes of Homer, Aeschylus and Sophocles, or in the eyes of Plato, Aristotle and Socrates, or for that matter in the eyes of Virgil, Dante and Shakespeare, or Augustine, Thomas Aquinas and the Scholastics. The whole legacy of civilized culture down the ages has been a synthesizing of art and philosophy in the service of reality. And, of course, the very notion that Homer, who gave us Achilles, Hector, Odysseus, Penelope and so many others, had a retarded "idea of the individual person" is laughable. It is in fact the consequence of Vernant's own misreading of the morality and theology of Homeric myth, a flaw which is fatal to his whole thesis.

Myth and Thought among the Greeks is also characterized by the author's imposition of his own dogmatic relativism upon the Greeks (and upon his readers). We are told, for instance, that "[t]here is not, nor can there be, a perfect model of the individual, abstracted from the course of the history of mankind, with its vicissitudes and its variations and transformations across space and time" (p. 18). This betrays nothing less than pure illiteracy as regards the author's approach to myth. Homer gives us Penelope, Dante gives us Beatrice, and Shakespeare gives us Cordelia, all of whom disprove Vernant's dogmatic denial of their existence as perfect models of the female individual. This blessed trinity of idealized femininity is itself a reflection, either via prefigurement or re-presentation of the Marian archetype presented by what Tolkien would call the True Myth of Christianity. And, of course, we have Christ Himself as the perfect model of the individual. One does not need to be a Christian to see this mythical truth; one simply has to empathise with, even if one doesn't sympathise with, the notions of moral perfection presented to us. Vernant is seemingly incapable of either empathy or sympathy. He is left, like Pilate, uttering *quid est veritas* and washing his hands as the moral passion of the myths unfold before his unseeing eyes.

Homer and Sophocles knew better than Pilate and Vernant. They were pagans not relativists and, as such, they knew that truth not only exists but that it is metaphysical and therefore transcends physical reality. This is why they give us blind seers such as Teiresias or Oedipus who see with the eyes of wisdom and faith even though they cannot see the purely physical things around them. Homer and Sophocles knew that Teiresias and Oedipus see better than the likes of Pilate and Vernant because they see the *truth*. Relativists, on the other hand, are blinded by their faith in narcissistic nihilism. They are neither theists nor polytheists but simply old-fashioned idolaters, idolizing themselves as the arbiters and touchstone of the "truth" that is mere opinion. Such people are not eyeless but clueless.

In a true reading of the timeless myths of antiquity we do not find distance and dissonance between ourselves and our ancestors but resolution and resonance. We can be at home with Homer because Homer is as homely as we are. He experiences the exile of life and desires the community and communion of Home, in its physical and its metaphysical sense. The relativist is not at home with Homer because he believes that man's homelessness is not due to exile but to the non-existence of Home. Homer knew better; so did Virgil, Dante, Chaucer, Shakespeare and Tolkien. They knew the connection between Everyman and the Everlasting Man. The relativist knows only Lennon's Nowhere Man.

Vernant is something of a veritas-vampire, sucking the spirit and truth from myth and leaving only the dust and ashes of psycho-babble. Switching metaphors, he can be said to have the hand of a cheapened

Midas. Everything he touches turns to dross. It is easy to relegate myth to mere metaphor but Vernant commits a far greater sin. He reduces myth to mere mechanics. As such, we are not presented with a living myth, nor even the corpse of a myth, but merely a lump of broken machinery. This is what Vernant claims to be the forging of "new paths" whereas, in truth, it is merely the following of a blind alley. His work is truly abysmal, literally, in the sense that it creates an abyss between us and the Greeks. Those wishing to cross the abyss should take one of the many bridges that unite us with our wise and esteemed ancestors. I would recommend Tolkien or Lewis as bridges we should take or, perhaps, more recently-built bridges such as that provided by Louis Markos in his new book, *From Achilles to Christ: Why Christians Should Read the Pagan Classics* (InterVarsity Press 2007). Far from moving "from myth to reason," which is the title of the last part of Vernant's book, we should follow more trusted guides and find the reason in the myth.

16. THE MIDDLE AGES

As time goes on, the "middle ages" is exposed as an inadequate name for the period in history that it purports to describe. As with other labels, such as "the Enlightenment" and "the age of Reason," the label says more about the men who did the labeling than about the thing being labeled. Thus, for example, "the Enlightenment" was the name that those who considered themselves "enlightened" gave to the eighteenth-century philosophers with whom they agreed in order to distinguish themselves from the ignorance of the "unenlightened" past. Similarly "the age of Reason" was a name that these same "enlightened" people gave to their own age to distinguish it from the unreasonable or "irrational" ages that preceded it. Implicit in such labeling is the priggish presumption that the whole of humanity lacked enlightenment and reason until these arrivistes arrived on the scene. Hence, by implication, Socrates, Plato, Aristotle, Augustine and Aquinas are "unenlightened" and "irrational."

Clearly these priggish arrivistes have tainted the very language that historians employ. It is, for instance, risibly ironic that the rationalist labeling of history as "ancient," "mediaeval" and "modern" is as irrational as is rationalism itself. The term "modern" was invented to distinguish the present from the past without the apparent realization that the present instantly becomes the past. As the "modern," which derives from the Latin for "just now" *(modo)*, slips further into the past it becomes ipso facto far less "modern." Thus, the "modern" now encompasses everything that has happened in the past five hundred years or more (and counting). Historians have sought to fix this absurdity by dividing the past half millennium into the "early modern" and "modern" periods. No doubt, eventually, they will have to invent the term "mid-modern" to distinguish the early-early-modern from the not-so-early modern, et cetera ad absurdum.

The "middle ages," as a label, is less absurd than the "modern" in the sense that it does at least define its place *between* two other ages. Yet to speak of the period between the fall of the Roman Empire and the fall of Constantinople as the "middle ages" is to presume something definitive and delineating in both events. Although the fall of these great empires is of great importance and had cataclysmic consequences, Christendom existed prior to the first cataclysm and continues beyond the second. Similarly western civilization precedes the former and survives the latter. The Church straddles the abyss between the "ancient" and the "modern," and the edifice of civilized art and philosophy has its foundations in the ancient Greeks and towers over the swamps of modernity like a colossus of common sense in an age of banal futility. This historical transcendence challenges the presumption that history is separated by seismic shifts that define one period from another.

In truth, the Church, and the civilization that she has nurtured and nourished, cannot be defined or confined by a specific historical label. She is not simply "mediaeval" or "middle-aged." Although she was indubitably a palpable presence in the mediaeval period, as she had been in the period that preceded it, she was also palpably present in the so-called "early modern" period, her wisdom, virtue and beauty shining forth with spectacular splendour during the flowering of the Counter-Reformation. Nor has she been absent in more recent times. Indeed, it could be argued that "modernity" is best defined as the secular rebellion against the Church. From Henry VIII's destruction of the monasteries and his formation of a state church, to the anti-clerical violence of the French and Russian Revolutions, and the persecution of the Church by the German Nazis and Spanish Republicans, the world has waged a relentless war of attrition against the Mystical Body of Christ.

And yet modernity is not much different from the middle ages in this respect. When Henry VIII had St. John Fisher and St. Thomas More put to death in 1535 (in the "early modern" period), it reminded many people of Henry II's role in the murder of St. Thomas Becket in 1170 (at the height of the "middle ages"). And, of course, the martyrdom of the saints, whose blood has been spilt across every century in each of the "ages," reminds us of the archetypal martyrdom of Christ Himself upon the Cross. The world has always hated Christ and His Church, as Christ Himself told us it would. As such, we should not be surprised to discover that each "age" of history seems remarkably similar to our own age.

In every age, the same war is waged between good and evil, which is to say that every age manifests its essentially unchanging humanity. Men are made in the image of God, which means that they value virtue as a good and view vice as an evil; but men are also Fallen, which means that they are prone to succumb to the vice that is their own worst enemy and the worst enemy of their neighbour. This striving for the good and temptation to evil runs through the heart of every man and is, in consequence, at the heart of every human society in every age. Failure to understand this unfailing truth has led to a comedy of errors, not least of which is the folly of the aforementioned "Enlightenment" with its slavish and credulous belief in the perfectibility of man through his own efforts and through the machinations of human society in the form of large and intrusive government. The result of such credulity has been the systematic extermination of millions of people on the altar of "enlightened" ideologies and the "progress" they preach. These millions of innocent victims have been sacrificed to the fantasy of a future "golden age" by "progressives" who pursue it as though it were the golden fleece and who idolise it as though it were the golden calf. Since these "progressives" are always looking forward to a mythical future, they do not heed the perennial lessons of the unchanging wisdom of the past.

At this juncture we should add a cautionary word about those "regressives" who believe that there was a "golden age" in the past. Certain types of "neo-mediaevalist" fall into this category. For such "regressives" everything was wonderful in the middle ages. They point with due reverence to Chartres Cathedral and show due deference to the monastic and mendicant orders that proliferated in mediaeval times. This is all to the good. Only a philistine fails to appreciate the majesty of the Gothic, and only a scoundrel pours scorn upon the religious life. Yet one perusal of Dante's divinely inspired *Comedy* or Chaucer's perambulatory *Tales* will dissuade anyone from seeing the middle ages as a "golden age." For every mediaeval saint in Dante's Paradise, there is a corresponding mediaeval sinner in his Hell. For every San Paolo and San Francesco there is a Paolo and Francesca. For every saintly mediaeval Parson on Chaucer's Pilgrimage there is a dastardly Pardoner; for every honest Plowman there is a dishonest Miller. The litany of sin and scandal is as horrific in the "middle ages" as in any other age, though certainly no worse than in our own times.

For this reason, the middle ages should not be studied as an outdated artefact, or as a mere curio. On the contrary, the middle ages are very much alive in the sense that they accurately reflect undying truths. Where the middle ages are right they are extremely right, as in the faith of St. Francis or the philosophy of Aquinas. This union of *fides et ratio* resonates through all ages with the romance of realism. On the other hand, where the middle ages are wrong, they are extremely wrong, as in the corruption and tyranny of many of its rulers. Yet the errors of the middle ages teach us valuable lessons about the corruption and tyranny endemic to rulers in all ages.

Ultimately the middle ages are important because they mirror the truth about humanity in the holiest of its heights and in the decadence of its depths. In reflecting the truth through its mirroring of humanity, it holds up the mirror to us also. It shows us ourselves. It speaks to us as an immortal neighbour whose deathless life beckons us from beyond the grave with the gravitas of undying truth.

17. THE HEALTHY WYRDNESS
OF THE ANGLO-SAXONS

It is one of the tragic ironies of modern-life that the words "Anglo-Saxon" and "Protestant" are often seen synonymously. It is also one of modern-life's perversities that the term "Anglo-Saxon Protestant" is often pre-fixed with the word "white" to make the racially charged and acrimonious acronym "WASP": "White Anglo-Saxon Protestant." It's enough to make the most mild-mannered Anglo-Saxon Catholic more than a little waspish!

The irony springs from the fact that Anglo-Saxon England was profoundly Catholic, to such a degree that the saintly Englishman, Boniface, helped to evangelise Pagan Europe, while his contemporary, the truly venerable Bede, exhibited the high culture that Saxon England enjoyed in abundance. Whilst the former converted the Germans to Christ, the latter excelled in Latin and Greek, and classical and patristic literature, as well as Hebrew, medicine and astronomy. Bede also wrote homilies, lives of saints, hymns, epigrams, works on chronology and grammar, commentaries on the Old and New Testament, and, most famously, his seminal *Historia Ecclesiastica Gentis Anglorum* which was translated into Anglo-Saxon by King Alfred the Great. At the time of his death in 735 Bede had just finished translating the Gospel of St. John into Anglo-Saxon. Almost six hundred years later, Dante expressed his own admiration for Bede's achievement by placing him in the *Paradiso* of his *Divina Commedia*. Thus, even at the dawning of the Anglo-Saxon era, England was a beacon of Christian enlightenment. So much for the so-called Dark Ages!

The epic poem, *Beowulf,* probably dates from the early eighth century, making it contemporaneous with the lives of Saints Boniface and Bede. This wonderful and wonder-filled narrative is animated by the rich Christian spirit of the culture from which it sprang, brimming over with allegorical potency and evangelical zeal. It also conveys a deep awareness of classical antiquity, drawing deep inspirational draughts from Virgil's *Aeneid*, highlighting the Saxon poet's awareness of his place within an unbroken cultural continuum.

The continuum remains unbroken. Twelve hundred years after the Saxon *scop* recited the saga of Beowulf to packed mead-halls, a scholar of Anglo-Saxon at Oxford University was using the ancient poem as one of the major inspirations for his own latter-day epic, *The Lord of the Rings*. J. R. R. Tolkien, sharing the same ancient faith as his Anglo-Saxon ancestors, knew that the truths conveyed in *Beowulf* continue to speak across the centuries with crystal-like and crystallised clarity.

Although *Beowulf* is the best known poem in Old English it is by no means the only poetic jewel in the Anglo-Saxon crown. "The Ruin," "The Wanderer," "The Seafarer" and "The Dream of the Rood" have each strode across the continuum of the centuries with the consummate ease that is the mark of all great art. The timely and timeless reminders of man's mortality are almost ubiquitous in these poems, palpitating like the heartbeat at the poetic core of life itself . . .

> Earthgrip holds them—gone, long gone, fast in gravesgrasp . . .
> . . . sank to loam-crust.

Yet if the Anglo-Saxons were close to death, always aware as Tolkien reminds us that they were "mortal men doomed to die," they were also close to life, in the sense that they were truly alive. They were close to nature, living off the fruits of the loam-crust until in the fullness of time sinking into it. Thus the imagery is primal, dealing with the primal realities of man's dependence on nature. Hail, falling on "the frost-bound earth," is described as the "coldest of grains." Fishermen are the ploughmen of the sea, who "drive the foam-furrow" to harvest the sea's fruit. The Seafarer is close to the creatures of the earth, with whom he shares an intimate communion, invoking his knowledge of birds and beasts to incant potent images of the "clinging sorrow" of his "breast-drought" . . .

> . . . for men's laughter
> there was curlew-call, there were cries of gannets,
> for mead-drinking the music of the gull . . .

> And the cuckoo calls him in his care-laden voice,
> scout of summer, sings of new griefs
> that shall make breast-hoard bitter . . .

> Cuckoo's dirge drags out my heart,
> whets will to the whale's beat
> across wastes of water: far warmer to me

are the Lord's kindnesses than this life of death
lent us on land.

How much more alive were these Anglo-Saxons than are we moderns! They lived in a world that was harsh and hard, but at least it was real. We live in our computer-generated demi-worlds, centred on ourselves, utterly addicted to the artificial life-support machine which drips the anodyne into the anoesis of our comfortably numb minds. How can we experience the beauty of this Old English poetry if we have never heard a curlew, or a gannet, or a cuckoo, or a gull? How can we experience Keats if we have never heard a nightingale, or Shelley if we have never heard a skylark? Oh for a sobering dose of reality that will re-connect us with the real!

And what is true of the natural is equally true of the supernatural. Unlike us moderns, the Anglo-Saxons were closely connected with the supernatural realities underpinning human existence. They called these realities "wyrd," a word which has decayed into the much weaker "weird." *Wyrd* was more than merely weird. It was the intimate, almost palpable, presence of Providence in the lives of men, the closeness and connectedness of God to the destiny of His creatures.

Who liveth alone longeth for mercy,
Maker's mercy. Though he must traverse
Tracts of sea, sick at heart,
—trouble with oars ice-cold waters,
the ways of exile—Wyrd is set fast . . .

In the earth-realm all is crossed;
Wyrd's will changeth the world.
Wealth is lent us, friends are lent us,
man is lent us, kin is lent;
all this earth's frame shall stand empty . . .

For the modern in his electronic dream-world this is but foolishness. He has no concept of wyrd. For him the wyrd is just weird, or, worse, merely absurd. Our ancestors' closeness to the natural and the supernatural is merely a sign of our ancestors' ignorance or barbarism. Or so the modern perceives. But then the modern perceives very little because he is covered with too many artificial accretions to be able to experience, and therefore perceive, the real.

The modern is right in one respect at least. He is right in perceiving that the Anglo-Saxons were primitives. He is right, however, for the wrong reasons. His error lies in his perception that the primitive is synonymous with the barbaric or the ignorant. It is indeed the irony of ironies that his belief that the primitive is synonymous with the barbaric or the ignorant is actually the product of his own barbarism and ignorance. In truth, the Anglo-Saxons are primitive while he, the modern, is barbaric and ignorant. One who is primitive is one who never loses sight of the prime realities, the first things, upon which all else rests. As an adjective *prime* relates to the chief things, the most important things; as a noun it means the state of highest perfection. A primitive never loses sight of the most important things nor of the state of highest perfection which, properly understood, is the Godhead. It is the ignorant and the barbarian who lose sight of these things.

Let us leave the modern to his barbarity and his ignorance and let us return to the healthy wyrdness of the Anglo-Saxons. The conclusion of "The Seafarer" is the conclusion that any sagacious Primitive will draw as the primal lesson of life. It is a lesson that needs to be learned from life before death forces its conclusion upon us.

> A man may bury his brother with the dead
> and strew his grave with the golden things
> he would have him take, treasures of all kinds,
> but gold hoarded when he here lived
> cannot allay the anger of God
> towards a soul sin-freighted.

18. THE FAITH OF MERRIE ENGLAND

Faith of our Fathers, Mary's prayers
Shall win our country back to Thee;
And through the truth that comes from God,
England shall then indeed be free.

It is a true joy to be associated with the resurrection of this anthology of mediaeval English prayers.[8] It is a joy not merely because it is resplendent with the cream of mediaeval English spirituality, though it is; nor is it a joy simply because it serves the practical purpose of being a wonder-filled prayer book for everyday use, though it does. Apart from these joys, it is also a joy to all true Englishmen because it is truly English, in the true sense of what being English really is. (I write as a native-born Englishman and hope that my American readers will indulge me in this particular joy.)

Let's begin by discussing what England is not. It is not Britain, whether Britain be considered "Great" or otherwise. The holy Englishmen who wrote the prayers in this book had no concept of "Britain." They were English, pure and simple, and were purely and simply the better for it. Furthermore, and this is the crux of the matter, they were all Catholics. They were all Catholics because there was nothing else to be. In Chaucer's England, as in Chaucer's *Canterbury Tales*, England was divided between good Catholics and bad Catholics. There were no non-Catholics (or at least non-Catholics were so few in number and influence that they can be safely ignored). The good Catholics, knowing that if something is worth doing at all it is worth doing well, were growing in holiness and were destined for heaven; the bad Catholics, knowing, as Chesterton knew, that if something is worth doing at all it is worth doing badly, were probably on their way to purgatory. And, paradoxically, the good Catholics were sometimes bad Catholics, and the bad Catholics were sometimes good Catholics, because purgatory, whether it be on this side or the other side of the grave, is part of everyone's path to heaven. And, of course, there were those who were such bad Catholics that, knowing that the thing was worth doing but choosing not to do it, were probably destined for hell. The wicked, like the poor, are always with us, at least until and unless we get to heaven.

The point, however, is that to be English is to be Catholic. From the anonymous author of *Beowulf* to the anonymous author of *Sir Gawain and the Green Knight* we have a heritage of several centuries of Catholic culture. *Beowulf* and *Sir Gawain*, and everything in between, are forged together by the Faith that fathered them. We don't know who wrote these works and it doesn't seem to matter. We don't know their names but we do know their Creed. They believe what we believe and are united with us in a union, and Communion, that is greater than time and space. A Catholic Englishman, alive today, has much more in common with the Anglo-Saxon author of "The Dream of the Rood" than he has with the vast bulk of those who happen, by a sheer accident of history, to be walking around at the same time and sharing the same piece of earth that used to be England. Time and space are but accidents; eternity is of the essence.

These mysteries are the very warp and woof of the web of wyrd that unites all Englishmen, and indeed all men of good will, across the ages. And these are the mysteries that unite the prayers to be found in this volume. From the words of Julian of Norwich to those of St. Edmund of Canterbury we are taken into ourselves and out of ourselves, weaving the mysterious threads of introspection and extroversion into the seamless garment of revealed truth. And, what is more, and to switch metaphors, we can take this spiritual mystery tour in the safe knowledge that we will not get lost. It is Catholic and, as such, is oriented towards the well-spring of its divine source. This cannot be said of all spiritual "mysteries." Mysticism, if it is not paradoxically liberated by the constraints of orthodoxy, is dangerous. Indeed, it is not only dangerous but perilous, because, as Ronald Knox reminds us, the wrong sort of mysticism begins in mist and ends in schism.

Sadly, England fell victim to the wrong sort of mysticism and it is no coincidence that England was swallowed up by Britain at the very moment that she began to have her faith stolen from her. It is Henry VIII who begins to build the navy even as he is destroying the monasteries, bent on self-aggrandizement and the imperialism which is its bitterly destructive fruit; it is Henry VIII, Cromwell and William the Usurper who rape Ireland in the cause of Britain. It is Edmund Spenser in *The Faerie Queen* who eulogises the concept of "Britain" and idolizes Queen Elizabeth. The birth of Britain would be the death of an independent England, as it was the death of an independent Wales, Scotland and Ireland. England would take a lot of killing, however. Between the 1530s and 1680s hundreds of true Englishmen, all Catholics, were put to death for their faith. And then, just when England appeared to be dead, there was something of a resurrection in the form of the Catholic Revival under Newman, Hopkins, Chesterton, Belloc, Waugh, Tolkien and others. England is not dead. Perhaps she is only sleeping. Perhaps we await the Return of the King. Perhaps. And yet perhaps this is little more than wishful thinking. Perhaps England is not dead, but dying. Perhaps she is not only sleeping but is sleepwalking to the abyss.

These are all questions for another discussion. This book celebrates a healthy time before Little England was overshadowed by Great Britain. It was a healthier time, and a holier time. It was the time of England's virginity, before she was raped by the Reformation. As we enjoy the innocence and the wisdom of these prayers, we are not merely transported back to a healthier and a holier time, we are perhaps transformed by the experience into something akin to the saints whose prayers we are enjoying. Enjoy this journey into Merrie England and the sojourn with her saints. And remember that even if England is dead or dying her saints are very much alive.

19. THE PRIEST'S HOLE

As a hobbit in exile my heart's hearth remains in the Shire; and, to be specific, to the English shire of Norfolk in East Anglia.

For many people, the restfully rolling landscape of East Anglia will bring to the mind's eye the works of John Constable whose depiction of haywain and mill have become timelessly evocative rustic icons. Constable's landscapes are to the mind's eye what Beethoven's Sixth Symphony is to the mind's ear—a sensual celebration of the pastoral idyll which places pasture and peasant in perfect and permanent union. Implicit in the composition of both the landscape painting and the symphonic score is the vision of humanity harmonising with Creation in a hymn of living praise to the Creator.

Whenever I have the opportunity to revisit the thatched coyness of rarely visited villages, viewing churches and pubs that border lovingly groomed village greens, I wonder why these eastern parts of England are so often overlooked. The picturesque coastal towns and villages of Norfolk and Suffolk are heaven-havens of Hopkinsesque serenity in which the landscape's inscape is almost palpable. Aldeburgh, once the home of Benjamin Britten, and Southwold, still the home of the justly celebrated Adnams ale, are paradoxically dwarfed by the diminutive charm of Walberswick, nestling shyly at a bashful distance from the bustling world, and by the desolate charm of Dunwich, most of which has long since sunk beneath the waves.

There is, however, one special sacred space to which this particular hobbit makes a pilgrimage whenever he returns to the Shire. Oxburgh Hall, a place which embodies the unbroken spirit of Catholic England, fills my heady heart with reverence and revelry, commingling heartfelt humility with heartskipping joy so that the desire to kneel in silence battles with the urge to jump and sing. This mystical and powerful sense of peace and elation is connected to the fact that Oxburgh Hall feels like home, and Home, in its truest and fullest sense, is the most sacred place of all.

Needless to say, Oxburgh Hall is not "home" in any literal or mundane sense. It is the ancestral home of the Bedingfield family, noble lords who have counted royalty amongst their associates. As far as I am aware, I have not the least drop of blue blood flowing through my veins, though, as the son of a carpenter, I can perhaps claim a mystical equality with the noblest of my countrymen. Oxburgh Hall is home because it has always been a bastion of Catholicism in England, and it is as an Englishman and as a Catholic that I claim kinship with the Bedingfield family.

Throughout the centuries, in spite of all the persecutions of the penal years, the Bedingfields kept the Faith, spurning the lure of heresy and the allure of worldly preferment which had enticed most of their fellow countrymen to rebel against Christ's Mystical Body. In an age of trial, tribulation and treachery they emerged as heroes of the Recusant Resistance.

Today, amidst the many treasures to be found at Oxburgh Hall, the most dramatic is the Priests' Hole, secreted beneath the stone floor of one of the upper rooms. Climbing into this hideaway one can feel, with the thrill of chilling reality, the perils of being part of the Catholic underground in Elizabethan England. Here the priest could hide from the prying eyes of the Queen's cohorts, knowing that, if he were discovered, he would face torture and death.

Asking for the prayers of St. Thomas More and St. John Fisher, and feeling the presence of the Forty canonized Martyrs and the eighty-five beatified Martyrs of England and Wales, any pilgrim who clambers down into this holiest of hobbit holes will know that it is a magical cave into which saints have crawled on their journey to the ultimate Home that every healthy heart desires.

20. THE COUNTER-REFORMATION

O, be some other name!
What's in a name? That which we call a rose
By any other word would smell as sweet . . .

Although Juliet had other things on her mind than philosophy when she uttered these impassioned lines, she is nonetheless asking a profound philosophical question. It is a question so profound that it touches not merely the heart of her Romeo, but the heart of philosophy itself. What *is* in a name? Is a name, or a word, merely a conventional sign that serves as a label for the thing it signifies, as Saint Augustine and others have asserted? Or is a name, or a word, something that expresses abstract concepts which have no real existence beyond the name itself, as the more radical nominalists and relativists maintain?

Clearly Juliet is on the side of the Saint, and the saints, in her understanding that "a rose by any other word would smell as sweet." She knows that the rose, as a thing, is real and that the word is merely a label that we have tagged on to the thing, so that we can talk about it, and think about it. Romeo is also on the side of the saints when he responds to her that he, like the rose, by any other word would smell as sweet:

I take thee at thy word.
Call me but love and I'll be new baptized.
Henceforth I never will be Romeo.

Why this long philosophical perambulation in an essay on the Counter-Reformation? The answer is in the Counter-Reformation itself, which, by any other name, would still smell as sweet as incense. The name itself is perhaps an ugly label for such a beautiful thing. Although it describes a period in history in which the Church was countering the Protestant Reformation, it is so much more than the mere reaction that the name signifies. It was magnificent, majestic, magisterial, and so much more glorious than the thing it was "countering." It was also, in a very real sense, a Catholic Reformation and was not, therefore, in this sense, a "counter-reformation" at all. From the reforms of the Council of Trent to the fruits of a new generation of saints, such as St. Ignatius Loyola, St. Philip Neri, St. Vincent de Paul, St. Teresa of Avila, St. John of the Cross and a heavenly host of others, the Catholic Reformation of this period was filled with the Spirit that had animated earlier Catholic Reformations, such as those heralded by St. Francis and St. Dominic three hundred years earlier.

In contrast to this true Reformation, the so-called Protestant "Reformation" was more of an anti-Catholic Reaction, a Protestant Counter-Reformation! Indeed the word "Reformation" is such a misleading label for the immeasurable damage to Christendom wrought by Luther, Calvin and their cohorts that it should be exposed as an utter misnomer. Judging the thing for what it is, the works of Luther et al. should be called the Deformation or even the Defamation, since their results have been to deform Christian Europe and to defame the heritage of Christian unity which had been guarded by the Church for more than a thousand years.

Another truer word for the Reformation would be the Rupture, since it has led not merely to religious division but to the fragmentation of the Protestant denominations into a plethora of sub-dividing particles. Looking at the history of the past five hundred years it can be seen that Protestantism is an explosion of faith, not in the positive sense of the fruits of "reform" but in the negative sense of a violent disintegration of one body of Reformers under Luther into thousands of individual denominations. And, as with any explosion, the individual pieces do not simply fragment, they move further and further away from the Centre. And so it is that the new (de)formed "churches" are becoming more eccentric, or, as our ancestors in the Counter-Reformation would have named them, more heretical. Only the Rupture could have spawned the Rapture!

As we witness the disintegration of the misnamed Reformation, dare we see some mystical significance in the past five hundred years of religious conflict? Might we not see the Reformation as a catastrophe through which God had worked His mystical will? Tolkien invented a word, eucatastrophe, to describe the good that God brings out of evil; it is the good which could not have happened without the evil that preceded it.[9] A eucatastrophe is the *felix culpa*, the blessed fault or fortunate fall, from which God brings forth unexpected blessings. Thus the catastrophe of the Fall brought forth the eucatastrophe of the Redemption, and the catastrophe of the Crucifixion brought forth the eucatastrophe of the Resurrection. Might it not be equally true that the catastrophe of the Reformation brought forth the eucatastrophe of the Counter-Reformation?

If, as Christians, we believe that Christ calls us to be One, in His Name, it is hard to see how the accelerating fragmentation of Protestantism can be an authentic work of His Holy Spirit. The Counter-Reformation, on the other hand, reverberates down the ages as a living testimony of the promise of Christ that He will never abandon His Church. As the Reformation dissolves into the oblivion that it has earned for itself, the Counter-Reformation remains as living proof that the Gates of Hell will not prevail against Christ's Mystical Body.

21. AFTER SHAKESPEARE:
ENGLISH LITERATURE FROM 1616 TO 1800

For more than a thousand years England shone like a beacon of Catholic truth, its light penetrating to the farthest corners of Christendom. In the third century, during the Roman occupation, England's first martyred saint, St. Alban, was put to death in the Hertfordshire town that still bears his name. After the Romans left England, or Albion as it was then called, in the fifth century, vestiges of Roman Christianity remained, particularly in the north of the country, in spite of the influx of pagan Germanic tribes. In 596, Pope Gregory the Great sent St. Augustine of Canterbury to England to evangelize the Anglo-Saxons. The success of his mission was such that England became one of the major Christian nations of mediaeval Europe. Churches sprang up across the land, in every village, and shrines such as Walsingham and Canterbury became major pilgrimage destinations, attracting pilgrims from across Europe. This springtime of the Faith in England saw the flowering of Old English poetry, such as *Beowulf*, "The Dream of the Rood," "The Seafarer" and "The Wanderer," and the emergence of a host of saints, from Cuthbert and the Venerable Bede to an array of female saints as formidable as their names suggest: Etheldreda, Withburga and Alkelda!

The Norman Conquest of 1066 caused major upheavals to the political structure of England but did nothing to diminish the Christian fervour of its people. In the centuries that followed, great works of literature such as *Sir Gawain and the Green Knight* and *The Canterbury Tales* exhibited the Catholicism at the heart of mediaeval English culture. Nothing, it seemed, could separate the English from their age-old Faith in Christ and His Church.

And then came the totalitarian tyranny of Henry VIII who declared himself head of the church in England, in defiance of not only the Pope but of the wishes of the vast majority of his subjects. He put dissidents, such as St. John Fisher and St. Thomas More, to death, systematically desecrated the shrines of the saints, and destroyed the many monasteries that graced the English landscape. For the next 150 years saints were put to death in England for no other crime than defiantly practicing their Catholic Faith. There are now forty canonized martyrs of England and Wales, eighty-five beatified martyrs, and hundreds of other martyrs who have not been officially recognized by the Magisterium of the Church. In the midst of this anti-Catholic pogrom, the giant figure of William Shakespeare emerges as a witness to the horrors that surrounded him and his fellow Catholics. Much has been written about Shakespeare's Catholicism, both in terms of the evidence discernible in the facts of his life and the evidence to be gleaned from the meaning of his plays. Yet it is often thought that he represents, paradoxically, not only the zenith of English Catholic literary achievement but, at the same time, the setting of its sun. It is almost as though Shakespeare is a super nova, a star that is brighter than all the others because it is dying. He is an explosion of brilliance followed by utter darkness.

Yet is this so?

It is certainly the case that the centuries following Shakespeare's death represented a new dark age in which God was declared dead, or dying, and Man was declared god, or, at least, in which Man had declared himself the measure of all things and the master of his own destiny. The theological pride at the darkened heart of this age can be seen by the supercilious names that it gave itself. It declared itself the Age of Reason, thereby snubbing the truly philosophical ages that had preceded it, thumbing its nose at the towering influence of Athens (Socrates, Plato and Aristotle), and the definitive position of Rome (St. Augustine, St. Thomas Aquinas, etc.). The Age of Reason had no need of these true pillars of Reason. Like a restless adolescent, it turned its back on its parents, and the wisdom of its elders, and declared itself independent.

Another name that the so-called Age of Reason gave itself was the Enlightenment, declaring, in effect, that the world had been in the dark until it came along with its "enlightened" views. Truly such an age, characterized by priggishness and pride, should be more truly called an endarkenment, an age that prides itself in shutting itself off from the light of wisdom, from the authoritative *gravitas* of tradition, and from the indissoluble marriage of *fides et ratio*.

Clearly the "Age of Reason" and the "Enlightenment" are misnomers. They are names that the age gave itself in an act of precocious chutzpah. They are names that carry more than a suggestion of self-justification, self-righteousness and snobbishness. They are purely subjective terms, as inaccurate in the service of objective discourse as would be the riposte of calling the age the "Endarkenment." These labels are all very well from the perspective of rhetoric but what is needed is a term that both sides can agree upon, a term that the protagonist and antagonist can accept as *objectively* accurate. Objectively speaking, the age should really be called the age of Disenchantment. The word, *enchantment*, derives from the Latin, *cantare*, to sing, or *cantus*, song, and the disenchantment of the Enlightenment was the shift from seeing nature as creation, i.e., as a beautiful work of art *sung* into existence by God, to nature as something merely mechanical and, later, merely meaningless.

In the age of Disenchantment, the wholeness and oneness of Christendom is lost in a progressive fragmentation of thought that continues to this day. From its earliest manifestation in the decay of the Christian humanism and neo-classicism of the Renaissance, and its coming of age in the pride of the self-named Enlightenment, to its self-defeating victory in the nihilistic nonsense of deconstructionism, the age of Disenchantment represents the triumph of barbarism over civilization. On the assumption that civilization is preferable or superior to barbarism, it could be said that the age of Disenchantment represents a move in the wrong direction.

Although the culture has become fragmented and disintegrated in the age of Disenchantment, destroying the unity of the age of Christendom, the presence of Christendom within the age of Disenchantment can be seen in the magic or miracle of Re-enchantment. Many of the greatest works of art in recent centuries are not the products of disenchantment but of re-enchantment. The works of Shakespeare, Dryden, Samuel Johnson, Blake, Coleridge, Wordsworth, Sir Walter Scott, Dickens, Dostoyevsky, Chesterton, Lewis, Tolkien, Waugh and T. S. Eliot, to name but an illustrious few, are inspired by a rejection of disenchantment and a desire for re-enchantment. And what is true of literature is true of painting (the Pre-Raphaelites), architecture (the Gothic Revival), and music (Bruckner, Mahler, Mendelssohn, Messiaen, Arvo Pärt, etc.). This disillusionment with disenchantment represents a refusal to believe that reality is only the cold mechanism of the materialist or the meaningless mess of the nihilist; it is an awakening to the enchantment of reality, perceiving it as a miraculous harmony of being, a song, a Great Music, the Music of the Spheres. Hence the employment of "disenchantment" as the operative description of the process that calls itself the Enlightenment.

One other misconception that needs addressing is the presumption that the period from Shakespeare's death, in 1616, to the genesis of the English

Romantic movement at the turn of the nineteenth century represents a period of utter Disenchantment, in which cold rationalism had eclipsed the enchanting power of beauty and faith. It is often believed that the Romantics represented a sense of Re-enchantment that the previous two centuries had seemingly lost. Although there is an element of truth in such a belief, and although the Romantic movement would give birth to various manifestations of neo-mediaevalism, such as the Gothic Revival, the Pre-Raphaelites and the Oxford Movement, it would be an unjust over-simplification to assume that there was nothing but disenchanted darkness in the two centuries following Shakespeare's death. The period from 1616 to 1800 included the heyday of the Metaphysical Poets (Donne, Herbert, Crashaw, etc.), the dark and disturbed genius of Milton, the satirical orthodoxy of Dryden and Pope, and the sheer wit and wisdom of Samuel Johnson. As an age that exhibited the perennial power of re-enchantment in a culture dominated by disenchantment, it is not dissimilar to our own.

Shakespearean England passed away with the passing of the Bard, but it did not signal the death of England, or the death of her Faith. The age of Dryden was followed by the age of Pope, and these were followed by the age of Johnson. Yes, there is life after Shakespeare, and it's a life worth celebrating.

22. TRUTH IN FICTION:
THE ART OF THE NOVEL

It is said, quite truly, that truth is stranger than fiction. It is, however, equally true to say that the strangest thing in fiction is the truth. This is not to say that truth is strange to fiction and is strange when we find it there. Quite the contrary. It belongs in fiction as an integral and inextricable part of the story; so much so, that we can talk about truth as being the very heart of the story, the invisible yet palpable force that infuses the fictional narrative with the life-blood of meaning. No, the reason that the strangest thing in fiction is the truth, is that the truth in fiction is beguilingly elusive whilst being immanently present. Although it is the very life of a story, it is all too easy to neglect or deny its presence, or even its existence. It is, therefore, essential that we learn to see the truth in fiction and to recognise its role as the conveyer of applicable meaning, the bridge that connects the fictional story with the real story in which we are living.

So how do we recognise the truth in fiction? First, as in life, we need to distinguish between the two types of truth; between the physical facts and the deeper metaphysical truth. With regard to the former, every fictional story must conform to the facts that govern our lives in this world. We have to be able to recognise reality in the fictional characters that are introduced to us by the author. They have to be believable; they must be credible. They have to be *real* people even if they are only realized in the imagination. Furthermore, the *real* imaginary characters have to live in real, believable places. If, for instance, we are reading an historical novel about the wild west, we will not tolerate our gun-toting hero, riding home from the range at sundown and switching on the television with the remote! Even fiction must conform to believable fact. And this rule must be followed even in the realm of fantasy or science fiction. If an eight-headed monster attacks a five-legged alien, in a landscape of orange mountains capped with purple snow under a turquoise sky resplendent with green clouds, we will still picture in our mind's eye real heads, however ugly, and real legs, however oddly positioned beneath the torso. We will know or presume, unless told otherwise, that the head contains eyes and a mouth, and the legs are for walking, or perhaps running as fast as possible considering the nature of the eight-headed beast in hot pursuit. The mountains will be mountains, regardless of their colour, and the clouds will be clouds. We can change the colour of things, or multiply them, but the things are still things that are *facts* in our world. If the alien landscape is so alien that we can't imagine it, the story will be unintelligible, and indeed untellable.

So much for the physical facts, the solid material, or nitty-gritty, with which the story is told; what about the metaphysical truth that breathes the breath of life and meaning into the story? This is more difficult to discern. We all recognise a cloud when we see one but we don't always recognise a philosophy, even when the philosophy is much less nebulous than the cloud. If we are blind to metaphysics, we will not see the metaphysical truth pulsating through a story even if it stares us in the face. And this is the problem facing modern man in his reading, or misreading, of classic literature. He no longer sees as the author of the work sees and is therefore blind to the deepest meaning that the author's work reveals.

The modern critic is bogged down in Dante's inferno because he doesn't see the efficacious and edifying power of repentance in Dante's purgatory. He is stranded in hell because he doesn't understand the theological brilliance of Dante's vision of heaven. Moving into the age of the novel, the modern critic sees only the decorative decorum of the social etiquette of Jane Austen's novels and not the decorous dignity of the edifying Christian morality that transcends the ornamental trappings. He sees only the highly-strung emotions of the characters in the romantic novels of the Brontë sisters without perceiving the orthodox Christianity that informs the works. He sees only the (homo)sexual undertones of *Brideshead Revisited* and not the workings of divine grace that is the supernatural thread binding the novel together. He sees *The Lord of the Rings* as an escapist fantasy not as "a fundamentally religious and Catholic work," to quote the author's own description of his timeless epic.

The tragedy of the modern critic is that he refuses to see through any eyes except his own. He believes that his eyes see more clearly than anyone else's, even those of the novelist himself. His self-centred vision allows him to see nothing but his own prejudices reflected back to him. A novel can teach him nothing because he is convinced that he has nothing to learn. Every novel is not a window through which he can perceive reality through the visionary eyes of the artist, but only a narcissistic mirror in which he sees only images of himself and his own ideas.

Let's leave our poor deluded critic admiring himself in the glass.

As for the rest of us, let's see the truth in fiction by seeing through the eyes of the author (as far as possible).[10] In doing so, we will escape from the vanity of the mirror of illusion and will step miraculously through the looking-glass of true perception into a wonderland in the presence of genius.

23. THE ROMANTIC REACTION

What is Romanticism? Is it right or wrong? Is it right or left? Is it revolutionary or reactionary? What *is* it? Such questions are not academic, nor are they unimportant. On the contrary, they help us to understand the world in which we live.

In the "Afterword" to the third edition of *The Pilgrim's Regress* C. S. Lewis complained that "Romanticism" had acquired so many different meanings that, as a word, it had become meaningless. "I would not now use this word . . . to describe anything," he complained, "for I now believe it to be a word of such varying senses that it has become useless and should be banished from our vocabulary." *Pace* Lewis, if we banished words because they have multifarious meanings or because their meaning is abused or debased by maladroit malapropism we should soon find it impossible to say anything at all! Take, for example, the word "love." Few words are more abused, yet few words are more axiomatic to an understanding of ourselves. John Lennon and Jesus Christ do not have the same thing in mind when they speak of love. One puts a flower in his hair and goes on an hallucinogenic trip to San Francisco; the other has a crown of thorns placed on His head and goes to His death on Golgotha. The one goes astray, the other shows the Way. C. S. Lewis understood this of course. He understood it so well that he wrote a whole book on the subject. In *The Four Loves* he sought to *define* "love," And what is true of a word such as "love" is equally true of a word like "romanticism." If we arc to advance in understanding we must abandon the notion of abolishing the word and commence instead with defining our terms. Lewis, in spite of his protestations, understood this also, proceeding from his plaintive call for the abolition of the word to the enumerating of various definitions of it, claiming that "we can distinguish at least seven kinds of things which are called 'romantic.'" From four loves to seven romanticisms, Lewis was not about to abandon meaning, or the *mens sana*, to men without minds or chests.

Since Lewis's seven separate definitions of romanticism are a little unwieldy, it is necessary to hone our definition of romanticism into an encompassing unity within which the other definitions can be said to subsist. What makes romanticism distinct; or, to return to our initial question, what *is* it? According to the *Collins Dictionary of Philosophy*, romanticism is "a style of thinking and looking at the world that dominated nineteenth-century Europe." Arising in early mediaeval culture it referred originally to tales in the Romance language about courtly love and other sentimental topics, as distinct from works in classical Latin. From the beginning, therefore, 'romanticism' stood in contra-distinction to "classicism." The former referred to an outlook marked by refined and responsive *feelings* and thus could be said to be inward-looking, subjective, "sensitive" and given to noble dreams; the latter is marked by empiricism, governed by science and precise measures, and could be said to be outward-looking.

Having defined our terms, albeit in the broadest and most sweeping sense, we can proceed to a discussion of the ways in which human society has oscillated between the two alternative visions of reality represented by classicism and romanticism. First, however, we must insist that the oscillation is itself an aberration. It is a product of modernity. In the middle ages there was no such oscillation between these two extremes of perception. On the contrary, the mediaeval world was characterized by, indeed it was defined by, a theological and philosophical unity which transcended the division between romanticism and classicism. The nexus of philosophy and theology in the Platonic-Augustinian and Aristotelian-Thomistic view of man represented the fusion of *fides et ratio*, the uniting of faith and reason. Take, for example, the use of the figurative or the allegorical in mediaeval literature, or the use of symbolism in mediaeval art. The function of the figurative in mediaeval art and literature was not intended primarily to arouse spontaneous *feelings* in the observer or reader, but to encourage the observer or reader to see the philosophical or theological significance beneath the symbolic configuration. In this sense, mediaeval art, informed by mediaeval philosophy and theology, is much more objective and outward-looking than the most "realistic" examples of modern art. The former points to abstract ideas which are the fruits of a philosophical tradition existing independently of either the artist or the observer; the latter derives its "realism" solely from the feelings and emotions of those "experiencing" it. One demands that the artist or the observer reach beyond themselves to the transcendent truth that is out there; the other recedes into the transient feelings of subjective experience. The surrender of the transcendental to the transient, the perennial to the ephemeral, is the mark of post-Christian, and therefore post-rational, society. It is the mark of the beast.

The mediaeval fusion of faith and reason was fragmented, theologically, by the Reformation, and, philosophically, by the secularizing humanism of the Late-Renaissance. Romanticism and classicism can be said to represent attempts to put the fragments of post-Christian humptydumptydom together again. They are attempts to make sense of the senselessness of fragmented faith and reason.

The superciliously self-named "Enlightenment" was the philosophical Phoenix-Frankenstein that rose from the ashes of this fragmented unity. It represented faithless "reason," or, more correctly, a blind faith in "reason" alone. In much the same way that the theological fragmentation of the Protestant Reformation had led to a rejection of scholastic *ratio* in its enshrining of *fides* alone, so the philosophical fragmentation of the Renaissance-Enlightenment had led to a rejection of *fides*, enshrining *ratio* alone. A belief that man had dethroned the gods of superstition led very quickly to the superstitious elevation of man into a self-worshipping god. Eventually it led to the worship of the goddess Reason at Notre Dame Cathedral in Paris during the Reign of Terror that followed the French Revolution, the first manifestation of rationalist totalitarianism.

If the Enlightenment was characterized by scientism and skepticism, i.e., the worship of science and the denigration of religion, the Romantic Reaction against the Enlightenment would be characterized by skepticism about science and by the resurrection of religion. Romanticism would emerge, in fact, as the reaction of inarticulate "faith" against inarticulate "reason"; heart-worship at war with head-worship. It was all a far cry from the unity of heart and head that had characterized Christian civilization. The Romantic Reaction would, however, be a significant step in the right direction, leading many heart-searching Romantics to the heart of Rome. This was, at least, the case in England and France, though in Germany it led, via the genius of Wagner and the madness of Nietzsche, to the psychosis of Hitler.

The Romantic Reaction in England could be said to have had its genesis in 1798 with the publication of *Lyrical Ballads* by William Wordsworth and Samuel Taylor Coleridge. Published only nine years after the French Revolution, the poems in *Lyrical Ballads* represented the poets' recoil from the rationalism that had led to the Reign of Terror. Wordsworth passed beyond the "serene and blessed mood" of optimistic pantheism displayed in his "Lines Composed a few miles above Tintern Abbey" to a full embrace of Anglican Christianity as exhibited in the allegorical depiction of Christ in "Resolution and Independence." Coleridge threw down the allegorical gauntlet of Christianity in "The Rime of the Ancient Mariner," and, in his "Hymn before Sunrise in the Vale of Chamouni," he saw beyond majestic nature (*O Sovran Blanc!*) to the majesty of the God of nature:

> Who made you glorious as the Gates of Heaven
> Beneath the keen full moon? Who bade the sun
> Clothe you with rainbows? Who, with living flowers
> Of loveliest blue, spread garlands at your feet?—
> God! let the torrents, like a shout of nations,
> Answer! and let the ice-plains echo, God!
> God! sing ye meadow-streams with gladsome voice!
> Ye pine-groves, with your soft and soul-like sounds!
> And they too have a voice, yon piles of snow,
> And in their perilous fall shall thunder, God!

In their reaction against the Enlightenment and its monstrous son, the French Revolution, Wordsworth and Coleridge had leapt over the errors and terrors of the previous three centuries to re-discover the purity and passion of a Christian past, leapfrogging heresy to find orthodoxy. This pattern of reaction would be repeated in the various manifestations of neo-mediaevalism that would follow in the wake of Wordsworth's and Coleridge's Romanticism. The Gothic Revival, heralded by the architect, Augustus Pugin, in the 1830s, and championed by the art critic, John Ruskin, twenty years later, sought to discover a purer aesthetic through a return to mediaeval notions of beauty. The Oxford Movement, spearheaded by John Henry Newman, Edward Pusey and John Keble, sought a return to a purer Catholic vision for the Church of England, leapfrogging the Reformation in an attempt to graft the Victorian Anglican Church onto the Catholic Church of mediaeval England through the promotion of Catholic liturgy and a Catholic understanding of the sacraments. The pre-Raphaelite Brotherhood, formed some time around 1850 by Dante Gabriel Rossetti, John Everett Millais, William Holman Hunt and others, sought a purer vision of art by leapfrogging the art of the Late-Renaissance in pursuit of the clarity of mediaeval and Early-Renaissance painting which existed, so the pre-Raphaelites believed and as their name implied, prior to the innovations of Raphael.

Perhaps the most important poetic voice to emerge from the Romantic Reaction is that of Gerard Manley Hopkins, who was received into the Catholic Church by John Henry Newman in 1866, twenty-one years after Newman's own conversion. Influenced by the pre-Reformation figures of

St. Francis and Duns Scotus, and by the counter-Reformation rigour and vigour of St. Ignatius Loyola, Hopkins wrote poetry filled with the dynamism of religious orthodoxy. Unpublished in his own lifetime, Hopkins was destined to emerge as one of the most influential poets of the twentieth century following the first publication of his verse in 1918, almost thirty years after his death.

Although these manifestations of Romantic neo-mediaevalism transformed nineteenth-century culture, countering the optimistic and triumphalistic scientism of the Victorian imperial psyche, it would be wrong to imply that Romanticism always led to mediaevalism. The neo-mediaeval tendencies of what might be termed Light Romanticism were paralleled by a Dark Romanticism, epitomized by the life and work of Byron and Shelley, which tended towards nihilism and self-indulgent despair.

If Wordsworth and Coleridge were reacting against the rationalist iconoclasm of the French Revolution, Byron and Shelley seemed to be reacting against Wordsworth's and Coleridge's reaction! Greatly influenced by *Lyrical Ballads*, they were nonetheless uncomfortable at the Christian traditionalism that Wordsworth and Coleridge began to embrace. Byron devoted a great deal of the Preface to *Childe Harold's Pilgrimage* to attacking the "monstrous mummeries of the middle ages," and Shelley, in his "Defense of Poetry," declared his loathing of Tradition by insisting that poets were slaves to the zeitgeist and that they were "the mirrors of the gigantic shadows which futurity casts upon the present." Slaves of the spirit of the Present, and mirrors of the Giant presence of the Future, poets were warriors of Progress intent on vanquishing the superstitious remnants of Tradition. Perhaps these inanities could be excused as being merely the facile follies of youth, especially as there appeared to be signs that Byron yearned for something more solid than the inarticulate creedless deism espoused in "The Prayer of Nature," and signs also that Shelley's militant atheism was softening into skylarking pantheism. Their early deaths, and the early death of their not-so-dark confrere, Keats, cut them off in the very life-throes of their groping for the light of meaning in the darkness of their self-centred and self-defeating grappling. Stealing upon them like a thief in the night, death has preserved them forever as icons of folly who often, almost in spite of themselves, attained heights of beauty and perception.

In essence, in comparing Wordsworth and Coleridge with Byron and Shelley, we see a parting of the ways between the high road of Light Romanticism and the low road of the Dark Romantics. Yet if we were to assume that the parting of the ways was permanent and that, as with

Kipling's East and West, "never the twain shall meet," we would be wrong. The two roads of Romanticism have more in common with the high road and the low road that lead to the "bonny, bonny banks of Loch Lomond" or, perhaps more appositely, they converge at last where all roads lead—at Rome. For, as befits a romance, Romanticism, even Dark Romanticism, often leads to Rome. The Byronic influence of Dark Romanticism crossed the channel and found itself baptized in the Decadence of Baudelaire, Verlaine and Huysmans, all of whom plumbed the depths of despair, discovered the reality of hell and recoiled in horror into the arms of Mother Church. Baudelaire was received into the Church on his deathbed, Verlaine converted in prison, and Huysmans, having dabbled with diabolism, ended his life in a monastery. The principal difference between the Dark Romanticism of Byron and Shelley and the Decadence of Baudelaire, Verlaine and Huysmans is that the former delved into the darkness of their own ego with nothing but Nothing to illumine their musings, whereas the latter delved deep into their own inner darkness with the light of theology. The former were lost in circumlocutions of self-centred circumnavigation, the latter discovered the Beast that dwelt in the bottomless pit of self-obsession and, beating their chests, knelt at last before the Christ that their own sins had crucified. The French Decadence was also characterized by its preoccupation with symbolism, which was itself a return to the mode of communication employed in mediaeval art.

If Dark Romanticism had crossed the channel in Byronic guise, metamorphosing into the symbolism of the French Decadence, it re-crossed the Channel under the patronage of Oscar Wilde, who was an aficionado of Baudelaire and Verlaine. Somewhat bizarrely and perhaps perversely, Wilde had read Huysmans's recently published Decadent masterpiece, *À Rebours*, during his honeymoon in Paris, a novel which would greatly influence his own Decadent tour de force, *The Picture of Dorian Gray*. As with their French predecessors the doyens of the English Decadence also found their way to the Catholic Church, turning their back on debauchery and modernity in favour of traditional Christianity. Apart from Wilde himself, who was received into the Church on his death-bed, other leading figures of the English Decadence who "poped" include Aubrey Beardsley, Lionel Johnson, John Gray, Ernest Dowson and even the *enfant terrible* of the 1890s, Lord Alfred Douglas. It can be seen, therefore, that the high road and the low road converged into the Roman Road of conversion. The high road of sanctity was followed by such as Newman and Hopkins, both of whom became Catholic priests, whereas the low road of sin, the path of the Prodigal Son, was taken by a host of French and English Decadents. For, as Oscar Wilde never tired of reminding us, even the saints were sinners and all sinners are called to be saints.

From the publication of *Lyrical Ballads* in 1798 to the death of Oscar Wilde in 1900, the Romantic Reaction could be seen, for the most part, to be a reaction against the rationalist and anti-religious superciliousness of the Enlightenment. For all its follies and foibles it staggered falteringly in the right direction and only occasionally lost its way.

Let's conclude by returning to our original questions. What is Romanticism? It is the generally healthy reaction of the heart to the hardness of the head. Is it right or wrong? It is often right, though sometimes wrong, but, in the words of that greatly misunderstood Romantic, King Lear, it is "more sinned against than sinning." Is it right or left? It has always been too wise to fall into the idiocy of classifying itself thus. Political concepts of left and right are the products of the irrational "rationalism" of the French Revolution; it is the language of the parliament of fools. True Romanticism, like true Classicism, has always concerned itself with matters of right and wrong, being content to leave the rhetoric of left and right to scoundrels and charlatans. Is it revolutionary or reactionary? It depends, of course, on how we are defining our terms. If, however, we are referring to political revolutions of the ilk of 1789 and 1917 it is counter-revolutionary and splendidly reactionary, at least in its English manifestation. What *is* it? It is an effort to rediscover what has been lost; a groping in the depths and the darkness of modernity for the light of truth that tradition preserves. For, as Oscar Wilde reminds us, "we are all in the gutter but some of us are looking at the stars."

24. ROME AND ROMANTICISM

If Rome is a mystery, so is Romanticism. If Rome, as the Eternal City, is so much more than the temporal city situated in the heart of Italy, Romanticism is so much more than romance, at least in the wine-and-roses sense in which it is celebrated on St. Valentine's Day. If Rome is more than mere superstition, Romance is more than mere schmaltz. There is, therefore, at the very outset of any discussion on the relationship between Rome and Romanticism a difficulty of definition. What *is* Rome; what *is* Romanticism?

The first thing to be understood is that Rome is more real than Romanticism. Rome is substantially real, Romanticism is a mere accident. Rome, as the Eternal City, is the Heavenly Jerusalem. If Rome, as Heaven, is the goal, She is also, as the Church, the means of achieving the goal. As the Mystical Body of Christ, She is the Way, the Truth and the Life. If this is true—and it is—it is true whether we believe it or not. God's existence is not contingent upon our believing in Him. We do not live in a relativist universe, even if we insist on calling ourselves relativists. Reality is not dependent upon us, we are dependent on It. Rome is real, whether we like it or not, or whether we believe it or not.

So far, so good. But what of Romanticism? Why is it less real than Rome?

Romanticism is less real because it only exists as a response to, or a reaction against, something else. It does not have an existential autonomy that is independent of the things to which it is responding, or against which it is reacting. Romanticism is said to be a reaction against classicism, as exemplified in early mediaeval culture by those works of literature in the vernacular, i.e., the Romance language (from whence the word "romance" derives), as opposed to works in classical Latin. According to this primal understanding of the word, Dante can be seen as being a classicist and as being a romantic at one and the same time. In revering Virgil and selecting him as his guide and mentor he is clearly placing himself in the classical tradition, yet in choosing to write in the modern vernacular, as distinct from Latin, he is making himself a romantic.

Similarly, Romanticism is said to be rooted in *feelings*, making it subjective in its approach to reality, whereas classicism is governed by what might be termed an objective approach to reality. If this is so, the great Christian mystics, such as St. John of the Cross or St. Teresa of Avila, can be said to be romantic in the intensity of their mystical experiences and yet practitioners of classicism in their continuing adherence to objectively verifiable doctrinal orthodoxy.

The apparent contradictions, or paradoxes, continue. If later manifestations of Romanticism can be said to be a reaction against the emergent scientism and skepticism of the Enlightenment, Jean Jacques Rousseau, the philosophical father of the French Revolution, is both a Romantic in his reaction against scientism and a child of the Enlightenment to the degree that he accepted the Enlightenment's rationalism and its religious skepticism. In this way, the French Revolution can be seen as being both a Romantic reaction against the Enlightenment and a product of it.

And so it goes on. Wordsworth and Coleridge reacted against the materialism of the Enlightenment by embracing, first, pantheism and then neo-mediaevalist Christianity, whereas Byron and Shelley reacted against Wordsworth and Coleridge by becoming anti-Romantic Romantics!

If this is all a little confusing, it is meant to be. Romanticism is as confusing as it is confused. It responds. It reacts. And it changes shape and colour as it does so. One might almost call Romanticism a chameleon. Yet it is less real than a chameleon, which has substantial reality. It is less real than the metaphor of the chameleon, which, as a chimera of the imagination, also has a *type* of substantial reality derived from a substantially real archetype. Romanticism is in fact not so much the chameleon itself, as the mere colour of the chameleon. It is not a thing but a colour; it is a mere pigment of our imagination. It is not one colour but a whole spectrum of colours. It is a rainbow created from the splitting of the white light of philosophical unity that preceded it. Its spectrum ranges from dark to light. At its darker extremities it is the colour of Rousseau's noble savage; it is the colour of the French Revolution; it is the blood-red hue of *la Terreur* that followed in the Revolution's wake; it is the colour of the philosophy of Schopenhauer and Nietzsche; it is the colour of Auschwitz and the Gulag Archipelago. It is also, towards the lighter end of its spectrum, the colour of Coleridge and Wordsworth, of Scott and Stevenson, and of Ruskin and Rossetti; it is the colour of the music of Berlioz, Bruckner and Liszt; and, in its brightest hue of all, it is the colour of conversion, lighting the path of many towards the Church of Rome.

And this brings us back to Rome and Romanticism. To switch our metaphors, Romanticism can be likened to a river, or, more precisely, to two rivers. One is the river of no-return, the river of dark romanticism that meanders into the meaningless swamps of deconstruction and beyond. The other is the eternal Tiber of the imagination, romanticism's river of light that flows, if it is followed to its end, to the very heart of the Eternal City.

25. THE VICTORIAN AGE

G. K. Chesterton devoted the first part of his book, *The Victorian Age in Literature*, to examining what he termed "The Victorian Compromise." He was alluding to the spirit of pragmatism which was one of the chief characteristics of nineteenth-century England. Yet the essence of the Victorian Conundrum, of which Chesterton was a perspicacious observer, had as much to do with ineradicable Contradiction as with pragmatic Compromise. The age of Victoria (1837–1901) saw the rise of Empire and also the rise of anti-imperial nationalism; it saw the apparent triumph of industrialism and yet also the rise of an entrenched anti-industrialism; it saw the triumph of capitalism and the birth of Marxism; it was the age of Darwinian science but also the age of Dickensian romance; it was the age of an emboldened atheism and yet the age of resurrected religion; it was the age of disillusioned agnosticism but also the age of returning Catholicism. It was all these things, a cacophonous clash of contradictions masquerading as compromise.

For most people perhaps, the Victorian Age was the age of Empire. It was the age of ascendant British Imperialism, culminating in the Boer War at the end of the century in which the might of Empire, serving the powerful mining interests in South Africa, sought to crush the resistance of Afrikaans farmers. It was in 1900 at a meeting opposing the Boer War that Hilaire Belloc and G. K. Chesterton first met, founding their friendship on a belief that John Bull was a bully. Yet he was a bully who had already had his day because, as the sun set on the Victorian Age, it was also setting on the British Empire.

There was, however, another Empire which made its mystical return to England during the Victorian Age. The Catholic Church, the mystical heir of the Roman Empire, rose over the Victorian horizon three hundred years after it had seemingly set forever over the distant horizon of Elizabethan England.

The Resurrection of Rome began with the Insurrection of Romanticism, the latter of which was a reaction against the arrogance and presumption of the eighteenth-century Enlightenment. As this Romantic reaction flowered into various forms of neo-mediaevalism, the Catholic Cultural Revival was born. Amongst the early converts was Augustus Pugin, who was received into the Church in 1833, and, as a leading light in the Gothic Revival, was responsible for the design of many new Catholic churches, most notably the new Catholic cathedral in Birmingham. His book, *True Principles of Christian Architecture*, published in 1841, did much to revive Gothic architecture in England.

Four years later, in 1845, John Henry Newman was received into the Church, arguably the most important convert of the whole Victorian period. He is widely considered to be one of the finest prose stylists of the nineteenth century and his many exceptional literary works include his semi-autobiographical novel, *Loss and Gain*, published in 1848, which charts a young man's path to Rome, and his masterful *Apologia pro Vita Sua*, published in 1865, in which he makes a stylistically beautiful and yet intellectually rigorous defence of the Catholic faith. Regarding the latter of these two works, Hilaire Belloc wrote that its importance "is due to the fact that it puts conclusively, convincingly, and down to the very roots of the matter, the method by which a high intelligence . . . accepted the Faith." With the conversion of Newman the Catholic Church found itself back at the centre of English intellectual life for the first time in two hundred years.

A year after the publication of the *Apologia* Newman received a young man by the name of Gerard Manley Hopkins into the Church who was destined not only to become a Jesuit priest but to become arguably the greatest and most influential poet to emerge from the Victorian Age. In sublimely beautiful poems, such as "The Wreck of the Deutschland," he would combine in seamless splendor the Franciscan philosophy of Duns Scotus with the mysticism of St. Ignatius Loyola. Unfortunately his poetry is so densely rich in double-entendres, onomatopoeia and alliteration that it is almost untranslatable into other languages. As such, this most wonderful poet is almost unknown beyond the English-speaking world, a sad fact that not only deprives the greater part of the world of his singularly beautiful voice but also obscures the extent of his undoubted cultural influence in Anglophone cultures, an influence which can be said to rival that of T. S. Eliot.

Hopkins, however, was only the most illustrious of a long line of literary lights who converted to Catholicism during the Victorian Age. Others included Coventry Patmore, who would exert a considerable influence on the young C. S. Lewis, and many of the major poets of the *fin de siècle* including Ernest Dowson, Lionel Johnson and John Gray. Aubrey Beardsley, the artist of the *fin de siècle* who in his short life became so important and such an influence on his contemporaries that Max Beerbohm dubbed the 1890s "the Beardsley Period," was also received into the Church shortly before his death in 1898. Apart from Beardsley the most important figure of the *fin de siècle* was the allegedly incorrigible Oscar Wilde who finally consummated his lifelong love affair with Catholicism with his reception into the Church on his deathbed in 1900.

On 22 January 1901 Queen Victoria died. On the day of her funeral, Chesterton reflected on the nature of his patriotism: "It is sometimes easy to give one's country blood and easier to give her money. Sometimes the hardest thing of all is to give her truth." In the new century, Chesterton would give her truth and, in so doing, he would be following in the foot-steps of Pugin, Newman, Hopkins and the host of others who had returned to the faith of their fathers and sought to persuade their fellow countrymen to do the same. For all its other claims to fame, the Victorian Age deserves to be remembered, first and foremost, as the age which gave birth to the Catholic Revival.

26. THE TWENTIETH CENTURY REVISITED

Actually I am a Christian, and indeed a Roman Catholic, so that I do not expect "history" to be anything but a "long defeat"—though it contains . . . some samples or glimpses of final victory.
— *J. R. R. Tolkien*

[T]ogether through ages of the world we have fought the long defeat.
— *Galadriel*

It's been more than a decade since the twentieth century's demise; more than a decade since that late lamented century joined its many predecessors in the long line of the "long defeat" of humanity of which Tolkien spoke.

Perhaps enough sand has now sifted through Time's hourglass, and enough dust has settled on the surface of those recent events, to enable us to look back with an objective eye on the last century and the lessons it has to teach. It began optimistically, if by optimism we mean the naïve assumption that humanity was not enduring the long defeat (the objective consequence of the Fall) but was on the verge of enjoying the final victory (itself a consequence of the Fall as the self-deceptive "fruit" of Man's desire to be God). The optimism found expression in the rise of Marxism, both in its pure unadulterated form, communism, and in the superficially more attractive form of socialism, communism's equivocating sister. The Marxist intelligentsia, epitomized by the Fabian Society, began the twentieth century on the crest of a triumphalist wave, certain of the eventual collapse of capitalism and the subsequent dawning of an age of social justice which would be implemented by a benignly all-powerful State. Marxist purists even believed that this would constitute the end of history, the final triumph of man in the permanent dictatorship of the proletariat. Man, liberated from the primitive shackles of feudalism and the transitional injustice of capitalism, would live happily ever after in a never-ending communist utopia. How amusingly naïve and childish this now sounds, a hundred years later.

At the heart of this utopian nonsense is the belief in "progress"; roughly defined as a blind faith in humanity's continual ascent, unguided by anything or anyone except its own inherent genius and its own inherent goodness, from the primitive swamps of "superstition" (religion) to the noble heights of "science" (not really "science" at all, but scientism, the superstitious belief in the unerringly benevolent power of technology).

A famous and enthralling intellectual battle was fought out in England during the 1920s by H. G. Wells and George Bernard Shaw, as the champions of "progress," and by G. K. Chesterton and Hilaire Belloc, as the champions of the "unprogressive" permanent things. Twenty years later, as the full horrors of the Second World War came to light, Wells admitted defeat in his last book, *The Mind at the End of its Tether*, a work of deflated idealism and pessimism that was effectively a recantation of his earlier works of inflated optimism. He was defeated, ultimately, not by the arguments of Chesterton and Belloc, which he remained too blind to see, but by the horrors of the twentieth century. His optimism about a brave new world of bright new technology was laid waste by blitzkrieg, by technologically-assisted genocide and by the atom bomb.

Tolkien, never one to be blinded by the promises of technology, had experienced, as a combatant in the First World War, what he called the "animal horror" of the Battle of the Somme, and was under no illusions about the destructive consequences of the animal horror of the Second World War:

> I have just heard the news . . . Russians 60 miles from Berlin . . . The appalling destruction and misery of this war mount hourly: destruction of what should be (indeed is) the common wealth of Europe, and the world . . . wealth the loss of which will affect us all, victors or not. Yet people gloat to hear of the endless lines, 40 miles long, of miserable refugees, women and children pouring West, dying on the way. There seem no bowels of mercy or compassion, no imagination, left in this dark diabolic hour . . . The destruction of Germany, be it 100 times merited, is one of the most appalling world-catastrophes . . . Well the first War of the Machines seems to be drawing to its final inconclusive chapter—leaving, alas, everyone the poorer, many bereaved or maimed and millions dead, and only one thing triumphant: the Machines. As the servants of the Machines are becoming a privileged class, the Machines are

going to be enormously more powerful. What's their next move?

Their "next move" was the fortification, with nuclear bombs, of the Iron Curtain that descended across Europe after the war. As the fires of World War chilled into Cold War, the servants of the Machines promised "Mutually Assured Destruction" (MAD!) to each other. In the meantime, the all-powerful "benign" States of communist China and the Soviet Union were using technology to murder their own "dissident" citizens on a scale of which tyrants from less-technological ages could have only dreamed. Stalin and Mao murdered dozens of millions, beside which even Hitler's inhuman atrocities seem amateurish by comparison. Hitler, however, was defeated before his diabolic work could be completed; Stalin, Mao and their successors had much more time to perfect the art of mass murder in the service of "progressive" utopia. The facile fantasies of the Fabians and their ilk had become nightmares, their dreams broken on the broken bodies of the victims of "progressive" ideology.

Marxism does not have a monopoly on "progress," of course, and "progressive" utopias come in many other guises and disguises. If the mask of Marx has been removed to reveal the ugly death's head lurking beneath its seemingly attractive propaganda, the mask of Mammon has been much more successful in concealing the skull skulking behind its cosmetic surgery. The self-worshipping "democracies" of the "free" world have already killed more people than the combined efforts of Stalin, Mao and Hitler in their legalizing of the abomination of abortion.

From genocide to infanticide it would seem that the twentieth century was intent on suicide, killing itself in an orgy of self-abuse. It died, however, of old age, after its five-score years had elapsed, older but apparently none the wiser from the experience of its excesses. In its crass credulity and its inability to see any merit beyond the meretricious, the century had much in common with many of its predecessors. The "long defeat" is awash with centuries as bad and barren as this last addition to the listless list. Writing of the sixteenth century, Chesterton bemoaned the "cold queen of England . . . looking in the glass" and the "shadow of the Valois . . . yawning at the Mass," berating a time in which a decadent Europe was failing to respond to the threat of Islam. *Plus ça change . . .*

Plus ça change indeed! *Plus ça change, plus c'est la même chose.* The more things change, the more they remain the same. In the final analysis, the most notable thing about the twentieth century is its remarkable similarity to its predecessors. The same pride, envy, greed, lust . . . The same selfishness. The same old humanity making the same old mistakes. No progress, only the same old mistakes repeated *ad nauseam*. Or, as Chesterton would have put it, responding to the naïve "progressive" presumption of H. G. Wells, merely the everlasting men making the everlasting mistakes. Putting the matter into a theological nutshell, merely the Fallen falling; sinners, sinning. *Plus ça change.*

There is, however, one important difference; a difference so noteworthy that it demands that we sit up and take notice. It is a difference summed up by the Catholic convert and socio-economic visionary, E. F. Schumacher, when he commented that modern man had become far too clever not to be wise. Schumacher was alluding to the fact that the increase in technology has made man potentially far more destructive, yet he is turning his back on the philosophy and theology necessary to teach him how to use his new powerful tools with the prudence necessary. Modern man is like a seven-year-old with a machine gun; he lacks the wisdom and virtue to be playing with the technology he has at his disposal. It does not bode well for the new century that spreads itself threateningly before us.

No matter. The "long defeat" of Fallen Man will continue as it has always done. Human history is not so much a race with time as a dance with destiny, and the dance will continue until the Lord of the Dance brings the Music to an end. Until then we must always remember that the Music has an end. It has an end in both senses of the word; it has finality, at least in its temporal manifestation, and it has purpose. Knowledge of the end is the beginning of wisdom. Nor must we forget that this knowledge of the end is itself the "glimpse of final victory" to which Tolkien referred. We must never lose sight of the promised victory, even in, especially in, the midst of the long defeat. Christ promised His Church that the gates of Hell will never prevail against Her, and the Church, like Galadriel, has fought the long defeat "through ages of the world," through many, many centuries. The twentieth century is merely the latest. The dark forces of the Mordor of Modernity are powerful, seemingly all powerful, but, as Frodo exclaims at the crossroads, "They cannot conquer forever!"

27. LIGHT AMID THE RUINS:
LITERATURE IN THE TWENTIETH CENTURY

We live in times in which "progress" is not only seen as a good but as a god. It is not to be questioned. It is not to be resisted. It is believed to be omnipotent, omnipresent, and omniscient. It cannot be stopped. It as an idol to which every knee must bow. Don't get in its inexorable way or you will be crushed by its onward march. Kowtow. Surrender. There is no other choice.

So we are told by the dogmatists of "progress."

And yet we are being told a lie; a most outrageous and damnable lie. The notion of "progress" is a creed for the credulous. It is a trap for the trite-headed and trivia-oriented; a net for the naïve; a gospel for the gullible. Don't be taken in.

In reality, we are living in regressive times in which the onward march of technology, and the technolatry that worships it, is accompanied by the backward march of mankind toward barbarism. The past century may be no different from its predecessors in the sense that it is characterized by the same old sins, but in terms of the sheer scale of the sins committed it was the most barbaric and murderous in human history, surpassing the bloodiest excesses of any previous age. The past had its torturers but nothing as gruesome as the tortures devised by the KGB or the Gestapo. The past had its bloody battles in which men killed men with the primitive weapons at their disposal but they had no "weapons of mass destruction." The "primitive" past knew nothing of the "progressive" use of blitzkrieg, or scorched earth, or mustard gas, or biological weapons, or atom bombs. Rome was sacked by the barbarians, but it wasn't flattened like Hiroshima, Nagasaki, or Dresden. The past had its dungeons, but it knew nothing of concentration camps; it had no Auschwitz or Belsen, no gas chambers, no gulag archipelago. The "primitive" past had its homicide, but it took "progress" to refine the diabolical art of genocide.

One would think that the enunciation of such close-to-home truths would open the eyes of the most gullible of "progressives." Alas! We underestimate their gullibility. With willful blindness and supercilious self-deception, today's "progressive" will tell us that he has learned the lessons of the immediate past. He will tell us that the rise of Marxism and Nazism were merely brief setbacks on man's onward and upward march toward a golden age of rationalism, ushered in by science, in which humanity will at last be liberated from the shackles of religion and superstition. It will do no good to remind him that this is exactly what the Marxists and Nazis were saying a hundred years ago. The communists, genuflecting before the "infallible" teaching of Lenin and the Hegelian certainties of history, were ushering in the final golden age in which the dictatorship of the proletariat would end all injustice. The Nazis, genuflecting before the fulminations of the Führer and the Nietzschean certainties of the übermensch, were ushering in a Thousand-Year Reich in which the Aryan master race would finally come of age: the golden age of the golden-haired. In the event, of course, the dictatorship of the proletariat led to nothing but the dictatorship of the Party, and the Thousand-Year Reich fell after only twelve years of destructive and self-destructive madness.

But what has this to do with today's holier-than-thou "progressive"? Nothing whatsoever, he will plead in his own defence. Washing his hands of the faith of his own "progressive" fathers, today's "progressive" will declare himself innocent. And yet, if anything, he has more innocent blood on his hands than either the communists or the Nazis. Since the insanely sanctimonious sixties, when the "progressive" new age came of age, millions of babies have been butchered in a silent slaughter as abysmal as anything devised by Hitler or Stalin. Indeed, Hitler and Stalin, for all their heinous crimes, never went so far as to say that an individual had the right to choose to kill another individual. The right to choose to murder someone, or to choose to rape someone, or to choose to steal from someone, has never been officially sanctioned in law, even by the greatest tyrants in history; yet today's "progressives" have enshrined in law an individual's right to choose to kill a baby. And this "progressive" plague of infanticide is being spread throughout the world wherever the "progressive" creed is preached successfully. If this is "progress" it is only "progressive" in the sense that a cancer can be said to be "progressive." It is a "progressive" disease that attacks and kills the most blameless and innocent members of society. Hitler has been replaced by Herod. Is this progress?

And apart from the infanticide, today's "progressives" also promote the kind of eugenics that previously had been the preserve of mad Nazi scientists like Josef Mengele. Babies are systematically exterminated simply because they are deemed to be "defective." Children with Down syndrome and other "imperfections" are routinely killed in the womb so that the race can be purified of all such *üntermenschen*. Is this progress, or merely the return of barbarism? Only the most credulous of "progressives" could believe that it is anything but the latter.

And amid the ruins of "progress" it is art that sheds the light of truth most powerfully. As science has all too often aided and abetted the return of the barbarian, it is art, and particularly literature, that has proved the voice of the resistance. From the political novels of Chesterton at the beginning of the last century to the defiant and lonely heroism of Solzhenitsyn as the century "progressed" toward its ignominious end, great writers have shone great light on the evils and ruins of modernity. As science developed the weapons of mass destruction that made the First World War the most barbaric in history, poets like Wilfred Owen and Siegfried Sassoon protested that such techno-wars, in which machines crush men, are crimes against humanity. As "progress" led to the police state and the concentration camp, novelists like Aldous Huxley, George Orwell, and the aforementioned Solzhenitsyn exposed the dark underbelly of "progressive" ideology. It took the aquiline vision of the dystopian artist to expose the myopia of utopia.

As the "progressives" heralded the new dawn of socialism, or Nazism, or secular fundamentalism, T. S. Eliot exposed the fatuousness of a "progress" that spawned only a lifeless wasteland fit not for heroes but for "hollow men." Eliot's poetic exposé of the wasteland of "progress" was echoed in the fiction of such literary luminaries as C. S. Lewis, J. R. R. Tolkien, and Evelyn Waugh. These few, these happy few, have refuted futility. Like candles shining forth in the "progressive" gloom, they show us the light beyond the grasp of the dark ages in which we live. This is art at its best; not merely art for art's sake but art for God's sake. Thank God for such art.

PART III
LITERARY LANDSCAPES

28. CATHOLIC SOCIAL THOUGHT AND LITERATURE

Subsidiarity, as defined in *The Catechism of the Catholic Church*, is a central pillar of Catholic social doctrine developed in papal encyclicals such as *Rerum Novarum* (Leo XIII, 1891), *Quadragesimo anno* (Pius XI, 1931) and *Centesimus annus* (John Paul II, 1991). As such, it might be assumed that any discussion of subsidiarity and literature would tend to focus on the manifestation of subsidiarist ideas in the period between Leo XIII's original groundbreaking encyclical in 1891 and John Paul II's reiteration of these principles a century later. It would, however, be wrong to assume that the principles of subsidiarity originated in the late nineteenth century with Leo XIII or that such principles had not been present in literature until after Pope Leo's encyclical had been published. In essence, and in its broadest applicable sense, the principle of subsidiarity can be said to have originated with the words of Christ that we should render unto Caesar that which is Caesar's and render unto God that which is God's. The key to discerning the role of subsidiarity is, therefore, summed up in the title of a book by Jacques Maritain, published in 1930, entitled *The Things that are Not Caesar's*. If "Caesar" represents worldly power or authority, it is a question of discerning and defining the limits of such power. When the power of the state, or the power of commerce, encroaches upon that which is rightfully God's, or rightfully Man's in his true ordered relationship with God, it is a usurpation of political or economic authority that should be condemned and resisted. A Christian is always a subsidiarist to the extent that he insists that there are limits to Caesar's power and, indeed, that there are areas of life in which Caesar has no rightful power at all.

An early literary exposition of this broadest definition of subsidiarity is to be found in *The City of God*, St. Augustine's masterful dissection of paganism, in which the values of the "world" and that of Christianity are set apart in such a way that Christendom emerges as the new order rising from the ruins of the falling Roman Empire. In Book XIV of *The City of*

God living "by the standard of man" is distinguished from living "by the standard of God," the former being animated by selfishness, "like the Devil," the latter by selflessness. It is, indeed, no exaggeration to say that the foundation of the Church's teaching on subsidiarity is laid by St. Augustine, using Scripture as his building blocks, in his exposition of "the character of the two cities," the City of God and the City of Man, and the character of the "two kinds of love" that create them:

> We see then that the two cities were created by two kinds of love: the earthly city was created by self-love reaching the point of contempt for God, the Heavenly City by the love of God carried as far as contempt of self. In fact, the earthly city glories in itself, the Heavenly City glories in the Lord. The former looks for glory from men, the latter finds its highest glory in God, the witness of a good conscience. The earthly lifts up its head in its own glory, the Heavenly City says to its God: "My glory; you lift up my head." In the former, the lust for domination lords it over its princes as over the nations it subjugates; in the other both those put in authority and those subject to them serve one another in love, the rulers by their counsel, the subjects by obedience. The one city loves its own strength shown in its powerful leaders; the other says to its God, "I will love you, my Lord, my strength."

It's almost as if St. Augustine was prophesying and preempting the work of Machiavelli, the great advocate of the earthly city, more than a thousand years before the latter published *The Prince*, the bible of anti-subsidiarity.

In his work *On Christian Doctrine* S. Augustine lays the philosophical foundations for the reading of reality allegorically, thereby inspiring generations of future writers to employ allegory as a means of conveying reality, or truth, through the medium of literature.

The first great work of Christian literary allegory was *The Consolation of Philosophy* by Boethius (*c.* 475–524) in which the author converses with his "nurse," Philosophy, in both prose and verse. Written during the author's imprisonment and shortly before his execution for alleged treason against the new "Caesar," the Gothic emperor Theoderic, *The Consolation of Philosophy* highlights the mutability and transience of all earthly fortune and illustrates that true security is to be found in virtue alone. In its insistence upon the dichotomous chasm that separates true satisfaction which can only be found in Christ and the elusive and ultimately illusory pursuit of happiness in the material or worldly sense, Boethius's classic established a leitmotif which recurs in Christian literature thereafter. *The Consolation of Philosophy* was hugely popular and hugely influential throughout mediaeval Europe and its light shone in the work of many later writers, most notably perhaps in that of Dante and Chaucer, the latter of whom translated Boethius into English from the original Latin.

Chaucer was not, however, the first Englishman to translate *The Consolation of Philosophy*. Five hundred years earlier it had been translated into Old English by King Alfred the Great (849–*c.* 900) who, as a Catholic ruler, had sought to practice what Boethius preached. Apart from saving Christian England from complete destruction at the hands of the Pagan Danes, King Alfred sought to promote the good of his people in accordance with Christian principles. It is, therefore, no surprise that, apart from Boethius, he also translated the *Pastoral Care* of Gregory the Great into English.

Anglo-Saxon England, prior to the Norman Conquest, was so subsumed within the wider culture of Christendom that those poems from the period that have survived—"The Wanderer," "The Ruin," "The Seafarer," etc.—exhibit concepts of human society entirely in harmony with the philosophical *consolations* offered by Boethius. Ironically it is not until the decay of Christendom in the late middle ages that Catholic social thought is seen more prominently in literature, protruding in protest against its abuse.

Dante's *Divine Comedy* is probably the most important work of literature ever written, and it is also the most important literary work from the perspective of Catholic social doctrine. The poet's journey through Hell, Purgatory and Heaven is awash with socio-political commentary seen through the eyes of a profound, and profoundly orthodox, poet who is, in turn, looking through the lens of St. Thomas Aquinas's *Summa Theologiae*. With St. Thomas as his mentor and guide, Dante examines the abuse of political power and the injustice it causes in the light of a fully integrated understanding of the human person and human society, placing politics within the wider domain of theology and philosophy. This timeless manifestation, in art, of the perennial nature of human society, rooted in an understating of human personhood, retains its relevance. Modern political commentaries on Dante, and particularly Dorothy L. Sayers's own notes to her translation of the *Comedy*, continue to shed light on contemporary social and political problems. Dante is not merely an incomparable poet and a fine theologian, he is also a master of the socio-political.

The perennial relevance of Dante's perceptive dissection of human politics and society was summarized with succinct adroitness by Dorothy L. Sayers in her *Introductory Papers on Dante*, published in 1954:

That the *Inferno* is a picture of human society in a state of sin and corruption, everybody will readily agree. And since we are today fairly well convinced that society is in a bad way and not necessarily evolving in the direction of perfectibility, we find it easy enough to recognize the various stages by which the deep of corruption is reached. Futility; lack of a living faith; the drift into loose morality, greedy consumption, financial irresponsibility, and uncontrolled bad temper; a self-opinionated and obstinate individualism; violence, sterility, and lack of reverence for life and property including one's own; the exploitation of sex, the debasing of language by advertisement and propaganda, the commercializing of religion, the pandering to superstition and the conditioning of people's minds by mass-hysteria and "spell-binding" of all kinds, venality and string-pulling in public affairs, hypocrisy, dishonesty in material things, intellectual dishonesty, the fomenting of discord (class against class, nation against nation) for what one can get out of it, the falsification and destruction of all the means of communication; the exploitation of the lowest and stupidest mass-emotions; treachery even to the fundamentals of kinship, country, the chosen friend, and the sworn allegiance: these are the all-too-recognisable stages that lead to the cold death of society and the extinguishing of all civilized relations.[11]

It is significant, and perhaps not altogether surprising, that this quotation by Sayers was cited at length by E. F. Schumacher, the most influential populariser of subsidiarist ideas in the past half century, in his book *A Guide for the Perplexed*. "What an array of divergent problems!" Schumacher exclaimed after quoting this passage. "Yet people go on clamouring for 'solutions,' and become angry when they are told that the restoration of society must come from within and cannot come from without."[12] Schumacher was a world-renowned economist who made subsidiarity the creed of a whole generation following the publication, in 1973, of his international bestseller, *Small is Beautiful*. How refreshingly decorous it is, therefore, that he should have found a mentor in the Thomistic genius of Dante whose incomparable *tour de force*, the *Divine Comedy*, is a fantasia of moral and political potency, the applicability of which to the "real world" is undiminished in its relevance in spite of the centuries that have elapsed since its composition. Rooted in an unchanging moral order which underpins all just concepts of political philosophy, Dante's vision retains a clarity and charity that should be at the centre of all studies of a socio-political nature. This being so, it is to be regretted that Dorothy L. Sayers's deeply perceptive analysis of the political relevance of Dante to the dire needs of the modern world is all too sadly neglected by students of political philosophy. The fact that the world in its worldliness produces political philosophers more at home with the tenets of Machiavelli's *The Prince* than with those of Dante's *Comedy* says more about the folly of the world than it does about the pertinence of either work.

In England, *Sir Gawain and the Green Knight*, an Arthurian romance by an unknown late-fourteenth-century writer, highlighted the decay of mediaeval knightly virtue into the merely formal and pharisaical decorum of chivalrous courtesy. Although the anonymous writer does not condemn chivalry and, indeed, treats it with due deference and courteous decorum, his purpose in the telling of the tale of Sir Gawain's temptation is to point out that chivalry is distinct from, and must be subservient to, virtue. The highest goal to be achieved by knight and commoner alike is sanctity, which is to be achieved by keeping one's sights on eternal verities as opposed to transient social conventions, however worthy the latter might be. If, at its highest, chivalry could be seen as synonymous with sanctity, at its lowest and least worthy it was an excuse for the rationalizing of sins such as pride or adultery. Courtly love had evolved from the cult of Our Lady to the cult of the Lady (meaning any Lady) until, in the final decay of *amour courtois*, it had become a form of ritualized seduction or adultery, merely cultivation of the Lady for the purposes of self-gratification. On a societal level this decadence manifested itself in the passing of the Christocentrism of the mediaeval period and its replacement by the humanism of the Renaissance with its self-professed switching of emphasis from the divine to the merely human. In the process Europe had passed from the veneration of the Virgin to a venereal adoration of Venus. It was this very process of decay that inspired the subtext of *Sir Gawain and the Green Knight*. It was also clearly on Dante's mind as he purified his love for Beatrice in the *Divine Comedy*, ensuring that his Lady always acted as an intercessor for him in Heaven. Far from decaying into an object of his own lustful ambitions, Dante's Beatrice becomes a type of the Blessed Virgin. His Lady pointed to Our Lady; the Particular in the service of the Universal.

It was against this same backdrop of late mediaeval decay that Geoffrey Chaucer wrote the *Canterbury Tales*. Chaucer's panoramic exposition and exposé of late-fourteenth-century England serves now, as it served then, as a damning indictment of the culture in which he lived. In the General Prologue to the Tales he contrasts the wretched moral state of most of his fellow pilgrims with the admirable Parson, who sets a Christ-like example to everyone he meets: to his parishioners, to the other pilgrims and to Chaucer's readers. Significantly, however, the other character who shines forth admirably is the Clerk of Oxenford who is as other-worldly in his love for philosophy as is the Parson in his love for the Faith. Chaucer's intention is clear. As a disciple of Boethius and of Dante, he is illustrating that Faith and Reason are united in the service of the Good and the True. His other characters are failing morally because they have not only lost a full grasp of their Christian faith but have also lost a clear vision of Christian philosophy. Immorality is not merely an affront to good faith, it is an affront to good reason.

By the time that St. Thomas More was writing his satirical *Utopia* in the early years of the sixteenth century the decay had really set in. This work, the subtlety of which continues to confuse its readers half a millennium after it was first published, exhibits a brilliant and cultured mind musing over the problem of politics—and not merely the politics of its own day but politics in the abstract and perennial sense *à la* Plato and Aristotle. The employment of irony throughout the work makes a literal reading dangerous, and the deliberate obliquity makes any reading of its true meaning difficult. Furthermore it is clear that the novel's narrator, Hythlodaeus, whose name translates from the Latin as a "dispenser of nonsense," should not always be taken seriously. It is equally true, however, that More allows him to say things, on occasion, that we are meant to take seriously. The trick to achieving a true understanding of the work is, therefore, to discern when to take More and his narrator seriously and when to simply enjoy the joke he is having at the expense of the follies of his age.

As with Boethius, Dante and Chaucer before him, More is seeking to hold a mirror to fallen human nature so that we may see and know ourselves better. As a true philosopher in the classic tradition he knows that it is necessary to ask questions before we can know the answers. In this sense *Utopia* begs more questions than it answers. It is not a blueprint but a touchstone. It does not seek to show the plans of a future utopian society but seeks to show us how to judge our own society from the perspective of eternal verities.

St. Thomas More's *Utopia* was the last glorious flowering of the literature of Catholic England. Fifteen years after its publication, Henry VIII had declared himself "Supreme Head of the Church in England" and, in 1535, More was martyred for his adherence to the Catholic faith. Thereafter the obliquity employed by More became obligatory for the new generation of Catholic writers who sought to express themselves during the period of persecution that followed. Those who chose to be more candid were endangering their lives. St. Robert Southwell, a Jesuit poet writing at the end of the sixteenth century during the reign of Elizabeth I, returned to the spirit of Boethius as a means of gaining consolation for himself and of conveying it to others. Many of his poems convey this consoling spirit but none more so than "Content and Rich," a verse which could serve as a foreword to Boethius in its advocacy of spiritual resignation in the face of political injustice and tyranny. Like Boethius, St. Robert Southwell was executed, being hanged drawn and quartered in 1595, having been tried and condemned as a priest.

Many of these Boethian themes were taken up by William Shakespeare, a contemporary of St. Robert Southwell, who was raised in a recusant Catholic family and who probably remained a Catholic throughout his life. Unlike Southwell, however, Shakespeare chose the path of subtlety and obliquity, succeeding in both to a degree that even the wily More would have been hard pressed to emulate. Many of Shakespeare's plays, as well as his enigmatic poem "The Phoenix and the Turtle" and several of his sonnets, deal with political themes in a way that implies sympathy with the plight of the Catholic "dissidents" living in the totalitarian atmosphere of Elizabethan and Jacobean England. Many of the plays deal with treachery, intrigue, doubtful claims to the throne and with the triumph of tyranny, all themes with politically charged connotations, but it is in the recurring theme of self-sacrifice and the consoling power of virtue in an unjust world that Shakespeare's work resonates with the persecuted plight of his Catholic compatriots.

Shakespeare's Catholicism manifests itself as a dialectic against secularism and the secularist state more than as a dialogue with Protestantism. The dynamism of this underlying dialectic is centred on the tension between Christian conscience and self-serving, cynical secularism. Whereas the heroes and heroines of Shakespearian drama are informed by an orthodox Christian understanding of virtue, the villains are normally Machiavellian practitioners of secular *realpolitik*. In this sense, and paradoxically perhaps, the Catholic meta-drama represents one of the most "modern" aspects of Shakespearian drama in terms of its applicability to the contemporary world. His works are awash with references to the usurpation of rightful power by illegitimate Machiavels. In consequence the virtuous characters have to battle with their consciences as they struggle with the demands of raw power and its insistence that the "rights" of the ruler, imposed from above, have priority, in terms of *realpolitik* if not in terms of traditional concepts of virtue, over the "rights" of those who are subject to it. In this sense, many of Shakespeare's works can be seen to be fundamentally subsidiarist in nature, particularly in the way in which his heroes and heroines resist the imposition of unjust power, and in the way that such power is implicitly or explicitly condemned through the inherent dynamic of the plot and its denouement.

In *King Lear* the subsidiarist meta-drama is present from the very first scene when the king promises political power to those who "love us most." Lear, symbolic of the state, demands all. There can be no room for other loves. Immediately his self-serving daughters, Goneril and Regan, outdo each other in sycophantic promises of absolute allegiance. It is left to Cordelia, the youngest daughter, to "Love, and be silent." She loves her father but cannot "heave [her] heart into [her] mouth," uttering platitudes to curry favour beyond that which her conscious dictates is decorous. Unlike the feigned or affected affection of her sisters, her love is "more ponderous than [her] tongue"; it is genuine and will not debase itself with falsehood or flattery. She will love the king "according to [her] bond, no more nor less." She cannot offer the king (or state) any allegiance beyond that which her conscience dictates is appropriate morally. The parallels with the position that Catholics (and Protestant non-conformists) found themselves in during the reign of Henry VIII, and in Shakespeare's time under Elizabeth and James, is patently obvious. When Henry VIII declared himself supreme head of the Church of England, effectively making religion subject to the state, his subjects were forced to choose between conforming to his wishes, and thereby gaining his favour, or defying his will and incurring his wrath. Only the most courageous chose conscience before concupiscence; most chose to please the king and ignore their conscience. There are always more Gonerils and Regans than there are Cordelias.

The near destruction of Catholicism in England during the persecution of the sixteenth and seventeenth centuries appeared to signal the final extinction of Catholic literature within the English tradition. Yet, against all the odds, it would be English literature, perhaps more than any other, which would come to champion Catholic social thought in the modern era.

The promulgation by Leo XIII of the Papal Encyclical *Rerum Novarum* in 1891 would have a profound influence upon the new generation of Catholic writers who came to the fore in the early twentieth century. G. K. Chesterton and Hilaire Belloc championed the Pope's vision of subsidiarity, dubbing it distributism. Chesterton's novel, *The Napoleon of Notting Hill*, championed small businesses and small nations against the power of cosmopolitanism, distilling distributist ideas and metamorphosing them into romantic literature. This novel, along with Belloc's *The Servile State*, would have a significant influence on the young George Orwell who regurgitated their gist in agnostic form in his late works, *Animal Farm* and *Nineteen Eighty-Four*.

Chesterton's *The Man who was Thursday* was a reaction against the decadence of the previous decade and against nihilism in both its philosophical and political guises. Its employment of a dark and nightmarish scenario to administer a hopeful antidote to the poison of nihilistic despair was emulated by T. S. Eliot in 1922 with his employment of similar dark imagery to relay his own hopeful message of Catholic Christianity in *The Waste Land*. Following his conversion to Anglo-Catholicism in 1928 Eliot's orthodox Christian critique of the evils of modernity, both politically and culturally, became more didactic and more forthright in its condemnation of philosophical materialism and its consumerist ramifications.

J. R. R. Tolkien's *The Lord of the Rings* combined the distributism he had imbibed from Chesterton with his own disdain for technolatry to forge a myth of unforeseen power. Its critique of Lord Acton's maxim that "power tends to corrupt and absolute power tends to corrupt absolutely" is memorable not merely for its condemnation of the abusers of power but for its positive vision of the principles of subsidiarity, illustrating the way that power should be used and the limits of its legitimate usage. These principles are particularly prevalent in Tolkien's depiction of the Shire which is, at one and the same time, a nostalgic idolization of Saxon England (the subsidiarity that had been) and an imaginative depiction of an idealized society living in accordance with Catholic social teaching (the subsidiarity that could and should be). Other facets of Catholic social teaching in *The Lord of the Rings* include the Christian brotherhood of the Fellowship of the Ring and, in contrast to this virtuous example of human society, the abusive power of Isengard and Mordor, which can be seen on the purely political level as representations of Nazism and Soviet communism, each of which represent the very antithesis of subsidiarity.

Tolkien's friend, C. S. Lewis, also wrote many works in which he used the medium of fiction to "smuggle" religious ideas into the minds of his readers. The influence of Tolkien, as well as of Chesterton, is evident in Lewis's work, not least in the condemnation of modernism and in the implicit acceptance of Catholic social teaching in the form of subsidiarity. It is, for instance, significant that one of the heroes in Lewis's science fiction novel, *That Hideous Strength*, is described as a distributist.

It is remarkable that Catholic social thought, as expressed in papal encyclicals such as *Rerum Novarum*, should find expression so evocatively and imaginatively in many of the greatest works of the past century. Little could Pope Leo XIII have realized when writing his critique of communism and capitalism that his ideas would inspire, directly or indirectly, works as magnificent as *The Lord of the Rings*.

29. ENGLISH ROADS TO ROME

One of the biggest problems afflicting modern England is her lack of knowledge of herself. Due to what Hilaire Belloc called the "ignorant wickedness" of the "tom-fool Protestant history"[13] with which she has blinded herself, England gropes and flails in the darkness of her self-constructed materialist dungeon. She finds herself in this sorry position because she has lost sight of who she truly is. And she has lost sight of who she truly is because she has forgotten who she truly was. Her problem is one of amnesia.

For more than a thousand years, from her Roman infancy as Albion, and her first martyr, St. Alban, through to the treachery of Henry VIII and his cohorts, England was inseparably united with Christ and His Catholic Church. In her Anglo-Saxon youth she gave us sublime poetry, such as *Beowulf* and "The Dream of the Rood," and a holy host of saints too numerous to mention, whose names emblazon the countless churches dedicated to them which are strewn like manna across her landscape.

In the eleventh century, England was ruled by St. Edward the Confessor, a veritable paragon of Christian kingship, and it was during his reign, in 1061, that the Blessed Virgin appeared to a noblewoman at Walsingham in Norfolk, an apparition that is the crowning moment in all of England's history and the greatest blessing that she has ever received. The heavenly apparition and the reign of the saintly king served as the pyrotechnic climax to Anglo-Saxondom, a supernova that burned at its brightest as it passed away. Five years after the apparition and in the same year as Edward's death, England was conquered by the Normans, heralding the setting of the sun on England's Anglo-Saxon ascendency.

For some, such as J. R. R. Tolkien, the Norman Conquest was an unmitigated disaster that destroyed something beautiful and irreplaceable; for others, such as Hilaire Belloc, the Conquest was a glorious rebirth that enabled England to grow into the fullness of her mediaeval splendour. Either way, England was as Catholic and as devoted to her faith after the Conquest as she had been before it. England became known as Our Lady's

Dowry, and Walsingham became one of the principal pilgrimage sites of the whole of Christendom.

Nothing, it seemed, could rip England away from her faith, a faith that had refined and defined her.

Then came the so-called English Reformation, a Machiavellian revolution that robbed England and her people of their Christian birthright. Unlike the Protestant Reformation in Europe, the so-called "Reformation" in England had nothing to do with the difference between Catholicism and Protestantism and everything to do with the cynical determination of Henry VIII to have his own wicked way. And unlike the Reformation in Europe, there was little popular support for anti-Catholic "reform." The people did not want the new "church" that Henry had forced upon them and resented its oppression and its suppression of the Old Faith. In defiance of the king and his henchmen, England remained Catholic in spirit, even if not in its forbidden practice. It took 150 years of brutal and merciless persecution, including the martyrdom of hundreds of faithful Catholics, to browbeat the English into final submission.

And yet it is said that the blood of the martyrs is the seed of the Church and this is as true of England as it was of the Church of the Roman catacombs. In the resistance of the saints is the resurrection of the sinner. And this is where the present volume comes in.[14]

Documenting those who have taken the "roads to Rome" in the years since the Reformation, the present volume encompasses converts from Scotland, Wales and Ireland, as well as those from England. This is as it must be, and should be, because England's destiny became entangled with those of her British neighbours in the wake of the Reformation (for better or worse). The Crown of Ireland Act of 1542 made the Kings of England (Henry VIII and his successors), Kings of Ireland also. In 1603, the accession of James I of England (James VI of Scotland) united the thrones of England and Scotland, thereby forming the United Kingdom of England, Scotland and Ireland, symbolized in the adoption of the crosses of St. George, St. Andrew and St. Patrick as the composite parts of the Union Flag (or Union Jack as it is now more commonly known). Wales is not represented on the nation's flag, indicative of the contemptuous way in which England annexed her diminutive western neighbour, an injustice that the Welsh nationalist convert, Saunders Lewis, lamented with acerbic eloquence.

For almost five hundred years countless Englishmen and their fellow Britons have rediscovered the Faith of their Fathers, converting to

Catholicism and thereby entering into communion with their nation's past and its true being. Here we should stress that "true being" is about being true to England's God-given inheritance. The present volume is a priceless testament to those many converts who have kept the flame of faith burning through the centuries. There are the most famous of the Victorians, such as Newman, Patmore, Hopkins, Johnson, Dowson and Wilde, and the most celebrated of the last century's converts, such as Chesterton, Baring, Knox, Noyes, Waugh, Greene, Guinness, Sitwell and Sassoon. And yet the most famous are only the tip of an illustrious iceberg that has been hidden beneath the surface of the ocean of literature on Britain's recent Catholic history. This diving and delving beneath and beyond the surface is the chief strength and value of this particular volume. Here we see, meticulously assembled, a far more comprehensive list of British converts to Rome than has ever been published before. For this reason alone, *Roads to Rome* deserves a place on the shelves of every British Catholic, and indeed on the shelves of every Catholic in the English-speaking world. It serves as an inspiration and an *aide mémoire*, reminding us of who we truly are, as Catholics and as Englishmen, Scotsmen, Irishmen or Welshmen. And lest we forget, these roads to Rome do not leave the British Isles to follow a foreign path to a foreign religion. On the contrary, these roads to Rome go straight through the heart of every man to the Home that every man's heart desires.

Let's end as we began with the words of Hilaire Belloc, a cradle Catholic whose mother, *née* Parkes, is one of the converts featured herein:

> The Faith, the Catholic Church, is discovered, is recognized, triumphantly enters reality like a landfall at sea which at first was thought a cloud. The nearer it is seen, the more is it real, the less imaginary: the more direct and external its voice, the more indubitable its representative character, its "persona," its voice. The metaphor is not that men fall in love with it: the metaphor is that they discover home. "This was what I sought. This was my need." It is the very mould of the mind, the matrix to which corresponds in every outline the outcast and unprotected contours of the soul. It is Verlaine's "Oh! Rome—oh! Mere!" And that not only to those who had it in childhood and have returned, but much more—and what a proof!—to those who come upon it from over the hills of life and say to themselves "Here is the town."[15]

30. LITERARY PRIESTS

All roads point at last to an ultimate inn, where we shall meet
Dickens and all his characters: and when we drink again it shall
be from the great flagons in the tavern at the end of the world.
                                                    —G. K. Chesterton[16]

One wonders what Chesterton's Father Brown and Graham Greene's whisky priest would say to each other were they to meet in Chesterton's fantastic tavern at the world's end. What would these two unforgettable individuals, who would appear to have absolutely nothing in common except their priesthood, say to each other? What would we see and hear if we were flies on the wall at such a meeting? Perhaps we would see the whisky priest sitting disconsolately over his flagon of ale, wishing that he could exchange it for a bottle of cheap Kentucky bourbon. Looking up, his tired, bloodshot eyes might meet those of Father Brown. "You know," he mumbles, "we are more inclined to regret our virtues than our vices, but only the most honest will admit this."[17] Father Brown might place his own tankard on the table between them, his gratitude for the foam-flecked nectar reinforcing a profound sense that he is unworthy of the gift he is imbibing. In the presence of such undeserved blessings, the whisky priest's words seem almost blasphemous. "I don't regret any virtues except those I have lost," mutters Father Brown. His thoughts are at least as sad as those of the whisky priest but his sadness is of a very different sort. His is the sadness of humility, the sorrow that leads to contrition; the whisky priest's is the sadness of pride, the sadness of Milton's Satan whose greatest sorrow is that he cannot escape from himself: "Which way I fly is Hell; myself am Hell."[18]

The abyss between these two types of sadness is as wide as the chasm that separates the inferno from paradise. Never the twain shall meet. But this begs an unsettling question: If the sorrow of the whisky priest is akin to the sadness of Satan does this mean that the whisky priest belongs in hell? Heaven forbid; or heaven forbid, at least, that we should ever have the pride and audacity to place him there. His near heroic death and grudging acts of self-sacrifice might be said to have snatched him from Satan's grasp and the reader is surely meant to give him the benefit of the doubt. Nonetheless, one can't help feeling irritated by the whisky priest's unrelenting joylessness, which is as unbelievable in a work of fiction as it is in the world of fact. The witness of real-life martyred priests, such as St. Edmund Campion and St. Robert Southwell, illustrate and illuminate the joy-filled courage with which these real men of faith met their martyrdom. A cursory perusal of Campion's famous "Brag" or Southwell's glorious poetry disperses the acrid aroma with which Greene surrounds his fictional martyr.

Let's leave the whisky priest in the company of Father Brown, his literary and priestly antidote, and let's fly to another part of Chesterton's apocalyptic tavern. Passing over Chesterton himself, deep in conversation with Dickens amidst the motley company of the latter's fictional characters, we might alight on the ceiling above another gathering of literary priests. There we might see the impeccably spoken Jesuit, Father Mowbray, conversing convivially with the gritty Glaswegian, Father Mackay. Perhaps their discussion centres on the flightiness of the Flytes as they revisit Brideshead, reminiscing about their respective roles in the novel in which Waugh had placed them.

Flying on a little further, we come across Father Elijah discussing apocalyptic intrigues with several priests from the fiction of Robert Hugh Benson. At the next table, Biersach's Father Baptist confers with Father Luke Scott, from Piers Paul Read's *Death of a Pope*, about the dangers of modernism and liberation theology. Standing at the bar, a large group of men in Elizabethan garb are laughing heartily. Amongst them is the fictional martyr, Father Robin Audrey, from Benson's *Come Rack! Come Rope!*, but the others are real historical figures, including the aforementioned Campion and Southwell, along with a host of other jovial English Martyrs. The joviality increases as Father Brown joins the company having just heard the whisky priest's confession.

At this point, our vision fades. It was, after all, only a dream, albeit a dream inspired by the imagination of G. K. Chesterton, who was very much awake when he imagined or "dreamed" it. Such dreams, in some manner or form, may come true but not presumably in every detail. It is, for instance, hardly likely that there would be any flies on the wall of such a heavenly tavern! If we were ever admitted to such a tavern we would presumably have to join the conversation like everyone else and not seek to become entomological eavesdroppers.

Having descended to earth with an unceremonious bump, our thoughts fall and falter from the heavenly sphere of the poetic to the mundane worldliness of the prosaic; settling finally on the level of the banal. We are reminded, for instance, that literary priests are like library books, which is to say that they can be categorized as fiction or non-fiction. Having taken our fictional flight of fancy with the fictional priests, we should not omit to mention those non-fictional priests who have given us such good literature. In our heavenly tavern, mingling with the fictional guests, we would surely find John Henry Newman and Gerard Manley Hopkins; Robert Hugh Benson and Ronald Knox.

Since there are no flies in such a tavern, and since we are not able to fly there ourselves, we will have to see Chesterton's tavern through the same eyes that he saw it; through the visionary eyes of the imagination. These are the eyes through which Chesterton first saw Father Brown and through which Michael D. O'Brien first saw Father Elijah. These are the eyes through which we also see these literary priests, and through which we see the deep truths that they convey to us. Like their non-fictional counterparts, these literary priests are ministers of grace blessing us with their sanctity and sagacity. Thank God for such blessings.

31. *IN PERSONA CHRISTI:*
THE PRIEST IN MODERN FICTION

There are two types of priests in fiction; those who are possible and those who are impossible. The former are figments of the imagination of Catholics, either practicing or lapsed; the latter are figments of the imagination of non-Catholics, whether Christian or otherwise. The former, though "fictional," are real men and real priests, whether saints or sinners, or both; the latter are phantasms, utterly impossible in any world beyond the ignorant fancies and fantasies of their creators. The former remain priests even when they behave in a very unpriestly fashion; they remain in character even when behaving uncharacteristically. The latter are never priests, even when dressed up to look like them; they are never bishops, even when mitred, but merely chimaeras in chimeres.

Although this sweeping assertion is true as a general principle, it should perhaps be modified and fine-tuned through the addition of nuance. It might be true, for instance, that some non-Catholics can produce real priests in their fiction, but they can only do so through an objective knowledge of the Faith assisted by such a high degree of empathy that it can be said that they have, in a sense, *become* Catholics, albeit temporarily, for the purposes of art. Conversely, some lapsed Catholics might have become so disillusioned with, and prejudiced against, the Faith that they are literally and literarily blinded by their belligerence; they can no longer see the thing as it is, or its priests as they are.

This whole issue was addressed with sober discernment by the Catholic novelist, Maurice Baring, and with rambunctious wit by Baring's great friend, G. K. Chesterton. In his last book, *Have You Anything to Declare?*, Baring wrote:

> It is utterly futile to write about the Christian faith from the outside. A good example of this is the extremely conscientious novel by Mrs. Humphry Ward called *Helbeck of Bannisdale*. It

is a study of Catholicism from the outside, and the author has taken scrupulous pains to make it accurate, detailed and exhaustive. The only drawback is that, not being able to see the matter from the inside, she misses the whole point.[19]

In Chesterton's novel, *The Man Who was Thursday*, the anarchist, Lucian Gregory, exposes his woeful ignorance of Catholicism in his pathetic effort to disguise himself as a bishop:

> "When first I became one of the New Anarchists I tried all kinds of respectable disguises. I dressed up as a bishop. I read up all about bishops in our anarchist pamphlets, in *Superstition the Vampire* and *Priests of Prey*. I certainly understood from them that bishops are strange and terrible old men keeping a cruel secret from mankind. I was misinformed. When on my first appearing in Episcopal gaiters in a drawing-room I cried out in a voice of thunder, 'Down! down! presumptuous human reason!' they found out in some way that I was not a bishop at all. I was nabbed at once . . ."[20]

In this depiction of the anarchist in disguise, Chesterton presents us with a metaphor for the non-Catholic or anti-Catholic novelist who tries to present a priest or bishop convincingly but only succeeds in exposing himself instead. Lucian Gregory's fictional bishop is utterly unconvincing. The portrayal is a betrayal.

Throughout the centuries, world literature has been plagued by a plethora of playwrights and novelists, who, like real-life Lucian Gregorys, have misrepresented the Faith in their work. From the anonymously authored *The Troublesome Raigne of King John* (printed in 1591) or John Webster's *The White Divil* (1612) to Schiller's *Maria Stuart* (1800) and Mary Shelley's *Frankenstein* (1818), right down to the present day with Dan Brown's inanely ubiquitous *Da Vinci Code*, Catholicism has been the victim of the prejudice and propaganda of those who know not the Thing that they condemn.

At this juncture it might be apposite to address the obvious riposte of non-Catholic or anti-Catholic authors and critics that perhaps their Catholic counterparts protest too loudly. Surely, they will no doubt argue, Catholic writers are at least as guilty of prejudice, and of propagandizing for the Faith, as others are guilty of prejudice and propaganda against it. In response, we need only assert that those writing from a Catholic perspective come in many shapes and sizes, from the conscientiously pious to the positively impious; and whether it be true that hell hath no fury like a woman scorned, it is certainly true that hell hath no fury like a lapsed Catholic's anti-Catholicism!

Nor should it be assumed that believing Catholics are incapable of objectivity, or that they never criticize the actions of their co-religionists. Dante and Chaucer, both deeply faithful Catholics in spite of the misreading of their work by many modern critics, were unremitting in their invective against bad Catholics. Dante places popes, bishops and priests in hell, and many more in purgatory; Chaucer pokes fun at the priggishness of the Prioress, the worldliness of the Monk, the avarice of the Friar, and the vanity of the Pardoner. Yet the evil of the bad Catholics in Dante's hell and purgatory serves merely to highlight the holiness of Beatrice, of the Blessed Virgin and of the saints in paradise; and the hypocrisy of Chaucer's bad pilgrims serves to accentuate the holiness of the Parson and the Ploughman, who are symbolic of the faithful clergy and the faithful laity respectively.

The role of symbolism in Chaucer or Dante is obvious; but no less obvious, at least to those who have eyes to see, is the essential symbolism inherent in the presentation of the priesthood in literature. The priest, it must be remembered, is mystically different from the rest of humanity in the sense that, at certain times, he is more than merely human; he is superhuman; he is, in a mystical sense, even divine; he is, at the altar and in the confessional, *in persona Christi*; he has powers beyond himself; powers that only God can give; powers that God ordains to give to the priest and to the priest alone. Yet priests are, at the same time, as human as the rest of humanity; as human and as sinful. If the Incarnate Christ was truly human, like us in all things *except* sin, the priest is also human and is like us in all things *including* sin. This places the priest in a unique position, and one that has made him a metaphor not only for Christ but for anti-Christ. The priest, at the altar and in the confessional, is *in persona Christi*; but the priest, as a sinner, is *in persona anti-Christi*. He can be a metaphor for Christ and for anti-Christ. By extension, he can serve as a metaphor for humanity, for Everyman. We are made in the image of God and are called to become Christ-like, yet we are fallen and broken in our sinfulness; we, as priests of a different ilk, are called to sacrifice ourselves on the altar of His Love, yet all too often we sacrifice others on the altars that we have erected to our Selves. We, like the ordained priesthood, can be *in persona Christi* or *in persona anti-Christi*, though not, of course, in the same way. It is this metaphorical dimension of the priesthood which has served as the

inspirational catalyst for many manifestations of the priesthood in literature; from the novels of Huysmans and Wilde in the nineteenth century, to
those of Joyce, Greene, Waugh and Walker Percy in the last century.

The timeless, and therefore perennially timely, significance of the
priest was presented by Cardinal Wiseman in his novel, *Fabiola: A Tale of
the Catacombs*, published in 1854, a year before Newman's own "tale of
the catacombs," *Callista: A Sketch of the Third Century*, was published.
Although Wiseman's Muse lacked the dexterity and subtlety of Newman's
the propagandistic dimension of the message he sought to convey in his
fiction was certainly as evident:

> We need not remind our readers, that the office then performed
> was essentially, and in many details, the same as the daily wit-
> ness at the Catholic altar. Not only was it considered, as now, to
> be the Sacrifice of Our Lord's Body and Blood, not only were
> the oblation, the consecration, the communion alike, but many
> of the prayers were identical; so that the Catholic hearing them
> recited, and still more the priest reciting them, in the same lan-
> guage as the Roman Church of the catacombs spoke, may feel
> himself in active and living communion with the martyrs who
> celebrated, and the martyrs who assisted at, those sublime mys-
> teries.[21]

This Sacrifice, Wiseman reminds his modern (Victorian) readers, is
the pivotal act of all history, past, present and future, offered for all humanity by the Eternal Priesthood, by those ordained to be priests forever
according to the order of Melchizedek. Such a sublime reality served as
imaginative grist to the metaphorical mill for Franz Kafka whose novella,
The Metamorphosis, can be seen, at its most perversely profound, as a
metaphor for the priesthood, albeit contorted and perhaps malicious.
Arguing persuasively for the underlying religious symbolism of Kafka's
novella, Kurt Weinberg insists that Gregor Samsa's transformation is a
"*negative transfiguration*, the inversion of the Transfiguration of Christ,
the Passion of an abortive Christ figure . . . If this is the case," Weinberg
continues, "then instead of *Metamorphosis* . . . *Die Verwandlung* would
have to be translated, in the spirit of Kafka, faithfully and ironically, as *The
Transfiguration* . . . indeed, even as *The Transubstantiation* . . ."[22]

The suggestion that translating *Die Verwandlung* as "metamorphosis"
is incorrect and is not in keeping with "the spirit of Kafka" is significant
and has wide-reaching implications with regard to the way the novella is

read and received. "Metamorphosis" accentuates a materialistic reading of the work, stressing the physical change of Samsa from being a man to being an insect, a sort of inverse metamorphosis in which the butterfly becomes the caterpillar; man as inverted invertebrate; Darwinian reductionism *par excellence*. Translating *Die Verwandlung* as either "transfiguration" or "transubstantiation" forces a spiritual reading of the work, taking it from the level of the physical to the metaphysical. As with the metamorphosis, however, the transfiguration is inverted: the Beautiful is transfigured into Ugliness; the Good is transfigured into Evil. Similarly, the transubstantiation is inverted; the bread and wine does not become the Flesh and Blood of God, but, on the contrary, the flesh and blood of Man (made in the image of God) becomes mere vermin. On this level, the level of the metaphysical, man is not metamorphosed into a beast, he is transfigured into something far worse than a beast; something spiritual, not physical; something not merely sub-human but anti-human; something satanic. Man *in persona anti-Christi*.

The fact that Gregor Samsa is a Christ figure, or perhaps more correctly, an anti-Christ figure, is borne out by the symbolism employed at several crucially significant points in the novella. He is wounded, ultimately fatally, by an apple, which leaves him "nailed to the spot," his body "stretched out . . . in a complete confusion of all his senses." His actual death palpitates with references to the Crucifixion, though, of course, the Crucifixion is itself inverted. The clock strikes three in the morning, not three in the afternoon, and as "his head sank down to the floor, and from his nostrils streamed his last weak breath," everything begins to grow light, instead of dark. It is, of course, significant that Gregor's "crucifixion" takes place at the end of March. It is Easter, and the novella ends with a "resurrection," though not Gregor's but his sister's who "got up . . . and stretched her young body."[23]

In the light of such symbolism it is surely significant that the German word, *ungeziefer*, in the novella's opening sentence, variously translated as "bug," "vermin," "dung-beetle" or "cockroach," derives etymologically from the late Middle High German *ungezibere*, *unziver*, and originally meant the "unclean animal not suited for sacrifice."[24] It is not surprising, therefore, that *ungeziefer*, unlike bug or beetle, carries with it echoes of the supernatural or the demonic. Samsa emerges, in his transubstantiation, as beingworthy of the sacrifice of the metaphorical Mass which is at the novella's symbolic heart. Yet he emerges as not only the victim of the Mass but the priest of the Mass also. It is clear that the novella is deeply autobiographical, and it is generally accepted that Samsa is a cryptogram for Kafka. Yet, if Weinberg is correct in his intimation that Samsa is also a phonetic contraction of the Czech words *sám* (alone) and *jsem* (I am), it can be seen that the author is making himself the priest of his own sacrifice, ascribing to himself the title of God Himself ("I am") and agreeing with God's Judgment in Genesis that it is not good to be alone. Thus, Kafka has enshrined himself, in his capacity as Artist, as the Priest, transfiguring his Art into the Mass that he is celebrating, if indeed one can be said to be "celebrating" such a dismal sacrifice. He makes himself the God-Man and makes literature a liturgy, the purpose of which is to reveal Himself to the world.

This brief discussion of Kafka's *Die Verwandlung* is far from exhaustive, of course, not least because the invocation of the devil at the beginning of the novella invites a Faustian, and therefore a more conventionally Christian, interpretation of the work's moral dimension. Be that as it may, its principal tropes all involve perversion through inversion, which is to say that conventional meaning is perverted through the inversion of the things associated with it. As such, it might be prudent to remind ourselves of the dangers inherent in such an approach to life and literature, the danger that the metamorphosis becomes a metaphormosis, the danger that we might become the very metaphor we're inventing. Put simply and bluntly, if we believe strongly enough that we are a cockroach we are in danger of becoming one!

In 1916, the same year in which *The Metamorphosis* was first published, James Joyce published *A Portrait of the Artist as a Young Man*, a work which, in many significant respects, is very similar to Kafka's novella. As with *The Metamorphosis*, the *Portrait* is clearly a self-portrait, exhibiting much that is autobiographical. As with *The Metamorphosis* it is an inverted transfiguration; the protagonist, Stephen Dedalus, being transfigured from a faithful Catholic, *in persona Christi*, who contemplates a vocation to the priesthood, into an anti-Catholic, *in persona anti-Christi*, who rejects the Catholic priesthood in order to embrace a new narcissistic priesthood that makes its sacrifices to Art. Throughout the novel, Joyce's attitude to the Catholic clergy transmogrifies from credulous awe, rooted in the priest's mystical power through the sacraments, (*Father Arnall knew more than Dante because he was a priest*)[25] to a satanic inversion of those powers in the scene in which the priest seeks to tempt Stephen to become a priest because of the power it will give him:

> To receive that call, Stephen, said the priest, is the greatest honour that the Almighty God can bestow upon a man. No king

or emperor on this earth has the power of the priest of God. No angel or archangel in heaven, no saint, not even the Blessed Virgin herself has the power of a priest of God: the power of the keys, the power to bind and to loose from sin, the power of exorcism, the power to cast out from the creatures of God the evil spirits that have power over them, the power, the authority, to make the great God of Heaven come down upon the altar and take the form of bread and wine. What an awful power, Stephen.[26]

In this bizarre discourse, we see pride (the original sin of Satan and of our first parents) appealing to pride; we see, in fact, a reflection of the pride of Satan tempting the pride of Man. Stephen "heard in this proud address an echo of his own proud musings," casting the priest in the role of Satan, *in persona anti-Christi*, and Stephen in the role of Man (Eve). Stephen rejects the temptation to the Catholic priesthood, though he eventually succumbs to the succubus of pride, making himself the priest of his own art-religion, declaring with Satan that "I will not serve":

I will not serve that in which I no longer believe whether it call itself my home, my fatherland or my church: and I will try to express myself in some mode of life or art as freely as I can and as wholly as I can, using for my defence the only arms I allow myself to use—silence, exile, and cunning.[27]

The parallels with Milton's Satan are striking and obvious, placing him *in persona anti-Christi* as the priest of his own self-idolatrous religion. He says as much when he compares his own "priesthood" to the Catholic priesthood, alluding contemptuously to "a priested peasant . . . who was but schooled in the discharging of a formal rite" whereas he was "a priest of eternal imagination, transmuting the daily bread of experience into the radiant body of everlasting life."[28]

As with Kafka, Joyce seemingly revels in the shock-value attached to sacrilegious and blasphemous imagery, and employs the same literary trope of perversion-through-inversion. As with Kafka, he is playing with his reader through these literary devices and toying with profound religious concepts seemingly for the sheer hell of it. There is, however, also a suggestion that Joyce has not entirely given up the (holy) ghost, leaving one foot hopefully in heaven, or at least in purgatory, even as he is dangling the other in hell, dabbling desperately with diabolism.

Although Kafka and Joyce were heralded as prophets of the avant-garde by the Bloomsbury group and other fashion-oriented critics, there was little intrinsically "new" in what they were doing. Charles Baudelaire was doing much the same thing sixty years earlier, and a later practitioner of the Decadent school, J. K. Huysmans, had boldly gone where Kafka and Joyce would go, only he had gone there thirty years earlier. In *À Rebours*, variously translated as *Against Nature* or *Against the Grain*, the protagonist, Des Esseintes, has a lurid fixation with the Catholic Church, which exceeds in its pure excessiveness anything ventured by Stephen Dedalus.

> The Demon, a powerful rival, now stood against an omnipotent God. A frightful grandeur seemed to Des Esseintes to emanate from a crime committed in Church by a believer bent, with blasphemously horrible glee and sadistic joy, over such revered objects, covering them with outrages and saturating them in opprobrium.
>
> Before him were conjured up the madnesses of magic, of the black mass, of the witches' revels, of terrors of possessions and of exorcisms. He reached the point where he wondered if he were not committing a sacrilege in possessing objects which had once been consecrated: the Church canons, chasubles and pyx covers. And this idea of a state of sin imparted to him a mixed sensation of pride and relief.[29]

Throughout this litany of "the pleasures of sacrilege" the real presence of the priest is seen in the Mass, the exorcisms, the consecrated objects, the chasubles and the pyx covers, none of which would have their existence or their sanctity without his ordained power.

Des Esseintes spends the duration of the novel enjoying or enduring an orgy of self-indulgence, "doing his own thing" to employ the jargon of a later hedonistic generation, and ends with a nauseous feeling of disgust with decadence and a deep desire for faith. *À Rebours* climaxes with a prayer, a *cri de coeur*, which sets the *leitmotif* for Huysmans's future novels: "O Lord, pity the Christian who doubts, the sceptic who would believe, the convict of life embarking alone in the night, under a sky no longer illumined by the consoling beacons of ancient faith."[30]

In the following novel, *Là Bas (Down There)*, Huysmans descends, through the travels and travails of his central character, the semi-autobiographical Durtal, into a demi-monde that leads to the very jaws of hell itself. He is led there by his lurid fascination for the occult in general and for the renegade priest-satanist, Canon Docre, in particular. We are told that "the spite of this priest was inordinate and his pride unlimited" and that he was "not displeased to be an object of terror and loathing, for thus he was somebody." The priest, through his presiding over the Black Mass, was committing "the most extreme of excesses for a believer, and Docre believes in Christ, or he wouldn't hate him so."[31] Towards the end of the novel, Huysmans describes a Black Mass in all its sacrilegious sickness, the graphic detail of which will shock and sicken the most hardened Catholic reader. Yet the horrific detail is not gratuitous but necessary. It shows us the abominable nature of the act of sacrilegious sacrifice, the abysmal reality that leads to the reality of the Abyss. It is as though the Black Mass opens the very jaws of hell itself, reminding those present that they are abandoning all hope by entering there. It is the point of no return. It is now or never, for the novel's protagonist, and for the reader: *Repent. Turn back. Or be damned forever.* It is at this point, in sheer revulsion, that we turn in horror from the grim reality of sin. It is at this point also that Huysmans shows the darkest of paradoxes, that the sordid can be edifying, a dark paradox that is re-presented in the works of Waugh, Greene, Flannery O'Connor, Walker Percy and in William Peter Blatty's *The Exorcist*. At the very end of *Là Bas* one of the characters reminds us that Father Ravignan had "proved that the wiliest thing the Devil can do is to get people to deny his existence."[32] As we finish the book we come to realise how much richer we are for the reminder.

Having read Huysmans's novels we are not surprised to discover that he spent the last years of his life in a monastery, any more than we are surprised to discover that Baudelaire converted on his deathbed or that Verlaine converted in prison. Each of these Decadent writers had walked to the very threshold of hell and, discovering it to be real, recoiled in horror into the arms of Mother Church. Similarly we are not surprised to discover that Oscar Wilde was received into the Church on his deathbed. We might have guessed as much from reading almost any of his plays, poems or short stories, but especially perhaps we might have prophesied his future conversion after reading his only novel, *The Picture of Dorian Gray*. This novel, one of the finest of the whole Victorian era, is a conflation or a confluence of two literary sources, Marlowe's *Dr. Faustus* and Huysmans's *A Rebours*, the latter of which Wilde had rather bizarrely read on his honeymoon in Paris. Like Faustus, Dorian Gray sells his soul to the devil, and, like Des Esseintes, he spends a life of decadent debauchery. Yet, even in the midst of the worst of his excesses, Dorian could never quite escape from the lure and allure of the Church, the Priesthood and the Holy Mass.

It was rumoured of him once that he was about to join the Roman

Catholic communion, and certainly the Roman ritual had always a great attraction for him. The daily sacrifice, more awful really than all the sacrifices of the antique world, stirred him as much by its superb rejection of the evidence of the senses as by the primitive simplicity of its elements and the eternal pathos of the human tragedy that it sought to symbolize. He loved to kneel down on the cold marble pavement and watch the priest, in his stiff flowered dalmatic, slowly and with white hands moving aside the veil of the tabernacle, or raising aloft the jeweled, lantern-shaped monstrance with that pallid wafer that at times, one would fain think, is indeed the *"panis cœlestis,"* the bread of angels, or, robed in the garments of the Passion of Christ, breaking the Host into the chalice and smiting his breast for his sins . . . As he passed out, he used to look with wonder at the black confessionals and long to sit in the dim shadow of one of them and listen to men and women whispering through the worn grating the true story of their lives.[33]

The satanic sting in the tail of this passage reminds us that the biggest barrier between Dorian and the Church is his own lack of repentance; and, furthermore, Dorian's desire to hear the confessions of others prefigures the furtive voyeuristic desire of Stephen Dedalus in Joyce's *Portrait* to do the same thing, envying the priest for his secret knowledge of other men's sins.

In *Finis Coronat Opus*, a little known short story by the poet, Francis Thompson, the protagonist, Florentian, sells his soul to the devil, setting a bust of Virgil on the altar in place of the crucifix, which he treads under foot, before sacrificing his Christian wife in return for the laurel of supremacy in the Poetic Arts. It is hard to see this story as anything other than a condemnation by Thompson of the deification of Beauty by the Aesthetic movement, as well as being a prophecy of the Art-worship of Joyce. One also suspects that the character of Florentian might even have been inspired by, and modeled on, Oscar Wilde. Similarly, Chesterton, in his essay, "The Diabolist," and in his novel, *The Man Who was Thursday*, is clearly in dialectical revolt against the darkness of the Decadents. It is, then, to Chesterton we look for a lighter, brighter role for the priest in modern literature. His invention of the character, Father Brown, inspired by his friendship with Father John O'Connor, represents the emergence not only of the priest-detective, but of the priest-philosopher, and, perhaps most refreshingly in the light of the darkness of so many other priestly characters in fiction, the emergence of sanity and sanctity. Nor should we forget the character of Father Michael, the mystical and mysterious monk in

Chesterton's *The Ball and the Cross*, who, like his archangelic archetype and namesake, defeats the devil almost single-handedly at the novel's climax.

There are, of course, a host of other memorable priests, gracing and disgracing the pages of literature, from the novels of Benson, Baring, Bernanos, Waugh and Greene, to those of John Morton Robinson, William Peter Blatty, J. F. Powers, Ralph McInerny and Michael D. O'Brien. The priest in fiction represents a potent presence, signifying the Real Presence of Christ, and sometimes His Real Absence. This sacramental mystique surrounding the priesthood enabled Walker Percy, in *Lancelot*, to make a priest the most powerful presence in the whole work, even though he is never seen and never utters a solitary word until the very final pages (and even then it is *only* a solitary word that he speaks). He is apparently unnecessary to the action, yet, at the same time, is indispensable as the only one who can make any meaningful sense of it. He is the personification of objective reality, seen as being synonymous with sanity, in a plot that is hopelessly entangled with the madness of relativism and its destructive ramifications. As the world of the protagonist collapses in a self-indulgent haze of sex, drugs and alcohol, he finds himself "confessing" (non-sacramentally) to the priest. His little world of godless self-indulgence is seen as a descent into madness. The priest, invisible but present, is outside the little world of relativism in which the plot unfolds. He inhabits the vast expanse of the objective reality beyond the reach of those trapped in their claustrophobic self-centred cosmoses. Unseen, unheard, unheeded, but always there; the invisible priest in Percy's *Lancelot* is a metaphor for Christ, standing on our behalf, *in persona Christi*, at the altar of reality, making sacrifice in the midst of the valley of tears and making sense of our life's exile. Perhaps Percy's priest also serves as a metaphor for the fictional priest *per se*. He is not significant in himself but gains his significance from the Thing he signifies. He is always more than himself, always signifying and representing something and Someone beyond himself, always pointing beyond the story to the Story Beyond.

32. CHILDREN'S LITERATURE: WISDOM IN WONDERLAND

"Once upon a time," said kind Uncle Chestnut, "we were all little children and we lived in a place called wonderland." Looking up from the book of fairytales that he was reading for the umpteenth time, he smiled sadly at his nephew. "The problem is that we forget that we were children and we lose sight of wonderland . . ."

"Enough!" exclaimed his nephew, who had recently completed his first semester at college. "Enough of such saccharine sentimentality! Enough of this Never-Never Land naïveté! That stuff is for innocent kids, uncle. You're old enough to know better. Isn't it time you grew up?"

Uncle Chestnut put the book to one side. "Innocent? Grown up? None of us were ever truly innocent and some of us never grow up."

"Well," said the nephew, whose name was Eustace, "I wish *you* would grow up!"

So, who is right? Uncle Chestnut? Or Eustace? Is wonderland merely a place for wishful thinking? Is it just for children? Shouldn't Uncle Chestnut put away childish things and just grow up?

The first thing we need to remember is that Christ Himself is a story-teller. He teaches many of His most important lessons through the telling of stories, or parables to give them their "grown-up" name. We think of the Prodigal Son perhaps, or the Good Samaritan, two fictional characters who, as figments of Our Lord's imagination, become figures of truth for all generations. He tells us stories because we are His children and these stories are the best way for us to understand what He means to tell us. If we will not become child-like, listening like children, we will not see the truth in the story, the moral that it teaches. The fact that the Prodigal Son or the Good Samaritan never existed in the "real world" but only as characters in the story does not make them less real. On the contrary, they become such powerful archetypes that there have been countless "prodigal sons" or "good Samaritans" in every generation since Christ first told the story.

And what is true of these stories can be true of other stories, each of which is the product of the God-given gift of the imagination. This is what Uncle Chestnut means when he praises wonderland and laments that we forget the wonderland we experienced as children. It is not that we forget that we *were* children, it is that we forget that we *are* children. There are some, to be sure, the victims of wicked stepmothers (or stepfathers), whose experience in wonderland was not much fun. There are others, led astray by ugly sisters or uglier friends, who turn their wonderland into a place of real ugliness. We forget, at our peril, that wonderland is not only full of wonders but wicked witches also. We forget that wonderland does not only contain wolves but, much more dangerous, wolves in sheep's (or grandma's) clothing. Wonderland is not a place of idyllic and unrealistic innocence or naïveté, as Eustace seems to believe, but a place where the virtuous struggle heroically against wickedness. In short, it is very much like the world in which we actually live.

But wait a minute, we can hear Eustace exclaim, the world in which we actually live does not have wolves that disguise themselves as granny. It does not have magic wardrobes through which we can pass into other worlds. It does not have beautiful princesses that sleep for a hundred years until a noble prince awakens them with a kiss. It does not have pumpkins that turn into carriages. At this point, Uncle Chestnut might remind his nephew that the world is full of wolves who disguise themselves as sheep or grannies. They include baby-kissing politicians, or advertising executives who launch marketing campaigns employing traditional values to sell poisonous products. He might also remind Eustace that every good book or good movie is a magic wardrobe that transports us to other worlds. Perhaps he might smilingly suggest that his nephew is himself a sleeping beauty who needs to be awakened by the kiss of goodness and truth. And as for pumpkins, Uncle Chestnut would insist that a pumpkin is more miraculous than a carriage and that we should learn to be as astonished at the appearance of the pumpkin on our plate as was Cinderella with the appearance of the carriage on the night of the ball.

On a more wistful note, the kindly uncle might warn his nephew that there are real dangers in not believing in the real magic of wonderland. There is a real danger that those who do not believe in dragons become dragons. There is a real danger that those who do not believe that Jack could slay the Giant become servants of the Giant and slayers of Jack. Such people, who are very successful in politics and law, are placed in the Giant's pocket and are used by him to ensure that Jack remains powerless and that the Giant's monopoly over the goose that lays the golden egg is safeguarded.

The cause of the singular blindness that prevents people from seeing the wisdom of wonderland is that people know their abc's but have forgotten their p's and q's, their *please* and *thank yous*. To say "please" is to ask for something in the proper manner, to say "thank you" is to show the appropriate gratitude. This is true of our relationship with our friends and family but is especially so of our relationship with God. It is no surprise that *please* is connected etymologically with *plea* and *plead* and is, therefore, connected practically to the reality of prayer. More importantly, the act of thanksgiving is a sign of our gratitude for the wonders of Creation and for the wonders of our existence within it. Giving thanks, showing gratitude, is a sign of humility and it is to the humble of heart that the vision of wonder is given. An ungrateful heart that believes it has nothing for which to be thankful is a proud heart incapable of wonder. As if by magic, wonderland becomes invisible to these proud-hearted souls. They cannot see it and therefore believe that it does not exist. This is, of course, the warped and defective logic of the relativist. For this sort of "realist" all reality is in the eye of the beholder. As such, all reality that they do not behold is ipso facto unreal: *"I do not see it, therefore it is not real."* Needless to say, such logic is childish and here we are reminded of the crucial difference between the childish and the childlike. The childish, lacking gratitude, fall into the sin of cynicism that blinds them to the beauty of truth; the childlike, grateful for the gift of life, see through the eyes of wonder and behold the wonderful wisdom of wonderland. And this beautiful vision is but a shadow of the Beatific Vision, the ultimate Wonderland where people truly live happily ever after.

33. HOW WE REDISCOVER REALITY THROUGH FANTASY

Any discussion of "reality" and "fantasy" must confront the implicit assumption inherent in the modern materialist *weltanschauung* that "fantasy" is unreal, and therefore irrelevant and impertinent. This misunderstanding was addressed with erudite eloquence by J. R. R. Tolkien in his definitive essay "On Fairy Stories." For Tolkien, fantasy literature conveyed a healthy trinity of virtues, namely Recovery, Escape and Consolation. "Recovery (which includes return and renewal of health) is a re-gaining . . . of a clear view," and was "seeing things as we are (or were) meant to see them." Fantasy literature accesses a reality beyond the mundane world of *facts*, allowing the qualitative to penetrate the merely quantitative, and enabling *meaning* to permeate the factual. It goes beyond seeing things only as they are, or as they seem to be; it sees them as they are meant to be. It does not accept the status quo, merely because it is the "real world," but explores the possibilities of different and better worlds. It transcends the barren limitations of "how things are" to explore the fruitful possibilities of "how things should be." This intrinsic idealism clearly has implications as regards the way that fantasy literature interrelates with reality.

Tolkien's discussion of "Escape and Consolation, which are naturally closely connected" focused on a defence of "escapism" against "the tone of scorn and pity with which "Escape" is now so often used: a tone for which the uses of the word outside literary criticism give no warrant at all." Detecting the ideological animus behind the critical animosity to "escape," Tolkien accused his accusers of seeking to imprison the imagination within the stifling walls of materialistic presumption. "Why should a man be scorned if, finding himself in prison, he tries to get out and go home? Or if, when he cannot do so, he thinks and talks about other topics than jailers and prison-walls? The world outside has not become less real because the prisoner cannot see it." Tolkien then implies that the materialistic critics are themselves the jailers, treating "the Escape of the Prisoner" as "the Flight of the Deserter": "Just so a Party-spokesman might have labeled departure from the misery of the Führer's or any other Reich and even criticism of it as treachery." The real reason, therefore, behind the prejudice against, and the hostility towards, fantasy literature on the part of many literary critics is purely a prejudice against, and a hostility towards, metaphysics in general, and Christianity in particular.

Having established the real relationship between fantasy and reality, a brief history of the genre of Christian fantasy literature will show how the truths it contains can be seen to be "applicable" to questions of human society.

The history of Christian fantasy goes back almost to the dawn of Christianity itself. Indeed, if one is to class the Book of Revelations as a work of fantasy, as an expression and exposition of the fantastically True and Real, it goes back to the dawn itself. Within the English tradition, *Beowulf* rose with the dawn of Anglo-Saxon Christianity and has shed its light across the centuries, its subtle blend of heroic epic narrative and applicable Christian allegory inspiring many later writers of Christian fantasy, not the least of whom was the aforementioned Tolkien who not only translated *Beowulf* into modern English but also borrowed from it bountifully in the writing of *The Hobbit* and *The Lord of the Rings*. As the Anglo-Saxon culture matured so did the Christian fantasy it produced, blossoming into multifarious Arthurian hues, most memorably perhaps in *Sir Gawain and the Green Knight*, a work of the late fourteenth century that wove wisdom and magic into a story designed to elucidate the relationship between chivalry and virtue. The authorship of *Sir Gawain and the Green Knight* remains a mystery but he was a contemporary of the great Geoffrey Chaucer whose *Canterbury Tales* have forged a place amongst the *illustrissimi* of world literature—this in spite of the fact that the work was unfinished at the poet's death. Chaucer succeeds in blending the grotesque and even gargoylic realism of "the ship of fools" motif with the allegorical employment of fantasy and fable. In the *Nun's Priest's Tale*, for example, he uses the fable of Chauntecleer and Pertelotte to re-enact the axial and axiomatic story of the Fall, stressing, by means of allegory, its perennial relevance, not merely theologically but sociologically and politically.

Another major milestone in the evolution of Christian fantasy was St. Thomas More's *Utopia*, published in 1516. The fact that "utopia," as employed by More, means "no place" or "nowhere" (from the Greek *ou*, meaning *not*, and *topos*, meaning *place*) as opposed to "good place" (from the Greek *eu*, meaning *good*, and *topos*, meaning *place*) is a fact all too often forgotten by modern critics who lack the subtlety to see the true intent of More's satire. Perceiving that More meant *eutopia* not *outopia* these critics have concluded quite erroneously that More was more of a humanist than he was a Christian or, even more absurdly, that he was a proto-communist or a proto-ecumenist. For a man who willingly laid down his life for his friends and his faith such conclusions lack all credibility. Although More used the medium of Christian fantasy as a vehicle for voicing criticisms of the cruelty and corruption of the times in which he lived, his purpose in writing the satire went beyond the temporal to the eternal. In the final analysis, More's *outopia* can be seen much more as a *dystopia* than a *eutopia*, depicting a world of self-evident absurdities based upon erroneous conceptions of reality.

In writing his *Utopia* More established a whole new genre of fantasy literature, the utopian or dystopian fantasy, in which imaginary worlds are created as a reflection of the real world. From Swift's *Gulliver's Travels* to Orwell's *Nineteen Eighty-Four* More's originality has inspired generations of writers to hold a utopian mirror to the world in which they lived.

34. APOCALYPTIC VISIONS: FAITH & SCIENCE FICTION

Properly understood, in the broadest etymological sense, science is merely knowing or seeing. Thus the omni-*science* of God means that He is all-knowing, or all-seeing. He knows everything. As such, God is the absolute and perfect scientist. He sees all that there is to see, and knows all that there is to know. It is, therefore, no surprise that theology, the study of the Word of God, is a true science. Indeed it is the truest science. It enables us to see through the eyes of the One who sees perfectly, even if our limited perception necessarily dims our perspective. We cannot know as He knows but at least we are knowing what He wants us to know, albeit imperfectly. That which God reveals is *meant* to be *known*. It is, therefore, the most *meaningful science*.

Similarly philosophy is truly a science because it sees with the eyes of reason. It does not, however, see reason as an end in itself, which is the reductive error of the rationalists, but as a means by which the lover of wisdom may see the splendor of truth (*veritatis splendor*). Reason is the eye with which we see; truth is the object seen.

The fact that the true science of theology and philosophy has been marginalized in the modern world is a sure indication that the modern world has lost its way. Quite literally, it has ceased being truly scientific. It cannot *know* reality and, in consequence, it cannot know where it is or where it is going.

So what went wrong? How did modernity lose its way? What caused its blindness?

The root of the problem resides in modernity's acceptance of a narrower vision of reality. Instead of seeing the fullness of truth, which is natural and supernatural, physical and metaphysical, material and spiritual, it sees only a part of the picture; its surface and not its depth. It refuses to see that which is revealed by God (theology) and insists on seeing only a small part of the truth that philosophy sees. It sees only *natural* philosophy, that part of philosophy that excludes the supernatural and the metaphysical from its field of vision. Thus a mere fragment of the true science of philosophy, a small part of the picture, has eclipsed the whole, enabling modernity to mistake the fragment for the totality. It can be seen, therefore, that modernity is narrow-minded and blinded by its own tunnel vision. This blindness is clear from the fact that modernity sees natural philosophy and science as synonymous. Hence the modern definition of "science" excludes all modes of knowing or seeing except the purely physical. It recognizes nothing except three dimensions (or four if we wish to consider time as an additional dimension) perceived by five senses. This is all that there is to *know* or *see*.

At this juncture the increasingly impatient reader is no doubt wondering what any of this has to do with "apocalyptic visions" or "faith and science fiction." The answer lies in the fact that science fiction, for all its use of science in the modern sense, is informed by science in the older, traditional sense. It is theology and philosophy that inform and inspire the best science fiction, regardless of how many spaceships, time machines and five-legged aliens are employed in the plot.

Gulliver's Travels, perhaps the progenitor of the sci-fi genre, has weird alien creatures, such as the platonic equine houyhnhnms and the bestial humanoid yahoos, and presents us with the "scientific" wonders of floating islands and the "scientific" blunders of mad scientists. Yet it was not written merely to exercise a scientific imagination but to exorcise the nonsense of modernism and scientism, the latter of which might be defined as the idolizing of natural science as the arbiter of all truth. Swift, a profoundly tradition-oriented Christian, uses science in his fiction to expose the follies of the emergent scientism of his day.

In the same fashion, Aldous Huxley's *Brave New World* exposes the pernicious nature of scientism in the novel's depiction of a culture neutered by "progress." Its characters are corrupted by the comforts of technology and rendered comfortably numb to the realities of life. Long before society's lurch into cyber-space, Huxley was warning of the dangers inherent in the substitution of reality for virtual reality.

If Huxley offers a timely reminder of the dangers of self-absorbed consumerism, facilitated by technology, George Orwell in *Nineteen Eighty-Four* warns of the dangers of totalitarianism. His futuristic masterpiece embodies the wisdom of Lord Acton's maxim that power tends to corrupt and absolute power tends to corrupt absolutely. Although the clear and present danger of communism and fascism has faded, Orwell's futuristic nightmare still serves as a powerful witness against the evils of secular fundamentalism.

C. S. Lewis's Space Trilogy uses the genre of science fiction to engage with the follies and fallacies of scientism and to convey timeless philosophical and theological truth as an antidote to the poison of materialism. In *Out of the Silent Planet* he exposes the facile shallowness of the scientism of H. G. Wells; in *Perelandra* he re-presents the primal apocalypse of Man's initial Fall, employing it as a vehicle for theological exploration; and in *That Hideous Strength* he exposes the scientism of the modern academy as ultimately demonic in its pride and its willful hatred of the truth.

There is of course an ironic paradox at the heart of this so-called "science fiction." It is not simply that the modern science in such novels is put at the service of ancient wisdom, the true science that has been forgotten, or that the futuristic points to the past, it is that the science in the fiction points to the God of science who is the truth in fiction.

The apocalyptic vision in science fiction is akin to the *memento mori* in mediaeval art. It reminds us of the Four Last Things: Death, Judgment, Heaven, and Hell. And these last things remind us of the first things, most importantly the primary reality that we are made in the image of God to love and serve him in this life that we may be with Him forever in the next.

The last things lead us to the first things. The first shall be the last and the last shall be first. And so it is that the greatest science fiction points us not merely to the stars but to the One who made the stars. It takes us beyond Alpha Centauri to the Alpha and Omega.

35. WHATEVER HAPPENED TO THE CATHOLIC LITERARY REVIVAL?

One of the most encouraging phenomena of the last two centuries is the Catholic Literary Revival, which, in its gestation period, from 1798 to 1845, saw the rise of neo-mediaevalism, beginning with Coleridge's *Mariner* and Scott's chivalrous heroes, and ending with Pugin's Gothic Revival and Newman's Oxford Movement. After its forty-seven years in the womb of neo-mediaeval culture, the Catholic Literary Revival could be said to have been born, in 1845, amidst the controversial pangs of Newman's conversion. This heralded what may be termed the Newman Period in the Revival, dating from 1845 until the great man's death in 1890. Apart from Newman himself, this period was graced with the presence of other eminent convert literati, including the poets, Coventry Patmore and Gerard Manley Hopkins, the latter of whom is perhaps the finest and most important poet of the whole Victorian period.

Following Newman's death there was the Decadent interlude of the *fin de siècle* in which a host of Catholic converts, such as Wilde, Beardsley, Dowson and Lionel Johnson, came to the Church via the dark and dangerous path of sin. In doing so, they were following in the footsteps of a previous generation of French converts, such as Baudelaire, Verlaine and Huysmans, each of whom had also taken the same dark path to conversion.

The period from 1900 to 1936 could be called the Chesterbelloc Period, in which the giant figures of G. K. Chesterton and Hilaire Belloc presided over a golden age of literary converts, including R. H. Benson, Ronald Knox, Maurice Baring, Christopher Dawson, Roy Campbell, Evelyn Waugh, Graham Greene and T. S. Eliot. (Although Eliot was technically an Anglo-Catholic who never crossed the Tiber his work is, to all intents and purposes, as Catholic as anything written by his Roman contemporaries.) From 1936 to 1973 we enter the Inklings Period, in which the formidable presence of J. R. R. Tolkien and C. S. Lewis dominate. (Lewis, like Eliot, was an Anglican and not a Catholic, but his work, which is overwhelmingly orthodox, sits very comfortably alongside the work of his Catholic contemporaries.) Eminent literary converts during this period include Edith Sitwell, Siegfried Sassoon, Muriel Spark and George Mackay Brown. In America, this period also saw the emergence of those two fine writers, Flannery O'Connor and Walker Percy.

What an array of talent! What a procession of literary giants! And yet one is left wondering what has happened to the Catholic Literary Revival in the past thirty years or so. Did it come to an end with the death of Tolkien in 1973? If so, why; if not, where are the signs of the Revival's continuance today?

It is sad but true that the Revival is not what it was. There are no literary giants of the calibre of Newman, Hopkins, Chesterton, Belloc, Waugh, Lewis or Tolkien today. Why is this? Does it have something to do with the malaise that followed in the wake of the second Vatican Council? Perhaps, up to a point. "Much water has flown under Tiber's bridges, carrying away splendour and mystery from Rome, since the Pontificate of Pius XII," lamented Sir Alec Guinness, himself a Catholic convert. It would, however, be an over-simplification to blame everything on the rampant modernism that followed Vatican II. After all, much water has also flown under the bridges of the Seine, the Thames and the Potomac since the death of Pius XII in 1958, carrying away much of what remained of Western civilization. Indeed, so much has passed away in the past half-century that we have seen Eliot's Waste Land prophecy that London Bridge was falling down and that the "unreal cities" were doomed to self-destruct being fulfilled before our eyes. Whatever else can be blamed on the modernist zeitgeist posing as the so-called "spirit" of Vatican II, the "spirit" of the Council cannot be held responsible for the tidal wave of ethno-masochistic self-hatred which characterized the 1960s and beyond. If anything, one might suggest that the latter was responsible for the former. And this brings us back to our discussion of the Catholic Literary Revival. If it is true that there are no great Catholic writers today, it is equally true that there are no great secularist writers either. Where are today's Orwells, Wodehouses and Shaws? The fact is that Chesterton was correct when he said that the "coming peril" was "standardization by a low standard." Chesterton, like Eliot, was a prophet whose prophesies are coming true before our eyes. We live in a dumbed-down sub-culture where excellence is shunned in favour of the banal and the inane. What place is there for the great and the true in such a desert of inanity? Is there no hope of a literary revival and of cultural renewal in such a wasteland?

These questions are answered by history. The great and the true can thrive in the desert. Christ triumphed in the desert, as did John the Baptist, and as did the Fathers of the Church. And what is true of God and His Catholic saints is true of Catholic writers. Shakespeare rose phoenix-like from the ashes of the Machiavellian desert of Elizabethan politics; Newman rose from the ruins of Anglicanism; Chesterton ascended from the wasteland of heresy; and Eliot sang like a latter-day Jeremiah from the wreck of post-war England.

A desert, or wasteland, is in need of water, as Eliot reminds us, and the Church is the living water that refreshes the sojourner in the desert of (post)modernity. It is, therefore, not altogether surprising that we are beginning to see the emergence of a new generation of Catholic writers in the very midst of today's hostile culture. All is not lost and there is much to be won. As we begin to see the twilight of the secularist gods, these signs of the renewal of the Catholic Literary Revival are heralds of the dawn. London Bridge is falling down but the bridges of Rome remain.

PART IV
LITERARY PORTRAITS

36. SHAKESPEARE'S CHALLENGE
TO CONTEMPORARY CULTURE

In the history of western civilization, which now stretches back almost 3,000 years, there has been a wealth of great writers. Many poets and authors spring to mind. From the classical period of pagan antiquity we think, perhaps, of Aeschylus, Aristophanes, Catullus, Euripides, Homer, Horace, Lucretius, Ovid, Theocritus, and Virgil; from the mediaeval period we think of Boccaccio, Boethius, Chaucer, Dante, Petrarch, and the anonymous authors of *Beowulf*, *The Song of Roland*, and *Sir Gawain and the Green Knight*; and from the so-called modern period we think of Calderón de la Barca, Cervantes, Dickens, Dostoyevsky, Goethe, Milton, Molière, Schiller, Shakespeare, Tolkien, and Tolstoy, to name but an illustrious few. Yet from each of these periods, one name emerges as supreme. From the classical period it is indubitably Homer, even though Virgil's influence was greater than Homer's during the mediaeval period; from the middle ages it is indubitably Dante, whose *Divina Commedia* is arguably the greatest poem ever written; and in the modern period it is indubitably Shakespeare, whose superlative achievement is incomparable.

Of this triumvirate of literary giants, Homer's legacy was at the heart of neo-classicism and is still at the heart of the best liberal arts programs in the academy. On the other hand, Dante's legacy, though gargantuan, is now largely ignored. His "relevance" to the modern world is questioned on the presumption that his Thomistic philosophy and theology has been superseded by the philosophy of the "Enlightenment." When Dante is read or studied at all, it is almost invariably only the *Inferno*, and rarely the *Purgatorio* or the *Paradiso*. This singular blindness is not without its ironic twist: The modern world is seemingly at home in the nihilistic atmosphere of Hell but is uncomfortable with the penitential atmosphere of Purgatory and completely baffled by the sheer beauty and majesty of Paradise. As C. S. Lewis reminds us in *The Great Divorce*, God doesn't send anyone to Hell; those in Hell send themselves there; they are there of their own volition. The modern world is only at home in Dante's Inferno because it is itself a Hell in which egocentric self-obsession obscures the wider spiritual panorama of self-sacrificial and penitential heroism and the salvation it brings. Modernity is a stranger to Purgatory and Paradise but recognises Hell as Home.

If Homer's legacy is largely academic and Dante's is largely ignored, Shakespeare's legacy is seemingly culturally ubiquitous. His influence is certainly greater now than it was in the century or so after he died, and seems to be as great in the twenty-first century as at any time since he first became *en vogue* in the early 1700s. The secret to Shakespeare's endurance is rooted in the way that his works connect the old "mediaeval" world of faith with the new "modern" world of doubt, and, more important, the way in which this connection of faith and doubt signifies the war between belief and unbelief that rages in the heart of every man in every generation. In short, Shakespeare is still read because he is still relevant. Yet this is not the sole reason for his perennial popularity. Let's not forget that Dante is still relevant and yet is not read.

Whereas Dante is didactically theological, and therefore clearly partisan, Shakespeare is never overtly didactic and his theology is always subsumed with subtlety within the fabric of the drama. Whereas Dante tells us a cautionary tale, lecturing us about the dangers of sin, the necessity of repentance, and the beauty of virtue, Shakespeare weaves his tales of sin, repentance and virtue, without lecturing us about anything. In doing so, he succeeds in stealing past those watchful dragons of modernity, to employ C. S. Lewis's powerful phrase, which make it their business to censure or censor all signs of Christian preaching or morality in literature or art. His reason for such subtlety is clear enough. In Elizabethan and Jacobean England it was illegal to discuss contemporary politics or religious controversy on the stage. Shakespeare had no option but to steal past the watchful dragons of state censorship as he endeavoured to weave political and religious significance into his plays. The Bard's struggle to be true to his own beliefs without being censored is the dramatic tension that permeates every one of his plays. There is, however, a danger inherent to Shakespeare's subtlety. If he managed to circumvent the state censorship of his time through the circumspection of his plots, he also seems to have managed to confuse the critics with regard to the true meaning of his works.

No one is more misread and misrepresented than William Shakespeare. His plays are interpreted as being nihilist, relativist, romantic, cynical, racist, anti-racist, homosexual, feminist, sexist, Christian, un-Christian and anti-Christian, depending on the penchants and prejudices of the individual critic. As such, Shakespeare, arguably the greatest writer who has ever lived, is made the slave or servant of the prejudices of his readers. And since his readers are pygmies in his presence we can be sure that we are being short-changed. If only we could see the plays through the eyes of the genius who wrote them we would really be able to grow in the presence of his wisdom.

How can this be done? How can we see through Shakespeare's eyes? The answer is obvious and yet all too often overlooked by modern Shakespeare scholars. Quite simply, if we wish to see through Shakespeare's eyes we need to know as much as possible about Shakespeare himself, and as much as possible about the time and culture in which he lived. This was the goal of my own book, *The Quest for Shakespeare* (Ignatius Press, 2008). The facts of Shakespeare's life point inescapably to the fact that he was born into a staunchly Catholic family at a time when Catholicism was illegal, that he remained a discreet but probably secretly practising Catholic throughout his life, and that he died defiantly Catholic. These facts form the bedrock reality upon which any true understanding of his plays must be based.

If Shakespeare was a Catholic, and was greatly influenced by the Catholicism of his parents and the persecution that surrounded the practice of Catholicism in his day, it forces us to re-read the plays in an entirely new light. In the past, the perceived lack of knowledge of the personhood of Shakespeare had enabled critics to treat him as a *tabula rasa* upon which they could write their own prejudiced agenda. For the proponents of "queer theory" he becomes conveniently homosexual; for secular fundamentalists he is a proto-secularist, ahead of his time; for "post-Christian" agnostics he becomes a prophet of post-modernity. It was all so easy to mould Shakespeare into the critics' own image when the Bard was a myth but now that he is emerging as a man, a living person with real beliefs, such distortion becomes more difficult.

For "post-modern" Shakespeare scholars the emergence of tangible evidence for the Catholic Shakespeare is not only a challenge but a threat. If he was a Catholic, he becomes irritatingly anti-modern. From the perspective of the modernist and post-modernist, Shakespeare emerges as an unenlightened and recalcitrant reactionary. From the perspective of tradition-oriented scholars, the evident clarity of moral vision that they had always perceived in the plays becomes more explicable and more clearly defined.

Throughout the plays Shakespeare's Catholicism manifests itself in a philosophical dialectic with the emergent atheism (*de facto* if not always *de jure*) of the embryonic Enlightenment. Although allusions to the doctrinal disputes of the Reformation and Counter Reformation are present in the plays, they are eclipsed by the overarching dialectic with secularism. Shakespeare's heroes and heroines are invariably adherents of tradition-oriented philosophy and religion, motivated in their choices and their actions by an implicit understanding of Christian orthodoxy and a desire to conduct themselves with traditional virtue. His villains, in contrast, are machiavels, disciples of the new cynical creed of Machiavelli, who are motivated solely by a self-serving desire to get what they want. Shakespeare's greatest heroines, such as Cordelia, Portia, Desdemona and Isabella, exhibit a self-sacrificial love emblematic of the Christian saint. His great villains, such as Edmund, Goneril, Regan and Cornwall in *King Lear*, King Claudius in *Hamlet*, Iago in *Othello*, or the demonically twisted Macbeths, are all philosophical iconoclasts, ripping to shreds Christian philosophy and openly defying orthodox moral theology.

In *Hamlet*, Shakespeare defends the Christian realism of Augustine and Aquinas against the nascent relativism of the late Renaissance. In Polonius's famous advice to his son, we see the enunciation of a philosophy of life rooted in self-serving relativism, a philosophy that would lead to his son's unwitting and ultimately fatal manipulation by King Claudius. Hamlet, on the other hand, begins with an egocentric tendency towards skepticism and nihilism but grows in wisdom through his prevailing adherence to the objectivity of Christian realism. His growth from this solid foundation in philosophy to a revitalized faith, the latter of which is evoked and invoked by his reference to the Gospel as the play approaches its providential climax, is the triumph of traditional virtue over the Machiavellian *realpolitik* of Polonius and King Claudius.

Hamlet can be seen as a companion piece to *Macbeth*, the latter of which is the inversion of the former. Whereas Hamlet is tempted to despair but grows in the light of realism, Macbeth begins in triumph but descends into the darkness of nihilism, declaring that life "is a tale / Told by an idiot, full of sound and fury, / Signifying nothing." Hamlet overcomes Machiavellianism through the power of Christian realism and virtue, Macbeth loses his power, and his reason, through his succumbing to relativism and the Machiavellianism it spawns. Macbeth is, therefore, an anti-Hamlet. Whereas Hamlet ascends purgatorially, through the acceptance of suffering, so that the noble Horatio can say with confidence following

Hamlet's death that flights of angels are singing him to his rest, Macbeth descends, through his enslavement to pride and personal ambition, to an inferno of his own devising.

In *King Lear* the same theme of purgative suffering is pursued in the midst of a political dynamic animated by what the Church would now call subsidiarity. Cordelia's decision to retain a virtuous silence in defiance of her father's wrath and at the cost of her disinheritance and exile, is rooted in a principled refusal to bestow unto Caesar that which is not rightfully his. Her courage in the face of draconian secularism is reminiscent of the example of Antigone in Sophocles's *Oedipus Cycle* but also of St. Thomas More's refusal to kowtow to the secular fundamentalism of Henry VIII or, more generally, of the refusal of England's Catholics to abandon their faith in the face of ruthless state-sponsored persecution.

The Merchant of Venice explores several political themes but its over-arching dynamic is the tension that exists between the worldliness of Venice and the other-worldliness of Belmont, epitomized in the respective philosophies of Shylock and Portia. The venality of Venice demands that the Law be employed to crush the malefactor with merciless abandon; the wisdom of Belmont insists that mercy must prevail or "none of us should see salvation." Once again, secularism (Venice) is seen to be at loggerheads with Christian orthodoxy (Belmont) and, once again, Shakespeare comes down solidly on the side of the latter.

Shakespeare's condemnation of usury in *The Merchant of Venice* serves as further evidence of his Catholicism, not only in its conformity with the Catholic Church's traditional teaching on the subject but in its implicit criticism of Calvinism for sanctioning the practice of usury. Since there was no Jewish presence in England in Shakespeare's time, the Jews having been expelled by Edward I three hundred years earlier, and since usury was practiced almost exclusively by Puritans, it has been suggested by several scholars that Shakespeare's characterization of Shylock is a veiled caricature of a Puritan. Such artistic subterfuge would have been necessary due to the Elizabethan government's ban on the portrayal of contemporary political and religious controversy on the stage.

Further evidence of the Bard's Catholicism is evident in his attitude towards monarchy and kingship. It is noteworthy, for instance, that the plays written during the reign of Elizabeth I are preoccupied with questions of legitimacy. Many Catholics questioned the legitimacy of Elizabeth, arguing that her father's relationship with Anne Boleyn was adulterous. It is equally noteworthy that such questions of legitimacy become less prevalent in the plays written after the accession of James I, whose legitimacy was not in question. Instead, the Jacobean plays are far more concerned with the essence of kingship itself. King James advocated the Divine Right of Kings, whereby a king's subjects were duty-bound to obey the monarch at all times, even if he behaved tyrannically. At the other end of the political spectrum the radical republicanism of the Puritans sought the abolition of the monarchy. Against these two extremes, Catholic political philosophy represented a via media in which monarchy was seen as a legitimate form of government but in which the monarch was considered to be as subject to the moral law as were his subjects. The political philosophy of Shakespeare's late plays reflects the Catholic position. King Lear's usurping of powers beyond his rightful jurisdiction leads to disaster and widespread injustice. His radical conversion on the heath, reminiscent of the equally radical conversion of St. Francis, signifies his acceptance and embrace of his own mortality and sinfulness. Yet his acceptance of the mystical equality that he shares with his subjects, under God, does not negate the reality of his kingship, nor the rights and responsibilities that accompany it. He has ceased to be a bad king and has become a good king, but he remains a king.

Shakespeare's most powerful depiction of a good king is his description of St. Edward the Confessor in *Macbeth*. Set against the self-serving Machiavellian machinations of Macbeth, the English king's sanctity, and the miraculous healing power that accompanies it, serves as an iconic antidote to the poison of tyrannical ambition.

In recent years, from Leo XIII's *Rerum novarum* (1891), Pius XI's *Quadragesimo anno* (1931), John Paul II's *Centesimus annus* (1991), and Benedict XVI's *Caritas in veritate* (2009), the Church has delineated its social teaching in terms of subsidiarity. Such teaching on the role and responsibility of secular power is explored with timely and timeless resonance in the works of the world's greatest playwright.

In an age in which Christians find themselves fighting in defence of life, liberty and marriage, Shakespeare emerges as a powerful voice for the culture of life against the Machiavellianism of the culture of death and its poisonous relativism. In an age of diabolical scandal, from *in utero* infanticide to the destruction of marriage, the Bard of Avon is on the side of the angels.

37. MAJOR OR MINOR POETS?
EXAMINING THE LITERARY STATURE
OF SOUTHWELL AND CRASHAW

*Here lies Robert Peckham, Englishman and Catholic, who, after England's
break with the Church, left England not being able to live without the Faith
and who, coming to Rome, died not being able to live without his country.*[34]

Robert Peckham's epitaph in the church of San Gregorio in Rome encap-
sulates the plight of England's Catholics during the decades of persecution
following the English Reformation. It also serves as a resonant introduction to Robert Southwell and Richard Crashaw, two of the foremost
Metaphysical Poets, who, being Catholic in very anti-Catholic times, faced
the same dilemma as Robert Peckham. Southwell, a Jesuit priest, was
arrested, tortured and put to death after his return to England; Crashaw, a
convert to Catholicism, chose a reluctant life of exile, dying, like Peckham,
in Italy. Although both poets suffered in the flesh for their faith during their
own lifetime, it is the suffering of their respective reputations after their
deaths that should animate the historian and the critic. As outsiders, bêtes
noire, who were considered "traitors" by their contemporaries and by the
Whig historians who wrote the officially accepted version of post-
Reformation English history, Southwell and Crashaw remained objects of
suspicion and hostility for many years after their deaths. Excommunicated
from the patriotic company of "true Englishmen," their reputation carried
an odour of ordure that threatened to exile their works to the margins of the
literary canon. The quest for objective judgement on the work of Southwell
and Crashaw is, therefore, also a quest for justice for the poets themselves.

In spite of their historical position as outsiders, or even outlaws, with
respect to the mainstream of English cultural life, and in spite of the fact
that they were on the losing side in a history that had been shamelessly
written by the victors, Southwell and Crashaw were, by the end of the

nineteenth century, fully acknowledged as important and significant poets. This renewal of interest in their work reflected the wider cultural acceptance of England's Catholics in the wake of Catholic emancipation in 1829 and it is likely that Southwell's and Crashaw's respective reputations benefited from the Catholic cultural revival that followed John Henry Newman's conversion to Catholicism in 1845.

A brief survey of several twentieth-century anthologies of poetry will show the perceived place of Southwell and Crashaw in the more recent past, compared to that of John Donne and George Herbert, the two poets popularly perceived to be the true giants of metaphysical poetry. Sir Arthur Quiller-Couch in his seminal if not definitive *Oxford Book of English Verse* (1900) included two poems by Southwell (four pages) and seven by Crashaw (fifteen pages). This compares to seven by Donne (eight pages), and six by Herbert (four pages). George Lacey May, in his anthology of *English Religious Verse*, published in 1937, included three poems by Southwell and five by Crashaw, compared to five by Donne, and nine by Herbert. Helen Gardner's canonical Penguin Classics edition of *The Metaphysical Poets* (1957) includes three selections of Southwell's verse and nine selections of Crashaw's. This compares to forty-one by Donne and twenty-four by Herbert. It should be noted, however, that the nine poems by Crashaw were longer cumulatively than the two dozen by Herbert (27 pages as opposed to 23). The *Oxford Anthology of English Poetry*, selected by John Wain (1990), included only a solitary poem by Southwell, the seemingly ubiquitously anthologized "Burning Babe," and five by Crashaw. This compares to eleven by Donne and nine by Herbert. Descending from the relatively sublime to the occasionally ridiculous, *The Nation's Favourite Poems*, published by the BBC in 1996, anthologized the hundred most popular poems for which the British public had voted in a nationwide poll the previous year. The list included some indubitably worthy verse, including three by Hopkins, though not his masterpiece, "The Wreck of the Deutschland," and five by Eliot, though curiously not *The Waste Land* or *Four Quartets*, and a veritable who's who of other major English poets, including both Brownings, Blake, Brooke, Burns, Chesterton, Coleridge, Housman, Keats, Kipling (the overall winner with "If"), Longfellow, Owen, Poe, Sassoon, Shakespeare (of course!), Shelley, Tennyson, Wordsworth, and Yeats, to name an illustrious sample. Sadly there were also a few modern poems on the list that are memorable as objects of venal vulgarity rather than as verse. As for the Metaphysical Poets who remained popular amongst the fin de siècle British public, John

Donne, George Herbert, and Andrew Marvell were all included. Southwell and Crashaw were not.

The overall impression to be gleaned from this admittedly impression-istic exercise is that Southwell has always been a relatively minor figure in these anthologies, though present in each of them with the exception of the democratically dumbed-down selection by the BBC. It is also noteworthy that Crashaw's star seems to have waxed under the scholarly patronage of Quiller-Couch, who places Crashaw above both Donne and Herbert in terms of the space he devotes to their respective verse. Indeed, he devotes more space to the verse of Crashaw than he does to Donne and Herbert combined. Helen Gardner also shows great respect for Crashaw's poetic achievement. Although her selection of Crashaw's poetry is dwarfed by the dominant presence of Donne, she reflects the judgement of Quiller-Couch in devoting more space to Crashaw than to Herbert.

Crashaw's poetic presence begins to wane in Wain's selection, indica-tive of the radical shift towards secular fundamentalism and away from religious tradition that had encompassed the wider culture by the last decade of the last century, and which is reflected by the absence of Southwell and Crashaw from the BBC's popular vote of "favourite poems." This secular shift is evident in Wain's choice of Crashaw's verse, which sig-nificantly omits the majestic and magisterial "Hymn to Saint Teresa," included by both Quiller-Couch and by Gardner. Crashaw's "Hymn" palpi-tates with the burgeoning presence of the Catholic Counter-Reformation, and is a shining forth of the Church Militant in prosodic prayer. One won-ders whether Wain, blind to the poem's Baroque brilliance, and possibly blinded by his own prejudice, could not bring himself to include such a work in his selection, finding its strident spirituality distasteful to his mod-ernist and secularist sensibilities. This distaste and disdain for triumphalist faith on the part of modern critics is at the heart of the distaste and disdain for the poetry of Southwell and Crashaw that characterises most (post)modern criticism of their work. It is the critical impasse between forthright faith and indomitable doubt.

It is, however, not so easy to dismiss the criticism of T. S. Eliot, a writer whose Catholic sensibilities might have predisposed him to accept and appreciate the spirituality of Southwell's and Crashaw's verse. Yet, in his essay on the Metaphysical Poets, published in 1921, and his essay on "Religion and Literature" published fourteen years later, he is less than wholly enthusiastic. Indeed, compared to the evident respect with which Crashaw is held by Quiller-Couch and Gardner, both of whom are at least

Eliot's equal in scholarly stature, he is positively lukewarm in his appraisal. Employing "devotional" as a pejorative adjective, he lauds Donne's poetry above the "devotional verse" of Herbert, Vaughan, Southwell, and Crashaw:

> For the great majority of people who love poetry, *"religious* poetry" is a variety of *minor* poetry . . . I think that this is the real attitude of most poetry lovers towards such poets as Vaughan, or Southwell, or Crashaw, or George Herbert, or Gerard Hopkins.
>
> But what is more, I am ready to admit that up to a point these critics are right. For there is a kind of poetry, such as most of the work of the authors I have mentioned, which is the product of a special religious awareness, which may exist without the general awareness which we expect of the major poet . . . I do not pretend to offer Vaughan, or Southwell, or George Herbert, or Hopkins as major poets: I feel sure that the first three, at least, are poets of this limited awareness.[35]

Interestingly, and tellingly, Eliot lists Gerard Manley Hopkins with these inferior "devotional poets," a jarring and incongruous juxtaposition considering the chasm of more than two centuries that separates them, and considering the innovatively "modern" character of Hopkins's verse. This odd and jarring juxtaposition prompts one to wonder whether Eliot's patronizing denigration of Hopkins might have been motivated by an element of professional or artistic jealousy. Such a suspicion is heightened by the fact that Eliot was passing this judgement in 1935, when Hopkins was at the very height of his fashionable popularity and when he was being heralded by many as the greatest of "modern" poets, an accolade that popular critical opinion had bestowed on Eliot during the previous decade. In any event, it is obvious that Eliot's dismissal of Hopkins as a "minor poet" is not in harmony with the judgement of most critics and throws into question his dismissal of the other "minor" poets with whom Hopkins is listed. The fact is that Eliot is a much greater poet than he is a critic, a fact that must be insisted upon and which is surely confirmed by his earlier rash dismissal of *Hamlet* as an "artistic failure":

> So far from being Shakespeare's masterpiece, the play is most certainly an artistic failure. In several ways the play is puzzling, and disquieting as is none of the others. . . . We must simply

admit that here Shakespeare tackled a problem which proved too much for him. Why he attempted it at all is an insoluble puzzle . . .[36]

Apart from the foolish audacity of dismissing arguably Shakespeare's greatest play as a "failure," Eliot is also guilty of a critical non sequitur in apparently connecting the alleged "failure" with the "puzzling" and "disquieting" aspects of the play. A play, or poem, can be both puzzling and disquieting without being a failure, something of which the author of "The Waste Land" should scarcely need reminding! There is also a hint of arrogance in Eliot's claim that Shakespeare might have bitten off more than he could chew in tackling *Hamlet*. Had Shakespeare really "tackled a problem which proved too much for him" or had he simply tackled a problem that proved too much for the critic? And as for "insoluble puzzles," it is important to remember the crucial difference between a puzzle that is really, objectively, insoluble, i.e., it has no solution, from a puzzle that is only insoluble to the individual attempting to solve it. In the latter case the problem is not with the puzzle but with the one who is puzzled! And this, ultimately, is the kernel of Eliot's problem in understanding the play, namely that since Eliot does not understand the play himself there is, ipso facto, nothing to understand.

This peripatetic aside has been necessary to establish that even major poets are not necessarily competent critics and that, on the contrary and to paraphrase Eliot himself, they may possess only a limited awareness without the general awareness we expect of a good critic. In order to highlight Eliot's limited awareness of the true merit of the poetry of Southwell and Crashaw, it will be helpful to analyze his critique of religious poetry and to compare it with the critique of Helen Gardner. Having done so, we will be able to judge Southwell's and Crashaw's verse in the light of Gardner's apprehension and Eliot's misapprehension of the true nature and purpose of metaphysical poetry.

In his essay on the Metaphysical Poets, Eliot differentiated between the "intellectual" poetry of Donne and Lord Herbert of Cherbury and the "reflective" poetry of Tennyson and Browning. Since the Victorian poets had followed in the wake of the subjectivist meanderings of the Romantics, who had placed the *reflective* sensibility of the poet over the cold rationalism of the philosopher, one would think that Eliot's distinction is based upon the division between the pre-Cartesian "intellect" of the Metaphysical Poets and the Romantic reflective "feeling" of the

Victorians. Yet this was emphatically *not* what Eliot meant. He was not distinguishing between the "*intellectual*" inheritance of the Greeks and the mediaeval Scholastics, on the one hand, and the "*reflective*" legacy of the Romantics, on the other. On the contrary, the "intellectual" dimension of Donne's poetry had, in Eliot's view, nothing to do with the expansive realist objectivism of Plato, Aristotle, Augustine and Aquinas, but was connected to the way in which the poet used his thoughts:

> A thought to Donne was an experience; it modified his sensibility. When a poet's mind is perfectly equipped for its work, it is constantly amalgamating disparate experience; the ordinary man's experience is chaotic, irregular, fragmentary. The latter falls in love, or reads Spinoza, and these two experiences have nothing to do with each other, or with the noise of the typewriter or the smell of cooking; in the mind of the poet these experiences are always forming new wholes.[37]

For those who know Eliot's *The Waste Land*, it is difficult to read these lines without the image of that poem's "typist" coming to mind, especially once we remind ourselves that this essay was being written at the same time that Eliot was working on his poem. The noise of the typewriter, the smell of cooking, the tawdry pretence of love combined with the Spinozan indifference to the debilitating passions it provokes; the chaotic, irregular, fragmentary experience of the ordinary person, lacking any apparent meaning except that which is bestowed upon it by the mind of the poet forming new wholes from the scattered fragments. When we read "The Waste Land" we witness the poet grappling with doubt, floundering in falsehood and groping for truth. We witness a poet making sense of the chaos and shoring up the fragments against his ruin in a way that portends conversion.

Life, or rather the experience of life, is, for Eliot, a succession of kaleidoscopic fragments that form figurative patterns in the mind of the poet. The fragments of experience become figments of imagination that metamorphose into figures of truth. This, for Eliot, is what he describes in the later essay on "Religion and Literature" as "the general awareness which we expect of the major poet," and this, therefore, is presumably what is lacking in the merely "devotional" poetry of "minor" poets like Southwell and Crashaw. The problem associated with such a notion of what constitutes a true or major poet is that it subjects all poetry to the realm of subjective experience, thereby disqualifying the purely objective, i.e., that which is not dependent upon subjective experience. In practice, and in spite of Eliot's profession of Catholic Christianity, this is a surrender to relativism. It subjects art to the *experience* of the artist and not to the truth that transcends that experience. It makes the artist the master of his art and not its servant. And this is the reason for Eliot's relegation of Southwell and Crashaw from the regal realm of the major poets to the provincial principality of the minor versifiers. In their adherence to doctrine or dogma, i.e., to a truth that transcends their subjective experience, and in their expression of that doctrine or dogma in their poetry, they break Eliot's golden rule. Their poetry lacks "experience" and is, therefore, merely "devotional" or "religious" in the narrow sense that Eliot prescribes to those terms. In expressing their "special religious awareness," to employ Eliot's terminology, they are betraying the "general awareness," rooted in personal experience, which is the mark of the great poet. In being true to a truth beyond themselves they are failing in true self-expression.

The problem at the irrational heart of Eliot's aesthetic is satirized sublimely by Jane Austen in *Sense and Sensibility*. Sense, in the sense in which Austen employs it, is obedience to objective truth, i.e., that which exists whether we know it or not or like it or not; sensibility, on the other hand, is the ultimately foolish endeavour of ignoring truth in favour of our feelings, the subjecting of ourselves to what we feel about things whether those things are true or not. In this sense, the sensibility that Eliot praises in the poet can be perilous. In divorcing experience from an informing philosophy that makes sense of it, we are left with only the subjective experience itself, and we have only ourselves and our feelings about the experience to guide us. God help us!

In order to illustrate the inadequacy of Eliot's aesthetic, and thereby defeat and deflate his negative critique of Southwell and Crashaw, let's return to Eliot's essay on the Metaphysical Poets. He states that the poets of the seventeenth century "possessed a mechanism of sensibility which could devour any kind of experience."[38] What one wonders is "a mechanism of sensibility"? The materialist would point no further than the physical organs of the body; our eyes, ears, nose, mouth and skin are our only mechanisms of sensibility, he would tell us, conceding perhaps that the cognitive function of the brain coordinates the data collected by this mechanism in a manner that makes sense of it. Eliot was not a materialist, of course, and this cannot have been his meaning. Unfortunately, however, he does not tell us what he means. We are offered the phrase, "a mechanism of sensibility," and are told simply that the particular type of such a mechanism possessed by Donne et al was such that it could "devour any kind of experience." Incidentally, as a related aside, it should be noted that the devouring of any kind of experience is not necessarily very healthy. The experience of the aforementioned typist in Eliot's poem is a case in point. If the devouring is a deflowering who or what is being devoured and by whom? Did she devour the experience or was she devoured by it? Such questions bring to mind the insatiable appetite for the devouring of experience that characterized the Decadents, whose creed was summarized by Walter Pater's declaration in the "Conclusion" to his *Studies in the History of the Renaissance* that life was merely a drift of momentary acts and that, in consequence, each act must be experienced to the full and each moment magnified. Life should be lived for the instant, seeking "not the fruit of experience, but experience itself."[39] The destructive consequences of such an experience-devouring creed can be seen in the work of the disillusioned disciples of Decadence, such as Baudelaire, Verlaine, Huysmans, Dowson, and Wilde. And yet this magnifying of experience beyond the bounds of philosophy or theology seems dangerously close to the sort of Plateresque poetic experience that Eliot appears to be advocating.

But to return to the mystically undefined "mechanism of sensibility," we might presume, reasonably enough, that such a mechanism must be the philosophy or theology whereby we not only devour experience but, more to the point and more fruitfully, how we digest the experience (and excrete that which is harmful) in order to grow from it. This, however, does not appear to be what Eliot had in mind. Donne and the other Metaphysical Poets whom Eliot admired shared essentially the same philosophy and theology as the Christian poets who preceded them and those that came after. Yet Eliot seems to be saying that Donne's generation possessed something singularly and peculiarly its own, something that set it apart from all that came before and all that came after. Unfortunately he fails to tell us what exactly it is. The fact that it cannot be a philosophy or theology is made abundantly clear from the astonishingly sweeping statement in the later essay on "Religion and Literature" that "Christian poetry . . . has been limited in England almost exclusively to minor poetry" ever since the time of Chaucer.[40] In short, and let's embrace the enormity of this statement, Eliot is dismissing almost all the Christian poetry written over a period of more than half a millennium as "minor poetry." As "minor poets," Southwell and Crashaw would appear to be in very good company!

Having been perplexed by the elusively undefined "mechanism of sensibility" we need to continue with our reading of Eliot's essay in order to fathom what exactly he is saying. Our first clue comes with the blaming of Milton and Dryden for the dispossession of poetry of this mysterious "mechanism": "In the seventeenth century a dissociation of sensibility set in, from which we have never recovered; and this dissociation, as is natural, was aggravated by the influence of the two most powerful poets of the century, Milton and Dryden."[41] These two literary giants had helped refine the language but, Eliot argued, their influence had also desensitized it: "while the language became more refined, the feeling became more crude."[42] Although, once again, Eliot fails to explain himself, it is perhaps possible to deduce what he means. He seems to be saying that the works of Milton and Dryden lacked the sensitivity of Donne, presumably an allusion to the somewhat dramatic and didactic tone of Milton's epic and Dryden's satires. If this is so, we are beginning to see why it is that Southwell and Crashaw are not valued by Eliot in the way in which he values Donne. Like Milton and Dryden, Southwell and Crashaw had a didactic purpose. Their work was designed to be inspirational, to inspire devotion. Indeed, in Southwell's case, his poetry was clearly an extension of his pastoral ministry, the outpouring of the fruits of his ordained vocation as a priest-poet. Compare this didactic approach to Eliot's assessment of the greatest attribute of the "major" Metaphysical Poets: "[T]hey were, at best, engaged in the task of trying to find the verbal equivalent for states of mind and feeling."[43] If this is the major attribute of "major" poets, at their "best," it's no wonder that Eliot denigrates Southwell and Crashaw and regrets the influence of Milton and Dryden. The exposition of the transubstantial reality of Christ's Presence in Southwell's "Of the Blessed Sacrament of the Altar" is not in the least concerned with "trying to find the verbal equivalent for states of mind and feeling." Does this disqualify it from being a major poem? Crashaw's "Hymn to the Name and Honour of the Admirable Saint Teresa" aims higher than the mere verbalizing of feelings. Is it therefore a failure? Milton's *Paradise Lost* paved the way for later writers to examine the psychology of evil, particularly in Milton's characterization of Satan, yet this was clearly not the poet's primary purpose or his principal achievement (in spite of the efforts of critics from Blake and Shelley onwards to suggest otherwise). Does Milton's preoccupation with the re-telling of a biblical story in the epic tradition of Homer and Virgil preclude his spending sufficient time ruminating on his own state of mind? If so, and in the light of Eliot's criteria for what is "best" in Metaphysical poetry, does Milton's preoccupation with descriptive narrative detract from the poetic credentials of his epic? Does it desensitize the language? Does Dryden's masterful allegorical and dialectical defence of Catholicism in *The Hind and the Panther* lack sufficient introspection to be considered great art? Is this Eliot's principal reason for the denigration of "devotional" and "religious" poetry? Does he happen to prefer poetry to be psychological and allusively obscure, and not theological and doctrinally direct? The answer is to be found in Eliot's own words: "The poet must become more and more comprehensive, more allusive, more indirect, in order to force, to dislocate if necessary, language into his meaning."[44] In short, Eliot calls for the forsaking of the illustrative for the allusive, the direct for the indirect, and location for dislocation. In Eliot's critical vocabulary it seems that the more "comprehensive" a poem is, the less comprehensible it will tend to be. Few would deny that Eliot put these principles into admirable and sublime practice in the composition of *The Waste Land* but they do not constitute a universal law of prosody. They are a statement of aesthetic preference, a question of taste, but not a dogma that defines good poetry from bad, or major poetry from minor. Eliot might not like the presence in poetry of the didactic, the descriptive or the devotional but Eliot's likes and dislikes do not define what constitutes good poetry. Homer and Virgil were descriptive, and Dante, whom Eliot acknowledges quite rightly as the greatest of all poets, is didactic, descriptive and devotional in due and decorous proportion, uniting the three in a formal unity which, like the rhyme scheme he chooses, reflects the Trinity Itself.

Another aspect of Eliot's singularly modern sensibility that serves indirectly to vindicate the poetic status of Southwell and Crashaw is his Baudelairean understanding of the soul. Praising Racine as the great master of seventeenth century French literature and Baudelaire as the great master of the nineteenth, Eliot describes them as "the greatest two psychologists, the most curious explorers of the soul" and compares them favourably to Milton and Dryden whose "dazzling disregard of the soul" might be considered a further example of their negative influence on English literature: "Those who object to the 'artificiality' of Milton or Dryden sometimes tell us to 'look into our hearts.' But that is not looking deep enough; Racine or Donne looked into a good deal more than the heart. One must look into the cerebral cortex, the nervous system, and the digestive tracts."[45] The problem with such a critique is that it constitutes an insufficient understanding of the nature of the soul. It is humanism in its most reductionist sense. The soul is not merely the psyche, in the sense that "psyche" is understood by modern psychology. It is not to be understood by plumbing the depths of the ego but by acknowledging its source and its destiny in its Creator. It is indeed true that Baudelaire plumbed the depths of the ego-psyche in ways that few, if any, poets had plumbed before. He had gone deeper, or at least he had gone lower. But Baudelaire found that the heart, or, for that matter, the cerebral cortex, the nervous system, and the digestive tracts, could not go deep enough. They were insufficient for a true understanding of the soul. In the end, he discovered, to his horror, that when you dig deep enough into the flesh as an end in itself, carnally or figuratively, you find the Devil. And having made the discovery, he recoiled in disgust into the saving arms of Mother Church. In short, Baudelaire discovered, after all his searching, the truth about the soul that can be discovered at the heart of the poetry of Southwell and Crashaw. Indeed, if Baudelaire had read Southwell he could have plumbed the depths of true psychology (psyche + logos) in the sense that Southwell's Jesuit training had imbued his poetry with the insights of Ignatian spirituality. Similarly, if Baudelaire had read Crashaw he could have been drawn to the depths of the soul to be found in the profound mystical theology of St. Teresa of Avila and St. John of the Cross. In any event, Baudelaire, by a circuitously sinful route, discovered the deepest truths that were second nature to Southwell and Crashaw. The consummation of Baudelaire's quest was his conversion to Catholicism. Later Decadents, such as Verlaine, Huysmans, Dowson, Lionel Johnson, Beardsley and Wilde, all consummated their quest in the same fashion, through their reception into the Church. And, of course, a few short years after Eliot wrote his essay on the Metaphysical Poets, he too would find the peace that passeth understanding in Catholic Christianity, though in his case in its "Anglo" manifestation.

Since Eliot's own psyche was in flux at the time he wrote his critique of the Metaphysical Poets, and since his own conversion to Christianity, which would give added coherence and cohesion to his thoughts, was still five years in the future, we should perhaps not vilify him too much for his critical blindness. Indeed, it is not the vilification of Eliot but the vindication of Southwell and Crashaw that has been the purpose of our engagement with the former's criticism.

Let's conclude with Helen Gardner, one of the great scholars of the Metaphysical Poets, who, as we have seen, showed great deference to the work of Southwell and Crashaw, though particularly the latter. Gardner concentrates on the role of the conceit, describing it as the "most immediately striking feature"[46] of metaphysical poetry. Her artfully succinct definition of the metaphysical conceit is worth quoting as a key that helps us understand metaphysical poetry in general, and, therefore and by extension, the poetry of Southwell and Crashaw:

> A conceit is a comparison whose ingenuity is more striking than its justness, or, at least, is more immediately striking. All comparisons discover likeness in things unlike: a comparison becomes a conceit when we are made to concede likeness while being strongly conscious of unlikeness. A brief comparison can be a conceit if two things patently unlike, or which we should never think of together, are shown to be alike in a single point in a single way, or in such a context, that we feel their incongruity. Here a conceit is like a spark made by striking two stones together. After the flash the stones are just two stones. Metaphysical poetry abounds in such flashes . . .[47]

Gardner's definition of "conceit" is remarkably similar to the Chestertonian understanding of "paradox," a fact that becomes immediately apparent if the former word is replaced by the latter in the above passage. Indeed the parallels between the use of the conceit by the Metaphysical Poets and the use of paradox by Chesterton are so striking that one feels that Chesterton should be redefined as a metaphysical novelist or as a metaphysical essayist. It is, therefore, scarcely surprising that Eliot dismisses Chesterton's novels as "Propaganda" (the upper case "p" is Eliot's emphasis) in the same essay on "Religion and Literature" in which he denigrates Southwell and Crashaw as "minor poets."[48]

Gardner also differs from Eliot in her exposition of the didactic dimension of metaphysical poetry that the employment of the conceit represents: "A metaphysical conceit . . . is not indulged in for its own sake. It is used . . . to persuade, or it is used to define, or to prove a point." And again:

> In a metaphysical poem the conceits are instruments of definition in an argument or instruments to persuade. The poem has something to say which the conceit explicates or something to urge which the conceit helps to forward . . . I have said that the first impression a conceit makes is of ingenuity rather than of justice: the metaphysical conceit aims at making us concede justness while admiring ingenuity.[49]

Gardner's eloquent description of the defining characteristic of metaphysical poetry contradicts, confutes and ultimately negates Eliot's whole critique. The didacticism of paradox that defines metaphysical poetry is found in abundance in Southwell and Crashaw and it is this very presence, its very mark of success, that Eliot seems to dislike. So be it. Eliot is wrong and the stature of Southwell and Crashaw as poets of merit is vindicated. This would be no great revelation to Shakespeare who seems to have been influenced to some degree by Southwell, particularly it would seem in the writing of *The Merchant of Venice* and *Romeo and Juliet*, and also in his early poem, *The Rape of Lucrece*.[50] Yet it must be conceded that few poems in Southwell's corpus reach the heights to which Donne, Herbert and Crashaw ascend, when writing at their best. Indeed, even the most ardent of Southwell's admirers might grudgingly agree with Gardner's criticism that he is "too dogged in his conceits and in his verse, one line padding at the same pace after another."[51] At the same time, admirers of Crashaw would echo Gardner's enthusiasm: "how vividly he dramatizes, rather than narrates, the story of St. Teresa, and invokes the weeping Magdalene: and how vigorously he urges the hesitant Countess of Denbigh against delay."[52]

Ultimately, critics as demanding of respect as Arthur Quiller-Couch have placed Crashaw at the very pinnacle of achievement. Southwell, on the other hand, is clearly less admired. Even though he merits a place in any reputable anthology of metaphysical poetry, and is more than merely a minor poet, he is perhaps not quite a major poet either. Perhaps he might whimsically be called a major minor poet, or perhaps a minor major poet. Crashaw, on the other hand, is a major poet of the first order whose work should be taught and read wherever major poetry is admired and appreciated.

38. NEWMAN, MANNING AND THEIR AGE

In a flash a sort of ripple ran along the line and all these eccentrics went down on their knees on the public pavement . . . Then I realized that a sort of little dark cab or carriage had drawn up . . . and out of it came a ghost clad in flames . . . lifting long frail fingers over the crowd in blessing. And then I looked at his face and was startled with a contrast; for his face was dead pale like ivory and very wrinkled and old . . . having in every line the ruin of great beauty.

The "ghost clad in flames" was Cardinal Manning, a prince of the Church enshrined as an ageing Prince Charming in the memory of an ageing G. K. Chesterton writing more than fifty years after the event. In Chesterton's memory of his childhood encounter with the Cardinal, Manning is not merely clothed in the scarlet of his ecclesial office but is also clad in the clouds of romantic legend. At the other extreme, Lytton Strachey, in his notorious book, *Eminent Victorians*, robed Manning in a cloak of hypocrisy under which the ambitious Cardinal concealed the treacherous dagger of intrigue. To the charitable Chesterton, Manning was a hero, perhaps even a saint; to the cynical Strachey, the same man was a villain worthy of vilification. It could be argued that these judgments reveal more about the men doing the judging than the man being judged. Chesterton perceived the truth in broad sweeping strokes of fanciful colour in which history was, above all, a good story, in which inimitable heroes fought iniquitous dragons; Strachey, as the founder of the modern school of hackiography,[53] subjugated the broader truth to narrow fact in which historical figures are seen as icons to be smashed in an iconoclastic debauch of cynical revisionism.

As for Manning himself, he made many enemies but was heralded at his death as "the people's cardinal." Even Strachey was forced to acknowledge Manning's huge popularity at the time of his death in January 1892, though he was evidently perplexed as to the reason for it:

> The route of the procession was lined by vast crowds of work-
> ing people, whose imaginations, in some instinctive manner,

had been touched. Many who had hardly seen him declared that in Cardinal Manning they had lost their best friend. Was it the magnetic vigour of the dead man's spirit that moved them? Or was it his valiant disregard of common custom and those conventional reserves and poor punctilios, which are wont to hem about the great? Or was it something untameable in his glances and in his gestures? Or was it, perhaps, the mysterious glamour lingering about him of the antique organisation of Rome? For whatever cause, the mind of the people had been impressed . . .

Why, one wonders, does Strachey gloss over the most obvious reason for Manning's popularity: his tireless work for the poor and the downtrodden?

Barely two years earlier, in September 1889, Manning had played a crucial role in the ending of the Dock Strike when, after weeks of delicate negotiation, the 81-year-old cardinal finally obtained for the dockworkers the bare justice for which they had asked. On 14 September, "the Cardinal's Peace" was signed, ending the strike and confirming Manning as a hero of the working class. A few years earlier, in 1885, he had been a member of the royal commission on the housing of the poor, and a year later was appointed to the royal commission on education. His social vision was gaining international recognition and it is widely believed that Manning's social teaching, and his practical example, were influential upon Pope Leo XIII's writing of the famous social encyclical, *Rerum novarum*, published in 1891, shortly before Manning's death.

As well as being a tireless defender of the poor, Manning was also an indefatigable defender of the Pope and he played an influential role at the First Vatican Council in 1870 in the discussions that led to the formal promulgation of the doctrine of papal infallibility.

Having succeeded Cardinal Wiseman as Archbishop of Westminster in 1865, Manning was the head of the English hierarchy and therefore the leader of England's Catholics during a period of great revival. And yet, in many ways, the revival of which he was the *de jure* leader could be said to have had a *de facto* leader in the person of his great contemporary, and sometime rival, John Henry Newman. Although the two men had so much in common, being graduates of Oxford and fellows of Oxford colleges, and being Anglican ministers who converted to Catholicism, they also had many differences.

Newman's conversion in 1845 can be seen as the real starting point of the Catholic Revival, heralding a wave of high-profile conversions, of which Manning's in 1851 was but one of many. Newman's brilliance was universally acknowledged, even by his enemies. His famous sermon on "Development in Christian Doctrine," which he preached in February 1843, has become the benchmark for the study of doctrinal development, elucidating the teaching authority of the Catholic Church in the light of the Church's claim to be the Mystical Body of Christ. His discourses on liberal education, delivered to Catholic audiences in Dublin in 1852, as he prepared to become rector of the new Irish Catholic University, would be published two years later as *The Idea of a University*, a book that remains one of the finest and most eloquent works advocating the efficacy of an integrated liberal arts education. To this day, Newman's influence can be seen in the founding of new Catholic centers of higher education, such as Ave Maria University in Florida, Christendom College in Virginia, and Thomas Aquinas College in California.

His greatest contribution to philosophy is his seminal work, *The Grammar of Assent* (1870), the product of twenty years' labour, which highlighted the rational foundations for religious belief and the inadequacy of empiricism. His *Apologia pro Vita Sua* (1864) is arguably the greatest autobiographical spiritual aeneid ever written, with the obvious exception of St. Augustine's incomparable *Confessions*.

Years earlier, in 1848, only three years after his reception into the Church, Newman had foreshadowed his *Apologia* with his first novel, *Loss and Gain*, a fictionalised semiautobiographical account of a young man's quest for faith amid the scepticism and uncertainties of early-Victorian Oxford. He also addressed the issue of conversion in his historical novel, *Callista: A Sketch of the Third Century*, published in 1855.

As a prose stylist, the critic George Levine judged Newman as "perhaps the most artful and brilliant prose writer of the nineteenth century," a judgement seemingly echoed by James Joyce, via Stephen Dedalus, in *A Portrait of the Artist as a Young Man*. Newman was also one of the finest poets of the Victorian age, writing poems, such as "The Sign of the Cross," "The Golden Prison" and "The Pilgrim Queen," which rank alongside the best verse of his illustrious contemporaries. His most ambitious poem, *The Dream of Gerontius*, later the inspiration for an oratorio by Sir Edward Elgar, was greatly admired by C. S. Lewis, who drew on what he called its "right view" of purgatory as one of the inspirational sources for his own purgatorial excursion in *The Great Divorce*.

Considering the sheer depth and breadth of Newman's brilliance it is not surprising that he has outshone Manning's own considerable achievement. To the eyes of posterity, if not necessarily in the eyes of their own age, Manning is seen as walking in Newman's more illustrious shadow.

In paying homage to the age of Manning and Newman, it would be a sin of omission not to mention another illustrious convert who is now justifiably revered but who was completely unknown during his own lifetime. This is Gerard Manley Hopkins, a Jesuit priest, received into the Church by Newman himself in 1866, who was destined, thirty years after his death, to become one of the most influential poets of the following century. Hopkins's verse, inestimable though not inimitable, is imitated the world over by budding poets seeking in vain to emulate the majesty and magnificence of the Jesuit master's sprung rhythm and mystical vision of inscape. As a poet he had no equal among his contemporaries, and perhaps only T. S. Eliot is his rival among the generations of poets who have followed in his wake. Hopkins' magnum opus, "The Wreck of the Deutschland," is one of the greatest poems of all time, not only in its form but in the celestial heights of mystical theology to which it ascends.

And so we see in the powerful presence of Manning, Newman and Hopkins a triune triumvirate of converts who made an indelible mark on the minds and hearts of the age in which they lived and who continue to inspire those who are trying to emulate their magnificent example in today's darkened world. Of these three giants of faith, Manning remains the least known and the least celebrated and yet, on this the bicentenary of his birth,[54] he emerges from the shadow of his more famous brethren to take centre stage. We will end, as we began, with a vision of Manning. We began with Chesterton's vision; we will end with Belloc's:

> It was my custom during my first days in London, as a very young man . . . to call upon the Cardinal as regularly as he would receive me; and during those brief interviews I heard from him many things which I have had later occasion to test by the experience of human life . . . and Manning did seem to me (and still seems to me) much the greatest Englishman of his time. He was certainly the greatest of all that band, small but intensely significant, who, in the Victorian period, so rose above their fellows, pre-eminent in will and in intellect, as not only to perceive, but even to accept the Faith.

39. NEWMAN'S BEATIFICATION

An interview with the Zenit news agency on the occasion of the beatification of John Henry Newman by Pope Benedict XVI in September 2010.

Benedict XVI had never presided over a beatification ceremony until that of Blessed John Henry Newman on Sunday. Why do you think the Pope chose Cardinal Newman in particular to single out with this gesture?

The Holy Father was certainly paying a special tribute to Blessed John Henry Newman in his decision to preside personally over the beatification ceremony. I believe it to be a reflection of the Holy Father's personal admiration for Newman, a great theologian who has exerted a huge and significant influence in the century or more since his death. Indeed Pope Benedict has acknowledged Newman's role in his own spiritual and intellectual development.

I believe also, however, that Pope Benedict sees the figure of Newman as a powerful witness to the modern world whose life and work have the power to assist the Church in her re-evangelizing of the secularized culture of England in particular and Europe in general. As such, I think that the Pope's decision to beatify Newman personally was connected to his desire that the beatification would take place in England, thereby facilitating the papal visit. There is no doubt that his visit to the United Kingdom provoked a rabid reaction from the secular fundamentalists who appear to be in the ascendant but, as we have seen, it also served as a catalyst for a nationwide catharsis. During the four days of engagements, millions of people in England and Scotland truly opened their hearts to the Pope and his message of faith and reason Amidst the quagmire of a decaying culture, the Holy Father's words shone forth as a beacon of sanity and sanctity.

In his homily at the beatification ceremony, the Pope specifically mentioned Blessed John Henry Newman's appeal for an "intelligent, well-instructed laity." Could you say something more about this?

The Pope was referring to Newman's role as a trailblazer in the push to empower the laity to take their place alongside the priesthood in the mission to evangelize the secular culture. Newman believed that the laity needed to be well-instructed in all aspects of the Faith so that every Catholic could defend the Church and its mission in an increasingly secular culture. In his work on the needs and nature of Catholic education, much of which was published in his important work, *The Idea of a University*, Newman emerges as one of the finest and most eloquent advocates of an integrated liberal arts education for the laity. The underlying and underpinning principle of such an education is that the Catholic laity must be well versed in theology, philosophy, literature, and history, and that they must be able to see how each of these intellectual disciplines informs the other. One cannot understand the history of western civilization or the great works of art and literature that it has bequeathed to posterity without understanding the philosophy and theology that was the wellspring of the civilization itself. This great and axiomatic truth of education has been lost by the secular academy but has become the animating principle behind the revival in the liberal arts and in the restoration of the so-called Great Books to the curricula of many colleges, particularly in the United States. Newman's influence in this revival cannot be overstated. The "intelligent, well-instructed laity," the chief beneficiaries of this revival in education, will be well prepared to defend the Faith and evangelize the culture.

The Pope also spoke about Blessed John Henry Newman's example of priestly life and ministry. In your opinion, what aspects of his priestly testimony are most noteworthy?

A major aspect of Newman's philosophy was that a living faith must be lived faithfully. He believed that a life of sanctity was the greatest and surest witness to the truth of Christianity. Although this is true for all Catholics, it is particularly true for those who have the priestly vocation. The absence of such sanctity is a great cause of scandal, as can be seen in the fallout surrounding the instances of sexual abuse carried out by wayward and fallen priests.

Newman's own life as a priest was exemplary, serving to illustrate the power of the priestly ministry if lived in accordance with the call to holiness implicit to the ministry itself. Although Newman is best known as an intellectual whose works of literature, history, philosophy and theology have exerted a profound influence, the Holy Father was reminding us that he was also a priest who ministered to his flock with the caritas that saves souls and wins them to heaven.

Could you say something about your own reflections, as one who has spent significant time studying Newman, regarding the beatification ceremony?

As an admirer of Newman, as an Englishman, and, more to the point, as an English Catholic convert, I was simply overjoyed by his beatification. Newman is rightly considered to be the father of the Catholic Revival and the seismic power of his conversion continues to reverberate throughout the English-speaking world. The number of converts who owe their conversion, under grace, to Newman, at least in part, are too numerous to mention. As such, a few will suffice to illustrate the point. Gerard Manley Hopkins, arguably the finest poet of the Victorian era, was received into the Church by Newman in 1866. Oscar Wilde fell under Newman's spell as an undergraduate and continued to admire him throughout his life. Wilde's ultimate deathbed conversion, the culmination of a lifelong love affair with the Church, was due in part to the beguiling presence of Newman's enduring influence. Hilaire Belloc and J. R. R. Tolkien both studied at the Birmingham Oratory School, which had been established by Newman, the former during Newman's own lifetime and the latter in his ghostly shadow a few years after his death. In both cases, Newman's role in their Christian formation contributed to the faithful fortitude that animated their lives as Catholic writers of the utmost importance. Others such as Graham Greene, Evelyn Waugh and Muriel Spark could be mentioned amongst the many others, documented in my book *Literary Converts* (Ignatius Press), who owed their conversion, at least in part, to Newman's benign influence. Last, and indubitably least, I must mention that Newman's beautiful and profound *Apologia pro Vita Sua* played a significant role in my own path to conversion.

What do you see as Blessed John Henry Newman's most important message to Catholics today?

Newman's most important message to today's Catholics is conveyed in the many works in which he affirms and elucidates the inextricable bond between faith and reason.

In his famous sermon on *Development in Christian Doctrine* he illustrates the paradoxical way in which the Church engages the mutability of the world with immutable doctrinal truth. In *The Idea of a University* he affirms the efficacy of an integrated liberal arts education in which faith and reason (*fides et ratio*) elucidate the splendor of truth (*veritatis splendor*). In *The Grammar of Assent*, his greatest contribution to philosophy, he highlights the rational foundations for religious belief and the inadequacy of empiricism. His *Apologia pro Vita Sua* is perhaps the greatest autobiographical spiritual aeneid ever written, with the obvious exception of St. Augustine's incomparable *Confessions*. In the *Apologia*, as in his semi-autobiographical novel, *Loss and Gain*, he illuminates how the path to faith is lit by the light of reason.

Although Newman is one of the finest writers of the Victorian period, whose poetry and fiction warrant a place amongst the greatest works of this golden age in English literature, he is nonetheless most important today as an exemplar of the rational-faithful mind. In today's beleaguered world in which the twin errors of faithless reason (secular fundamentalism) and irrational faith (Islamic fundamentalism) are a dark and portentous presence, we need giants such as Blessed John Henry Newman to remind us of the indissoluble marriage between true faith and true reason.

40. TURNING WINE INTO MARSH-WATER: A SORDID LIFE OF OSCAR WILDE

Neil McKenna, *The Secret Life of Oscar*. New York, Basic Books, 2005.

Oh dear, oh dear, oh dear. Oscar Wilde must be turning in his grave at this smutty biography. It stinks. It has something of the stench of the gutter, or the faecal fetidness of marsh-water. "We are all in the gutter," says Lord Darlington in *Lady Windermere's Fan*, "but some of us are looking at the stars." This sordid biography has no interest in the stars. It is rather at home in the gutter. It reminds one insistently of that inveterate swamp-dweller, Gollum, in *The Lord of the Rings*, who, despising the stars and hating the sun, grubs around in the dark, grunting gutturally in his quest for decaying flesh to guttle. As with Gollum, this book seems to have a predilection for decaying flesh, or at least for flesh that revels in decay. It revels in what it reveals. Decadence is desirable: the life of the shadows out of the sight of the sun, or the light of the stars.

"You knew what my Art was to me," Wilde wrote from Reading gaol to Lord Alfred Douglas, "the great primal note by which I had revealed, first myself to myself, and then myself to the world; the real passion of my life; the love to which all other loves were as marsh-water to red wine. . . ." Clearly Wilde believed that his true self, his true value was to be found in his art. By contrast, many of his modern admirers, Judas-like, have betrayed their Master with a kiss and have sold his Art for the thirty pieces of silver to be made from gossiping about (male) prostitutes.

This particular biography is certainly not concerned with Wilde's art, which is hardly surprising considering that his art almost invariably looks to the stars, even if it sometimes looks at them from the gutter. Salomé is in the gutter; she is addicted to the lust of the flesh. She is maddened by it; it maddens her. She kills the object of her lust, St. John the Baptist, and is herself killed by one, Herod, for whom she is an object of lust. Lust is disordered. It kills those who allow themselves to be enslaved to it. Dorian

Gray is in the gutter and does his best to stay there. In so doing he destroys his own life and the lives of all those who have the misfortune to know him. His addiction to lust kills him as surely as it kills Salomé. His portrait, the mirror of his soul, the voice of his conscience, shows him the ugliness of his sin and calls him to continence. It rebukes him. It shows him the diseased reality of the gutter and points silently to the stars. Dorian Gray prefers the gutter and dies there in despair. The same essentially Christian moral message is present throughout the rest of Wilde's work; in his plays, his fairy-stories, and in his poem, *The Ballad of Reading Gaol*, in which his conversion whilst serving his two-year prison term is recounted:

> And thus we rust Life's iron chain
> > Degraded and alone:
> And some men curse, and some men weep,
> > And some men make no moan:
> But God's eternal Laws are kind
> > And break the heart of stone . . .

> Ah! happy they whose hearts can break
> > And peace of pardon win!
> How else may man make straight his plan
> > And cleanse his soul from Sin?
> How else but through a broken heart
> > May Lord Christ enter in?

To reiterate, McKenna's biography is not concerned with Wilde's art, and it is significant that none of the laudatory blurbs on the dust-jacket mention Wilde's literary achievement. Nor is the book interested in Wilde's life-long quest for spiritual fulfillment and truth. The biography doesn't care for Wilde's desire to "make straight" his life, only its own twisted desire to keep his life "bent," or as a reviewer in the London *Times* put it: "McKenna makes an impassioned case for re-gaying Wilde." Put bluntly, the objective truth must surrender to the demands of the gender agenda at the queer heart of McKenna's work. Wilde desired to "cleanse his soul from sin," this book is determined to keep it sinful and dirty, desecrating it, as it were, and were it possible (which it isn't), necrophilically. Wilde desired to let Christ in; this book is at pains to keep Him out. There is no interest in Wilde's life-long attraction to the Catholic Church and his desire for the peace that conversion would bring. Wilde's love for Christ and the Church is, in McKenna's biography, the love that dare not speak its name.

Those who know Wilde well, know his works well; and those who know his works well know that his reception into the Catholic Church on his deathbed was the logical and theological consummation of his life-long love affair with Christ and the Church. After the scandal that brought about his downfall, Wilde remarked wistfully that his decision to turn his back on Rome as a young man was ultimately disastrous. "Much of my moral obliquity is due to the fact that my father would not allow me to become a Catholic," he confided to a journalist. "The artistic side of the Church would have cured my degeneracies. I intend to be received before long." Having read Wilde's work, and having seen how close he came to conversion on several occasions throughout his life, Wilde's many Christian admirers know that it would have been odd if he had not finally succumbed to the Passion that puts all other passions to shame. The only surprise is that it took him so long to follow his head to its long-standing conclusion and his heart to its Home.

This is as nothing to McKenna. Ignoring Wilde's insistence that his Art was "the love to which all other loves were as marsh-water to red wine," McKenna's biography pours out the wine of Wilde's art as a libation to the marsh-water. It is also worth noting that in the same letter to Lord Alfred Douglas in which Wilde spoke so plaintively of wine and marsh-water, he referred to the homosexuality that had been the bane of his life during the 1890s as his "pathology," his sickness. Clearly, any "re-gaying" of Wilde would be very much against his will! And this brings us back to our imaginary vision of Wilde turning in his grave. With "friends" like these, the ghost of Wilde might be tempted to mutter plaintively, who needs enemies?

"Every great man nowadays has his disciples," Wilde wrote, "and it is always Judas who writes the biography." He also wrote in the Preface to *The Picture of Dorian Gray* that "those who find ugly meanings in beautiful things are corrupt without being charming." This, he added, "is a fault." This is a faulty biography. It is corrupt. It lacks charm.

41. WILFRID WARD:
A MAN FOR ALL SEASONS

Dom Paschal Scotti, *Out of Due Time: Wilfrid Ward and the Dublin Review*, 1906–1916. The Catholic University of America Press, 324 pp.

A book should not be judged by its cover; nor, perhaps, should it be judged by its opening pages. The opening pages of this particular book are plagued by the sort of wooly-mindedness that Wilfrid Ward devoted his life to combating. It does not do him justice; and, indeed, it does him a veritable injustice when it implies that he subscribed to views that he would indubitably have spurned or condemned. Yet, and to reiterate, a book should not always be judged by its opening pages. *Out of Due Time* is full of fascinating facts about the intellectual climate of Edwardian and early Georgian England, and, specifically, about the Catholic contribution to that climate as expressed in the pages of the *Dublin Review* under Wilfrid Ward's editorship.

Let's begin, however, with the nonsense that litters the first chapter.

Alarm bells are set ringing on the very first page when it is claimed by the author that Ward's "greatest desire was to see the reconciliation of the Church and the world." Since no effort is made to define what is meant by "the world" in this context, we are left wondering what this statement means, and fearing, perhaps, that it means what we think it means. This is an early example of what might be termed intellectual impressionism, namely a failure to provide clear definitions of the terms under discussion and a spurning of clear delineation of meaning in favour of a fuzzy and foggy "feel-good" factor. It springs from the assumption that conflict is always bad—or, worse, impolite—and that it should be avoided at all costs, and also from a desire to reconcile ourselves with the prevailing tendencies of the modern world in order to remain "relevant" to the fads and fashions of the time. This is not the way that Wilfrid Ward thought or acted. He would, in fact, have agreed with G. K. Chesterton, an occasional contributor to the *Dublin Review* under Ward's editorship, who insisted that we did not need a Church that will move with the world but a Church that will move the world. *Pace* Dom Scotti, Ward's "greatest desire" (after his desire for Heaven, presumably) was *to reconcile the world to the Church.* This is a world away (and a heaven and a hell away) from the reconciliation of the Church and the world. One necessitates good old-fashioned evangelization, engagement with the culture in order to enlighten and convert it; the other implies compromise, accommodation and perhaps even surrender. Ward wanted the former and utterly rejected the latter.

Ward's father, the enigmatic and robust William George Ward, is criticized through the employment of an array of curiously juxtaposed adjectives, such as "extreme and dogmatic" and "papal and rigid," which say more about the author's liberal prejudices than they do about W. G. Ward. This fuzzy-minded "correctness" descends inexorably into the realm of the *reductio ad absurdum.* If dogma is extreme, every believing Catholic who recites the Creed is an extremist! In similar vein, the author's later implicit criticism of W. G. Ward for his "triumphalism" represents a further descent into the regions of malapropian "correctness": "Ward's view of the Church was always triumphalist: no matter her human imperfections, she was the ark of salvation and the locus of divine truth, and nothing could diminish his respect and loyalty to her." Since "triumphalism" is only ever used in a derogatory sense, denoting a presumed superiority and a supercilious, gloating arrogance towards others, and since presumably this is the sense in which Dom Scotti is using it, one can only assume that a belief in the Church as "the ark of salvation and the locus of divine truth" is somehow an example of arrogant and supercilious bigotry. It is also noteworthy that Dom Scotti later, in a derogatory sense, refers to those who are "ultraorthodox," seemingly oblivious to the logical absurdity of the very juxtaposition of "ultra" and "orthodox." One is either orthodox or one is not. It is impossible to be "ultra-orthodox." At least it is impossible unless the word is taken literally, or rather radically, in compliance with its etymological components, in which case it means "beyond orthodox," a better word for which is "heresy." One who is "ultra-orthodox" is a "heretic." One suspects that this is not the meaning the author intended.

As one proceeds doggedly through the opening chapter it feels, at times, as though one has entered a twilight zone between Lewis Carroll and George Orwell, oscillating between the "curiouser and curiouser" musings of Alice and the deceptive art of doublethink. Thus, comparing Wilfrid Ward to Fr. George Tyrrell and Baron Friedrich von Hügel, the author describes Ward as the "least adventurous" of the three. Considering that Fr. Tyrrell was destined to be excommunicated as a modernist it seems that "adventurous" is a synonym for "heretic." Such a conclusion is reinforced by Dom Scotti's seeming sympathy towards Tyrrell's point of view, stating that Fr. Tyrrell felt that Ward "had not sufficiently separated himself, in principle, from the extreme right." What, one wonders, is meant by "extreme right" in such a context? One might hope that Dom Scotti is referring to Ward's doctrinal orthodoxy, which was extremely right, as opposed to Tyrrell's modernism being extremely wrong. One knows, alas, that this is not the case. Only the "extreme and dogmatic" and the "papal and rigid" are narrow enough to define ideas in terms of right and wrong. Dom Scotti is not speaking of anything as insensitive and intransigent as right and wrong, with all its moralistic associations, but about right and left. The terms are not those of antediluvian morality but post-Enlightenment politics. Once something is described as being "extreme right" it can be sneered at and dismissed, thereby avoiding the onerous task of defining terms and arguing one's own position. Ward's tradition-oriented and anti-modernist Catholic associates are on the "extreme right" and, as such, can be dismissed without the necessity of intellectual engagement. They are "extreme right" and are, *ipso facto*, anathema. The irony of such "broad-minded" inverted-McCarthyism is self-evident.

And thus endeth the first chapter. Thereafter there is, for the most part, much improvement and much less nonsense. Chapter two begins with a good historical overview of English Catholicism in the nineteenth century including an enlightening discussion of the Cisalpine Movement. Again, however, the author's view is often an impediment to a full understanding of the facts being presented. What, for instance, is one to make of his bizarre comparison of the essential characteristics of the Enlightenment with those of the Church? "While the Enlightenment emphasized man's untrammeled reason (Kant's *sapere aude*) and the necessity of intelligibility, the Church was built on the superiority of revelation, the authority of tradition, and the intrinsic value of mystery." The presumption that the "untrammeled reason" of the Enlightenment always remained trammeled by "the necessity of intelligibility" is curious, though perhaps arguable, but the suggestion, implicit in the contradistinction being stressed, that the Church was in some way hostile to reason and the necessity of intelligibility, is plainly at variance with the whole scholastic tradition which places *fides et ratio* in necessary harmony, the intelligibility of the one always being a buttress to the other. The emphasis on the Church's insistence on the superiority of revelation implies a belief in the inferiority of reason, a view that would not have been held by St. Augustine or St. Thomas Aquinas, or by Wilfrid Ward. Similarly, the assertion that the Church was built on "the intrinsic value of mystery" is not true, at least if the statement is taken literally and in isolation. Mystery has no intrinsic value *per se*. Its value is connected to, indeed trammeled by, orthodoxy. Without the necessary connection between mystery and orthodoxy, the former is not trustworthy and its intrinsic value questionable. It was, I believe, Ronald Knox who quipped that mysticism begins in mist and ends in schism. This, of course, is not always true, but it is true that the greatest mystics, such as St. Teresa of Avila and St. John of the Cross, were profoundly orthodox, as were their mystical experiences.

In spite of such impediments to the full enjoyment of the work, it is full of much that scholars of the period will find enlightening. The better parts of *Out of Due Time* represent an engaging and highly informative journey through an intellectually invigorating decade, as seen in the pages of the equally invigorating *Dublin Review*. The chapter on the modernist crisis is, as one might expect, deficient and defective in places, though full of interesting detail. The chapters on "Politics" and "Society" are well-written and, for the most part, well-reasoned, and the chapter on "Literature" is a veritable delight, presenting us with a procession of the *illustrissimi* and lesser literary lights of the period: Chesterton, Belloc, Wells, Francis Thompson, R. H. Benson, Compton Mackenzie and Arnold Lunn, to name but several. *Out of Due Time* is worth purchasing for the chapter on literature alone.

In the final chapter the author reveals his reason for giving the book its title. "Ward was, in many ways, a man born out of due time. In his political and social conservatism, he was born too late, and in his openness to theological trends, too early." Such a woeful attempt to turn Wilfrid Ward into a "trendy," a slavish follower of fashion, is reminiscent of another book, recently published, about Wilfrid Ward's daughter. In *The Living of Maisie Ward* by Dana Greene (University of Notre Dame Press, 1997) the author succumbed to the temptation to paint her subject in the colours of her own choosing with little regard for Ward's true colours as a staunch and resolute defender of Catholic orthodoxy against modernism. Now, with the publication of this new book, the sin against the daughter has been revisited upon her father. In truth, Wilfrid Ward was not a man born out of due time but was a man for all seasons.

Whether it is right to judge a book by its cover, it may sometimes be right to judge it by its title. This book has the wrong title because it is large-ly a wrong-headed book about a right-headed man. Writing of Wilfrid Ward, Dom Scotti unwittingly hits the nail on the head and, thereby and equally unwittingly, hits the nail into the coffin of his own defectively "trendy" conclusion: "Like his father, his mind was firmly grounded in dogma and first principles; he disliked flabbiness and muddled thinking . . ." Quite so. *Out of Due Time* spurns dogma and is full of flabbiness and muddled thinking. Wilfrid Ward would not have liked it.

42. COME RACK! COME ROPE!
A MINOR CLASSIC

Robert Hugh Benson was born in 1871, the youngest son of E. W. Benson, a distinguished Anglican clergyman who counted the Prime Minister, William Ewart Gladstone, amongst his friends. In 1882, when Benson was eleven years old, his father became Archbishop of Canterbury. Having taken Anglican orders himself, it was Benson who read the litany at his father's funeral in Canterbury Cathedral in 1896. The son, however, was not destined to follow in his father's footsteps. In 1903, after a period of conscientious self-examination, the details of which were elucidated masterfully in his autobiographical apologia, *Confessions of a Convert*, Benson was received into the Catholic Church. Thereafter, for the next eleven years until his untimely death in 1914, he was a tireless defender of the Catholic Church and a prolific novelist and man of letters.

In *Come Rack! Come Rope!*, first published in 1912, the whole period of the English Reformation is brought to blood-curdling life, the terror and tension gripping the reader as tightly as it grips the leading characters, who witness courageously to their faith in a hostile and deadly environment. According to the Jesuit, Philip Caraman, it "quickly became established as a Catholic classic" and remains "perhaps the best known" of Benson's novels, although his futuristic tour de force *Lord of the World* is surely its literary equal and the lesser known *Richard Reynal, Solitary* remains sadly and undeservedly neglected.

The inspiration for the novel came from the account of the Fitzherbert family in Dom Bede Camm's *Forgotten Shrines*, published in 1911, and from Benson's own visit, in the same year, to the Fitzherbert house in Derbyshire, where he preached at the annual pilgrimage in honour of the Catholic priest-martyrs, Blessed Nicholas Garlick and Blessed Robert Ludlam, who were executed in 1588. From the blood of these martyrs came the seed of Benson's story. The novel's title is taken from the famous promise of St. Edmund Campion that he would remain steadfast, "come rack, come rope." Campion was executed in 1581.

As for its historical accuracy, opinions appear to be divided. Father Caraman wrote that Benson had "remained most faithful to his sources" and Hugh Ross Williamson remarked that Benson's "invented personages" were created "within the orbit of known truth, leaving us to feel, correctly, that they could have lived and acted as Benson makes them." Williamson continues:

> The whole epoch leaps to life and if any reader should object that this picture of Catholic England under the Elizabethan Terror savours a little of melodrama, there is the author's own unchallengeable answer: "If the book is too sensational, it is no more sensational than life itself was to Derbyshire folk between 1579 and 1588."

Hilaire Belloc, on the other hand, begged to differ. Although he was, for the most part, a great admirer of Benson's work, writing on one occasion that he believed that Benson would "be the man to write some day a book to give us some sort of idea what happened in England between 1520 and 1560," Belloc complained that the description of daily life in *Come Rack! Come Rope!* was inaccurate, resembling life in the eighteenth, not the sixteenth, century.

Casting these differences aside, the novel is, in any case, much more than mere historical fiction. It is a great romance, a great love story. It is a story that shows the romance of Rome and the true greatness of a noble and self-sacrificial love between a man and a woman. The love between Robin and Marjorie, the two principal characters, is a love far greater than that between Romeo and Juliet. Their love for each other has none of the possessiveness of Shakespeare's "star-cross'd lovers" and everything of the purity and passion of Lear's Cordelia. As a love story alone, *Come Rack! Come Rope!* deserves its place in the canon.

As for the novel's climax, one must agree with Hugh Ross Williamson that "it is impossible not to be moved by the last chapter which, as far as I know, has never been bettered as an account of an Elizabethan martyr's execution." For potency and poignancy, the novel's climactic moment compares in literary stature with the final, fateful moments of Lord Marchmain in Waugh's masterpiece, *Brideshead Revisited*. And if Benson's finale lacks the subtlety of Waugh's denouement it matches it for dramatic tension.

Why, one wonders, does Benson's mini-masterpiece, which warrants comparison with the works of Waugh, remain largely unknown? One suspects that it has a good deal to do with the sad and sorrowful, and sinful and cynical, times in which we live. In healthier times, for which we can hope and pray, it will be regarded as the minor classic that it is.

43. PAST PRESENT:
HILAIRE BELLOC & THE EVANGELISING POWER OF HISTORY

History . . . should above all explain: it should give "the how and the why." It is the business of history to make people understand how they came to be; what was the origin and progress of the state of which they form a part; what were the causes which influenced each phase of change from the beginning almost to our own time.

— Hilaire Belloc[55]

The truth will set us free. So says Christ. Yet if this is so, which of course it is, it follows that falsehood will enslave us. Falsehood in history prevents us from understanding our past and, in consequence, our present.

Properly understood, history is a chronological map that shows us not only where we have come from but also where we are, and how we got here. It is also possible to project where we are likely to be going in the future by drawing the line of knowledge on the chronological map from where we have come from to where we are now, and extending the line into the realm of future possibilities. In this sense history can also be a prophet. It increases our knowledge of the past, present and future. This, however, is only true if the chronological map is accurate. If it has been drawn by those with prejudiced perceptions or a prejudiced agenda it will only succeed in getting us lost. There are few things more dangerous than an inaccurate map, especially if we find ourselves in perilous terrain.

Perhaps at this juncture we need to proceed from Christ to Pilate. We need to pass from Christ's assertion that the truth will set us free to Pilate's question: What is truth? In the context of the study of history, the truth requires the knowledge of three distinct facets of historical reality, namely historical *chronology*, historical *mechanics* and historical *philosophy*, i.e., *when* things happened, *how* things happened and *why* things happened. The last of these, though it is dependent factually on the other two, is the most important. If we don't know why things happened history remains devoid of meaning; it makes no sense. As such, historians must have knowledge of the history of belief. They must know *what* people believed *when* they did the things that they did in order to know *why* they acted as they did. They must have empathy with the great ideas that shaped human history, even if they don't have sympathy with them. This whole issue was addressed with great lucidity by Hilaire Belloc, perhaps the most important historian of the twentieth century (with the possible exception of Christopher Dawson):

> The worst fault in [writing] history . . . is the fault of not knowing what the spiritual state of those whom one describes really was. Gibbon and his master Voltaire, the very best of reading, are for that reason bad writers of history. To pass through the tremendous history of the Trinitarian dispute from which our civilization arose and to treat it as a farce is not history. To write the story of the sixteenth century in England and to make of either the Protestant or the Catholic a grotesque is to miss history altogether.[56]

Clearly frustrated at this supercilious attitude towards the past that blinded many historians, Belloc offers a practical example of its effects upon scholarship:

> There is an enormous book called Volume 1 of a *Cambridge History of the Middle Ages*. It is 759 pages in length of close print . . . It does not mention the Mass once. That is as though you were to write a history of the Jewish dispersion without mentioning the synagogue or of the British Empire without mentioning the City of London or the Navy . . .[57]

In order to avoid the chronological snobbery that presumes the superiority of the present over the past and which causes this lack of proportion and focus, historians must see history through the eyes of the past, not the present. They must put themselves into the minds and hearts of the protagonists they are studying; and to do this adequately they must have knowledge of philosophy and theology in order to *understand* their own academic discipline and in order to remain disciplined in their study of it. An ignorance of philosophy and theology means an ignorance of history.

Hilaire Belloc's principal legacy as an historian falls into three areas.

First, is his seminal struggle with H. G. Wells over the "outline of history"; second, his groundbreaking refutation of the prejudiced 'official' history of the Protestant Reformation; and finally his telescopic and panoramic study of the "great heresies."[58]

Belloc's war of words with H. G. Wells over the latter's publication of *The Outline of History* was one of the most controversial and notorious academic battles of the twentieth century. Belloc objected to his adversary's tacitly anti-Christian stance, epitomized by the fact that Wells had devoted more space in his "history" to the Persian campaign against the Greeks than he had given to the figure of Christ, but it was the underlying philosophy of materialistic determinism in Wells's *History* which was most anathema to him. Wells believed that human "progress" was both blind and beneficial; unshakeable, unstoppable and utterly inexorable. History was the product of invisible and immutable evolutionary forces that were coming to fruition in the twentieth century. Human history had its primitive beginnings in the caves,[59] but was now reaching its climax in the modern age with the final triumph of science over religion. The emergence of science from the ashes of "superstition" heralded a new dawn for humanity, a brave new world of happiness made possible by technology. Obviously such an approach precluded any serious or objective consideration of the great ideas that had forged human history since, in Wells's view, these ideas were shaped by the superstition and ignorance which had been superseded by humanity's "progress" towards modernity.

Wells's "outline" had been, to Belloc, like a red rag to a bull. It was, therefore, no great surprise that Belloc charged. He accused Wells of prejudiced provincialism claiming that "in history proper," Wells "was never taught to appreciate the part played by Latin and Greek culture, and never introduced to the history of the early Church." Furthermore he suffered "from the very grievous fault of being ignorant that he is ignorant": "He has the strange cocksureness of the man who only knows the old conventional text-book of his schooldays and mistakes it for universal knowledge."[60] The controversy reached a conclusion and a climax in 1926, when Belloc's articles refuting Wells's history were collected into a single volume and published as *A Companion to Mr. Wells's "Outline of History."* Wells responded with *Mr. Belloc Objects*, to which Belloc, determined to have the last word, replied with *Mr. Belloc Still Objects*. At the end of the controversy, Belloc claimed to have written over 100,000 words in refutation of the central arguments in Wells's book. As such, Belloc could be likened not so much with a charging bull as with a biting bulldog that refuses to let go.

The lasting legacy and lingering lesson of the war of words between Belloc and Wells is its exemplification of the fact that one's philosophical presuppositions will invariably colour one's understanding of the "outline of history." Belloc understood the beliefs of the past and, as such, could discern why people acted as they did; he could see *why* things happened as well as *when* and *how* they happened. Wells, on the other hand, regarded the beliefs of the past as superstitious and dismissed them superciliously. His chronological snobbery prevented his analysis of history from rising above the *when* and *how*, and since the *when* and *how* are influenced by, and perhaps determined by, the *why*, Wells's understanding was inevitably deficient in these areas also.

Belloc's war with Wells also represented an encapsulation and embodiment of the clash between "progress" and tradition, a clash which was summarized succinctly by the Catholic poet, Roy Campbell: "The orgy of irresponsible innovations and inventions—which . . . now threatens to become a Gadarene stampede of headlong and irresistible impetus—was regarded as something beneficial and called 'progress,' which it certainly is, being downhill and completely without brakes: the most rapid and disastrous "progress" ever witnessed."[61]

Campbell's words had the benefit of hindsight, being written in 1949, a quarter of a century after the Belloc-Wells controversy, and a few short years after the fruits of "progress" had led to the atrocities of Hitler and Stalin and the dropping of nuclear bombs on Hiroshima and Nagasaki. Belloc had foreseen that a credulously optimistic faith in "progress" could lead to "sheer darkness" and "strange things in the dark," whereas Wells believed that "darkness" was a thing to be found in the "dark ages" of the past whereas the future held the promise of "enlightened" scientific thinking. It would take the horrors of the Second World War to open his eyes to the evils that could be unleashed by science in the service of "progressive" ideologies. Shaken out of his "progressive" dementia, Wells's last book, written shortly before his death in 1946 and entitled, appropriately, *The Mind at the End of its Tether*, was full of the desolation of disillusionment. In the end, Wells's "progressive" optimism, already defeated in debate by Belloc, was defeated in practice by reality itself.

In the wake of the controversy with Wells, Belloc became increasingly preoccupied with historical questions. "In history we must abandon the defensive," he had written in 1924, at the height of the war with Wells, ". . . We must make our opponents understand not only that they are wrong in their philosophy, nor only ill-informed in their judgement of cause and effect, but out of touch with the past: which is ours."[62] From this time onwards, Belloc's historical work would be less concerned with European history than with the history of England in the sixteenth and seventeenth centuries. There were notable exceptions, such as *Joan of Arc* in 1929, *Richelieu* in 1930 and *Napoleon* in 1932, but in general Belloc now concentrated his attention and his passion on aspects of English history. Commencing with the first of four volumes of *A History of England*, he also wrote specific books on many of the main characters and key events of the English Reformation. These included *Oliver Cromwell* (1927), *James the Second* (1928), *How the Reformation Happened* (1928), *Wolsey* (1930), *Cranmer* (1931), *Charles the First* (1933), *Milton* (1935) and *Characters of the Reformation* (1936).

In the preface to his *Shorter History of England* (1934), Belloc sought to explain why he thought that the study of the English Reformation deserved greater emphasis than had been customary. Explaining why he had given much more space to "the Transformation of England through the total change of her religion in the sixteenth and seventeenth centuries . . . than to the nineteenth," he added that this was necessary "if one is to present a true scheme of the past: to present 'the how and the why.'"[63] These general comments were expanded upon in the introductory chapter of *Characters of the Reformation*, in which Belloc insists that the English Reformation had a profound impact upon Christendom as a whole:

[The] severance of England from Europe and from Christendom was . . . the pivotal matter of the Protestant advance. On it the partial success of the religious revolution everywhere depended. Hence the necessity for beginning by an understanding of the *English* tragedy, failing which the disruption of Europe and all our modern chaos would never have appeared.[64]

The importance of England's break with Rome is made manifest by Belloc's insistence upon its "pivotal" place in the "break-up" of Christendom.

The break-up of united western Christendom with the coming of the Reformation was by far the most important thing in history since the foundation of the Catholic Church fifteen hundred years before.

Men of foresight perceived at the time that if catastrophe

were allowed to consummate itself, if the revolt were to be successful (and it was successful) our civilization would certainly
be imperiled and possibly, in the long run, destroyed.

That is indeed what has happened. Europe with all its culture is now seriously imperiled and stands no small chance of
being destroyed by its own internal disruption; and all this is
ultimately the fruit of the great religious revolution which
began four hundred years ago.

This being so, the Reformation being of this importance, it
ought to form the chief object of historical study in modern
times, and its nature should be clearly understood even if only
in outline.[65]

Belloc's frustration at the anti-Catholic bias of the Whig historians in
their treatment of the Reformation was expressed in a letter to his daughter in which he complained that "most people are still steeped in that false
official history which warps all English life."[66] Elsewhere he complained
about the "weary work [of] fighting this enormous mountain of ignorant
wickedness" that constituted "tom-fool Protestant history."[67]

If Belloc's crusade to spread a true understanding of the Reformation
was invaluable so was his other great crusade in the field of history: his
mapping, in *Survivals and New Arrivals* (1929) and *The Great Heresies*
(1938), of the war of ideas that had forged the history of Europe and
beyond. It is in this sphere that we see Belloc the historian emerging as a
prophet, particularly with regard to his warnings about the renewed threat
of Islam. It is, for instance, almost chilling that Belloc wrote of the lifting
of the Moslem siege of Vienna "on a date that ought to be among the most
famous in history—September 11, 1683."[68] It is a date that Christendom
has forgotten, to its shame, but which the militants of Islam had apparently remembered. "It has always seemed to me possible, and even probable,
that there would be a resurrection of Islam and that our sons or our grand-
sons would see the renewal of that tremendous struggle between the
Christian culture and what has been for more than a thousand years its
greatest opponent."[69] These words, written more than sixty years ago, went
unheeded. Today they resound like the death-knell of Europe.

Hilaire Belloc's vision of the past enabled him to see the future. Today,
more than ever, our culture needs to heed his words. The evangelizing
power of history is that it teaches us about ourselves and about our enemies. The more one understands history the more one ceases to be

Protestant, wrote Newman. It is equally true that the more one understands history the more one ceases to be a liberal secularist. Our culture of death is doomed to die. The future will belong to Christ or Mahound. The choice is ours. The final words are Belloc's:

> In such a crux there remains the historical truth: that this our European structure, built upon the noble foundations of classical antiquity, was formed through, exists by, is consonant to, and will stand only in the mould of, the Catholic Church.
> Europe will return to the Faith, or she will perish.[70]

44. BELLOC'S *THE FOUR MEN*

Hilaire Belloc wrote on literally anything and everything, "literally" being meant quite literally. His book *On Anything*, published in 1910, had been preceded the previous year by his book *On Everything*. He also published *On Nothing* in 1908 and *On Something* in 1910. Then, in 1923, he took the omnivorous whimsy to its utmost conclusion, publishing *On*. Such volumes display Belloc's versatility as an essayist, illustrating not only the many facets of his Catholicism but also his catholicity of taste on anything, everything and, most beguilingly, on nothing in particular. Thus, for instance, he writes "On the Pleasure of Taking Up One's Pen," "On Ignorance," "On Tea," "On Them," "On Death," "On Experience," "On Sacramental Things," "On Song," "On the Rights of Property," "On Old Towns" and, appropriately enough at the conclusion of one of the volumes, "On Coming to an End." In the pages of these meandering miscellanies one discovers more about Belloc the man than is discernible in any of his other works except for those hauntingly personal pilgrimages of the soul, *The Path to Rome* (1902), *The Four Men* (1912) and *The Cruise of the Nona* (1925), in which the author waxes wistful and whimsical on the first things, the permanent things, the last things, and in general on the things (and the Thing) that give meaning to, and make sense of, anything and everything else.

These three "pilgrimages," taken together, might be dubbed "travel-farragoes," a distinct literary genre in which Belloc excelled. They are, at one and the same time, both travelogues and farragoes; linear narratives connected to a journey interspersed with seemingly random anecdotal musings on anything and everything. The overriding structure of each of these three works is, therefore, animated by the creative tension between the forward momentum maintained by the author's account of his pilgrimage and the inertial force of the tangential interruptions. As such, Belloc's travel farragoes are not for those who are in a hurry but for those who wish to saunter with the author in the leisurely pursuit of those things that are worth pursuing at leisure; and those things worth pursuing at leisure are, of course, the very things that are worth spending our whole lives getting to know better.

Although *The Path to Rome* was, according to Belloc's own appraisal, the best book he ever wrote, there is little doubt that *The Four Men* warrants a place of distinction as one of the finest works of this finest of writers. Although it was not published until 1912, Belloc seems to have embarked on it as early as 1907, originally planning to call it "The County of Sussex." In 1909 he told Maurice Baring that it would describe "myself and three other characters walking through the county; the other characters are really supernatural beings, a poet, a sailor and Grizzlebeard . . . they only turn out to be supernatural beings when we get to the town of Liss, which is just over the Hampshire border."[71]

Since he embellished his journey with imaginary characters it is not fanciful to suggest that he also invented the dates on which the journey was made. Whatever the facts of the matter, it is clear that Belloc had evidently walked the whole route at some time or other and that he knew every inch of the way. The facts, however, should not obscure the deeper truth for which the book was written. In writing *The Four Men*, Belloc provides a metaphorical and therefore metaphysical path through Sussex to accompany his earlier path to Rome.

The Path to Rome and *The Four Men* are pilgrimages conveying a soul's love for the soil of its native land, which in the former case is the macrocosmic "Europe of the Faith" in which Belloc was raised and in the latter case is the microcosmic Shire in which he was also raised. Home, like Rome, is a "holy place" and *The Four Men* is full of spiritual premonitions of "the character of enduring things" amid the decay of time:

> . . . it has been proved in the life of every man that though his loves are human, and therefore changeable, yet in proportion as he attaches them to things unchangeable, so they mature and broaden.
>
> On this account . . . does a man love an old house, which was his father's, and on this account does a man come to love with all his heart, that part of earth which nourished his boyhood. For it does not change, or if it changes, it changes very little, and he finds in it the character of enduring things . . .
>
> And as a man will paint with a peculiar passion a face which he is only permitted to see for a little time, so will one passionately set down one's own horizon and one's fields before they

are forgotten and have become a different thing. Therefore it is that I have put down in writing what happened to me now so many years ago, when I met first one man and then another, and we four bound ourselves together and walked through all your land, Sussex, from end to end. For many years I have meant to write it down and have not; nor would I write it down now, or issue the book at all, Sussex, did I not know that you, who must like all created things decay, might with the rest of us be very near your ending. For I know very well in my mind that a day will come when the holy place shall perish and all the people of it and never more be what they were. But before that day comes, Sussex, may your earth cover me, and may some loud-voiced priest from Arundel, or Grinstead, or Crawley, or Storrington, but best of all from home, have sung Do Mi Fa Sol above my bones.[72]

One is struck upon reading these wistfully eloquent words from the preface to *The Four Men* with their similarity to the preface to *The Path to Rome*, published ten years earlier.[73] Belloc began the earlier book by recounting an unexpected encounter with the valley of his birth, conveying his pleasant surprise that "the old tumble-down and gaping church" that he had loved in his youth had been renovated so that it appeared "noble and new." This pleased him "as much as though a fortune had been left to us all; for one's native place is the shell of one's soul, and one's church is the kernel of that nut." In both books, therefore, Belloc lays the foundations of what might be termed the "theology of place" from the very outset.

This understanding of the spiritual significance of "home," this theology of place, is such a recurrent theme in Belloc's work that it could be said to be almost omnipresent. Few writers have felt so intensely the sense of exile, and hence the love of home, to the degree to which it is invoked by Belloc. From the love of Sussex at the heart of *The Four Men* and in poems such as "Ha'nacker Mill" or "The South Country," to the love of Europe in general, and France in particular, evoked in *The Path to Rome* and in poems such as "Tarantella," his work resonates with the love of earth as a foreshadowing of the love of heaven. It is in this soil-soul nexus that the nub of Belloc's profundity is to be discovered. It manifests itself in the tension between permanence and mutability, and finds infectious expression in the perfect balance between wistfulness and whimsy. Although these qualities are to be found in all of Belloc's work, as expressions of the very spirit of the man himself, they are to be found to an exceptional degree in *The Path to Rome* and *The Four Men*.

In my introduction to the Ignatius Press edition of *The Path to Rome*, I wrote that "*The Four Men* rivals it, and perhaps surpasses it, as a vehicle for Belloc's wit and wisdom, or as an outpouring of his irrepressible personality." Since Belloc considered *The Path to Rome* his best work, it seems that I am in disagreement with the great man himself in such effusive praise of *The Four Men*. No matter. Even if we are to defer to Belloc's own judgment, it is no small thing to be Belloc's second best, or even his third best book.[74] In any event, like all of Belloc's books, it deserves to be read and re-read by all who hunger for the "enduring things" in an age of deplorable change.

45. THE RESURRECTION OF
G. K. CHESTERTON

"The reports of my death have been greatly exaggerated," quipped Mark Twain upon hearing that his obituary had been mistakenly published in a newspaper. Although it must have been a strangely flattering experience for the great American writer to read of his own demise when he was still very much alive, it is even more flattering that he is still alive long after his death. Such enduring fame represents a far greater tribute than any obituary could offer. It is in this way that we mortal men, doomed to die, attain a level of immortality. And, for the faithless man, this is the only immortality there is. This was the immortality of which Hilaire Belloc was writing when he wrote, with mischievous whimsy:

> When I am dead, I hope it may be said:
> His sins were scarlet, but his books were read.

There is, however, an obverse side to the coin of posterity. Many writers who live and die in a blaze of celebrity are doomed to die a second death, in the years after their passing, as their reputation, and the memory of their life and work, fades into the oblivion of public forgetfulness. C. S. Lewis, in his humility, was convinced that this was to be his destiny; that his books had been read during his own lifetime but that they would be forgotten, along with their author, in the years following his death. How mistaken could he be. According to his literary executor, Walter Hooper, "the number of Lewis's books which are read today is far in excess of anything that happened in his own lifetime."

It is certainly heartening that a Christian writer of Lewis's calibre should be enjoying such a renaissance and it is equally heartening that G. K. Chesterton, a writer who was at least Lewis's equal as an indefatigable defender of Christian truth, should be enjoying a similar renaissance of his own. "Twenty years ago, there were fewer than ten Chesterton titles in print," says Dale Ahlquist, President of the American Chesterton Society.

"Today there are over seventy, including new collections of previously uncollected material. More titles are coming out all the time." Ahlquist's enthusiastic optimism is matched by Tony Ryan, Marketing Director of Ignatius Press, one of the increasing number of publishers who are bringing out new editions of Chesterton's works. "Clearly the sales of books by, and about, G. K. Chesterton have skyrocketed in the last ten years," says Ryan, "which is truly great news for the Church and for Catholics everywhere because Chesterton was truly a prolific writer on many topics of crucial importance for the temporal and eternal good of the human race."

"Currently we have thirteen individual books in print by Chesterton at IP," Ryan continues, "including such classics as *Orthodoxy*, *The Everlasting Man*, *The Well and the Shallows*, and *What's Wrong with the World*. These titles and his others sell very well in both the Christian and in the secular markets. GKC truly has a wide appeal." In addition, Ignatius Press publishes several outstanding works *about* Chesterton, including *G. K. Chesterton: The Apostle of Common Sense* and *Common Sense 101: Lessons from G. K. Chesterton*, both by Dale Ahlquist, and IP is also responsible for the *Collected Works of G. K. Chesterton*, a critically acclaimed series that currently constitutes twenty-seven multi-title volumes, with more on the way. It was, indeed, with a sense of elated surprise that the present writer espied many volumes of the *Collected Works* in the private library of the great Russian writer and Nobel Prize winner, Aleksandr Solzhenitsyn, during a visit to Moscow to interview him.

Few would have predicted such an unlikely revival during the dark years of the sixties and seventies, when Chesterton's reputation was well and truly on the wane. During those years the flag was kept flying by a mere handful of Chesterton die-hards. In England, the irrepressible Aidan Mackey specialized in selling used copies of long out of print Chesterton titles to a relatively small number of aficionados. In the United States, Father Ian Boyd founded the *Chesterton Review* in 1974, in the centenary year of GKC's birth, and few imagined that such a journal could survive in the rising tide of modernist indifference that characterized the dark and dismal years which followed the Vatican Council. Today, almost forty years later, the *Review* continues to thrive under Fr. Boyd's tireless guidance, and has established a well-earned reputation as one of the most respected and learned literary journals in the academic market.

Back in 1980, when the present writer, as a teenager, was first introduced to Chesterton, it was easy to pick up editions of his works in used bookstores very cheaply. The generation that had read Chesterton was dying off and their children, seemingly indifferent to the literary heritage passed on to them, had sold their parents' books to the book-dealers. It was also not uncommon to see Chesterton titles that bore the stamp of convent libraries, seemingly sold off or given away by the religious orders in the belief that old-timers like Chesterton had no place in a church inebriated with the "spirit of Vatican II." It is not without a guilty sense of *schadenfreude* that one notes the death of these liberal congregations even as one notes the resurrection of Chesterton. With regard to the latter, it is interesting that first editions of Chesterton novels are now selling for more than $400 each, a far cry for the few pennies required in the 1980s.

There is another parallel between Chesterton and Lewis in the way that each was treated by liberal theologians in the "dark ages" before the salvific election of John Paul II. In much the same way that Chesterton was rejected by liberal congregations and modernist theologians, Lewis was increasingly rejected by the liberal ascendancy in the Anglican church. Walter Hooper recalled how even those who had been Lewis's greatest admirers, during his lifetime, had turned against him in the years following his death: "I was surprised to see what used to be a very Anglo-Catholic magazine from America now saying 'why did we ever read Lewis, he's far too doctrinal, he's far too Roman Catholic for us now'." Again, it is hard to resist a sense of *schadenfreude* in the knowledge that Lewis's star has been waxing while the falling star of Anglicanism has plummeted towards the abyss it has prepared for itself. It is, in fact, not difficult to imagine that, in the not so distant future, more people will be reading Lewis's books than will be attending Anglican services.

And, of course, those millions of avid readers of Lewis have none other than Chesterton to thank because, as Lewis freely admitted, Chesterton played a prominent role in Lewis's conversion. "In reading Chesterton . . . I did not know what I was letting myself in for," Lewis wrote in his autobiography, *Surprised by Joy*. "A young man who wishes to remain a sound Atheist cannot be too careful of his reading. There are traps everywhere . . . God is, if I may say it, very unscrupulous." Chesterton's influence over Lewis would continue to grow until Lewis's atheism finally crumbled beneath the inexorable logic and inestimable charm of Chesterton's apologia for Christianity in his masterful work, *The Everlasting Man*. "I read Chesterton's *Everlasting Man* and for the first time saw the whole Christian outline of history set out in a form that seemed to me to make sense." Thereafter, it was only a matter of time before Lewis's own conversion to Christianity and it is indeed an astonishing thought that if it had not been for Chesterton there would have been no Lewis.

It is an even more astonishing thought that if it had not been for Chesterton there might not have been a whole host of other writers who owe their conversions in some significant way (under grace) to GKC's wit and wisdom. Amongst those leading figures of the Catholic Literary Revival influenced by Chesterton on their path to Christ are Maurice Baring, Ronald Knox, Christopher Dawson, Theodore Maynard, Alfred Noyes, and Graham Greene. Dorothy L. Sayers told a friend that if it hadn't been for Chesterton she might in her schooldays have abandoned Christianity altogether. "To the young people of my generation GKC was a kind of Christian liberator," Sayers wrote in 1952, describing his impact as being "like a beneficent bomb."

In 1956, twenty years after Chesterton's death, Arnold Lunn, another literary convert, lamented the way that Chesterton's influence was waning and criticized his contemporaries for "forgetting the impact which his books made on the minds of the young men who were infected by the fallacy of Victorian rationalism." Lunn's fears were ultimately unfounded because reports of Chesterton's demise were to prove greatly exaggerated. Today, half a century after Lunn's lament, Chesterton's resurrection is a cause for celebration and perhaps, even, a temptation to triumphalism, that most unjustly berated of counter-reformation virtues.

"Besides sales being way up for Chesterton books, we are hearing about more and more conversions to Catholicism by people because they have read books by Chesterton," enthuses Tony Ryan. "And sometimes these conversions are truly amazing. Like the story of Dawn Eden, a secular Jew living an immoral lifestyle as a hard-core rock journalist, who happened, by chance, to read the Chesterton novel, *The Man Who was Thursday*. She was so stunned by the wisdom and truth in that book, that she read it two more times. Then she read everything she could get her hands on by Chesterton. The happy ending of that story is that Dawn Eden is now an on-fire Roman Catholic—thanks to the Great One, G. K. Chesterton. So not only have the works of GKC dramatically increased in sales in recent years, but the visible impact of those sales is something we are so excited about at Ignatius Press."

Dawn Eden's book, *The Thrill of the Chaste: Finding Fulfillment while Keeping Your Clothes On*, bubbles with the irrepressible rambunctiousness which its author no doubt caught from the contagious charm of Chesterton himself. Her talk at a recent Chesterton Conference in St. Paul, MN, entitled "The Girl Who was Thirsty: How Reading Chesterton Led to My Conversion," was one of the highlights of a conference that has become one of the largest literary gatherings in the world. The conference is itself a powerful witness of the Chesterton revival. In the 1980s fewer than twenty people gathered at the annual get-together of the Chesterton Society; today the conference attracts several hundred people, many traveling from as far as New Zealand, Australia and Europe. They come not merely for the many talks but for the incarnation of the Chestertonian spirit that permeates the conference. Homebrewed ales and homemade wines are in plentiful supply for the thirsty participants, at no cost, though bottled water must be bought! One can't help but feel that GKC would have approved. He was, after all, famous for declaiming that he didn't care where the water went if it didn't get into the wine! Such is the effervescence of the event that one senses the ghost of Chesterton presiding benevolently over the proceedings, invisible but nonetheless present, chuckling at Dawn Eden's jokes and toasting the bibbers of wine and ale with the ambrosial fare that he now imbibes as the reward for his earthly labours.

The annual conference is organized by the American Chesterton Society, an organization that is at the very hub of the Chesterton revival. Apart from the burgeoning size of the conferences, its website has also seen a huge increase in traffic. The site (www.chesterton.org) received 100,000 visitors in its first six years; in the following four years the number of visitors exceeded half a million, a phenomenal increase of more than eight hundred per cent.

The American Chesterton Society also publishes *Gilbert Magazine*, a populist journal that serves as a good counterpoint to the more academically rigorous and rigid *Chesterton Review*, and the society's president, Dale Ahlquist, presents a regular series, "G. K. Chesterton: The Apostle of Common Sense" on EWTN, the global Catholic television network. Presented with such an abundance of activity, one wonders whether there is another literary society anywhere in the world that can boast as many achievements in the past decade.

In the wake of this popular groundswell of interest in Chesterton's work, it is amusing to see the denizens of the miasma of (post)modernity seeking, like King Knut, to hold back the emerging wave of academic interest in Chesterton. "I am contacted by students all over the country and all over the world, both at the graduate and undergraduate level, who want to do theses or dissertations on Chesterton," says Ahlquist. "They've discovered Chesterton and the problem is that there are almost no faculty members who know anything about him, so getting an adviser is very difficult. The American Chesterton Society, of course, is one of the best resources to help these students. But here and there, even professors are starting to discover Chesterton, and even sneaking an occasional Chesterton text into a syllabus."

The present writer is one such professor who has not only discovered Chesterton but is forever indebted to him as being the greatest influence, under grace, on his conversion to Catholicism. I also teach Chesterton regularly in my class on twentieth-century literature, though at Ave Maria University it is scarcely necessary to "sneak" it onto the syllabus. *The Man Who was Thursday* is always the text with which I start the semester and we also study Chesterton's "Lepanto." In 2006, a "special topics" course on "Chesterton and Belloc" proved one of the most popular electives ever offered at AMU.

Chesterton is, without doubt, a huge hit with the new generation of undergraduates and this bodes well for the future. "An older generation that remembers studying Chesterton a long time ago is very pleased with this revival," says Ahlquist. "A young generation is very excited at the discovery of this astonishing writer. But the in-between generation is still quite mystified by it all."

If the revival of interest in Chesterton is cause for celebration and, indeed, cause for optimism about the future, dare one hope that even Hollywood might fall under his infectious influence? It's been more than fifty years since Sir Alec Guinness graced the movie theatres with his unforgettable portrayal of Chesterton's Father Brown, and more than thirty years since Kenneth More brought the priestly detective to British television screens. The subsequent cinematographic and televisual silence is, from a Chestertonian perspective, positively deafening! Perhaps, however, there is hope that GKC may be resurrected in these media also. The huge success of Peter Jackson's stunning, if flawed, film adaptation of Tolkien's *Lord of the Rings*, and the more recent success of Disney's dabbling with C. S. Lewis's Narnian Chronicles, might prove portentous. Clearly, at the very least, Hollywood is now alive to the fact that Christian literature, and Christian morality, makes money at the box office; and since, like Wilde's cynic, movie-moguls know the price of everything and the value of nothing, there is indeed hope for Chesterton's return to the silver screen. Certainly the surreal brilliance of *The Man Who was Thursday* or *The Ball and the Cross* would benefit greatly from the special effects now available to filmmakers, and an adventurous producer/director could work wonders with the fruits of Chesterton's luridly lucid imagination.

Is this wishful thinking? Quite possibly it is, not least because a good movie version of one of the great Chesterton novels would transport this particular moviegoer to Chesterton heaven! Whether or not such an ascension ever happens in the future, we can rest, for the present, in the safe assumption that Chesterton is alive and well in the twenty-first century. Like the Master whom he served, Chesterton is not to be found in the tomb. His place is not in the sepulchre reserved for the forgotten literati whose reputation is fading with the fads and fashions they followed. His place is on the honour roll of the living. Do not seek for him in the grave of the dead men of letters. He is not there. He is risen from the dead.

46. G. K. CHESTERTON:
FIDEI DEFENSOR

On November 24, 1521, Pope Leo X bestowed the title of *Fidei Defensor* (Defender of the Faith) on King Henry VIII. The honour was granted to the English king in recognition of his book *Assertio Septem Sacramentorum* (*Defence of the Seven Sacraments*), in which the King defended all the sacraments of the Catholic Faith, including the sacramental nature of marriage, and in which he asserted the supremacy of the Pope. The King's stance, known as the Henrician Affirmation, was considered an important weapon in the struggle against the Protestant Reformation in Europe, and especially against the ideas of Martin Luther. It was, therefore, hardly surprising that the Pope should seek to honour the English monarch for his services to the True Faith.

Within a few years, however, in one of the great ironies and treacheries of history, Henry VIII broke from the Catholic Church, declaring himself the head of the church in England. As if to add insult to infamy, he also profaned the sacrament of marriage, deserting his wife and daughter in favour of a scandalous adulterous relationship with Anne Boleyn, whom he would later have beheaded. Faced with such outrageous behaviour, it was scarcely surprising that Pope Paul III revoked the title of Defender of the Faith from such a Machiavellian tyrant and Henry was duly excommunicated.

This was not, however, to be the end of the irony and treachery. In an act of faithless defiance the English Monarchs continued to style themselves as "Defenders of the Faith" in spite of the title being revoked by the Church. Up to this day, the reigning monarch has continued to make claim to the title, *Fidei Defensor*, and the phrase is still to be found on all current British coins. More recently, in 1994, Prince Charles, as heir to the throne, has declared his desire to be known "as Defender of Faith, not *the* Faith." One wonders what sort of faith he is talking about. If he does not want to defend *the* Faith, does he not want to defend *the* God of Christianity?

Whose God does he want to defend? Does he want to defend everyone's god? Does he want to defend gods in general? Or is even this too dogmatic? Why should faith be restricted to a belief in God or gods? Why shouldn't we defend faith in dogs instead of gods? Perhaps even faith in dogs is a little too dogmatic. Why not cats? It would certainly seem that Prince Charles's vague and indefinable faith is more comfortable with dogs than dogma and more at home with cats than catechesis. His aversion to the definite article is an article of indefinable faith in God knows what. Such faith in anything is, in fact, faith in nothing in particular; and a faith in nothing in particular is, in particular, a faith in Nothing. Is Nothing worth defending?

The great G. K. Chesterton would have had great fun with the lunacy of Prince Charles. In *The Man Who was Thursday* he had mused mirthfully over the impenetrable circularity of the phrase that "nothing is worth doing," putting the nonsensical paradox into the mind and mouth of the corrupt and incorrigible Professor de Worms.[75] One can only surmise what fun Chesterton would have had with the folly of faith in nothing in particular, and the even greater folly of wishing to *defend* faith in nothing in particular. Surely Prince Charles is one "defender" that even Chesterton the great Defendant would have had difficulty defending.

All this is of course nonsense, a nonsense that leads to madness. The reductionism of ever decreasing circles leading to a downward spiral into the realm of the *reductio ad absurdum*.

In the light of all this nonsense one is reminded insistently of the phrase often attributed to Chesterton that people who don't believe in God do not believe in nothing, they believe in anything. Ultimately we can't believe in Nothing because "nothing" doesn't exist, and if we refuse *the* Faith in something we will be left with faith in anything. It is one of God's paradoxical jokes that credulity can be defined as the absence of a Creed.

Chesterton's friend Hilaire Belloc insisted with pugnacious certainty that "Outside [the Church] is the Night, and strange things in the Night." If we will not be creatures of the Light we will be creatures of the Night and followers of the strange things in the Night. "The issue is now quite clear," said Chesterton on his deathbed. "It is between light and darkness and every one must choose his side." There is no third way.

Shortly after Chesterton's death in 1936, Pope Pius XI sent a telegram, which was read to the vast crowd gathered for Chesterton's requiem Mass at Westminster Cathedral. In the telegram, the Pope described Chesterton as a "gifted Defender of the Catholic Faith." Ironically the secular press in

England refused to publish the Pope's telegram on the grounds that "the Pope had bestowed on a British subject a title held by the King." That the title of *Fidei Defensor* was originally bestowed upon the King by the Pope was either overlooked or forgotten. It was, in any event, singularly apt that Chesterton should be the first Englishman honoured by the Pope with the title of Defender of the Faith since Henry VIII had dishonoured the title four hundred years earlier. Choosing to be Outside, the King had condemned his nation and his descendants to a nocturnal existence in which many strange things emerged from the darkness, not least of which was the ironically named "Enlightenment"! One of the strangest things to emerge was the bizarre faithless faith in "faith" espoused by Prince Charles. In the midst of this right royal nonsense, Chesterton, a commoner, became the apostle of common sense. A light in the darkness of modern England, Chesterton deserved the title that the King had deserted. He was, and is, an indomitable Defender of the Faith.

47. THE BEST OF CHESTERTON

"I am interested in getting to know the works of G. K. Chesterton. Could you recommend a good place to start?" When I hear this question, one of the most frequently asked during my travels on the lecture circuit, I experience a sinking feeling deep inside. I am obviously not disappointed that my interlocutor desires to get to know Chesterton. (Perish the thought!) On the contrary, I am always delighted to learn of another would-be convert to the magic of GKC. The truth is that the sinking feeling overcomes me in spite of such delight, souring its sweetness. I have come to realise that this seemingly inexplicable sense of apprehension is caused by the knowledge that I have just been asked a question that is much easier to ask than it is to answer.

The first difficulty in answering such a question is that I need to know more about the person asking it before I am able to offer an adequate reply. Does he prefer fiction or non-fiction? Does he like poetry? Is he the type of reader who likes to battle with the big questions of metaphysics, or does he prefer the truth served up in bite-sized (or byte-sized) chunks? I feel that I would have to sit down with my interlocutor and become his inquisitor, preferably over a pint or two of ale or a glass or two of wine. Since time seldom affords us the luxury of such pleasures, it becomes necessary to cut to the chase. Therefore, and in the absence of all the necessary data, I offer the eminently sensible suggestion that he begins his study of Chesterton by buying my own biography of him! Such a solution has the added bonus of offering him the opportunity to instantly gratify his new-found enthusiasm for GKC by purchasing a copy of the said volume even as he speaks, ample stocks of which are available at the author's book-table at which he is presently standing.

In defence of such shameless salesmanship, and in defiance of those who wish to scoff, I explain that my biography is peppered throughout with liberal and lengthy quotations from many of Chesterton's works. These serve as an appetizer or a sampler of GK's considerable corpus, an hors d'oeuvre to his oeuvre.

But let's return to our original question and try to answer it in general terms in spite of our knowledge that every man is not Everyman and that, therefore, he will differ in his preferences from his fellow men. Should our interlocutor prefer fiction, he should be told that *The Man Who was Thursday* is indubitably Chesterton's finest novel but that, on the other hand, it is less accessible and perhaps less fun than *The Ball and the Cross*. It is certainly more confusing on a first reading, whereas *The Ball and the Cross* offers the reader an unabashed battle between its Catholic and atheist protagonists in decidedly unambiguous terms. If he prefers poetry, he should be introduced to *The Ballad of the White Horse* or to "Lepanto" but should not be deprived of the delights of Chesterton's less ambitious voyages into verse, such as "The Donkey," "The Fish," "The Skeleton," or "The Rolling English Road"; nor should he be allowed to overlook relatively unknown and priceless gems, such as "The Strange Music" and "The Crystal." If he wants to do battle with the great metaphysical truths underpinning reality, he should grapple with the acrobatic brilliance of *The Everlasting Man* or *Orthodoxy*. If he wants hagiography worthy of hallowing to the heights, he should read GKC's pen portraits of St. Thomas Aquinas or St. Francis of Assisi. And we have not even mentioned the works of literary biography, or the detective stories, or the works of history, politics or economics. Or the essays.

As to the last, it is a sorry fact that Chesterton's essays are sadly neglected in relation to the rest of his corpus, and this in spite of the fact that Chesterton is one of the finest essayists ever to grace the English language. And as for this particular essay, if it has allowed me to wallow self-indulgently in *la crème de la crème* of Chestertonian *belles-lettres*, I offer no apology for the indulgence. Indeed, if bathing luxuriously in the cream of Chesterton is a crime, it is a crime that everyone should commit. Let's all become partners in cream!

[Having soured the cream of Chesterton with the worst of puns, the author exits stage left, rather hurriedly, to a chorus of boos and hisses . . .]

48. THE NOVELS OF G. K. CHESTERTON AND C. S. LEWIS

The towering figures of G. K. Chesterton and C. S. Lewis straddle the twentieth-century literary landscape like beacons of faith and reason, shining forth in the fog and murk of modernity. Their combined legacy as indomitable Christian apologists in an age of skepticism is without equal in the English-speaking world. Taking up the mantle of their illustrious nineteenth-century forebear, John Henry Newman, who blazed the trail that they would follow, Chesterton and Lewis were in the vanguard of the Christian cultural revival that produced some of the greatest literary works of the past 150 years. Although both men are known for their lucid and accessible exposition of Christian doctrine in their works of non-fiction, most notably in Chesterton's *Orthodoxy* and *The Everlasting Man* and in Lewis's *Mere Christianity*, it would be true to say of both writers that some of their finest apologetics is to be found in their works of fiction.

Born in 1874, G. K. Chesterton burst upon the literary scene as a journalist and controversialist at the beginning of the last century and continued to pour forth works of effervescent wit and wisdom until his death in 1936. He was in every sense of the word a man of letters who indulged his magnificent and magnanimous gifts across every literary genre. As an essayist, he ranks among the finest stylists in the English language, peppering his prose with the lively spice of paradox. As a poet, he is remembered primarily for his poem "Lepanto," about the Christian victory over the Muslim fleet in 1571, and also for his poetic epic, *The Ballad of the White Horse*, which recounts the struggles of the Christian king, Alfred the Great, against the invading Vikings and their seemingly indomitable paganism. Other poetry, such as "The Donkey," "The Secret People," and "The Rolling English Road" remain well-known and well-loved and are often anthologized. He was also a literary critic of the first order writing studies of William Blake, Robert Browning and Geoffrey Chaucer. His study of Charles Dickens was greatly admired by T. S. Eliot, and his panoramic survey, *The Victorian Age in Literature*, remains the best introduction to this golden age of English letters.

Chesterton's biographies of St. Francis of Assisi and St. Thomas Aquinas were hugely popular and have remained so, the latter being judged by the celebrated Thomist, Etienne Gilson, as one of the finest studies of Aquinas ever written. As already mentioned, Chesterton's seminal apologetic works, *Orthodoxy* and *The Everlasting Man*, were hugely influential and have been cited by many converts as being instrumental on their journeys in faith.

No appraisal of Chesterton's legacy would be complete, however, without due consideration being given to the importance of his works of fiction. Best known for his invention of the priest detective, Father Brown, Chesterton was also the author of several full-length novels, each of which can be classified as a theological thriller. His first novel, *The Napoleon of Notting Hill* (1904), looks at the perennially important and perennially ignored issue of subsidiarity. As defined in *The Catechism of the Catholic Church*, the principle of subsidiarity stipulates that "a community of a higher order should not interfere in the internal life of a community of a lower order, depriving the latter of its functions, but rather should support it in case of need and help to co-ordinate its activity with the activities of the rest of society, always with a view to the common good." To define the term with less subtle finesse but with more succinct frankness, subsidiarity implies that small government is generally better than big government, and that small business is generally better than big business. In consequence, and as the *Catechism* makes clear, "the principle of subsidiarity is opposed to all forms of collectivism. It sets limits for state intervention. It aims at harmonizing the relationships between individuals and societies." It was this principle, taught by Pope Leo XIII in his encyclical *Rerum novarum* (1891) and championed by Chesterton and his friend Hilaire Belloc in their advocacy of what became known as distributism, which was the principal inspiration for Chesterton's first sortie into the realm of fiction. Another related source of inspiration was the Boer War (1899-1902) in which the might of the British Empire sought to crush the independent agrarian spirit of the Afrikaner nation in South Africa. Chesterton had opposed Britain's role in the war and much of the spirit of the small nation defying the large empire percolates through the pages of *The Napoleon of Notting Hill*. Amongst the novel's admirers was George Orwell, whose novel *Nineteen Eighty-Four* was inspired, at least in part, by Chesterton's book. It is curious, for instance, that Chesterton set *The Napoleon of*

Notting Hill in the year 1984 and it has been conjectured that this may have been the inspiration for Orwell's selection of this particular date for the setting of his own dystopian fantasy about big government crushing the spirit of freedom.

The Man Who was Thursday (1908) is generally considered to be Chesterton's greatest fictional achievement. Subtitled "a nightmare," it has been compared with Franz Kafka's nightmarish *Metamorphosis*. Making such a comparison, C. S. Lewis wrote that "while both give a powerful picture of the loneliness and bewilderment which each one of us encounters in his (apparently) single-handed struggle with the universe, Chesterton, attributing to the universe a more complicated disguise, and admitting the exhilaration as well as the terror of the struggle, has got in rather more; is more balanced: in that sense, more classical, more permanent . . ." In essence, *The Man Who was Thursday* is Chesterton's exorcizing of the spirit of nihilism which had led him to the brink of despair when he was a young man. Under the influence of the decadent aestheticism of Oscar Wilde, and seduced for a while by the radical pessimism of Schopenhauer, Chesterton had felt himself crushed by fundamental doubt in his youth. Emerging from this nihilistic nirvana and embracing the philosophy of Christian realism, Chesterton's great philosophical novel exposes the sophistry of irrational doubt with the clarity of faith and reason.

If *The Man Who Was Thursday* is Chesterton's deepest and most difficult novel, *The Ball and the Cross* (1910) is his brightest and most dazzling. It's a swashbuckling romp through England and France in which the two protagonists, an honest atheist and an honest Catholic, seek to fight a duel in defence of their principles. In endeavouring to do so, they find themselves at war with a world that puts convenience and pragmatism before self-sacrifice and principle. With its many twists and turns, the novel celebrates the value and virtue of the quest for truth amidst the worldliness of indifference.

Manalive (1911) contrasts the intrinsic wisdom of innocence with the willful naïveté of cynicism. Its main character, the symbolically named Innocent Smith, is misunderstood because his innocence is inaccessible to those around him. He is so innocent that they think he must be guilty and so honest that they believe he must be lying. The novel is, therefore, a meditation on the nature and supernature of sanctity and serves as an exposition of the reasons that saints are misunderstood by sinners and are indeed often martyred by them.

The Flying Inn (1914) is a rumbustious romp in defence of traditional

Christian freedom and conviviality in the face of the puritanism of Islam, on the one hand, and the secular asceticism of George Bernard Shaw and his ilk, on the other. Chesterton had criticized Shaw for his militant vegetarianism and teetotalism, and for his belief that the state should impose its puritanically socialist will on the populace. The novel likens the temperance movement in the west, with its demands for the outlawing of alcoholic beverages, with the intolerance of Islam. As such, it serves as a prophecy of the experiment in Prohibition in the United States and also as a warning against the rise of socialist intolerance, epitomized perhaps by the rise of Hitler who, as a non-smoker, a vegetarian, and a teetotaler, represented the sort of secular asceticism that Chesterton lampoons in the novel, especially in his characterization of the novel's antagonist, Lord Ivywood. Hitler, as a vegetarian teetotalitarian, could be seen as the character of Lord Ivywood taken to its logical extreme. At its deepest, therefore, *The Flying Inn* is a celebration of Christian freedoms against the forces of non-Christian and anti-Christian intolerance.

Like his illustrious forebear, C. S. Lewis was also a man of letters who wrote in many different literary genres. Born in 1898, he began with a fervent desire to be considered a poet but was disheartened by the lukewarm response that his poetry received from the critics. Thereafter, he abandoned poetry for prose and became known for works of literary criticism, as well as for works of Christian apologetics. Apart from his most influential work, *Mere Christianity*, he wrote several other important works of non-fiction, most notably *Miracles*, in which he makes a convincing philosophical case for the intervention of the supernatural in the natural order. He is, however, best known for his fictional works, most especially perhaps for *The Chronicles of Narnia* (1950–56), a series of seven novels written for children. Although ostensibly for a younger readership, the Narnian Chronicles are so full of profound theological and philosophical insights that they offer spiritual and intellectual nourishment to readers of all ages. In particular, the climax to *The Last Battle*, the final book in the series, contains some of the finest eschatological theology in the English language. It is indeed a proof of Lewis's genius that he can embed such mystical profundity within the text of a children's story.

Lewis's earliest sortie into fiction was *The Pilgrim's Regress* (1933), a formal allegory which is a largely autobiographical account of Lewis' own conversion from atheism to Christianity. Journeying from his childhood home in Puritania, representing the puritanical Calvinism that Lewis experienced as a child in Northern Ireland, the protagonist, "John," meets various personified abstractions, representing the ideas Lewis encountered in his journey towards conversion, including the spirits of the Enlightenment and of Romanticism, and the Spirit of the Age, the last of which is overthrown by Reason, personified as a beautiful maiden on a horse. Eventually, and reluctantly, John submits to Mother Kirk (Mother Church) and is baptized.

If *The Pilgrim's Regress* was clearly modeled after its progenitor, John Bunyan's *The Pilgrim's Progress*, a seventeenth-century formal allegory, *The Great Divorce* (1945) owes an obvious debt to Dante's *Inferno* in its exploration of the psychology of the damned. As we meet the various doomed souls, each of whom rejects the love of God and the grace being offered, it becomes clear that God does not condemn anyone to hell. Those in hell freely choose to go there, preferring the alienated Self to the Communion of Love. The same masterful understanding of the human psyche is present in *The Screwtape Letters* (1942), in which Lewis plays devil's advocate in order to expose the diabolical nature of sin.

The Space Trilogy, sometimes also known as the Cosmic Trilogy or the Ransom Trilogy, is a series of science fiction novels in which Lewis counters the progressivism and scientism of the previous generation of science fiction writers, such as H. G. Wells. In *Out of the Silent Planet* (1938), the first of the series, Lewis deploys the character of Elwin Ransom, a middle-aged philologist modeled on Lewis's friend J. R. R. Tolkien, to counter the ideas of Dr. Weston, a mad physicist modeled in part on the egocentric humanism of Wells and his ilk. Having been kidnapped by Weston and his accomplice Dick Devine, Ransom is taken to Malacandra (Mars), where the three men meet various strange beings, most notably the angelic eldila, whose wisdom exposes the shallow and narrowly bigoted nature of Weston's philosophical materialism.

In the second book of the Trilogy, *Perelandra* (1943), the action takes place on Venus to which Ransom has been sent to counter the designs of the Black Oyarsa of Thulcandra (Satan). He once again encounters his old enemy Dr. Weston, whose presence on the planet threatens the primal and unfallen innocence of the Lady, whom Ransom has been sent to protect. The novel then revolves around the dialectical engagement between Ransom and Weston, the former arguing for a traditional Christian understanding of the cosmos and the latter for an arrogant materialism that is eventually exposed as being satanic in its origin and purpose.

In the final book of the Trilogy, *That Hideous Strength* (1945), Ransom, who is now older and has become something of a mystic, is the voice of sanity and sanctity in a world darkened by the forces of materialism. Set against the backdrop of an England in the grips of scientism, the novel is kaleidoscopic in its mixing of seemingly incompatible literary genres. Ostensibly a science fiction story, it incorporates an Arthurian dimension in the presence of the resurrected Merlin, and presents a plethora of modern ideologies and philosophies in an unholy alliance against the forces of goodness and truth.

Lewis's final work of fiction, and the one that he believed was his best, is *Till We Have Faces* (1956), a retelling of the ancient myth of Cupid and Psyche from Apuleius's *Metamorphoses*. This is much more subtle than Lewis' other fiction in its handling of the allegorical dimension, leaving many of Lewis's admirers confused by its apparent obliqueness. At root, the novel is an exploration of the nature of faith, particularly from the perspective of one who lacks it. Lewis makes Psyche's palace invisible to mortal eyes and thereby presents a challenge to those who can't see it. The way in which Orual, the protagonist, responds to this hidden reality provides the dynamism of the plot.

Although Chesterton and Lewis approach the writing of fiction very differently, their novels serve the same purpose. Both writers aim to engage with the intellectual currents of the modern age in order to highlight the fallacious nature of modernity's view of reality and to show the perennial and prevailing wisdom of Christianity. Chesterton's swashbuckling adventures, awash with humour and almost dreamlike in their lurid surrealism, and Lewis's voyages to other planets and to the gloomy world of the afterlife are intended to awaken us from the nightmare of nihilism so that we can rise from our bed of sleep to the dawning of the miraculous day that God has given us.

49. ELIOT AND HIS AGE

As much as it might hate to admit it, the secular culture is greatly indebted to the Catholic Cultural Revival. From the roots of the revival in the Romantic reaction against the secular rationalism of the Enlightenment to the fruits of its mellifluous manifestations in the twentieth century, the Catholic Cultural Revival has bestowed its benisons on the hostile world in which it finds itself. Since T. S. Eliot is one of the fruits of this revival it is appropriate that we should look at his place within the larger literary landscape; it is fitting to see where he fits.

The stream of literary converts that formed the wellspring of the Catholic Revival makes for impressive reading: Newman, Patmore, Hopkins, Wilde, Baring, Benson, Knox, Chesterton, Greene, Eliot, Waugh, Campbell, Sitwell, Sassoon etc., etc. Although Eliot belongs in this list he is nonetheless something of an odd man out. Unlike the others he never submitted to Rome, preferring to declare himself a "Catholic" within the Church of England, a so-called Anglo-Catholic. His reason appears to have been rooted in an Anglophilia bordering on Anglomania. As a native American trying too hard to become an honorary Englishman, he imbibed the English prejudice against Rome and clung to the beleaguered belief that Anglicanism was somehow apostolic. As the neo-Thomist philosopher Jacques Maritain quipped, "Eliot exhausted his capacity for conversion when he became an Englishman."

In spite of such folly, Eliot *is* a Catholic writer, much more so than that other great convert to Anglicanism, C. S. Lewis, and much more than writers who are technically more "Catholic," such as Graham Greene. Whereas Greene toyed with heterodoxy, playing with fire for the sheer hell of it, one would search in vain for any infelicitous *faux pas* against orthodoxy in the works of Eliot. Greene, gangrened with doubt and self-loathing, lapsed into the folly of mortal sin, the fatal *felo-de-se*; Eliot, healed by faith and humility, rose to the fullness of grace, the fruitful *auto-da-fé*. Greene protested that he was not a Catholic writer but a writer who happened to be Catholic; Eliot ironically was very much a Catholic writer who happened not to be Catholic.

As for the age in which Eliot wrote, the 1920s and '30s, the age he condemned as a wasteland, it paralleled in many respects the wasteland that had provoked and inspired the Romantic reaction of Wordsworth and Coleridge more than a century earlier. Like his Romantic predecessors, Eliot was reacting against an atheistic anti-clericalism that had spawned a revolution. If Wordsworth and Coleridge were reacting against the debacle of the French Revolution, Eliot was recoiling from the debauchery of the Bolshevik Revolution. In "England, 1802" Wordsworth had described modern England as "a fen of stagnant waters," in which the wasteland of modernity takes the form of a swamp. Similarly the allegorical dimension in Coleridge's "The Rime of the Ancient Mariner" resonates uncannily with the fragmentary hints of conversion and resurrection which emerge in Eliot's *The Waste Land*. In both these works the deepest truths are revealed tantalizingly through their being re-veiled tarantellically in a web of wyrd-woven intensity.

Since "in my beginning is my end," as Eliot asserted at the beginning of "East Coker," paradoxically echoing and inverting the motto of Mary Stuart, I shall end as I began by reminding the secular culture that it is greatly in debt to the Catholic Cultural Revival. One of the finest poems of the eighteenth century, *me iudice*, is "The Rime of the Ancient Mariner," a poem which is awash with allusions to Catholic conceptions of grace; one of the finest poems of the nineteenth century is "The Wreck of The Deutschland" by Gerard Manley Hopkins, the Jesuit and mystic who showered the world with the innovative dynamism of orthodoxy in poesis. As for the finest poem of the twentieth century, it is hard to choose between *The Waste Land* and *Four Quartets*, both by T. S. Eliot. Whether one prefers the former, a jeremiad of unsurpassed subtlety, or the latter, an ecstasy worthy of the mystic flights of St John of the Cross, the conclusion remains the same and remains as unmistakable. T. S. Eliot is not merely a giant in his age but is a colossus who will cross the abyss of the ages. A great poet, and Eliot is surely one of the greatest, is not merely of "his age" but of all ages. *Atque in perpetuum, frater, ave!*

50. ROY CAMPBELL REMEMBERED

Roy Campbell exploded onto the British literary scene in May 1924 with the publication of *The Flaming Terrapin*, a vibrantly original tour de force that challenged the prevailing nihilism of the period with an unbridled zest for life. The sheer verve, vigour and irrepressible energy of the poem won over the critics, one of whom wrote with breathless excitement about the "exuberant relish of the sheer sonority and clangour of words, words enjoyed for their own gust, and flung down to fit each other with an easy rapture of phrase."[76] Almost overnight, the twenty-two-year-old had been rocketed into the ranks of the illustrissimi of English letters. And yet, almost ninety years later, posterity seems to have relegated him to a place among the lowly footnotes of twentieth-century literature, in which he is remembered more for his friendships and enmities with more illustrious contemporaries than as a poet in his own right. The impression that his legacy has left on twentieth-century literature is that of a muse that burst into glorious flame in a dazzling display of prosodic pyrotechnics and then fizzled out, or rather sputtered and sparked without ever really catching fire again. Such an impression is justified, up to a point, to the extent that Campbell seldom, if ever, reached the heights to which he ascended in *The Flaming Terrapin*. Whereas T. S. Eliot eclipsed the youthful brilliance of *The Waste Land* with the maturity of *Four Quartets*, his magnum opus, Campbell's youthful brilliance seems to eclipse all that followed it. It might almost be said that he never grew up, artistically speaking.

As with all sweeping statements the preceding one requires an element of qualification. If it is true that Campbell never improved upon the dash and dare of his earliest work, it is emphatically not true to dismiss his other work as being of little worth or even worthless. On the contrary, Campbell remains one of the major poets of the twentieth century and much of the rest of his corpus warrants a place in the cannon, its ignominious exclusion from which constitutes nothing less than a literary scandal.

Broadly speaking, Campbell's corpus can be divided into several periods. There are the African poems, the Provençal poems, the Spanish poems, the British poems, and the Portuguese poems.

It is in the African poems that Campbell comes closest to capturing the breathless brilliance of *The Flaming Terrapin*. In "Zulu Song," "Zulu Girl" and "The Serf" he displays a degree of formal discipline and lyrical flourish that is seldom achieved in much of his later verse, and in "The Sisters" he gallops erotically alongside his sexually charged subjects, handling his mount with tactfully suggestive dexterity. In "The Theology of Bongwi the Baboon" the poet indulges in theological subversion similar to that indulged in by Yeats in "An Indian Upon God" but does so with a playfulness that is utterly devoid of cynicism. On the contrary its joviality and *joie de vivre* have more in common with the satirical verse of G. K. Chesterton, which becomes apparent if Campbell's poem is read alongside "Race Memory (by a dazed Darwinian)," Chesterton's satire on a similar theme. There is no poetry written in the twentieth century that can match the best of these African poems for invigorating freshness and primitive intensity.

Campbell's muse rekindled something of this freshness after his escape from the puritanical prurience of the Bloomsburys in England and his discovery of the residual Catholicism of Provence. Settling near Martigues, Campbell fell in love with the briny earthiness of the peasants and fishermen with whom he assimilated with consummate ease. The Provençal poems reverberate with enthusiasm for his adoptive culture, embracing the primal matter of soil and sea as a means of seeing the soul of man. The purifying impact of Provence is seen in poems such as "Autumn," in which all is stripped away so that the "clear anatomy" is revealed in its quintessential simplicity, and it also surfaces in the religious imagery that begins to proliferate at this time. The presence of Catholic imagery in the absence of Catholic faith is exemplified most poignantly in the tranquil agnosticism of "Mass at Dawn," whereas the embryonic desire for faith is evident in the imagery of "Saint Peter of the Three Canals" in which the apparently faithless frivolity of the early verses makes way for the tacit acceptance or desire for faith implicit in its invocatory finale.

It was not, however, until the poet's arrival in Spain in 1933 that the Faith finally claimed the poet, or, at least, that the poet finally acclaimed the Faith,

> under the stretched, terrific wings,
> the outspread arms (our soaring King's) —
> the man they made an Albatross![77]

Campbell's conversion to Catholicism unfolds majestically in his sonnet sequence, "Mithraic Emblems," the earliest of which were written in

Provence and the last of which were written in Spain. Taken as a whole they display a soul in transit. Whereas the early sonnets show the poet groping with an uncomprehended and incomprehensible paganism, the later sonnets show an emergent Christianity that does not so much vanquish Mithraism as make sense of it. In the final sonnets, the sun is no longer a god to be worshipped, but only a symbol of the Son, the true God, who gives the sun its meaning and purpose. The Mithraic emblem is transformed by Christian typology and becomes Christ transfigured:

> Oh let your shining orb grow dim,
> Of Christ the mirror and the shield,
> That I may gaze through you to Him,
> See half the miracle revealed.[78]

Campbell's reception into the Catholic Church on 24 June 1935 confirmed him in his love for Spain, which he later described as "a country to which I owe everything as having saved my soul."[79] It also accentuated still further his alienation from the secularist ascendancy in British literature, an alienation that had been expressed with shrill abandon in his verse satire *The Georgiad* two years earlier. Campbell's conversion would also serve to alienate him from the new generation of socialist poets, such as Stephen Spender, W. H. Auden, Louis MacNeice and Cecil Day-Lewis, an alienation that would become bitterly combative when Campbell's vociferous support for Franco's Nationalist forces in the Spanish Civil War brought him into conflict with the equally vociferous support of the new generation of poets for the communist and anarchist Republican forces.

Campbell's position as an outsider was confirmed by his choice of the "wrong" side during the Spanish Civil War and he was never really accepted thereafter among England's literati, even after he returned to live in London at the end of the Second World War. There were exceptions, such as his friendship with J. R. R. Tolkien, C. S. Lewis, Edith Sitwell and Dylan Thomas, but for the most part Campbell had become something of a pariah. This is perhaps the real reason that he is seldom read and studied these days. It is not so much for any real or alleged deficiency in his poetry that he is neglected, as for a supercilious refusal to accept the dissident voice in an age of "political correctness."

Roy Campbell was a great poet but he was also a great man, in the sense that he was larger than life. Finding oneself in his company is to find oneself intoxicated with the pure pleasure of his presence. One would like to meet him in the flesh, perhaps in that tavern at the world's end that Chesterton mentions, in which we will meet "Dickens and all his characters." In the absence of such a celestial rendezvous, a meeting with Campbell in the terrestrial presence of his poems is pleasure enough.

51. TOLKIEN AND LEWIS:
MASTERS OF MYTH, TELLERS OF TRUTH

> "I have left behind illusion," I said to myself. "Henceforth I live in a world of three dimensions—with the aid of my five senses."
>
> I have since learned that there is no such world, but then, as the car turned out of sight of the house, I thought it took no finding, but lay all about me at the end of the avenue.[80]

Charles Ryder's thoughts upon leaving Brideshead for what he thought would be the last time, and his own later judgment on those thoughts, convey a great deal about the nature and supernature of the reality to which we are all subject. Like the young and naïve Charles Ryder, materialists insist that the supernatural is merely an illusion; only when we have "left behind illusion" are we able to see all that there is to see, the world of three dimensions—with the aid of our five senses. The problem, as Charles Ryder would come to realise, is that such a world is itself an illusion. There is no such world. The real world, as Hopkins reminds us, "is charged with the grandeur of God." There is simply no escaping His powerful omnipresence. "For God's sake," exclaims Charles Ryder to the Jesuitical Bridey, "why bring God into everything?" Ryder's question strikes the dauntlessly (theo)logical Bridey as "extremely funny." Whether Ryder knows it or not, God *is* in everything and "into everything." He is inescapable. Unavoidable.

It is the inescapable and unavoidable presence of God that makes myth such a powerful conveyer of reality. If the essential ingredients of reality, of life, are not physical but metaphysical, it follows that true stories must reflect these metaphysical realities. If goodness, truth, beauty and love are at the heart of all that is truly real, and if these things transcend the three dimensions and the five senses, it follows that stories must convey this essential transcendence in order to be real and true. Any story that fails to convey this mystical transcendence and remains solely within a world of three dimensions and five senses will not only be lacking in reality, it will be dead. Lifeless.

And so it is that J. R. R. Tolkien and C. S. Lewis are tellers of truth and masters of myth. The Ainulindalë in *The Silmarillion* is a hymn of praise to the Great Music of God's Creation, as is Aslan's singing of Narnia into Being in *The Magician's Nephew*. In their powerful and poetic evocation of the beauty and harmony at the heart of the cosmos, Tolkien and Lewis are singing in creative harmony with Dante's vision of Paradise and Lorenzo's reverence for the Music of the Spheres in *The Merchant of Venice*:

> Look how the floor of heaven
> Is thick inlaid with patines of bright gold:
> There's not the smallest orb which thou behold'st
> But in his motion like an angel sings,
> Still quiring to the young-eyed cherubins;
> Such harmony is in immortal souls;
> But whilst this muddy vesture of decay
> Doth grossly close it in, we cannot hear it.[81]

Tolkien, Lewis, Dante and Shakespeare share the knowledge that it is Love that moves the sun and the other stars, and that the cosmos is the first and greatest Love Song. These great writers live in an *enchanted* world which has been sung into existence. And here we need to remind ourselves that the word enchantment derives from the Latin *cantare*, "to sing," as in Gregorian Chant, and has nothing to do with the modern corruption of language which has made enchantment synonymous with bewitchment. (To hell with the Devil's deconstruction of language and heaven preserve us from his post-modern disciples in the academy!) And while we're on the thorny subject of language-abuse, we should insist that history is not about "superstition" and "enlightenment" but about "enchantment" and "disenchantment." The so-called "Enlightenment" was hardly enlightened in its rejection of the realism of Plato, Aristotle, Augustine and Aquinas in favour of the nominalism of William of Ockham. It was, however, disenchanted. It rejected that the cosmos had been brought into existence by a beneficent Creator, the Prime Mover, First Cause and Great Composer of the cosmos, and insisted instead that it was all a highly unlikely accident! It was not meant to happen, it was not made to happen, it simply "happened." There's no purpose, no meaning, no music. There's only the monotony of matter, a world of three dimensions perceived by our five senses. Such a world does not exist in reality, as Charles Ryder came to understand, but its non-existence does not prevent the credulous from believing in it. Such believers in Nothing have no music in their souls, no harmony in their hearts and, as Lorenzo reminds us, cannot be trusted:

> The man that hath no music in himself,
> Nor is not moved with concord of sweet sounds,
> Is fit for treasons, stratagems and spoils;
> The motions of his spirit are dull as night
> And his affections dark as Erebus:
> Let no such man be trusted. Mark the music.[82]

In the face of such faithless and irrational disenchantment Tolkien and Lewis have blessed us with powerful works of re-enchantment. They remind us that disenchantment is the False Myth, the ultimate Lie that denies the very cause and source of things, whereas, in contrast, re-enchantment reawakens us to the True Myth and the Great Music. This is true reason, and it is for this reason that Tolkien and Lewis, as masters of myth, can be trusted as tellers of truth.

52. NARNIA AND MIDDLE EARTH: WHEN TWO WORLDS COLLUDE

Back in 1997 several major opinion polls in the United Kingdom confirmed the place of *The Lord of the Rings* by J. R. R. Tolkien as the most popular book of the twentieth century.[83] A few years later, from the release of *The Fellowship of the Ring* in December 2001 until the release of *The Return of the King* two years later, Peter Jackson's three-part film version of Tolkien's epic became the movie phenomenon of the new century. Now, and no doubt inspired by the success of Jackson's blockbuster, Walt Disney Studios and Walden Media are in the midst of releasing films based on *The Chronicles of Narnia* in the hope that the children's classic by C. S. Lewis can emulate the success of Tolkien.

It is indeed singularly appropriate that Lewis should be following in the footsteps of his great friend, Tolkien, not least because, as we shall see, he was following in Tolkien's footsteps when he wrote *The Chronicles of Narnia*. It would in fact not be an exaggeration to describe Lewis as a follower of Tolkien, at least in the area of what might be termed their shared philosophy of myth. A look at the history of their friendship will illustrate how Lewis was greatly influenced by his friend and how Tolkien, for his part, benefited greatly from the encouragement he received from Lewis during his writing of *The Lord of the Rings*.

In his autobiography, *Surprised by Joy*, C. S. Lewis described how his first meeting with Tolkien had forced him to confront his own prejudices: "At my first coming into the world I had been (implicitly) warned never to trust a Papist, and at my first coming into the English Faculty (explicitly) never to trust a philologist. Tolkien was both."[84] Lewis's upbringing in the sectarian atmosphere of Belfast had coloured the way in which he perceived "papists" (Catholics) and the prejudice persisted long after his Protestant faith had dissolved. Having lost the lukewarm Christian faith of his childhood, Lewis was a somewhat reluctant atheist at the time that he and Tolkien had first met in Oxford in May 1926. Lewis's first impressions of Tolkien as "a smooth, pale, fluent little chap"[85] gave no indication that he saw in Tolkien someone with whom he was destined to form a long and enduring friendship. The touchstone of their friendship, and the touchwood that ignited it, was their shared love for mythology.

Tolkien, six years Lewis's senior, soon became not merely a friend but a mentor. In December 1929, Lewis wrote to a friend that he had been up until the early hours of the morning "talking to the Anglo-Saxon professor Tolkien . . . discoursing of the gods and giants of Asgard for three hours," adding that "the fire was bright and the talk was good."[86] If Lewis had found in Tolkien a kindred spirit who shared his love for the Norse myths, it seems that Tolkien also detected in Lewis a soul with whom he could share his own creative endeavours at myth-making. Taking Lewis into his confidence he lent him his poem on Beren and Luthien, two heroic characters who would be alluded to in *The Lord of the Rings* and who would finally emerge as central figures in *The Silmarillion* following its eventual publication almost half a century later. On 7 December, Lewis wrote to Tolkien expressing his enthusiasm:

> I can quite honestly say that it is ages since I have had an evening of such delight: and the personal interest of reading a friend's work had very little to do with it—I should have enjoyed it just as well if I'd picked it up in a bookshop, by an unknown author. The two things that come out clearly are the sense of reality in the background and the mythical value: the essence of a myth being that it should have no taint of allegory to the maker and yet should *suggest* incipient allegories to the reader.[87]

The last sentence has a particular resonance with regard to the work of both writers because it touches upon aspects of the philosophy of myth which inspired their creative vision and underpinned their respective literary works. Take, for instance, Lewis's denial, in the following letter to school-children written in 1954, that *The Chronicles of Narnia* were "allegorical" in any crudely formal or clumsily intentional way:

> You are mistaken when you think that everything in the books "represents" something in this world. Things do that in *The Pilgrim's Progress* but I'm not writing in that way. I did not say to myself "Let us represent Jesus as He really is in our world by a Lion in Narnia": I said "Let us *suppose* that there were a land

like Narnia and that the Son of God, as He became a Man in our world, became a Lion there, and then imagine what would have happened." If you think about it, you will see that it is quite a different thing.[88]

Clearly Lewis was at pains to distance the Narnian stories from the sort of formal or crude allegory of which *The Pilgrim's Progress* is perhaps the most obvious exemplar (although it is noteworthy that Lewis succumbed to the genre of formal allegory himself with great success in the semi-autobiographical *The Pilgrim's Regress*). It is also evident from his discussion of the issue in *The Allegory of Love* that Lewis understood that there is a crucial distinction between formal allegory and what could be called informal allegory, the latter being the allegory of applicable significance which is almost universally present, to one degree or another, in literature and beyond.

> Allegory, in some sense, belongs not to medieval man but to man, or even to mind, in general. It is of the very nature of thought and language to represent what is immaterial in picturable terms. What is good or happy has always been high like the heavens and bright like the sun.[89]

Lewis distinguished this broad definition of allegory from formal allegory, which he defined thus:

> . . . you can start with an immaterial fact, such as the passions which you actually experience, and can then invent *visibilia* [visible things] to express them. If you are hesitating between an angry retort and a soft answer, you can express your state of mind by inventing a person called *Ira* [Anger] with a torch and letting her contend with another invented person called *Patientia* [patience]. This is allegory.[90]

In fact, *pace* Lewis and in view of his earlier broader definition, this is not an instance of allegory *per se* but of *formal* allegory.

Perhaps at this juncture it might be helpful to look at the whole question of allegory, formal and informal, in more detail.

Saint Augustine wrote about the most basic level of allegory with unexcelled eloquence in *De doctrina Christiana* (*On Christian Doctrine*) in which he discussed "signs." In the case of all signs, the thing signified can only be ascertained through a process of quasi-allegorical applicability. One must know that a three-letter word, dog, signifies a certain type of four-legged mammal, or that the same three letters, when arranged in reverse order, signify the supreme being and creator of the universe (if the g is in upper case) or some lesser being of supernatural power (if the g is in lower case). In each case a leap of imaginative applicability needs to be made from the "dead" letter of the literal thing or things being used as signs to the "living" meaning signified. This involves allegory, at least in the broadest and most basic sense in which the word is used.

Moving from the most basic understanding of allegory to what could be seen as the strictest and most elaborate, Saint Thomas Aquinas asserted that there were four levels of meaning in Scripture, namely the literal, the allegorical, the moral and the anagogical. It is of course arguable that this four-fold exegesis is not applicable to literature as a whole and is only applicable to, and appropriate for, a theological reading of the Bible. Such a view was not shared by the author of arguably the greatest work of literature ever written. Dante insisted that his magnificent poem, *The Divine Comedy*, should be read according to Saint Thomas's four-fold method.[91] This is interesting within the context of our understanding of Narnia and Middle Earth because Dante's magnum opus is not a formal allegory. Dante, Virgil, Beatrice and the various individuals they meet on their travels are principally themselves. They are not mere personified abstractions. On the literal level, Dante is himself; it is only on the level of allegory that he can be seen as Everyman. Virgil is himself, or the ghost of himself; it is only on the allegorical level that he can be seen as the summit of human Reason or Wisdom unassisted by Christian Revelation. Beatrice is herself, albeit, no doubt, an idealized form of herself as purified by Dante's imagination; it is only on the allegorical level that she can be seen as signifying a Bearer of the Light of Grace. Similarly Dante does not meet seven deadly monsters named Pride, Envy, Lust, etc., representing the seven deadly sins, as he would have done had his work been a formal allegory; he meets real historical people who were guilty of these sins. In short, the story can be read purely on the literal level, and no doubt enjoyed as such, although it is greatly enriched when understood on the other levels of allegorical significance.

This discussion of the meaning and nature of allegory is essential to a true and deeper understanding of the work of both Lewis and Tolkien. Generally, though not exclusively, Lewis and Tolkien tended to use the word "allegory" in its formal sense. Thus Lewis in his letter to the schoolchildren could deny that Aslan is allegorical and Tolkien could say that he "despised" allegory and that *The Lord of the Rings* "is neither allegorical nor topical."[92] On the other hand, and on other occasions, Lewis could write that the "whole Narnian story is about Christ"[93] and Tolkien could write that "*The Lord of the Rings* is of course a fundamentally religious and Catholic work."[94] Since Christ is never mentioned by name in either Narnia or Middle Earth the Christian significance in both works is only discernible through leaps of imaginative applicability that is certainly allegorical in the looser and broader sense of the word. How else does one discern Christ in Narnia except through making allegorical connections? How else does one unravel the "fundamentally religious and Catholic" dimension in Middle-earth without seeking and discovering the levels of Christian allegory with which the works of Tolkien are awash?

In order to understand more fully these allegorical connections in the works of Lewis and Tolkien it is necessary to return to the philosophy of myth that they shared. Tolkien's philosophy of myth, destined to have such a profound influence on Lewis, was conveyed most memorably in his poem "Mythopoeia," which was written "To one who said that myths were lies and therefore worthless, even though 'breathed through silver.'" The "one" to whom this dedication referred was Lewis himself who had claimed that myths were merely beautiful lies during a conversation on mythology in Oxford in September 1931, a conversation that has now been enshrined as being pivotal to Lewis's final embrace of Christianity. "*No*," Tolkien had replied emphatically. "*They are not*"."[95] He followed this blunt rebuttal with a lucid exposition of the nature and supernature of mythology which can be summarized as follows[96]:

Since we are made in the image of God and since we know that God is the Creator, it follows that our creativity is the expression of the *imageness* of God in us. As such, all myths, as the product of human creativity, contain splintered fragments of the one true light that comes from God. Far from being lies they are a means of gaining an inkling of the deep truths of metaphysical reality. God is the Creator, the only being able to make things from nothing, whereas we are sub-creators, beings made in God's creative image who are able to partake of His Creative Gift by making new things from other things that already exist. Put simply, we tell our stories with words, God tells His Story with History. The fact that Facts serve the Truth is another way of saying that Providence prevails. In essence, Tolkien believed that Christianity is the True Myth, the myth that really happened. It is the archetypal myth that makes sense of all the others. It is the Myth to which all other myths are in some way a reflection, a myth that works in the same way as all the others except that it exists in the realm of fact as well as in the realm of truth.

For Tolkien the pagan myths, far from being lies, were, in fact, God expressing Himself through the minds of poets, using the images of their "mythopoeia" to reveal fragments of His eternal truth. Most astonishing of all, Tolkien maintained that Christianity was exactly the same except for the enormous difference that the poet who invented it was God Himself, and the images He used were real men and actual history.

Tolkien's arguments had an indelible effect on Lewis. Twelve days later, Lewis wrote to his friend, Arthur Greeves, that he had "just passed on from believing in God to definitely believing in Christ," adding that his "long night talk with . . . Tolkien had a good deal to do with it."[97] The full extent of Tolkien's influence can be gauged from another of Lewis's letters to Greeves, written only a month after the "long night talk":

> Now the story of Christ is simply a true myth: a myth working on us in the same way as the others, but with this important difference that *it really happened*: and one must be content to accept it in the same way, remembering that it is God's myth where the others are men's myths: i.e., the Pagan stories are God expressing Himself through the minds of poets, using such images as he found there, while Christianity is God expressing Himself through what we call "real things."[98]

Lewis would expand upon this core thesis in his exposition of the "pictures" of the pagans during Father History's discourse on the difference between the pagans and the Jews in *The Pilgrim's Regress*. It is, however, clear that he owed his initial inspiration to Tolkien's philosophy of myth. It is also clear that the conception of (sub)creativity which underpins this philosophy would have a profound and pronounced effect upon the approach of Lewis and Tolkien towards their own work. It was their shared belief in the *gift* of creativity that led to their dislike of formal allegory. For Tolkien and Lewis formal allegory constituted an abuse of the gift. If one has faith in the powers of the gift, derived from the power of the Giver, one will allow the gift the freedom it needs to breathe life into the creative work. In allowing a story to take on a life of its own a writer allows the gift itself—or, more correctly, the Giver of the gift—to add dimensions of truth beyond the conscious designs of the story-teller. By contrast, in seeking in his pedagogy and didacticism to dominate the reader, the writer of a formal allegory dominates the gift, thereby enslaving it and depriving it of much of its power.

Although Tolkien and Lewis were at such pains to distance their own work from the taint of formal allegory, there are clearly truths to be gleaned from the works that can only be deduced allegorically or, to employ the term that Tolkien preferred, can only be ascertained through a process of "applicability," the process of applying the truths that emerge in the story to the "real world" beyond the story. There are so many of these "applicable" moments in *The Lord of the Rings* that whole books have been written on the subject and there are many more waiting to be written.

The influence of *The Lord of the Rings* on *The Chronicles of Narnia*, and on Lewis's other works, is inestimable. Tolkien read each chapter of *The Lord of the Rings* to Lewis at the weekly meetings of the Inklings as it was being written, and one can only wonder at the wonderful and wonder-filled hours that Tolkien spent in Lewis's company explaining the work during the catalytic process of its creation. Certainly he found in Lewis one of its greatest admirers and advocates both before and after its publication. "The unpayable debt that I owe to him," Tolkien wrote of Lewis, "was not 'influence' as it is ordinarily understood, but sheer encouragement. He was for long my only audience. Only from him did I ever get the idea that my 'stuff' could be more than a private hobby."[99] This view of Lewis's importance as an "encourager" was reiterated by Tolkien in a letter to Professor Clyde Kilby in December 1965: "But for the encouragement of C. S. L. I do not think that I should ever have completed or offered for publication *The Lord of the Rings.*"[100] Lewis's own estimation of the work was expressed in a letter to Tolkien shortly after Lewis had read through the completed typescript of *The Lord of the Rings* in the autumn of 1949. It was, he asserted, "almost unequalled in the whole range of narrative art known to me."[101]

Tolkien's "unpayable debt" to Lewis was repaid more than adequately by Tolkien's positive influence on Lewis's own intellectual, spiritual and creative development. It is, however, a little surprising that Tolkien failed to sympathise with most of Lewis's work. If Lewis had been a great "encourager" to Tolkien he must have been greatly discouraged by Tolkien's lack of enthusiasm for his own efforts at fiction. In 1949, the same year that Lewis was enthusing about the finished typescript of *The Lord of the Rings*, Lewis began to read the first of his "Narnia" stories to the Inklings. This was *The Lion, the Witch and the Wardrobe*, destined to become one of the most popular children's books ever written. Tolkien was unimpressed. "It really won't do!" he exclaimed to Roger Lancelyn Green, a mutual friend who would later become Lewis's biographer. "I mean to say: 'Nymphs and their Ways, The Love Life of a Faun'!"[102] Later, Tolkien would write that it was "sad that 'Narnia' and all that part of C. S. L.'s work should remain outside the range of my sympathy."[103] Why, one wonders, should this be so?

Tolkien's almost obsessive perfectionism led to the expectation of very high standards and an intolerance of the efforts of those who failed to attain such heights. Tolkien must have been aware of his influence on Lewis and must have been aware also that Lewis's creation of Narnia was all too obviously a reflection, albeit a pale reflection in shallower creative waters, of his own creation of Middle Earth. The wistful gravitas of *The Lord of the Rings* grated with the whimsical gaiety of *The Lion, the Witch and the Wardrobe*; hence Tolkien's scoffing at the juxtaposition of mythical creatures worthy of respect, such as nymphs or fauns, with the descent into the vulgar vernacular, "and their Ways" and "Love Life." Similarly, Tolkien would probably have been decidedly uncomfortable with the insertion of inconsistent and incompatible objects into a mythical world, such as lampposts and umbrellas. As a cultural luddite who despised most manifestations of technological "progress" he would have looked upon the gate-crashing of these objects of modernity into the purity of a mythological world as pollutants of the world itself and of the imagination of the reader. Finally, Lewis's work, based upon what he termed "supposals," lacked the subtlety of applicability for which Tolkien strived. For all Lewis's denials that *The Chronicles of Narnia* were an "allegory," it is clear that Aslan is *always* a figure of Christ, albeit a Narnian manifestation of Christ, in all the stories and at each and every moment. Compare this with the subtlety with which Frodo, Gandalf and Aragorn *remind* us of Christ while always remaining themselves and while always being distinct from Christ, even at the moments when they most remind us of Him. Although, strictly speaking, Lewis is right to assert that the "Narnia" stories are not formal allegories, they can be seen to be closer to formal allegories than are the stories of Middle Earth. Put bluntly, one suspects that Tolkien's subtle sensibilities considered Narnia too close to "crude" or "formal" allegory for his liking. One suspects also that Lewis not only understood Tolkien's objections but agreed with them, at least in part. This was probably why Lewis considered his late work, *Till We Have Faces*, to be his "best book" and his "favourite of all my books."[104] In this book, sub-titled *A Myth Retold*, Lewis resists his natural inclination to didacticism and controls his desire to teach his readers a lesson. In consequence, he succeeds for the first time in submerging the allegory within the story with the subtlety that had hitherto eluded him.

In the final analysis, and in spite of Tolkien's criticism of Lewis's work, it would be wrong to suggest that Tolkien had not benefited as greatly as Lewis from their friendship, though in a different way. Tolkien's daughter Priscilla believed that her father owed an "enormous debt" to Lewis,[105] and his son, Christopher, was even more emphatic in his insistence that his father's friendship with Lewis was crucial to his creative achievement. 'The profound attachment and imaginative intimacy between him and Lewis were in some ways the core to it,' he said, adding that their friendship was of "profound importance . . . to both of them."[106] To put the matter in a nutshell, Lewis's debt to Tolkien is that if he had not known Tolkien he would not have written *The Chronicles of Narnia*; Tolkien's debt to Lewis is that if he had not known Lewis he would never have finished *The Lord of the Rings*. Paradoxically, we have Tolkien to thank for Narnia, and Lewis to thank for Middle Earth. Such are the benefits, the power and the glory when two worlds collude.

53. THE CATHOLIC GENIUS OF J. R. R. TOLKIEN

A good book, like a good wine, improves with age. This is so much the case that an objective critical judgment cannot be made on a great work of literature until it has had time to mature. And just as one should not judge a book by its cover, one should not judge a book's literary merit on the fact that it has made the bestseller lists. A book can be very popular at the time that it is published for all sorts of reasons that have little or nothing to do with its literary merit. It can titillate or scandalize, and there are always plenty of people seeking titillation or scandal; or it can follow the latest fads and fashions, and there are always plenty of people seeking to be fashionable; or it can be topical, and there are always plenty of people who are not able to see beyond the end of the news. And yet titillation and scandal are transitory. They serve the desire for instant gratification of our lower passions after which they are tossed aside. And fads and fashions are as facile and fragile as their followers are fickle and feckless. Fads fade because there is nothing as unfashionable as yesterday's fads. And as for topicality, it is as transient as titillation and scandal, and as fading as fashion. Yesterday's news is as newsworthy as yesterday's fashion is fashionable. It is forgotten as instantaneously as it was reported.

One of the finest things about *The Lord of the Rings* is that it made the bestseller lists and has stayed on the bestseller lists without succumbing to any of the pitfalls of popular fiction. It doesn't titillate or scandalize, nor does it follow fashion. In fact, and ironically, the only people scandalized by it are those followers of intellectual fads and fashions who are scandalized by how unfashionable it is! And as for topicality, Tolkien's story could not be further from the "stuff" of daily newspapers. It is not rooted in today's news, or even in yesterday's news, but in a world beyond the news. It is not rooted in contemporary times or in past times, but in all time. And yet this is the very root of its relevance. Fashions fade away and news ceases to be news, but the "stuff" of reality remains. Tolkien's epic goes to the heart of reality, to the heart of good and evil, to the heart of the unchanging human condition, to the heart of the spiritual realities that make sense of the physical world in which we live. It is not a slave of the zeitgeist but a servant of the Heiligen Geist. It is timely because it is timeless. Or, to put the whole matter in Tolkien's own words, "*The Lord of the Rings* is of course a fundamentally religious and Catholic work."

There we have it in a nutshell, and from the lips of the author himself. "*The Lord of the Rings* is of course a fundamentally religious and Catholic work." But how is it so? Or is it so? There's no mention of Christ anywhere in the story; or the Church; or any religion. Is it really as "fundamentally religious and Catholic" as its author maintains? Yes it is, and in ways that continue to surprise and astound the reader with each subsequent reading. It is so rich with religious and Catholic meaning that one could go on and on, seemingly forever, unraveling the multifaceted applicability of the doctrinal and spiritual truths that emerge from the story. It is, therefore, difficult to know where to end in any discussion of this Catholic masterpiece. It is easier, however, to know where to begin. Tolkien gives us the vital clue we need to begin to understand the "fundamentally religious" character of the work in the date on which the One Ring is destroyed. It is cast into the maw of Mount Doom on March 25, a date that is so significant that it serves as the key with which we can unlock the rest of the plot.

March 25 is the Feast of the Annunciation, the day on which the Word was made Flesh in the womb of the Blessed Virgin. As a date, March 25 is more salvifically charged than Christmas. Although Jesus was *born* on Christmas Day he was *conceived* at the moment of the Annunciation. The significance of this date was not lost on the mediaevals, many of whom believed that the Crucifixion also happened on March 25, thereby connecting the beginning of the life of Jesus with His death. The date was also adopted by some mediaeval cultures as New Year's Day, thereby connecting the date of the Incarnation and Crucifixion with the New Life of Redemption heralded by Christ's Resurrection. And what, exactly, is achieved by this triune act of Redemption (Incarnation, Crucifixion, and Resurrection)? It is nothing less than the liberation of man from the bondage of Original Sin. And what, exactly, is Original Sin? It is the One Sin to rule them all and in the darkness bind them, just as the Ring is the One Ring to rule them all and in the darkness bind them. The One Sin and the One Ring are both cast into the hellfire from which they were made on the same date: March 25.

From the supercharged significance of this one juxtaposition between

God's Creation and Tolkien's subcreation, the rest of the plot falls into place with ineffable orthodoxy. Frodo as the Ring bearer, the bearer of Sin, is also the Cross bearer. He is a Christ figure and, at the same time, an icon of Everyman who is called to take up his cross and follow Christ. He is called to carry his cross through the land of Mordor (the valley of death, the vale of tears or the via dolorosa) to Mount Doom (Golgotha). He is fed on his journey by the "magical" power of lembas, a clear allusion to the Blessed Sacrament. And this is to speak of the role of Frodo only. We have said nothing of Aragorn as an imago Christi, or of Gandalf. There is much more that could and should be said, but, as we have said already, it is much easier to know where to begin in any discussion of this wonderful work than it is to know where to end, if indeed there is an end. Since, however, one must make an end, there seems no better way of doing so than with Tolkien's own words about the Real lembas that fed his Christian imagination and inspired the genius of his Catholic Muse.

> Out of the darkness of my life, so much frustrated, I put before you the one great thing to love on earth: the Blessed Sacrament. . . . There you will find romance, glory, honour, fidelity, and the true way of all your loves on earth, and more than that: Death: by the divine paradox, that which ends life, and demands the surrender of all, and yet by the taste (or foretaste) of which alone can what you seek in your earthly relationships (love, faithfulness, joy) be maintained, or take on that complexion of reality, of eternal endurance, which every man's heart desires.[107]

54. TOLKIEN IN HEAVEN

The most incisive insights into Tolkien's understanding of Heaven are given in his important poem, "Mythopoeia," and in his equally important short story, "Leaf by Niggle." Apart from their undoubted literary merit, these two works serve as an exposition of Tolkien's philosophy of myth. Tolkien believed that human creativity was a reflection of Divine Creativity, the former being the image of the latter. Human imagination is God's image in us. Like God, we can create—or, more correctly and as Tolkien stressed, we can sub-create. God creates from Nothing by giving things existence; we sub-create by making new things from other things that already exist through the use of the imagination. In the conclusion of "Mythopoeia" Tolkien asserted his belief that this human creativity will be beatified in Heaven by its being made perfect. Souls in Heaven will still "renew/from mirrored truth the likeness of the True."

> Salvation changes not, nor yet destroys,
> garden nor gardener, children nor their toys.

Our human creativity is not destroyed in Heaven but perfected, in the absence of evil, into the unfallen splendour that it was meant to be.

> In Paradise they look no more awry;
> and though they make anew, they make no lie.
> Be sure they still will make, not being dead,
> and poets shall have flames upon their head,
> and harps whereon their faultless fingers fall:
> there each shall choose for ever from the All.

This poetic vision of the triumph of True Art in Heaven was re-presented in "Leaf by Niggle," a story which is the nearest Tolkien ever came to writing a formal allegory. The character of Niggle, a thinly disguised allegory of Tolkien himself, has spent his life trying to paint a landscape but has only managed to render one leaf to his perfectionist satisfaction. When Niggle dies he stumbles across his imaginary unfinished tree in Heaven.

Yet now it is Real. The fruits of his flawed imagination have been perfected and have become incarnate in Paradise. His art shares his crown of Glory.

The third place in which Tolkien's philosophy of myth finds heavenly expression is in the *Ainulindalë*, the Creation Myth at the beginning of *The Silmarillion*. In the Beginning, Eru, the One God, propounds themes of music to the angelic Ainur: "Of the theme that I have declared to you, I will now that ye make in harmony together a Great Music. And since I have kindled you with the Flame Imperishable, ye shall show forth your powers in adorning this theme, each with his own thoughts and devices, if he will. But I will sit and hearken, and be glad that through you great beauty has been wakened into song." God in the Primal Heaven of his Creation blesses his creatures with the twin gifts of Freedom and Creativity. As with the Alpha of the *Ainulindalë* before the birth of time, so with the Omega of Niggle's heavenly vision after death. In the beginning and in the end, among angels and mortals alike, the Creator is glorified in the beauty of Creation's creativity.

Whereas the essentially orthodox vision of Heaven described in "Mythopoeia," "Leaf by Niggle" and the *Ainulindalë* can be seen to be the fruits of Tolkien's Catholicism, the pseudo-heavens described elsewhere in his legendarium might appear to be less in harmony with his Christian beliefs. In fact, however, they emerge as being more harmonious with Christian orthodoxy than might perhaps be supposed. The halls of Mandos and the mystic West can be likened to the *limbus patrum*, the limbo of the fathers, which is the mystical place of waiting for all just souls who died before the coming of Christ. In Christian tradition, souls in the *limbus patrum* were in a state of happiness awaiting the Messianic Kingdom to be established upon Christ's Ascension into Heaven. Since Tolkien maintained that Middle-earth is our earth, not some strange planet in outer space, and since the tales he tells occurred long before the Coming of Christ, the similarities between the description of the halls of Mandos and the mystic West with Christian concepts of the *limbus patrum* resonate with Tolkien's evident desire to conform his legendarium to his religious beliefs.

55. MORGOTH:
THE SATANIC PRESENCE
IN MIDDLE-EARTH

In *The Road to Middle Earth*, T. A. Shippey describes "the history of Genesis" as the "most obvious fact about the design of *The Silmarillion*." Shippey compares Tolkien's Creation myth with "a summary list of doctrines of the Fall of Man common to Milton, to St. Augustine, and to the Church as a whole." Satan is, of course, a central figure in the story of the Fall of Man in *Genesis*.

Melkor, later known as Morgoth, is Middle-earth's equivalent of Lucifer, or Satan. Melkor is described by Tolkien as "the greatest of the Ainur" as Lucifer was the greatest of the archangels. Like Lucifer, Melkor is the embodiment of, and the primal perpetrator of, the sin of pride; like Lucifer he is intent on corrupting humanity for his own purposes. Melkor desired "to subdue to his will both Elves and Men, envying the gifts with which Ilúvatar promised to endow them; and he wished himself to have subjects and servants, and to be called Lord, and to be master over other wills."

The parallels with the Old Testament become even less mistakable when Tolkien describes the war between Melkor and Manwë, the latter of whom is clearly cast in the role of Lucifer's nemesis, the archangel Michael. Manwë is "the brother of Melkor in the mind of Ilúvatar" and was "the chief instrument of the second theme that Ilúvatar had raised up against the discord of Melkor."

The link between Melkor and Lucifer is made most apparent in the linguistic connection between them. As a philologist, Tolkien employs language to synthesize his own Satan with his Biblical archetype. The original spelling of Melkor, in the earliest drafts of the mythology, is Melko, which means "the Mighty One"; Melkor means "He who arises in Might"—"But that name he has forfeited; and the Noldor, who among the

Elves suffered most from his malice, will not utter it, and they name him Morgoth, the Dark Enemy of the World." Similarly Lucifer, brightest of the angels, means "Light Bringer," whereas the Jews named him Satan, which means "Enemy" in Hebrew. Linguistically, therefore, "Morgoth," "Satan" and "Enemy" share the same meaning. They are the same word in three different languages. "Morgoth" and "Satan" clearly represent the same primal "Enemy" of humanity. Tolkien's intention, both as a Christian and as a philologist, in identifying Melkor with Lucifer is plain enough.

In the earlier drafts of the mythology that pre-date the publication of *The Lord of the Rings*, Melkor's role parallels that of the Biblical Satan. He is the primal bringer of discord into Ilúvatar's Design and he harbours a desire to have dominion in the world contrary to the will of Ilúvatar. In the later versions of the myth, the role of Melko, now known as Melkor, becomes more complex, itself a reflection of Tolkien's increasing concern with theological intricacy, yet Melko-Melkor-Morgoth always remains essentially a depiction of Satan.

Taking his inspiration, perhaps, from the Book of Isaiah ("Thy pomp is brought down to the grave, and the noise of thy viols: the worm is spread under thee, and the worms cover thee. How art thou fallen from heaven, O Lucifer, son of the morning"—Isaiah 14:11–12), Tolkien says of Melkor: "From splendour he fell through arrogance to contempt for all things save himself, a spirit wasteful and pitiless . . . He began with the desire of Light, but when he could not possess it for himself alone, he descended through fire and wrath into a great burning, down into Darkness."

Shortly after this description of Melkor, Tolkien introduces Sauron, the Dark Enemy in *The Lord of the Rings*. Sauron is described as a "spirit" and as the "greatest" of Melkor's, alias Morgoth's, servants: "But in after years he rose like a shadow of Morgoth and a ghost of his malice, and walked behind him on the same ruinous path down into the Void." This brief depiction of Sauron in *The Silmarillion* unveils the evil power in *The Lord of the Rings* as being directly connected to Tolkien's Satan, rendering implausible a non-theistic interpretation of the book's deepest moral meaning.

In *Morgoth's Ring*, volume ten of *The History of Middle-earth*, Tolkien is preoccupied with the figure of Melkor-Morgoth. "Above all," wrote Christopher Tolkien in his foreword to *Morgoth's Ring*, "the power and significance of Melkor-Morgoth . . . was enlarged to become the ground and source of the corruption of Arda." Whereas Sauron's infernal power was concentrated in the One Ring, Morgoth's far greater diabolic power was dispersed into the very matter of Arda itself: "the whole of Middle-earth was *Morgoth's Ring*." The pride of Melkor-Morgoth had "marred" the whole of material Creation just as, according to the Christian doctrine of the Fall, the pride of Lucifer-Satan had marred the very fabric of the world.

If, however, the Shadow of Morgoth had fallen across the face of Middle-earth, marring it terribly, Tolkien asserts with Christian hope that the final victory would never belong to Morgoth. "Above all shadows rides the Sun," Samwise Gamgee had affirmed in the Tower of Cirith Ungol, and Tolkien uses the childlike wisdom of the hobbit to express deep theological truths. The Sun is a metaphor for Ilúvatar, the All-Father, God Himself, and the shadows a metaphor for evil. The final triumph of Good, i.e., God, and the ultimate defeat of Evil, was spelled out by Ilúvatar himself in the Ainulindalë, at the very beginning of Creation. Referring to Melkor's introduction of disharmony into the Music of the Ainur, Ilúvatar warned his Enemy of the ultimate futility of his rebellion: "And thou, Melkor, shalt see that no theme may be played that hath not its uttermost source in me, nor can any alter the music in my despite. For he that attempteth this shall prove but mine instrument in the devising of things more wonderful, which he himself had not imagined." Eventually Melkor will understand that all his evil actions have been the unwitting servant of unimaginable Providence. "And thou, Melkor, wilt discover all the secret thoughts of thy mind, and wilt perceive that they are but a part of the whole and tributary to its glory." Sauron is mighty, and Melkor is mightier still, but, as Frodo exclaimed at the Cross-roads, "They cannot conquer forever!"

56. DARKNESS IN MIDDLE-EARTH

In the beginning . . . the earth was a formless void and darkness covered the face of the deep . . . Then God said, "Let there be light"; and there was light. And God saw that the light was good; and God separated the light from the darkness. The opening lines of the first book of *Genesis* are paralleled by Tolkien in *Ainulindalë*, the Music of the Ainur, his own version of the Creation myth. Thus speaks Ilúvatar, the All-father (God), at the beginning of time: "'Therefore I say: *Eä!* Let these things Be! And I will send forth into the Void the Flame Imperishable, and it shall be at the heart of the World, and the World shall Be . . .' And suddenly the Ainur saw afar off a light, as it were a cloud with a living heart of flame . . .'" Light is, therefore, at the very heart of Creation and its absence, Darkness, is associated from the very beginning with evil. Thus Tolkien says of Melkor: "He began with the desire of Light, but when he could not possess it for himself alone, he descended through fire and wrath into a great burning, down into Darkness."

At its deepest this primal and primeval dichotomy of light and darkness is a reflection of orthodox Christian theology. St. Augustine and other great Christian philosophers and theologians have taught that evil has no existence of its own but is merely the absence of that which is good. It is, therefore, easy to see why Good is synonymous with, and symbolized by, light, whereas Evil is synonymous with, and symbolized by, the absence of light, i.e., Darkness. It is for this reason that Tolkien describes Sauron as "a huge shape of shadow" or as "a shadow of Morgoth." Like evil, a shadow has no existence of its own but is only visible insofar as it obstructs or hides the light. "Above all shadows rides the Sun," states Samwise Gamgee in the Tower of Cirith Ungol, reflecting Tolkien's own Christian understanding of the deepest theological truths. In Sam's hope-filled words, uttered in the midst of the terrible darkness on the edge of Mordor, the Sun can be seen as a metaphor for Ilúvatar, the All-father, God Himself, and the shadows a metaphor for the evil that cannot prevail.

In the meantime, however, the children of Ilúvatar (Elves and Men) are doomed, through the rebellion of Melkor (Satan), to dwell in his shadow. "[S]o great was the power of his uprising that . . . through long years in Arda [he] held dominion over most of the lands of the Earth." Yet from the very beginning the Elves are given the light of the stars as a promise of their final deliverance from the Darkness of evil. Varda, greatest of the angelic Valier, forged the brightest of the stars in the heavens to serve as an everlasting light over the darkness of Middle-earth. "It is told that even as Varda ended her labours . . . in that hour the Children of the Earth awoke, the Firstborn of Ilúvatar. By the starlit mere of Cuiviénen, Water of Awakening, they rose from the sleep of Ilúvatar; and while they dwelt yet silent by Cuiviénen their eyes beheld first of all things the stars of heaven. Therefore they have ever loved the starlight, and have revered Varda Elentári above all the Valar." Thus, in Tolkien's Creation myth, God chooses the moment that Varda finishes the forging of the stars, including the constellation of Menelmacar (Orion) "that forebodes the Last Battle that shall be at the end of days" (the final victory of light over darkness), as the time to bring the Elves into Being. Thereafter the Elves look to the stars, and to Varda, the maker of the stars, whom they call Elbereth, as a promise of the triumph of light over darkness, good over evil. If Samwise Gamgee, the hobbit, looks to the light of the sun as a promise of deliverance from Darkness, the Elves look to the light of the stars.

57. REDEMPTION IN MIDDLE-EARTH

The Redemption—the redeeming of humanity from the slavery of Original Sin through the Life, Death and Resurrection of Christ—was central and axiomatic to Tolkien's very understanding of the nature of reality. It is, therefore, not surprising that the Redemption serves as an omnipresent, if largely concealed, ingredient in Tolkien's legendarium.

Tolkien wrote that "successful Fantasy" offered "a sudden glimpse of the underlying reality or truth . . . a brief vision . . . a far-off gleam of *evangelium* in the real world." Tolkien, in his own work, offers his readers this sudden glimpse, this brief vision, this far-off gleam of the underlying reality or truth of the Gospel in a multitude of ways, multifarious and subtle. Such is his genius that his work bears most fruit when it is read in much the same way that Christians read the Old Testament, as a story that prefigures the truth which will be revealed in the New Testament. In much the same way that Old Testament stories point to the Redemption still to come so Tolkien's legendarium points in the same way to Christian truths still to be revealed.

In *The Lord of the Rings* Tolkien reveals that the Ring is destroyed on March 25, a date that is so significant to Christians that it could be called the date of the Redemption itself. Christians believe that the Annunciation and the Crucifixion took place on this day, the two events which, alongside the Resurrection, constitute Christ's Redemption of fallen humanity. As such, the Quest at the centre of *The Lord of the Rings* can be seen as a metaphor for the Redemption, most particularly with regard to Christ's dying for our sin. The ring-bearer takes up his burden (his Cross) and walks through Mordor (Death) to Mount Doom (Golgotha, the place of the Skull) where the power of the Ring (Sin) to enslave the people of Middle-earth (humanity) to the will of the Dark Lord (Satan) is destroyed.

The necessity of the Incarnation to the Redemption of fallen humanity was central to "The Debate of Finrod and Andreth" (*Athrabeth Finrod ah Andreth*) in *Morgoth's Ring*, volume ten of *The History of Middle-earth*. In this story, Andreth tells of the "Old Hope" that Eru (God) would enter into Arda in person to save Middle-earth from Melkor (Satan). Finrod understands instantly why such an Incarnation will be essential to the Redemption of the people of Middle-earth from Melkor's evil grip. Melkor-Morgoth's "marring" of Middle-earth can only be rectified by the physical intervention of God Himself. "I cannot see how else this healing could be achieved. Since Eru will surely not suffer Melkor to turn the world to his own will and to triumph in the end. Yet there is no power conceivable greater than Melkor save Eru only. Therefore Eru, if He will not relinquish His work to Melkor, who must else proceed to mastery, then Eru must come in to conquer him."

Morgoth's Ring was written after Tolkien had finished *The Lord of the Rings* and some of these finer theological points are not evident in the earlier work. Nonetheless it is clear that Tolkien had the Fall and the Redemption very much in mind at the time he was writing *The Lord of the Rings*. Since, for example, Original Sin is the One Sin to rule them all and in the Darkness bind them, the connection between the One Ring and the One Sin is evident and obvious. It is also made manifest, albeit enigmatically, in the character of Tom Bombadil. "Eldest, that's what I am," says Tom, adding that he "knew the dark under the stars when it was fearless—before the Dark Lord came from Outside." Tom is older than the Fall. He remembers when the world was innocent, before fear marred its happiness after the coming of the Dark Lord. Tom is Pre-Lapsarian. He pre-dates the Fall. It is, therefore, no surprise that he and presumably Goldberry, his wife, are the only creatures in Middle-earth over whom the One Ring (Original Sin) has no power. Clearly Tom Bombadil and Goldberry represent Unfallen Creation; they show the way things could have been if the Marring of Melkor (the Fall) had not happened. The fact that Tom and Goldberry represent primal Innocence and that Tom only has jurisdiction over his Garden remind us insistently of Adam and Eve, prior to the Fall.

Tolkien offers other clues pointing to the centrality of the Redemption in his legendarium. As a mediaevalist and a philologist he was well-versed in the relationship between typology and etymology. Take, for instance, Sauron. Etymologically it clearly echoes *sauros*, the Greek for lizard; typologically and iconographically, a lizard is interchangeable with "serpent" or "dragon," the symbol for Satan. Saruman also contains *saur* and might be said to translate anagrammatically as "Dragonman" (though etymologically it has its roots in the Mercian form of West Saxon, "Searu-man," which translates as "crafty man"). The philological wordplay continues with Wormtongue. The Old English word for dragon or serpent was *wyrm*;

hence Wormtongue translates as Dragontongue or Serpent-tongue. Note also how Gandalf addresses Wormtongue: "Down, snake! Down on your belly!," "See, Théoden, here is a snake!" Wormtongue "with a hissing breath" spits (venom?) before the king's feet.

Ultimately Tolkien shows the effect of redeeming grace through the development of his characters. Those who cooperate with the grace grow in virtue, becoming Christ-like; those who refuse to cooperate with the grace wither into pathetic parodies of the people they were meant to be. Gandalf the Grey lays down his life for his friends and is resurrected and transfigured as Gandalf the White. Strider passes the self-sacrificial tests of kingship and ascends the throne as Aragorn. Such is the reward of those who accept the gift of redemption and who respond heroically to the sacrifices demanded of them. On the other hand, those who deny the gift and defy the call to heroic self-sacrifice diminish into grotesque shadows of their former selves. Saruman withers into Sharkey; Gríma slithers into Wormtongue; and, perhaps most tragically of all, Sméagol fades into Gollum.

58. THE CHRONICLES OF NARNIA: DEEP MAGIC FROM BEFORE THE DAWN OF TIME

The release of the film adaptations of *The Chronicles of Narnia* represents another Christian victory in the culture war being fought for the minds and hearts of Americans. For years we have witnessed the moral decline of the movie industry, to such a degree that the very word "Hollywood" has become synonymous with moral obliquity. Recently, however, there has been a renaissance in good, solid moral movies. The stunning success of Mel Gibson's *The Passion of the Christ* is the most notable example of this moral renaissance but there have been significant successes for other wholesome films in recent years. The tremendous popularity of the Peter Jackson adaptation of *The Lord of the Rings* exhibited a great desire on the part of movie-goers for tradition-oriented morality devoid of the sickness of moral relativism and free from the propaganda of the new tacit totalitarianism of secular fundamentalism.

Tolkien and Lewis were great friends, and Tolkien, a life-long practicing Catholic, was instrumental to Lewis's conversion to Christianity in 1931. Following his conversion C. S. Lewis became one of the most indomitable Christian apologists of the twentieth century. His many books continue to sell by the million but none of them are more loved than his children's series, *The Chronicles of Narnia*, the first of which to be written being *The Lion, The Witch and The Wardrobe*. This work is certainly as religious as is *The Lord of the Rings*, and, indeed, the Christian dimension is even more obvious. Whereas Tolkien subtly subsumes the Christianity within the story, Lewis allows it to float on the surface, making it unmistakable and unavoidable.

In *The Lion, The Witch and The Wardrobe*, and throughout the other six titles in the *The Chronicles of Narnia*, the Lion, Aslan, is quite clearly a figure of Christ. He is unmistakably and indubitably so. This becomes particularly evident in Aslan's offering of himself to be sacrificed in the place of Edmund, who had betrayed his family and friends to the White Witch. The Witch reminds Aslan of the "Deep Magic from the Dawn of Time" which "the Emperor put into Narnia at the very beginning." Aslan, as the Son of the Emperor-beyond-the-Sea (God, the Father), knows the Deep Magic but allows the Witch to tell him, no doubt so that others can hear: "You know that every traitor belongs to me as my lawful prey and that for every treachery I have a right to a kill." Here the Witch reveals herself as a Satan figure, the primeval traitor to whom all treachery owes its ultimate allegiance. "And so," she continues, "that human creature is mine. His life is forfeit to me. His blood is my property." The Witch knows that she can't be robbed of her rights by mere force. The Deep Magic must be obeyed. Primeval Justice must be done. The sinner belongs to her. He stands condemned. With "a savage smile that was almost a snarl" she gives the doom-laden ultimatum: "unless I have blood as the Law says, all Narnia will be overturned and perish in fire and water."

"It is very true," says Aslan. "I do not deny it."

Aslan knows that the Deep Magic cannot be denied and that Justice must be done. He offers himself to be sacrificed in the place of the sinner, Edmund.

In the chapter entitled "The Triumph of the Witch" we see the Passion of Aslan. He has his Agony in the Garden; he is scourged; beaten; kicked; ridiculed; taunted. Finally he is bound and dragged to the Stone Table on which is written the Deep Magic. He is then laid on the Table, the altar of sacrifice, and the Witch raises the knife. Before striking the fatal blow she cannot resist the temptation to gloat:

> And now, who has won? Fool, did you think that by all this you would save the human traitor? Now I will kill you instead of him as our pact was and so the Deep Magic will be appeased. But when you are dead what will prevent me from killing him as well? . . . Understand that you have given me Narnia for ever, you have lost your own life and you have not saved his. In that knowledge, despair and die.

The irony resides in the fact that the Witch (Satan) only has knowledge of despair and death; hope and life are beyond her ken.

"But what does it all mean?" asks Susan following Aslan's resurrection.

"It means," replies Aslan, "that though the Witch knew the Deep Magic, there is a magic deeper still which she did not know. Her knowledge goes back only to the dawn of time. But if she could have looked a little further back, into the stillness and the darkness before Time dawned, she would have read there a different incantation. She would have known that when a willing victim who has committed no treachery was killed in a traitor's stead, the Table would crack and Death itself would start working backwards." Aslan, the sinless victim, saves the life of Edmund and, with him, the Life of every other "traitor" (sinner). The Death and Resurrection of Aslan has Redeemed the world!

Although the Passion and Resurrection of Aslan is the centerpiece of the Christian dimension in *The Lion, The Witch and The Wardrobe*, it is by no means the only example of profound Christian symbolism. To offer but one example, the chapter in which Aslan breathes life into the statues of the living creatures who had been turned to stone in the Witch's castle reminds us of Christ's harrowing of Hell and his release of the souls from Limbo.

The Deep Magic would re-emerge in the other books of *The Chronicles of Narnia*. From Aslan's creation of Narnia in *The Magician's Nephew* to the Apocalypse of *The Last Battle* in the final book of the series, C. S. Lewis presents us with perhaps the finest Christian children's literature of the twentieth century.

The new movie versions of *The Chronicles of Narnia* show how the Deep Magic can penetrate even to the darkened heart of Hollywood. The heart remains dark, however, and the Witch of this world is already plotting her next move. The culture war is not over. It will not be over until Time itself is over. Until then the Darkness will wallow in its own despair, dragging the treacherous into its self-centred orbit, and the Light will shine forth the Deeper Magic from Before the Dawn of Time and Beyond the End of Time. "The issue is now quite clear," said the great Catholic writer G. K. Chesterton on his deathbed. "It is between light and darkness and every one must choose his side." Chesterton chose his side, and C. S. Lewis chose the same side as Chesterton. Their choice was wise. Ultimately the side they chose is the winning side.

59. MAN AND EVERYMAN:
C. S. LEWIS'S ASCENT FROM FAITHLESS
RATIONALISM TO *FIDES ET RATIO*

The Abolition of Man, C. S. Lewis's masterful critique of the relativism that was as rampant in his day as it is in ours, represented the culmination of the author's quest for the quintessential meaning of man's being and purpose. Always a diligent searcher after truth, Lewis had climbed a long and arduous path from the faithless rationalism of his youth to the pinnacle of perspective from which *The Abolition of Man* was written. Following in Lewis's footprints—his ascent from denial to assent—will enable us to understand not only the arduous path that he had taken but the ardour with which he had taken it.

The long ascent began from the depths of the valley of doubt into which Lewis had descended following the loss of the lukewarm Christianity of his childhood. "And so, little by little, with fluctuations which I cannot now trace, I became an apostate, dropping my faith with no sense of loss but with the greatest relief."[108] By 1916 he was dismissing all religions with a seventeen-year-old's arrogant ignorance, stating that he believed in no religion because there was "absolutely no proof for any of them," adding that his atheism was merely a reflection of "the recognized scientific account of the growth of religions." Superstition had always "held the common people, but in every age the educated and thinking ones have stood outside it."[109]

In spite of his atheism, Lewis never sank into the quagmire of relativism. Believing philosophically in the Absolute he wrote in his diary on 6 July 1922 of his intention to write a dissertation on "the hegemony of moral value" and two years later read a paper of that title to the Oxford Philosophical Society. He was, therefore, a believer in the Absolute and an advocate of the Permanent Things long before his conversion to Christianity. It was this belief in, and desire for, Order which animated his objections to the aesthetic experimentation of the modern poets in general, and to T. S. Eliot in particular.

Lewis's didacticism and his desire for order and formality were at loggerheads aesthetically with the subtlety and obscurantism of Eliot's *The Waste Land* with its "heap of broken images." Lewis was seeking to unify "moral value," bringing all the pieces together according to the harmonizing principle of the Absolute, whereas Eliot was shoring up "fragments" of "broken images," scattering the pieces apparently at random. Appearances can be deceptive, however, and it would take Lewis many years before he finally came to accept Eliot as a kindred spirit. Eliot's *Modern Education and the Classics*, published in 1934, complemented Lewis's own "Reflections on Education with Special Reference to the Teaching of English" which was the sub-title of *The Abolition of Man*. Both works insisted that education could not be divorced from morality and that the latter must inform the former. Similarly Eliot's *The Idea of a Christian Society* (1939) and his *Notes Towards the Definition of Culture* (1948) dovetailed with Lewis's position as regards the necessity of Christianity to any genuine restoration of European culture. Most notably, Eliot's depiction of "The Hollow Men" in his poem of that title, published in 1925, prefigures Lewis's "Men without Chests" in *The Abolition of Man*. It is indeed a little odd that Lewis remained apparently blind to these multifaceted and multifarious similarities between his own work and that of one whom he deemed an "enemy."

This singular and peculiar blindness extended to other kindred spirits, such as Roy Campbell and Edith Sitwell, both of whom were satirized mercilessly in Lewis's *The Pilgrim's Regress*, the former as "the bearded singer" and the latter as "Victoriana," two of the "Clevers" in Eschropolis. Lewis would also attack Roy Campbell in his poem "To the Author of *Flowering Rifle*" and, as with his belated friendship with Eliot, would only later recognize his affinity with one whom he had presumed to be an enemy. Similarly, and although he had dismissed her so acrimoniously in *The Pilgrim's Regress*, one cannot imagine Lewis failing to appreciate Edith Sitwell's later poems, such as "Still Falls the Rain" or "The Shadow of Cain," the latter of which, being the first of her "three poems of the Atomic Age," resonates profoundly and disturbingly with the diabolical scientism of the N.I.C.E. in Lewis's *That Hideous Strength*. "The Shadow of Cain" was written in 1945, the same year in which *That Hideous Strength* was published, and both works share the same "merely Christian" response to the destructive triumph of technology over humanity in the "atomic" age. Lewis's original inspiration for the N.I.C.E—the National Institute of Coordinated Experiments—had been occasioned by the controversy surrounding the founding of an atomic plant near Blewbury, fifteen miles from Oxford;[110] Sitwell's "The Shadow of Cain" had been inspired by the dropping of the atomic bomb on Hiroshima and was about "the fission of the world into warring particles, destroying and self-destructive." Both works also employed the imagery of coldness as a metaphor for the atomic age long before the post-war nuclear impasse became known as the "Cold War." One of the diabolical materialists in *That Hideous Strength* is named Frost, accentuating the chilling hardness of his characterization, whereas Sitwell characterized her poem as a description of "the gradual migration of mankind . . . into the desert of the Cold, towards the final disaster, the first symbol of which fell on Hiroshima." According to Sitwell the first two pages of "The Shadow of Cain" "were partly a physical description of the highest degree of cold, partly a spiritual description of this."[111]

> We did not heed the Cloud in the Heavens shaped like the hand
> Of Man . . .
>   the Primal Matter
> Was broken, the womb from which all life began.
> Then to the murdered Sun a totem pole of dust arose
>   in memory of Man.

In these lines from "The Shadow of Cain" the similarities between Lewis's work and Sitwell's are made manifest; from the plaintive description of the Promethean arrogance of scientism, which is the "hideous strength" of the N.I.C.E. in Lewis's novel, to the sobering consequences of such hideous strength in the abolition of Man himself.

At this juncture it is worth emphasizing the close connection in Lewis's own mind between *The Abolition of Man* and *That Hideous Strength*. Both books were written in 1943, although the latter would not be published until two years later, and Lewis makes a distinct connection between them in his Preface to *That Hideous Strength*: "This is a 'tall story' about devilry, though it has behind it a serious 'point' which I have tried to make in my *Abolition of Man*." The connection, or the "point," or perhaps more accurately the connecting point, of both works is the dire consequences of rejecting the Natural Law in favour of a moral relativism rooted in Promethean Pride, the primeval or original sin which gives birth to all others. Put succinctly, free will is the strength at the heart of man but, at the same time and paradoxically, is also man's greatest weakness. If the freedom of the will is ordered, i.e., if it is in harmony with the Will of the One who bestowed the freedom in the first place, it is man's greatest strength. If, on the other hand, it is disordered, i.e., if it rebels against the Divine Will, it becomes his greatest weakness. Paradoxically, however, the weakness is strong, in the sense that it has great destructive and ultimately self-destructive power. At the moment that it ceases to be the true freedom which, as Edmund Burke insisted, "must be limited in order to be possessed," it becomes the anarchy which, as Oscar Wilde so memorably asserted, is "freedom's own Judas." Man betrays himself with a kiss when he kisses the mirror.

It is this Promethean self-centredness which is the "hideous strength." Pride is the hideous strength. And it is Pride which is at the root of the philosophical relativism which leads to the abolition of man. Put simply, the philosophical errors exposed by Lewis in *The Abolition of Man* lead to the diabolical idolization of science or "progress" which is the destructive driving force behind the N.I.C.E. in *That Hideous Strength*.

None of this is original to Lewis, of course; it is as old as Original Sin itself. It is, however, all too often forgotten in our meretriciously myopic age. Furthermore, and as we have seen, Lewis himself, as a young atheist, had not been averse to an element of "progressive" idolization of science, genuflecting before "the recognized scientific account of the growth of religions." He was led away from such scientism, in large part, by the benign influence of G. K. Chesterton, so much so that it is easy to trace the intellectual roots of *The Abolition of Man* and *That Hideous Strength* to ideas that Lewis might have learned from his reading of Chesterton.

Lewis had first read Chesterton whilst convalescing from an attack of "trench fever"'in a British Red Cross field hospital at Le Treport in France during the First World War. It was love at first sight:

> I had never heard of him and had no idea of what he stood for; nor can I quite understand why he made such an immediate conquest of me. It might have been expected that my pessimism, my atheism, and my hatred of sentiment would have made him to me the least congenial of all authors. It would almost seem that Providence, or some "second cause" of a very obscure kind, quite over-rules our previous tastes when It decides to bring two minds together. Liking an author may be as involuntary and improbable as falling in love . . . In reading

Chesterton, as in reading [George] Macdonald, I did not know what I was letting myself in for. A young man who wishes to remain a sound Atheist cannot be too careful of his reading. There are traps everywhere . . . God is, if I may say it, very unscrupulous.[112]

In the years after the First World War Lewis continued to read the works of Chesterton voraciously without ever succumbing to the fullness of their veracity. "Chesterton had more sense than all the other moderns put together; bating, of course, his Christianity."[113] Even as he was treating contemporaries such as Eliot, Campbell and Sitwell with unmerited contempt, Lewis was allowing Chesterton's religious orthodoxy to drip-feed itself into his heart without ever, consciously, admitting it into his head. "Then I read Chesterton's *Everlasting Man* and for the first time saw the whole Christian outline of history set out in a form that seemed to make sense."[114]

Chesterton had written *The Everlasting Man* as a response and riposte to H. G. Wells's *The Outline of History*. Wells's work, ostensibly an objective account of the history of the world, was in fact a retelling of history according to Wells's own philosophy of materialistic determinism. Its overriding presumption was that human society is "progressing" towards perfection and that, in consequence, the past is always and necessarily inferior to the present, as the present is necessarily inferior to the future.

Wells's *Outline of History* had an immense and immediate impact. It was lauded by those who shared Wells's philosophy as a thoroughly modern view of history, a view of history unshackled by the prejudices and superstitions of the past. It was history as if God did not matter. In 1923, Joy Davidman (who was destined many years later to become Lewis's wife) had read *The Outline of History* as an impressionable eight-year-old and had immediately declared herself an atheist.

Although Chesterton doesn't address Wells's work directly, it is clear that *The Everlasting Man* represents an alternative "outline of history" which was intended as an antidote to Wells's book and a rebuttal of his deterministic "progressive" thesis. In essence Chesterton was insisting that man is essentially unchanging, that human society isn't "progressing" inexorably, and that the health of any human society is directly dependent upon the practice of virtue and the avoidance of sin. A virtuous society might be said to be progressing, a sinful society might be said to be regressing; since, however, sin and virtue are dependent upon the freedom of the will there is nothing "blind" or "inexorable" about human history or human destiny. Chesterton's book could also be seen as a response to George Bernard Shaw's "progressive" Nietzscheanism, particularly in plays such as *Man and Superman*. Contrary to the Shavian or Wellsian belief that man was evolving or progressing into superman, or *übermensch*, Chesterton insisted that man was always in stasis; he was best understood in relation to Everyman, the archetype of his perennial unchanging self as observed through history and through the literature of the ages. The answer to the fallacy of *Man and Superman* was the felicity of *Man and Everyman*.

The triumph of Chesterton over Wells can be seen in Lewis's work by the negative characterization of those who espouse the Wellsian *weltanschauung*. In *Out of the Silent Planet* and, to a lesser extent, in *Perelandra*, the character of Dr. Weston is unmistakably a parody of Wells and others of his ilk, such as Shaw, J. B. S. Haldane and Olaf Stapledon. Perhaps more specifically, Weston can be seen as a parody of one of Wells's or Stapledon's fictional heroes. In *That Hideous Strength* the character of Horace Jules is clearly meant to remind us of Wells, though the name itself also suggests an allusive nod in the direction of Jules Verne. Mr. Jules is described as "a cockney," a clear allusion to Wells's lower middle-class origins on the outskirts of London, whose "novels had first raised him to fame and affluence." The ideas that Jules expounds with self-opinionated zeal are close and clear reflections of those espoused by Wells. Significantly Lewis shows that Jules's naïve philosophy of optimistic scientism is not merely deficient rationally but is being used by more sinister and ultimately demonic forces. Bad philosophy and its exponents become servants of evil.

If the villainous characters of Jules and Weston can be seen, in part at least, as fictional personifications of Wells, the hero of Lewis's Space Trilogy, Dr. Elwin Ransom, described as a middle-aged Philologist of Cambridge University, can be seen as a fictional personification of Lewis's great friend, J. R. R. Tolkien, who, when Lewis was writing his Space Trilogy, was a middle-aged philologist at Oxford University. "As a philologist I may have some part in him," Tolkien wrote to his son Christopher, speaking of Ransom, "and recognize some of my opinions and ideas Lewisified in him."[115] It was singularly apt that Lewis should pay tribute to his friend in this way, not least because Tolkien was perhaps the most important figure, with the possible exception of Chesterton and George Macdonald, on Lewis's ascent from faithlessness to faith. In what must have been the most important single conversation in Lewis's life, in Oxford in September 1931, Tolkien had convinced Lewis that myths were not "beautiful lies and therefore worthless," as Lewis had maintained, but that, on the contrary, they contained "splintered fragments" of the one true light and, as such, were priceless beacons of illumination in a darkened world. Within days of this conversation Lewis announced that he had finally come to accept the Christian God and that this conversation with Tolkien had been largely instrumental in his resolving of his final difficulties.

The conversation with Tolkien can be seen to have influenced the discussion of the *Tao* in *The Abolition of Man*, principally in the sense in which Lewis insists that the convergence of belief in various religions and myths illustrates that each contains these "splintered fragments" of truth. The underlying harmony and uniformity of the various belief systems handed down through the centuries of human experience points to their ultimate fulfillment in the one truth which is revealed in Christ. The experience of Man points to Everyman; and Everyman is perfected in Christ.

One wonders also whether Tolkien's exposition of the "splintered fragments" of truth to be found in myth had enabled Lewis to understand the "fragments" of "broken images" employed by his old "enemy" T. S. Eliot. Could he now understand how Eliot was using modernity mythopoeically, arranging the "broken images" to project the "splintered fragments" of truth to a broken and fragmented culture? It seems not. Lewis remained blind to the mythopoeic majesty of Eliot's *oeuvre*. As such, he was never able to learn from Eliot as he had learned from Chesterton and Tolkien during his ascent from faithless Rationalism to *Fides et Ratio*.

60. CYBER-SPACE:
HELL'S FINAL FRONTIER

Jim Forest, *The Wormwood File: E-Mail From Hell*. Orbis Books.

C. S. Lewis distinguished between "allegory" and what he called "supposal." Writing to a schoolgirl about the role of Aslan in *The Lion, the Witch and the Wardrobe* Lewis insisted that Aslan's role was "not, as some people think, an *allegory*. That is, I don't say 'let us represent Christ as Aslan.' I say, 'Supposing there was a world like Narnia, and supposing, like ours, it needed redemption, let us imagine what sort of Incarnation and Passion and Resurrection Christ would have there.'" Similarly Lewis insisted that his novel, *Perelandra*, was not an allegory but a "supposal." It was the imaginative expression of a supposition: "Suppose, even now, in some other planet there were a first couple undergoing the same that Adam and Eve underwent here, but successfully." Jim Forest, as an evident admirer of Lewis, has taken Lewis's idea of a "supposal" and has given us a splendid re-working of Lewis's "satanic" satire, *The Screwtape Letters*. Let's suppose, posits Forest, that the devil has an e-mail account, and let's suppose that he uses it for his own diabolical ends.

In *The Wormwood File: E-Mail from Hell*, Forest gives centre stage to Wormwood, the novice demon to whom Screwtape addressed his "letters" in Lewis's original book. Now, having been promoted (if "promotion" is the right word for advancement in Hell), Wormwood is in charge of his own novice demon, Greasebeek, who has the deviously devilish responsibility of securing the damnation of an ordinary young man. With admirable ingenuity, Forest has Wormwood leaping into cyber-space and finding himself at home amongst the pornography and other pernicious effluvia caught in the world-wide web.

Wormwood's e-mails to Greasebeek are full of the exhortations tinged with threats which had characterized the earlier "letters" he had received from Screwtape. "No wonder you let a month go by without a word. Your client's wife is pregnant? You told me she was only glancing into baby carriages. How could you have been so unaware of the direction in which things were moving?" Thus begins an e-mail to Greasebeek on the subject of "Choice," directed of course at persuading their "client" to persuade his wife to "choose" an abortion. "With a little effort on your part, your client will find himself convinced that the future of the marriage is in the balance unless his wife has an abortion. If she resists having an abortion, suggest that he flat out threaten to leave. He can tell her that she has no right to have a baby when he isn't ready and add that, if she insists on going ahead, it will be entirely her own project." He beseeches Greasebeek to "pay careful attention to terminology." He should encourage his client to avoid words like "unborn baby" or "unborn child" and refer to the child as an "embryo" or a "fetus." He should also avoid talking about "abortion" and speak instead about "terminating the pregnancy." This is the correct language of "choice." This is but one example of the many ways in which Wormwood and Greasebeek seek to undermine the work of their "client's" guardian angel. Ultimately, however, as with Lewis's original, the client escapes their clutches.

As with Lewis's prototype, *The Wormwood File* represents a literary trysting place at which the realms of satire, psychology and apologetics come together in creative collision. At times, Forest succumbs to some gratuitous spleen-venting, employing his demonic mouthpiece as a means of firing broadsides at the follies of modernity in a manner unbefitting the more subtle demands of the literary medium he has chosen. Unnecessary perhaps; unsubtle certainly: but at least he is venting his spleen in the right directions! For the most part, however, he manages to resist this temptation and allows the satire to speak on his behalf.

If Wormwood follows in the precipitous footsteps of his master, Screwtape, Forest follows in the edifying footsteps of his own master, Lewis. He stumbles occasionally and seldom reaches the heights that Lewis attained. Yet in spite of such obvious and perhaps inevitable deficiencies *The Wormwood File* remains a noble effort at a noble endeavour. Nor can Forest be accused of plagiarism in "stealing" Lewis's ideas. His reworking of *The Screwtape Letters* might not be able to boast any great degree of originality but, as Wormwood would no doubt take great pride in pointing out, there is nothing truly original, humanly speaking, except sin. Sin aside, every other work of man is an act of sub-creation, which is to say that it is something made from other things that already existed. This differentiation between Creation, which comes from God alone, and sub-creation, which is the image of God working in man, was a central axiom of the artistic philosophy of J. R. R. Tolkien, Lewis's great friend and mentor. Tolkien borrowed from the great myths of antiquity to sub-create his own myths of Middle-earth, and Lewis borrowed liberally from his great literary predecessors and contemporaries as a prop or prompt for his own imagination. Bunyan's ghost haunts the pages of *The Pilgrim's Regress*; Dante's daunting presence permeates *The Great Divorce*; H. G. Wells wanders through *Out of the Silent Planet*; Milton meanders through *Perelandra*; Charles Williams wallows in the weirdness of *That Hideous Strength*; and there is more than a modicum of Chesterton's *Orthodoxy* in Lewis's *Mere Christianity*. Is Forest guilty of "borrowing" somebody else's ideas? Yes indeed he is. Unashamedly so; unabashedly so. At least he does so in the knowledge that he is in very good company. Similarly *The Wormwood File* deserves to be in the very best company, perched on the bookshelf beside the works of C. S. Lewis, not as their equal but as their *confrère*.

61. THE JOY OF BEING SURPRISED BY C. S. LEWIS

I first stumbled across C. S. Lewis whilst fumbling around in a fog of ignorance. As an angry young man, filled to the brim with bitterness, I was
groping for fragments of light amid figments of darkness. The light had
first shone forth from the pages of a book by G. K. Chesterton, *The Well
and the Shallows*, in which the intellectually indefatigable GKC had van-
quished many of the idols of my prejudice. I began to perceive, dimly at
first, that the philosophy and theology of Christendom was the well of truth
from which European civilization had sprung whereas the ideas of modernity were mere shallows by comparison.

I developed a seemingly insatiable appetite for Chesterton, scouring
through second-hand bookshops for his works. It was on one of these
book-trawling expeditions that my eyes settled on a book called *Surprised
by Joy* by someone called C. S. Lewis. I had heard of C. S. Lewis, possibly as the author of *The Lion, the Witch and the Wardrobe*, a book I'd never
read, but I knew nothing about him. Perhaps I had read somewhere that he
was a Christian writer. Perhaps not. I'm not sure. The shadow of the years
has descended upon the surface of my memory. Either way, something
prompted me to take the book from the shelf. Turning to the index I
looked for references to Chesterton and, sure enough, his name was listed. My interest aroused, I turned, as the index directed, to page 147. As
my eyes read Lewis's words, my heart leapt, surprised by the joy of discovering a kindred spirit. "It was here that I first read a volume of
Chesterton's essays," Lewis wrote. "I had never heard of him and had no
idea of what he stood for; nor can I quite understand why he made such
an immediate conquest of me." Yes! This was exactly how I felt when I
had first read him. It was uncanny that someone in a field hospital in
France, during the First World War, more than sixty years earlier, could
have felt exactly the same way that I had upon discovering Chesterton. I
continued reading:

It might have been expected that my pessimism, my atheism, and my hatred of sentiment would have made him to me the least congenial of authors. It would almost seem that Providence, or some "second cause" of a very obscure kind, quite over-rules our previous tastes when It decides to bring two minds together.

Exactly! I couldn't have put it better myself. "Liking an author may be as involuntary and improbable as falling in love." Yes again! How did this man Lewis do it? He knew exactly how I felt about Chesterton. He knew it because he felt it too—in exactly the same way.

Lewis waxed lyrical about Chesterton for a further page or so, my heart continually leaping in joyful assent at his words, before he finally concluded with the following doom-laden words:

> In reading Chesterton . . . I did not know what I was letting myself in for. A young man who wishes to remain a sound Atheist cannot be too careful of his reading. There are traps everywhere . . . God is, if I may say it, very unscrupulous.

After reading these words I couldn't say that I hadn't been warned. Lewis was cautioning me that, in reading Chesterton, I was walking a dangerous path. Who knew where it might lead? The warning went unheeded. Not only did I not desist from reading Chesterton but I now added C. S. Lewis as a literary mentor. From now on, when trawling through the treasures in second-hand bookshops, I would be searching for titles by Lewis as well as those by Chesterton.

In reading Lewis's *Mere Christianity*, as in reading Chesterton's *Orthodoxy*, I learned that the Christian Creed provided the very credentials for truth itself. In reading Lewis's *The Problem of Pain*, as in reading Chesterton's *The Man Who was Thursday*, I began to perceive the sense to be found in suffering; and in reading *A Grief Observed* I saw the abstract arguments about suffering become incarnate in Lewis's own pain at losing his wife. In Narnia, as in Chesterton's *Manalive* and his Father Brown stories, I discovered the wonder of remaining child-like, and the wisdom that springs from this wonder-filled innocence. And, of course, in Lewis, as in Chesterton, there was so much more to discover. Finally, through their guidance, like John in *The Pilgrim's Regress*, I would lay myself at the feet of Mother Kirk. In reading the works of Lewis and Chesterton, and in the enjoyment of their company, I had crossed the threshold of hope and had entered Aslan's country.

62. THE LEGACY OF RONALD KNOX

David Rooney, *The Wine of Certitude: A Literary Biography of Ronald Knox*. San Francisco: Ignatius Press. 2009.

David Rooney's new study of one of the great twentieth-century apologists is as welcome as it is needed. Father Ronald Knox was one of the premier figures of the Catholic Literary Revival, deserving a place among the Revival's *illustrissimi*, such as Newman, Manning, Hopkins, Chesterton, Belloc, Tolkien, Waugh, Greene *et al*. Yet he has been sadly and unjustly neglected in the half-century since his death. His translation of the Bible into what he hoped would be "timeless English" is overlooked in favour of other, often worse, translations, and his other works, ranging across the spectrum of genres, are similarly unread and largely forgotten. It is, therefore, encouraging that we are seeing something of a Knox revival, a timely resurrection, in the wake of a revival of interest in the whole Catholic Literary Revival of which he was such a key player.

Baronius Press has recently secured the rights for the Knox translation of the Bible from the Diocese of Westminster and is currently in the process of producing a new complete edition, thereby bringing this literary gem back into print after several decades in the biblio-wilderness. In 2007 Ignatius published a major work on Knox's Apologetics by Father Milton Walsh, *Ronald Knox as Apologist: Wit, Laughter and the Popish Creed*, and in 2008 Ignatius published a comparative study of Knox and Lewis, also by Father Walsh, entitled *Second Friends: C. S. Lewis and Ronald Knox in Conversation?*. David Rooney's new literary biography is a welcome addition to this recent flurry of activity.

Rooney is to Knox what Dale Ahlquist of the American Chesterton Society is to Chesterton, an avid reader and amateur enthusiast who becomes, in time, an acknowledged expert. This book serves as testimony to Rooney's diligence in research, from the brief biography of the opening chapter to the sermons and retreats with which the volume concludes. In between, Rooney presents us with a comprehensive overview of the whole

Knox oeuvre, from the relative levity of his satire and detective fiction to the gravitas of his work as translator and apologist, mindful nonetheless that, as a disciple of G. K. Chesterton, Knox's levity always has gravitas, and his gravitas levity. For, as GKC reminds us, angels can fly because they take themselves lightly, whereas the devil falls by the force of gravity, i.e., by taking himself too seriously. Like his mentor, Knox was able to fly with the lightness of an angel because he never took himself as seriously as the topics he was tackling.

If *The Wine of Certitude* has one irritating weakness it is the disjointedness attached to excessive quotation. Throughout the length of the book, the flow of Rooney's dexterous prose is interrupted by chunks from Knox's own works. The reader, or at least this reader, would have preferred Knox's works to have been presented within the seamless garment of Rooney's narrative, rather than, at times, the narrative fading into little more than a segue between the quotations. This is, however, a mere quibble. Rooney has succeeded in doing what he evidently set out to do. He has given us a superb introduction to the life and work of Ronald Knox in a solitary volume. Anyone wishing to know more about this great defender and champion of the Faith need look no further than this timely tome.

63. THE LEGACY OF FRANK SHEED AND MAISIE WARD

Frank Sheed & Maisie Ward, *Spiritual Writings*, Selected with an Introduction by David Meconi, S.J. Maryknoll, NY, Orbis Modern Spiritual Masters Series, 2010.

First impressions can be deceptive. On first perusal this new selection of the spiritual writings of the great husband and wife team, Frank Sheed and Maisie Ward, seemed to suggest not merely a selection of their work but also a selective reading of it from a suspiciously modernist perspective. Suspicions were roused initially by the epigraph that serves as an appetizer for what is to follow. It is taken from Sheed's *Christ in Eclipse*:

> Christ is the whole point of the [Church's] functioning. We are not baptized into the hierarchy, do not receive the cardinals sacramentally, will not spend eternity in the beatific vision of the pope . . . Christ *is* the point . . .

There is, of course, nothing wrong with this statement. Indeed, and as one would expect from the pen of a consummate master of apologetics, the statement is resplendent in its orthodoxy. The problem is not the words themselves; it is their being plucked, out of context, from Sheed's gargantuan corpus to serve as the volume's epigraph, the curtain raiser for all that follows. Although strictly orthodox, the words convey, at least to those whose theological antennae are attuned to the manipulations of modernism, an implicit attack on the Church's hierarchy. Such suspicions are reinforced when the epigraph is read in connection with the list of other writers and thinkers who have previously had selections of their work published in the "Modern Spiritual Masters" series of which this volume is a part. These include a dazzling array of figures from across the religious spectrum, including Dietrich Bonhoeffer, Anthony de Mello, Mohandas Gandhi, Karl Rahner, Sadhu Sundar Singh, Albert Schweitzer,

Brother Roger of Taizé, Leo Tolstoy, Swami Abhishiktananda, and the Dalai Lama. Clearly the series is not merely ecumenical in the Christian sense of the word, intending to bring together Catholics and Protestants, but in the trans-religious and fundamentalist sense that seeks to bring together all religions, irrespective of the self-evident contradictions that each presents in relation to the others. To be fair, there were also genuine giants of orthodoxy amongst those considered "modern spiritual masters," including Mother Teresa, Edith Stein, St. Thérèse of Lisieux, Flannery O'Connor, and G. K. Chesterton; and there were other luminaries on the list deserving their place in such a series, such as Simone Weil, Caryll Houselander, and Jean Vanier. On the other hand, it was odd, to say the least, that the only modern Pope included in the series was John XXIII. The significant absence of the wonderful triumvirate of Piuses who have graced the twentieth century, and the exclusion of Paul VI, the Pope who outraged modernists with his promulgation of *Humanae vitae*, speaks volumes.

These first impressions seemed to suggest that this volume would be another attempt by modernists to claim the Sheed and Ward legacy as their own. In *The Living of Maisie Ward* by Dana Greene (University of Notre Dame Press, 1997), the author succumbed to the temptation to paint her subject in the colours of her own choosing with little regard for Ward's true colours as a staunch and resolute defender of Catholic orthodoxy against modernism. Later, with the publication of Dom Paschal Scotti's *Out of Due Time: Wilfrid Ward and the Dublin Review, 1906–1916* (Catholic University of America Press, 2006), the sin against the daughter was revisited upon her father. This crass revisionism needs to be rooted out and rectified whenever it raises its confused and confusing head. Clearly this latest volume in what would seem to constitute a Sheed and Ward revival needed to be judged in the light of these earlier abuses.

And yet, as we have said, first impressions can be deceptive.

The first indication that the anti-modernist antennae were twitching unnecessarily was the reassuring fact that the selection from Sheed's and Ward's writings had been made by Father David Meconi, one of that rare and precious breed of resolutely and courageously orthodox Jesuits who continue to rekindle hope in the venerable Society that bequeathed such martyrs to posterity as Saints Edmund Campion and Robert Southwell. In this respect, Meconi belongs in the illustrious company of his contemporary confreres, Fessio, Pacwa, Schall and Spitzer. His name on the cover served as confirmation that the selection was in safe and trustworthy hands.

In his acknowledgments, Meconi dedicates the volume to Walter Hooper, the Catholic convert and indefatigable defender of C. S. Lewis, whom Meconi describes as his "friend and erstwhile mentor." The connection with Lewis is significant because Meconi describes Frank Sheed as "perhaps the one twentieth-century apologist who was worthy to complement Lewis." Such a statement would appear to be sheer effrontery, affronting the sensibilities of those who claim Chesterton as the only modern Christian apologist to rival Lewis. Yet there is reason behind Meconi's apparent madness. Chesterton's work is not merely animated by his *joie de vivre* but by his *joie de mots*, a sheer love of language that leads him to take tantalizing tangents of paradoxical and pyrotechnic brilliance. Whilst these never fail to dazzle the reader, they do not always illuminate the subject with the pure and simple succinctness that many readers desire. Lewis's great gift, or, more correctly, one of his many great gifts, was his astonishing ability to elucidate difficult theological and philosophical concepts in plain and simple language that even the man on the street could understand. Frank Sheed, whose work with the Catholic Evidence Guild meant that he quite literally preached to the man on the street from a soapbox at Speakers' Corner in London and at other places, shares Lewis's gift for succinctness and clarity. As such, Meconi's judgment, in this respect at least, would seem to be validated.

Although Meconi's thirty-page introduction to the life and work of Frank Sheed and Maisie Ward is one of the highlights of the book, encapsulating their life stories, their love for each other, and their shared evangelical zeal, it is marred by the occasional factual error. Hilaire Belloc died in 1953, not 1954, as stated by Meconi, and, most egregious of errors, the young Maisie Ward could not have helped those injured "from the *Blitzkrieg* over British cities" during World War One because the blitz didn't hit British cities until World War Two. The creeping of such mistakes into the book will no doubt make Meconi wince (the present reviewer still cringes at the thought of a rudimentary error in the rendering of a common Latin phrase in one of his own books) and it must be said that the fault lies at least as much with his editors, who have served him badly in their failure to eradicate such errors before publication. Nonetheless, and in spite of the onerous responsibility of a reviewer to bring factual *faux pas* to light, Meconi's introductory essay remains a fine piece of work, setting the scene for the selection of quotes from the works of Frank and Maisie that follow. His short commentary, interspersed between the quotes, is also valuable and illuminating, particularly in his crucial contextualizing distinction between the authentic teaching of the Second Vatican Council and the so-called "spirit of Vatican II," the latter of which was not an incarnation of the Council itself but manifestations of anarchy committed in its name.

There does not seem much of a need in a review of a volume of selected writings to quote from the writings themselves. Such an exercise would constitute a selection of the selection, in which the reviewer plucks his favourite passages from the editor's own selection. Suffice it to say that Meconi's selection is superb. The congruence of Frank's and Maisie's writing on the subject of mystery in general and the mystery of the Trinity in particular serves as ample evidence that their marriage was one of minds and not merely of bodies. Frank's thought-provoking assertion that books of theology cannot elucidate the faith as much as the truths contained in the Missal illustrates his devotion to the Church's central and defining act of worship. There is much else besides. Maisie's affinity with the ideas of Tolkien and Lewis makes for joyful reading, and her discussion of the tortured presence of Christ in the works of Graham Greene and the dreadful consequence of His Real Absence in the work of Joyce are truly incisive. On the other hand, Frank seems to be guilty of bad ecclesiology in his lament, following the Second Vatican Council, that "vast numbers are not drawn to him, and other vast numbers seem to be moving away if not from Christ, certainly from his Body." How, one might ask, can one move away from Christ's Body without moving away from Christ? Such an error reminds us that Frank and Maisie do not speak infallibly. Like so many others, they were swept up by the delusional optimism that intoxicated so many Catholics in the wake of Vatican II, suffering from a glib naïveté that was the Church's equivalent of the "summer of love" and "flower power" of the hippies. Ultimately, however, Frank and Maisie are not defined by these temporary delusions but by a lifelong attachment to orthodoxy.

Let's end with some words of Maisie's that will serve as an appropriate counterpoint to Frank's lines about hierarchy with which we began this review:

> After Newman and Browning came Chesterton—in the long run the greatest influence of them all, especially because I could watch over the years his vision of the Church as it grew

clearer . . . He had seen that the saint grows only in the Church and draws his strength from that divine source. And he expressed it perfectly . . . when he wrote *ubi Petrus, ibi Franciscus*. The chief religion of authority is also the chief religion of the spirit . . .

"Where Peter is found, there is Francis." Where there is hierarchy, there is sanctity.

64. E. F. SCHUMACHER:
TRUE ECONOMIST

Almost forty years ago, in 1973, a German economist, living in England, wrote an international bestseller called *Small is Beautiful*. It had a huge impact. The book's author, E. F. Schumacher, became a celebrity overnight. He and his book became the icon of a new generation of environment-conscious politicians, economists and campaigners. The views expressed in Schumacher's book became so fashionable that Jimmy Carter, following his election to the presidency in 1976, invited Schumacher to the White House for a photo-shoot. Pictures of Carter and Schumacher, arm in arm, were splashed across the newspapers, indicating, so the president would have us believe, that he was in tune with the latest thinking on "economics as if people mattered," which was the sub-title of Schumacher's book.

There was, however, a secret behind Schumacher's book that his millions of admirers did not know. It was a secret that some of them would wish not to know. It was, in fact, a secret that many of them still want to keep secret. The secret is this. Schumacher was hugely influenced in his writing of *Small is Beautiful* by the teaching of the Catholic Church.

At first skeptical that the popes "in their ivory tower" could have anything of worth to teach him in the sphere of economics, he read Pope Leo XIII's *Rerum novarum* (1891) and Pope Pius XI's *Quadragesimo anno* (1931) and was astonished at the insight that the social teaching of the Church had to offer.

It was, however, the promulgation of another Papal Encyclical, Pope Paul VI's *Humanae vitae* (1968), which would have the most immediate impact on his life. This Encyclical prompted his wife and one of his daughters to seek instruction in the Catholic Faith. The message that *Humanae vitae* conveyed, wrote Schumacher's daughter, "was an affirmation and support for marriage, for women . . . who had given themselves entirely to their marriages and who felt acutely the pressure from the world outside that shouted ever louder that homebound, monogamous relationships were oppressive to women and prevented them from 'fulfilling themselves.'" Although, at the time, Schumacher did not feel able to follow his wife and daughter into the Church, he concurred with their view of the Encyclical. "If the Pope had written anything else," he told a friend, "I would have lost all faith in the papacy."

On 29 September 1971 Schumacher was finally received into the Catholic Church. Two years later his world bestseller, *Small is Beautiful*, was published, a work, both popular and profound, which almost single-handedly redefined the public perception of economics and its impact upon the environment. It is, in fact, ironic that the modern environmental or "green" movement derives its *weltanschauung* not from any "new age" philosophy or neo-pagan "religion" but from the expertise and wisdom of a world-renowned economist who found inspiration from the social doctrine of the Church.

Schumacher died on 4 September 1977, shortly before his second major work, *A Guide for the Perplexed*, was published, in which he sought to outline the underlying spirituality and philosophy from which the economic vision in *Small is Beautiful* is derived.

Schumacher's lasting legacy is to illustrate that "subsidiarity," the essence of the Church's social teaching as taught by successive popes, as defined in *The Catechism of the Catholic Church*, and as reiterated by John Paul II in *Centesimus annus* (1991), has worldwide popular appeal. It is, therefore, ironic that it is sometimes seen as the Church's best kept secret.

It was with this thought in mind that I decided to write *Small is Still Beautiful* as a way of showing how Schumacher's original book is as relevant today as it was when it was first published, if not more so, and as a means of making the Church's teaching known to the wider world. I changed the subtitle to "economics as if families mattered" to show that families are the most important units in any society, and to emphasise this message in the light of the concerted attacks on the family since Schumacher's book was written. The fact that Schumacher would have endorsed the change of title is evident from his wholehearted support of Pope Paul VI's encyclical on human life.

Schumacher's ideas exploded like a beneficent bomb, demolishing, or at least throwing into serious question, many of the presumptions of *laissez faire* economics. His insistence that the question of scale in economic life should not—and, indeed, morally speaking, could not—be separated from the overriding dignity of the human person, shifted the whole focus of economic thought away from impersonal market forces and back to the dignity of human life. The tendency of modern economics to genuflect before Mammon in the name of quasi-mysterious market forces, and to disregard the dignity of the human person, is ultimately not an economic question at all. It is a moral question. As such, we should not be surprised that the whole issue has concerned the Catholic Church for more than a century.

Schumacher warned of impending calamity if rampant consumerism and economic expansionism were not checked by human and environmental considerations. Like a latter-day prophet he asserted that humanity was lurching blindly in the wrong direction, that the pursuit of wealth could not ultimately lead to happiness or fulfillment, and that a renewal of moral and spiritual perception was essential if disaster was to be avoided. His greatest achievement was the fusion of ancient wisdom and modern economics in a language that encapsulated contemporary doubts and fears about the globalized world. He confronted the presumptions of modernity with the dynamism of tradition. He stressed that the wisdom of the ages, the perennial truth that has guided humanity throughout its history, serves as a constant reminder to each new generation of the dangers of self-gratification. The lessons of the past, if heeded, should always empower the present.

In practical terms Schumacher counteracted the idolatry of giantism with the beauty of smallness. People, he argued, could only feel at home in human-scale environments, of which the family was the archetype. If structures—economic, political or social—became too large they became impersonal and unresponsive to human needs and aspirations. Under these conditions individuals felt functionally futile, dispossessed, voiceless, powerless, excluded and alienated. He applied similar criteria with regard to technolatry, the idolization of technology. He felt that modern technology often pursued size, speed, novelty and violence in defiance of all laws of natural harmony. The machine was becoming master and not the servant of man, severing him from his natural environment and encasing him in an increasingly artificial world. As techno-man plugs himself into the latest electronic illusions he simultaneously disconnects himself from the real world and its very real problems.

As Schumacher observed: "Modern man does not experience himself as a part of nature but as an outside force destined to dominate and conquer it. He even tells of a battle with nature, forgetting that, if he won the battle, he would find himself on the losing side." We were given authority over our environment as stewards of the goodness it has to offer, not as locusts devouring what we have no intention of replenishing. The moral is easy enough to discern for those who have ears to hear. It is this: that, ultimately, small is beautiful because families are the small and beautiful building blocks of a healthy society, and because the earth itself is not only beautiful but small.

65. CHRISTOPHER DAWSON:
TRUE HISTORIAN

I first met Christopher Dawson during my research for *Literary Converts* (HarperCollins UK/Ignatius Press 1999). I had heard of him prior to my research for this particular book, but had never actually met him. When I did meet him it was not in the flesh, because he had already been dead for almost thirty years, but in the spirit of the truth that he served and elucidated. I recognized in Dawson a kindred spirit. It was not merely that he was one of the *illustrissimi* of literary converts of whom I was writing; nor that he was one of the most important Catholic historians of the past two centuries, taking his seat of honour in the company of Lingard, Acton, Belloc and the newcomer Eamon Duffy. It was also because he had *seen* history as few other historians had seen it. It was as though he had got beyond the nitty-gritty and the nuts-and-bolts and, to switch metaphors, had soared on eagle's wings to a height where the whole panoramic past came into breathtaking perspective. He was to history what E. F. Schumacher, another convert, was to economics. Just as Schumacher had seen beyond the mechanistic and materialistic understanding of economics, arriving at a meta-economics that transcended and transfigured conventional economic assumptions, so Dawson had seen beyond the mechanistic and materialistic understanding of history, arriving at a meta-history that transcended and transfigured conventional historical assumptions.

My first meeting with Dawson and my first meeting with Schumacher were true epiphanies. In both cases I was shown reality, as if for the first time, and, in so doing, enjoyed that wonderful experience of standing on one's head that Chesterton refers to as the only way of seeing things as they really are. It is the disconcerting disorientation that precedes reorientation. One stands on one's head and one realizes that, in fact, one is now the right way up for the first time, and, surprise of all disconcerting surprises, that, up until then, one had always been looking at reality upside down. This whole paradox was put more eloquently by Evelyn Waugh when he wrote that "conversion is like stepping across the chimney piece out of a Looking-Glass world, where everything is an absurd caricature, into the real world God made; and then begins the delicious process of exploring it limitlessly." Waugh was referring to his own conversion to the Catholic Church but the experience is as true of these lesser conversions: the conversion to a true perspective of history or economics.

Dawson is very much alive, more alive than many of the materialistic somnambulists walking around today. He is alive in the sense that his labours continue to bear fruit, and continue to open the eyes of the blind. He is also alive in that more important sense that lies beyond the grave.

I'll finish with one final observation: A true historian makes the past present by the light of the eternal omnipresent. According to this criterion, Christopher Dawson is a true historian *par excellence.*

66. THE GREAT I AM: ONTOLOGICAL OBJECTIVITY IN CAUSLEY'S "I AM THE GREAT SUN"

I am the great sun, but you do not see me,
  I am your husband, but you turn away.
I am the captive, but you do not free me,
  I am the captain you will not obey.

I am the truth, but you will not believe me,
  I am the city where you will not stay,
I am your wife, your child, but you will leave me,
  I am that God to whom you will not pray.

I am your counsel, but you do not hear me,
  I am the lover whom you will betray.
I am the victor, but you do not cheer me,
  I am the holy dove whom you will slay.

I am your life, but if you will not name me,
  Seal up your soul with tears, and never blame me.

It is tempting, on first perusal, to compare Charles Causley's sonnet, "I Am the Great Sun" (1955), with Roy Campbell's "To the Sun" (1936). Yet the similarities, though seemingly obvious, are deceptive. Take, for instance, their apparent similarity in form. Both appear to be sonnets, but Campbell's flagrant deviation from the Petrarchan or Shakespearean norms casts doubt on its true credentials, relegating it to the sphere of the pseudo-sonnet. The apparent similarity of subject is also deceptive. In Causley's sonnet the Great Sun is the I Am, i.e., God Himself, whereas in Campbell's poem the Sun is defined by the fact that he (or it) is not God but only a mere creature like the poet himself.

Oh let your shining orb grow dim,
Of Christ the mirror and the shield,
That I may gaze through you to Him,
See half the miracle revealed . . .

And what is true of the two poems is equally true of the two poets. Causley and Campbell appear to have a great deal in common but their apparent similarities serve to mask their deep and defining differences.

Let's begin with the obvious similarities.

Both poets were courageous in their resistance to the fashionable ascendancy of their day, choosing to champion traditional poetic form in defiance of the iconoclastic innovation of their modernist confreres. Campbell's long verse satires, written in heroic couplets, owed more to Dryden and Pope than to any of his contemporaries. Similarly Causley's resurrection of the ballad came at a time when modernist critical consensus had declared the form dead and beyond the pale, an archaism with which the modern poet would fraternize at his peril. Campbell and Causley, ever defiant of the temptation of many modern artists to enslave themselves to the zeitgeist, were absolutely brazen in their open fraternization with the formal enemies of modernism.

Both poets were also inspired by the synthesis of soil and soul, writing verse that is expressive of what might be termed the theology of place. Whether writing of his native South Africa, or the places he lovingly adopted, such as Provence, Spain and Portugal, Campbell's verse is always infused with the fusion of this soil-soul nexus in which the cultivation of the soil is seen as synonymous with the cultivation of the soul. This radical understanding of culture, so alien to the rootless cosmopolitan, was also implicit, though somewhat less impassioned, in Causley's quintessentially Cornish Muse.

Both poets also indulged their whimsy with carefree abandon, even when dealing with the usually solemn subject of religion. Such is the case with Campbell's "Saint Peter of the Three Canals" and Causley's "Mevagissey," the latter of which is so similar in tone and theme to the former that one suspects that the one served as inspiration for the other. Both poems resurrect the apostle, Saint Peter, and place him within the setting of a modern fishing village, Martigues in Provence and Mevagissey in Cornwall respectively. Here's Campbell:

For when the Three-in-One grow thrifty,
Saint Peter, he is One in Fifty,

Saint Peter, he is All in All!
And I have heard the fishers tell
How when from forth the jaws of hell
No other saint would heed their call,

Doomed wretches at the swamping rowlocks
Have seen a saintly Castor-Pollux,
Walking the waves, a burning wraith,
Speed to their aid with strides that quicken
As light as Mother Carey's chicken
Foot-webbed with Mercy and with Faith.

And here's Causley:

Peter jumped up in the pulpit
His hands all smelling of fish,
His Guernsey was gay with the sparky spray
And white as an angel's wish.

The seagulls came in through the ceiling
The fish flew up through the floor,
Bartholomew laughed as he cast off aft
And Andrew cast off fore.

Such similarities, though real and profound, should not disguise the fact that Campbell and Causley were seemingly at loggerheads in their theology, the one area which, above all others, really delineates the limits of one's perception of the cosmos. Campbell was a convert to Catholicism, the most institutional of religions in the sense that it claims to have been instituted by Christ Himself; Causley, on the other hand, declared himself unenamoured of any "organized religion," and denied that he was a Christian.[116] This difference of theology represents a real abyss between the two poets, the real presence of faith in one contrasting with its real absence in the other. Indeed, the abyss is present in the two ostensibly similar poems that we have just cited. Campbell ends his piscatorially Petrine whimsy with a prayer that serves as a prophecy of the poet's impending conversion, whereas Causley ends his whimsical encounter with St. Peter with the sobering and sickening anti-climax of disillusionment. Here's Campbell:

Be with me, then, when nights are lone
And from the pampas of the Rhône,

Thrilling with sleet, the great guns blow:
When the black mistral roars avenging
Increase the horse-power of my engine,
Hallow my petrol ere I go![117]

And here's Causley:

I walk all day in the dockyard
Looking for Captain Pete,
But there's not a marine or a brigantine
At the bottom of Harbour Street.

The boy-voiced boat, like summer,
Has sailed away over the hills
And I'm beached like a bride by the travelling tide
With a packet of seasick pills.

Neither poet is a practicing Christian when their respective poems are written, yet both seem to share a desire for faith. One voices the desire in prayer and receives the faith, the other remains prayerlessly silent and sees his vision break like a disconsolate wave on his beached desires. The abyss between the two visions is truly abysmal. It is as wide and fathomless as the ocean over which the poets peer longingly. One sees an empty and endless horizon but believes that there is a New World, out of sight but nonetheless really there, a world seen by the eyes of faith and confirmed by reason; the other sees the endless flat horizon of seemingly endless sea and believes that there is nothing beyond the horizon except another flat horizon until, eventually, we come to the end or edge of the world. Such is the chasm that separates the believer from the non-believer.

This is all very well, but what on earth (or in heaven) are we to make of Causley's sonnet, "I Am the Great Sun," to which we now belatedly return? How can a man without faith write such a poem? How do we read the poem in light of the poet's beliefs or lack thereof? Can a non-Christian write a truly Christian poem? If so, how? And what makes a poem Christian? These are all questions that must be asked and answered if we are to really understand the greatness of Causley's sonnet.

The answers to all the aforementioned questions can be found in Causley's achievement of *objectivity*, which is to say his ability to empathise *perfectly* with his subject. Here we must define our terms carefully by refining the definition of *empathy* in the *Oxford English Dictionary*. The *OED* defines *empathy* as "the power of projecting one's personality into (and so fully comprehending) the object of contempla-tion."[118] Such a definition contains an implicit relativism in the employ-ment of the projection of personality into the process of empathy. In pro-jecting our personality into an object we are ipso facto not empathizing with it but, on the contrary, are subjecting it to our subjective perception of it. True empathy should be defined as "the ability to subject one's personality to the object of contemplation so that it may be comprehend-ed objectively and dispassionately."[119] The former definition is subjec-tive: *What would I feel if I were in your position?* The latter definition is objective: *What must you be feeling?* It is the ability to truly empathise in the latter sense that Charles Causley possesses to quite an extraordinary degree and which is exhibited so sublimely in "I Am the Great Sun."

There is no better exponent of Causley's empathetic method than Dana Gioia who refers to it as "conscious objectification," a process of objectiv-ity answering "a deep need in Causley's imagination for impersonal, pub-lic subject matter":

> The subjects . . . or locations [of his poems] might be openly drawn from the poet's personal experience, but their treatment almost always reflects some conscious objectification . . . The poems may speak in the first-person, but the "I" is almost always a fictive character . . .
>
> His historical ballads . . . reject the notion that a poet creates a private reality in the context of his or her own poems . . . His work makes its appeal to a common reality outside the poem—usually an objectively verifiable reality of history or geogra-phy.[120]

Although Gioia is referring specifically to Causley's historical ballads, it is clear that this "conscious objectification" is present in the sonnet, "I Am the Great Sun," in an even greater sense. Indeed, it is "objectification" in its most extreme or primal form. In this sonnet, Causley strips away all masks of creative distance between himself and his subject, subjecting himself to his subject to such a degree that the subject becomes not only the object but the very Object, the very Thing that makes sense of every-thing else. Even the adoption of the first-person is the genuflection of the poet in the presence of the First Person to whom all other persons owe their being. The "I Am" in the sonnet is not the Cartesian "I" who thinks there-fore he is, but the ultimate "I Am" of Exodus 3:14 who is the very source of all thought. Causley's poem removes *all* masks, even the poet's own "bare bones" persona, so that we can move beyond the Cartesian *cogito ergo sum* (I think, therefore I am) to the Biblical *Ego sum qui sum* (I Am Who Am). It is this "I Am," the alpha and omega and the raison d'être of all else that is, who speaks to the poet and to the reader in Causley's masterfully crafted verse. The poet has succeeded so well in his aim of objectification that he has stepped outside of the poem itself, his voice voluntarily silenced in the Real Presence of Christ speaking from the Cross.[121]

The whole structure of the poem turns on the ontological relationship between God and his creatures: *I Am . . . but you . . .* God *is* and we only *are* because He is, but we fail to recognize our dependence on Him, or our debt to Him, or His love for us. On the contrary, as the poem unfolds we are described as being blind, ignorant, unjust, disobedient, faithless, willfully homeless, deserters, prayerless, deaf, treacherous, killjoys, and killers. He *is* but we will not *be* who we are meant to be. He *is* objective reality but we are blinded by our relativism from seeing Him and acknowledging Him. He is necessary and we only contingent, but we cherish those things that are contingent and not the one Thing that is necessary. The sonnet concludes with a devastating couplet in which we are told by Reality Himself that He is our very life and that we will only have ourselves to blame if we lose our lives in losing Him:

I am your life, but if you will not name me,
Seal up your soul with tears, and never blame me.

Returning to the questions that we posited earlier, we can answer that a man without faith can write such a poem only if he consciously objectifies his vision of things; he can do so only if he sees beyond his own subjective faithlessness to the reason inherent in faith. In this way a non-Christian can write a truly Christian poem if the non-Christian poet attains true empathy with his Christian subject; if he sees it as it is.[122] If a poet attains true empathy, i.e., true objectivity, he has thereby succeeded in separating his beliefs from his work. If so, and only if so, his beliefs or lack thereof are not relevant to the reading of the work.[123]

Charles Causley may not believe but he writes as though he does. As a veritable master of true empathy, he has stripped himself of the robes of his own subjective beliefs and has sacrificed his prejudices on the altar of objectivity. The artistic gift of such self-sacrifice is the Word becoming Flesh on the poet's naked bones.[124] In this light, the opening verse of Campbell's "Autumn" comes to mind:

I love to see, when leaves depart,
The clear anatomy arrive,
Winter, the paragon of art,
That kills all forms of life and feeling
Save what is pure and will survive.

Causley, perhaps, can be seen as the "autumnal" poet par excellence, a veritable paragon of art who shows us what is pure and what will survive in the clear anatomy of objectivity. His ability to escape the confines of self-constructed beliefs in order to see through the eyes of others makes him not only a paragon of art but a paragon of realism. As such, he serves as a guide to lead us beyond the labyrinth of myriad microcosmoses, each ruled by its own individual relativist god, which constitutes the self-delusional society of *homo superbus*. He is, to put the matter simply, on the side of the angels even if he doesn't believe in them.

67. FLANNERY O'CONNOR: MISFIT AND MYSTIC

One of the most memorable characters to emerge from the gargoylesque pen of Flannery O'Connor is the Misfit in "A Good Man Is Hard to Find." He is savagely psychopathic and yet, at the same time, savagely sane. "I call myself The Misfit," he said, "because I can't make what all I done wrong fit what all I gone through in punishment." In perceiving himself as a hapless victim of injustice, he appears to be a kindred spirit with that other "madman," King Lear, who declared himself "a man more sinn'd against than sinning."

The problem with which the Misfit struggles, in his case unsuccessfully, is the conundrum at the heart of life itself. Why do we suffer, and are we more sinned against than sinning? This was the conundrum at the very crux of Chesterton's novel *The Man Who was Thursday* which explores the mind's quest for meaning in the face of seemingly meaningless suffering. At the novel's end, the mysterious figure of Sunday emerges as a figure of the Divine, accused of inflicting so much apparently senseless pain. He is asked, "have you ever suffered?," to which he replies with the words of Christ: "Can ye drink of the cup that I drink of?" Although Sunday answers the question with another question, his question *is* the answer. It is the suffering of God Himself that makes sense of all suffering, and it is through the suffering of Christ that Christians find meaning and purpose in their own suffering. This axiomatic truth is at the sacred heart of the Christian's *acceptance* of suffering, an acceptance which Chesterton's friend, Maurice Baring, conveyed with sublime eloquence through the words of a character in *Darby and Joan*, the final novel he wrote before his own slow and painful death from Parkinson's disease:

> "One has to *accept* sorrow for it to be of any healing power, and that is the most difficult thing in the world . . . A Priest once said to me, 'When you understand what *accepted* sorrow

means, you will understand everything. It is the secret of life.'"[125]

This secret of life had been discovered by Fyodor Dostoyevsky, who believed that his life had been positively transformed by his sufferings as a prisoner: "It was a good school. It strengthened my faith and awakened my love for those who bear all their suffering with patience."[126] Dostoyevsky's great literary compatriot, Alexander Solzhenitsyn, underwent a similar transformation through his experience in the Gulag and, most particularly, through his near-death experience with cancer. By any stretch of the imagination, Solzhenitsyn's real-life experience of suffering at the hands of unjust jailers eclipses any injustice that we can imagine was suffered by the Misfit, yet, unlike the Misfit, Solzhenitsyn not only accepted his suffering but was grateful for its healing qualities. "Years go by, yes," Solzhenitsyn wrote to his wife from Ekibastuz labour camp, "but if the heart grows warmer from the misfortunes suffered, if it is cleansed therein—the years are not going by in vain."[127] During an interview with Bernard Levin in 1983, Solzhenitsyn declaimed that "suffering is essential for our spiritual growth and perfection." It was "sent to the whole of humanity . . . in sufficient measure so that if man knows how to do so he can use it for his growth."[128] Nowhere does Solzhenitsyn encapsulate the heart of this painful paradox more powerfully than in the recollection and recognition of the place of suffering in the religious conversion that was the pivotal moment in his life: "When at the end of gaol, on top of everything else, I was placed with cancer, then I was fully cleansed and came back to a deep awareness of God and a deep understanding of life. From that time I was formed essentially into who I am now. After that it was mostly evolution, there were no abrupt turns, no breaking directions."[129] Suffering had quite simply turned Solzhenitsyn around and set him down on the straight and narrow path. For Solzhenitsyn, *accepted* suffering does not only heal, it provides meaning to life itself. It does not only warm and cleanse the heart, it means that "the years are not going by in vain." The paradox is that suffering is not meaningless, as is claimed by the satanic accuser in Chesterton's *The Man Who was Thursday* or by the manically rational Misfit in "A Good Man Is Hard to Find," but that, on the contrary, and as disclosed by the priest in Baring's novel, it uncovers the secret at the heart of life. Far from being senseless, it actually makes sense of ourselves and our place in the cosmos. It is not needless but necessary.

All of this was known and embraced by Flannery O'Connor whose *acceptance* of her lifelong struggle with the debilitating effects of lupus is manifested throughout her work. Her experience of suffering, and the strengthening of faith and awakening of love that it heralded, could even be said to have been incarnated in her work, the pain serving as her Muse. "I have been through a lot and will see and experience even more—you shall see how much I will have to write about."[130]

Dostoyevsky's words could as easily have been O'Connor's.

In "A Good Man Is Hard to Find" the real absence of this acceptance, as revealed by the Misfit's complaints about the suffering that he had experienced, leads to a desire to inflict suffering on others. The anger that is the bitter fruit of the Misfit's non-acceptance is literally deadly, reaping havoc. And, significantly, the reason for his anger is rooted in theology, not psychology. His non-acceptance of suffering is a consequence of his non-acceptance of Christ's Death and Resurrection:

> "Jesus was the only One that ever raised the dead . . . and He shouldn't have done it. He thrown everything off balance. If He did what He said, then it's nothing for you to do but throw away everything and follow Him, and if He didn't, then it's nothing for you to do but enjoy the few minutes you got left the best way you can—by killing somebody or burning down his house or doing some other meanness to him. No pleasure but meanness," he said and his voice had become almost a snarl.

Solzhenitsyn lamented that the hedonistic modern world considered the acceptance of suffering as "masochism,"[131] yet here, in O'Connor's story, we see that the absence of such acceptance leads to sadism, and sadism of the most psychotic kind. The Misfit's words indicate that a refusal to follow the two great commandments of Christ, that we love the Lord our God, and that we love our neighbour, leads to anger and the inevitable killing of our God and neighbour. A failure to love God leads to the Crucifixion; a failure to love our neighbour as ourselves leads to hatred of our neighbour as our enemy (and a subconscious hatred of ourselves also, as can be seen beneath the surface of the Misfit's words). God is Love; if we will not have God we will not have love; and the absence of love is hatred, even if, in its slothful form, it makes a show of cynical indifference.

O'Connor presents us with another misfit in "Good Country People," a misfit who makes a dark art of cynical indifference. The ironically named Joy Hopewell even goes so far as to change her name to the deliberately ugly Hulga as a means of denying and defying the "joy" which was given to her at birth. In denying her Christian name she is denying Christianity itself, choosing the ugly alternative of nihilism instead. Hulga had declared war on "joy" as a bitter reaction to her losing a leg in a hunting accident as a child. Her whole philosophy of life is built on the bitterness of *unaccepted* suffering. Like the other Misfit, she feels that life has treated her badly and she hates life because of it, and, as for God, if He exists He is the One responsible for her hateful life. The sin of pride, the source of her bitterness, is made evident by the fact that she has effectively declared herself the god of her own cosmos, a fact revealed by O'Connor through the words of defiance that Hulga directs to her mother: "If you want me, here I am— LIKE I AM." This is clearly a thinly veiled reference to the name that God gives to Himself, when asked His name by Moses in the Book of Exodus: *I Am Who Am*. This could be translated as Hulga utters it: "I am—LIKE I AM." Hulga has not only changed her name, she has changed her religion. She now worships herself alone. She has declared herself god of herself. This, of course, is the *de facto* position of all relativists. In refusing to accept the existence of absolutes, including truth itself, they make themselves the sole arbiters of reality.

Deceived by her pride into believing that she is not deceived by anything, Hulga tells Pointer, the Bible salesman, that "I don't have illusions. I'm one of those people who see *through* to nothing." The delicious irony is that she is being deceived by Pointer even as she is speaking. As he steals her wooden leg, she vents her venomous spleen against him and the religion she believes he represents:

"You're a Christian!" she hissed. "You're a fine Christian! You're just like them all—say one thing and do another . . ."

Again, she is deceived by her credulous incredulity as Pointer responds indignantly that he doesn't believe "in that crap." His last words to her before disappearing with her leg are the final comical *coup de grâce*: "And I'll tell you another thing, Hulga, you ain't so smart. I been believing in nothing ever since I was born!"

As with all of O'Connor's fiction the key to understanding the work is to be found on the level of allegory. In "Good Country People," the wooden leg is both the crutch and the crux of the story.[132] It is the crutch upon which the whole story rests and the crux, i.e., cross, to which it points. The wooden leg is the cross that Joy/Hulga has been called to carry, that she is called to *accept* as Christ accepted His own Cross. In her refusal to accept her cross she sows the seeds of her own downfall. In refusing to accept her suffering with joy, it becomes the source of her bitterness, the root of her sin. Perhaps hell is full of forsaken crosses. Perhaps it is from these that the damned hang eternally.

The brilliance of O'Connor's use of the grotesque is that her stories bring the essential metaphysics to the surface. She presents us with gargoyles, such as the Misfit and joyless Hulga, in order to show us the face of the devil. Her grotesque conceits unmask the devil, to borrow the title of Regis Martin's excellent study of O'Connor,[133] by removing the mask of the mundane that obscures the struggle of good and evil at the heart of reality. It's as if she picks up the stone with which we've hardened our hearts in order to reveal the nest of cockroaches, or serpents, lurking beneath. "My subject in fiction is the action of grace in territory held largely by the devil," she tells us,[134] echoing the words of Dostoyevsky in *The Brothers Karamazov*: "The awful thing is that beauty is mysterious as well as terrible. God and the devil are fighting there, and the battlefield is the heart of man."[135] This is the battlefield of which O'Connor writes, and it's the most realistic battlefield of all because it's the one on which we're all fighting, whether we like it or not, or know it or not.

Flannery O'Connor is one of the brightest gems in the priceless crown of the Catholic Literary Revival. "The Catholic novel," she insisted, "is not necessarily about a Christianized or Catholicized world, but one in which the truth as Christians know it has been used as a light to see the world by."[136] According to this definition, she is herself a Catholic novelist par excellence. Her fiction is not set in a Christian or Catholic world but in dark grotesque worlds where, as Chesterton said, "the Christian ideal has not been tried and found wanting; it has been found difficult and left untried." She knows that her readers will only begin to see the beauty of a life with Christ by seeing the ugliness of a world without Him. She shows us the value of the light by showing us the darkness, reminding us that we do not value the good things in our lives, even our wooden legs, until we lose them.

"There is a moment in every great story," O'Connor tells us, "in which the presence of grace can be felt as it waits to be accepted or rejected, even though the reader may not recognize this moment."[137] The presence of grace can be felt on almost every page of the works of the inestimable Miss O'Connor who was herself a misfit, though of a very different ilk to the one in her story. She was a misfit in the sense that we are all misfits, which is to say, in the wonderful words of the *Salve Regina*, that she is a poor banished child of Eve, an exile in this vale of tears, a sojourner, a stranger in a strange land. Yet she was more of a misfit than most. As a Southerner from Georgia, she was a misfit in a Yankee-dominated world; and as a cradle Catholic in the staunchly Protestant and alienated South, she was a misfit among misfits. She was, therefore, an outsider looking into a world in which she did not really belong, and yet, gift of gifts, she could see that world from the inside and show that world itself in new and startling ways. She could do so because she was the Hillbilly Thomist who had cut her aesthetic teeth on Jacques Maritain's *Art and Scholasticism*. In short, she saw clearly because she saw through the eyes of the Church. In seeing through the edifying and inspirational eyes of Miss O'Connor, we see through the eyes of the Church Herself all the more clearly.

68. SOLZHENITSYN:
THE TRIUMPH OF WINSTON SMITH

It is almost a century since the forces of secular fundamentalism unleashed an anti-Christian pogrom on the people of Russia. Declaring the liberation of Man from God, the communists sought to murder the Mass, replacing it with mass murder. In the following decades, tens of millions were sacrificed on the altars of atheism as Man, unshackled from the constraints of Christian morality, showed the horrific deadliness of his "enlightenment." With perverse and infernal irony, men were slaughtered in the name of Man.

The seeming omnipotence of Man was reinforced by the monolithic State, the political Machine with which Man crushed men. This Man-Machine shoveled millions of men into death camps, feeding them like fodder to Man Almighty, the new god of materialism. This was the madness of Marxism, a madness that seemed to sweep the world before it in the first half of the last century. It seemed to be maddeningly charming, sweeping men off their feet and out of their heads. Its kiss was a curse, the kiss of death.

In the midst of this Marxist maelstrom, a child was born. His name was Alexander Solzhenitsyn. He was much like any other child of the Revolution. He was brainwashed by the Man-Machine's "education" program and became a clone of the system. He fought for the Machine during the Second World War, idolizing Stalin, the self-styled Steel-Man, who was Master of the Machine, and he witnessed the raping and pillaging of Prussia as part of the Steel-Man's bloodlustful revenge on the Germans. He then committed the heresy of criticizing the Steel-Man in a letter to a friend. Denounced as a blasphemer against Man he was sent to prison where he lost his faith in Almighty Man and where he discovered, for the first time, the exiled God.

Liberated from the slavery of subservience to a false god, Solzhenitsyn found his freedom whilst in prison. Turning his back on Man, he learned

to love men. The Will made Steel had been overthrown by the Word made
Flesh. Later, after almost dying of cancer, he found life in his near experience of death. It was this near-death experience that led to his final conversion to Christianity. In his death was his resurrection.

Now, aided by the Risen God, he was ready to harrow hell itself. He
was only one small man, seemingly powerless against the Soviet system,
but, aided by the God-Man, he was ready to take on the might of the Man-
Machine. Almost single-handedly, and almost miraculously, this one man
would play a major role in the overthrow of Man Almighty, at least in its
Soviet incarnation. His devastating exposés of the horrors of communism
in works such as *One Day in the Life of Ivan Denisovich* and the monumental *Gulag Archipelago* undermined the very faith-foundations of Marxism.
His books, and the living example of his courageous resistance against the
Machine's efforts to crush him, served as a beacon of light penetrating to
the heart of the darkness.

Today, after the Machine has ground to a halt, and after the statues of
the Steel-Man have been ignominiously toppled, it is easy to forget the
sheer enormity of Solzhenitsyn's achievement. Quite simply, what he did
was considered to be impossible. It was beyond belief that one man could
defy the communist State and survive. It was even more unbelievable that
he should not only survive but that he should play a significant role in the
State's downfall and that he should outlive the State itself. Solzhenitsyn's
life and example flew in the face of the "reality" of the "realists."

The destiny of the small man who dared defy the Man-Machine was
epitomized in the eyes of most pessimistic "realists" by the example of
Winston Smith in George Orwell's novel, *Nineteen Eighty-Four.*

Orwell's novel was published in 1948 when Solzhenitsyn was serving
his sentence as a political prisoner of the Soviet regime. As such, the figure of Winston Smith can be seen as being not merely a figure of
Everyman in his alienation from the Man-Machine (Big Brother), but as an
unwitting figure of Solzhenitsyn himself. According to the "realistic"
view, Winston Smith would not only be crushed by the Machine, he would
also betray every ideal, and everything he loved, in abject surrender to the
Almighty State. The triumph of Big Brother was inevitable; it was preor-
dained. It was Fate, and to deny or defy fate was fatal and futile. The fact
is that Orwell had failed to shake off the Hegelian determinism of his
Marxist past. He had long since become disillusioned with Marxism but
still believed that the forces of history were immutable and the triumph of
the Man-Machine inevitable. Orwell still believed, like his former

comrades, that the Man-Machine was omnipotent; he only differed from them to the extent that he hated the omnipotent god, whereas they admired it.

Solzhenitsyn, on the other hand, did not believe that the Machine was a god but merely a demon, or a dragon, a manifestation of evil. He did not believe in fate but in freedom; the freedom of the will and its responsibility to serve the truth. Fate was a figment of the imagination, but the dragon was real. Furthermore, it was the duty of the good man to fight the dragon, even unto death if necessary. Solzhenitsyn fought the dragon, even though it was thousands of times bigger than he was, and even though it breathed fire and had killed millions of people. He fought it because, in conscience, he could do nothing else. In doing so, he proved that faith, not fate, is the final victor. Faith can move mountains; it can move Machines that were thought to be gods; it can move and remove Big Brother.

Solzhenitsyn has re-written George Orwell's novel, using the facts of his life as his pen. He represents the victory of Winston Smith. And that's not all. He is also living proof that St. George slays the dragon; that David slays Goliath; and that Jack slays the Giant. The saints are alive, the Bible is true, and fairy stories are more real than so-called "realistic" novels. Truth is not only stranger than fiction, it has a happier ending.

69. THE ESSENTIAL SOLZHENITSYN

Edward E. Ericson, Jr., and Daniel J. Mahoney (eds), *The Solzhenitsyn Reader: New and Essential Writings 1947–2005*, ISI Books.

My own generation is perhaps the last to whom the figure of Alexander Solzhenitsyn looms as large as a legend. I have vague, hazy recollections as a boy, and as a teenager, of the man in the news who was seen as a hero against Soviet totalitarianism. I was eight when Solzhenitsyn was expelled from the Soviet Writers' Union, nine when he won the Nobel Prize for Literature, and thirteen when he was forced into exile, first to Switzerland and then to the United States. All that I really knew about the Russian at this time was that he was famous. His picture was as familiar to me as that of the most famous politicians. His imposing beard, his stern expression and his lofty brow made him instantly recognizable. He was, to employ the modern inane label, a celebrity. It was only later, when, at the age of around seventeen, I had first read *The Gulag Archipelago*, that I fully realized that the lofty brow was also a highbrow, that the imposing presence had as much to do with the wisdom of what he said as with the heroism with which he said it. And when I read Orwell's *Nineteen Eighty-Four*, at around the same time, it struck me that Solzhenitsyn was a real-life Winston Smith. With these experiences enshrined in my memories of him, it is easy to imagine how I felt, many years later, when Solzhenitsyn walked into the room, at his home near Moscow, to be interviewed by me for my biography of him. I felt as though I was in the presence of a living icon. It was as though Winston Churchill had walked into the room. One does not often have the chance to chat with a legend.

All of the foregoing serves merely as a preamble to a discussion of *The Solzhenitsyn Reader*, edited by those edifices of Solzhenitsyn scholarship, Edward E. Ericson, Jr., and Daniel J. Mahoney, both of whom had already established their credentials with previously published studies of the great man. These are men who know the man as few others in the world know him. They know his life and his works, and they fully appreciate his importance. They are, therefore, ideally suited to edit a volume of "new and essential writings."

The Editors' Introduction serves as a succinct biography of Solzhenitsyn's life for those unfamiliar with it, and as a brief and astute critical analysis of his thought, culminating in a section entitled "The Continuing Relevance of Solzhenitsyn."

Having established the context in which the works should be seen and read, the editors present us with their selection of what is "new and essential" in Solzhenitsyn's work. They commence with a selection of poetry from Solzhenitsyn's early period, depicting his experience of the second world war, and, subsequently, the ordeal of prison, of the Gulag and of internal exile. In their introduction to "Besed," chapter five of the epic poem *Dorozhen'ka* (*The Trail* or *The Way*), composed in prison between 1947 and 1952, they make a rare error in their seeming insistence that the narrative of the poem is strictly autobiographical. Although, as a whole, it should be read as an autobiographical narrative of Solzhenitsyn's experience, and the spiritual germination which arose from the cruelty and suffering depicted, there are surely times when the principal character of the narrative, Sergei Nerzhin, is a *composite* of Solzhenitsyn's experience, incorporating the actions of others that he had witnessed and, no doubt, the actions of others merely reported to him by a third party. It is, therefore, wrong to attribute everything experienced and enacted by Nerzhin as having been really, and in every detail, experienced and enacted by Solzhenitsyn *in person*. Such a reading denies the poet the artistic license he has no doubt employed and therefore sacrifices the literary on the altar of the literal. Worse, since Solzhenitsyn cannot be assumed to have done everything that Nerzhin does in the poem, it sacrifices literary truth on the altar of literal falsehood. Art is sacrificed to erroneous fact. It should be stressed, however, that such errors are rare and that the short introductions to each section are normally unerring in the safe critical hands of Messrs. Ericson and Mahoney.

There is another shadow that passes across this early section of poems. It is the shadow of which T. S. Eliot speaks in "The Hollow Men", the shadow that falls between the potency and the existence. More specifically, it is the shadow that falls between the potency of Solzhenitsyn's original poems and the existence of the translations. It is always a saddening and sobering realization, when reading poetry in translation, that we are reading something in which the original inspiration has been overshadowed by its falling into a foreign tongue. I was struck by this painful realization upon reading "Acatisthus," a veritable and irrepressible hymn of thanksgiving that evokes Solzhenitsyn's gratitude for his conversion to Christianity. Even if the translation is masterful, we know that something is missing, something is lost. And it is the thing that is lost, rather than the meaning that remains present, which we regret. It is the real absence of the *je ne sais quoi* beyond translation that touches us with its exiled beauty. The fall of the shadow of which Eliot speaks is nothing less than the shadow of the Fall. It is the babble of Babel. It is for this reason that it is worth learning Italian, not merely to converse as more than a mere tourist in Rome, but to be able to read Dante's *Divine Comedy* in the original language. Similarly, it is worth learning Russian merely so that we can read Solzhenitsyn in the original, not to mention Dostoyevsky, Tolstoy *et al.* Until such time, we are exiles in the shadowlands of literature. Although the foregoing applies to all of Solzhenitsyn's work, and to all foreign works in translation, it is particularly so in the case of poetry, in which language is distilled towards perfection, rather than in prose, in which the slack of linguistic looseness can be taken up by the translator and refashioned into something more closely akin to the original. It is for this reason that one is overcome with regret when reading these poems, a regret which, paradoxically, is heightened by the high quality of the translation. The more we are moved by their beauty, and they are truly beautiful even in the shade that shields them from their source, the more we pine for the chance to bask in the direct light of the original conception. None of this is the fault of the editors, of course, nor of the translators. It is simply part of the flawed cosmos in which we live.

In the section allotted to Solzhenitsyn's "Stories" it is good to see the inclusion of *Matryona's Home* and *Easter Procession*, the former a masterfully understated presentation of rustic sanctity, the latter a gratingly graphic depiction of urban vice and vacuity. The sections devoted to Solzhenitsyn's novels clearly created a problem for the editors, an unenviable one because ultimately an insoluble one. It would, of course, be unthinkable to exclude the novels from such a volume as this, but their inclusion in fragmentary form is far from ideal. Isolated chapters, published out of context, cannot possibly convey the sweep and swath of the plot's panorama, nor the swathes of layers with which its beauty and meaning are revealed. And yet the sin of vandalism involved in picking these novels apart is a lesser evil than the sin of omission that would have been committed in leaving them out altogether. The editors have, therefore, opted for the lesser of two evils and, since no other option was available to them, they are to be commended for so doing. One could perhaps play devil's advocate and wonder why *One Day in the Life of Ivan Denisovich* was omitted completely when, as such a short novel, it could have been included in its entirety, but my sympathies are with the editors' insistence that a place of suitable honour be reserved for the more voluminous works. How could one have an "essential" Solzhenitsyn without *The First Circle* or *Cancer Ward*, even if we have to make do with only fragments of each? It still irritates me that *Ivan Denisovich* is left out in the cold but I can fully understand the difficulties that the editors faced in making their selection. Perhaps this is grounds for requesting a companion volume entitled "More Essential Solzhenitsyn"!

Although the cutting and pasting of the novels leaves one with reservations, *The Gulag Archipelago* lends itself well to this selective text-dipping. Almost a hundred pages are dedicated to selections from the *Gulag* and it is sufficient, one feels, for a newcomer to get a taste for this monument to the monumental mania of the Soviet form of secular fundamentalism. For the vast bulk of Solzhenitsyn's readers who do not speak his native tongue, the selection from *March 1917* and *April 1917*, those parts of his epic, *The Red Wheel*, which have not yet been published in English, will be most welcome, as will be the selections from *Two Hundred Years Together*, his recent controversial study of the Jews in Russia. It was also heartening to see parts of *Russia in Collapse*, another recent work, but a little disappointing that space was not found for his earlier work, *Rebuilding Russia*, much of which retains its relevance, socio-politically, not merely for Russia but for the rest of the world also. Much of Solzhenitsyn's continuing relevance is to be found, however, in the lengthy section on his essays and speeches. Many of the defining moments in Solzhenitsyn's intellectual engagement with the modern age are to be found in this section: his Open letter to the Soviet Writers' Union; the Nobel Lecture; the call for "self-limitation" in one of his essays published in *From Under the Rubble*; and his valedictory address to the West before his return to Russia at the International Academy of Philosophy in Liechtenstein. And, of course, there is the indispensable and quintessentially definitive Harvard Address which, even today, can be employed as a touchstone or litmus test of true conservatism.

Since his return to Russia, Solzhenitsyn has returned to poetry, specifically to the writing of prose poems, or miniatures, as the Editors prefer to call them. Some of these are sublime, and allow us to reach further into the soul of the man. *The Solzhenitsyn Reader* ends, therefore, as it began, with poetry. This is as it should be. Solzhenitsyn might be as austere as a monk, as stern as a prophet, as astute as a sage, as indefatigable as an athlete, and as mighty as a warrior—all characteristics which are exhibited in this admirable *Reader*—but deep down in the soul of this exile is the beauty of the poet. It is here, in the prosodic depths, that the essential Solzhenitsyn is to be discovered.

70. GRAHAM GREENE AND GEORGE W. BUSH: OLD WORLD CYNICISM MEETS NEW WORLD NAÏVETÉ

There was something bizarre, indeed something almost surreal, about George W. Bush's recent reference to Graham Greene's novel, *The Quiet American*, in his speech in Kansas City to the National Convention of the Veterans of Foreign Wars. Attempting to draw a parallel between the conflict in Vietnam and the current conflagration in Iraq, Bush criticized Greene's suggestion that the "quiet American's" patriotism was dangerously naïve:

> In 1955 . . . Graham Greene wrote a novel called *The Quiet American*. It was set in Saigon, and the main character was a young government agent named Alden Pyle. He was a symbol of American purpose and patriotism—and dangerous naïveté.

Bush's unexpected sortie into the fictional world of Greene was itself dangerously naïve, especially as several commentators had already suggested that Bush was little more than a real-life incarnation of Alden Pyle. It was also both bemusing and amusing to see Bush reference a work that almost everyone presumed he had never read. Certainly, if he had read *The Quiet American*, he would not have made the rudimentary error of referring to Pyle as the novel's "main character," a distinction that belongs to the character of Thomas Fowler, a disillusioned and cynical English journalist. Such is the pitiable state of American politics in these sorry days that an uncultured President relies for his semblance of erudition on equally unlettered speech writers.

Be that as it may, *The Quiet American* will serve as a good place to look at the relative merits of messieurs Bush and Greene, and will serve as a meditation on the relationship between New World naïveté and Old World cynicism. If, for example, there is a great deal of George W. Bush in the transparent (and dangerous) shallowness of Alden Pyle, there is more than a hint of Graham Greene in the world-weary depths of Thomas Fowler. Pyle is certain that "Democracy," "Freedom" and "America" are not only inseparable but that they are synonymous. It is almost as though they form an indivisible Trinity, as holy as the Trinity of the Christians and as worthy of praise. This quasi-religious zeal turns every war for "Freedom" and "Democracy" into a jihad, with Pyle emerging as a fanatic for the cause of "America" in much the same way that the new breed of Muslim terrorists emerge as fanatics for "Islam." It must be said, however, that Pyle is much more likeable than any Islamic fanatic, and is even dis-armingly charming in his simple, unquestioning faith in the Motherland. Parallels with Bush are not only palpable, they positively palpitate from the pages of *The Quiet American*!

But what of Thomas Fowler, the pathetically apathetic wastrel whose jaded presence dominates the novel? He is almost the antithesis of Pyle, the anti-Pyle. Whereas Pyle is puritanical and abstemious, Fowler is an opium-addicted Baudelairean decadent. Whereas Pyle is an idealist, albeit an idealist enslaved by an ideology (ironically like his communist ene-mies), Fowler is cynically indifferent to all ideals. Whereas Pyle is deco-rously prim and proper in his dealings with women, and particularly in his chivalrous dealings with Phuong, the woman at the centre of his and Fowler's desires, Fowler is unremittingly self-serving in his carnal rela-tions, deserting his wife and children and seeing in Phuong little more than a comfortable and convenient ménage, indulging her as an addictive habit which, like his opium habit, allows him to escape temporarily from his responsibility to reality. Whereas Pyle is motivated by an illusory heaven on earth, a heaven of "democracy" and "freedom" (again, ironically, like his communist enemies), Fowler shuns heaven and purgatory and desires only the adulterous hell of Paolo and Francesca in Dante's *Divine Comedy* (referring to an unwanted promotion which would force him to return to England, Fowler muses that "Dante never thought up that turn of the screw for his condemned lovers. Paolo was never promoted to Purgatory."). Pyle is willing to be a martyr for his false heaven; Fowler tells heaven (and pur-gatory) to go to hell! Who then is worse: the puritanically idealistic Pyle, or the morally iconoclastic Fowler? What is worse: the messianic Americanism of George W. Bush or the jaded, ethno-masochistic death wish of most of the leaders of Europe? New World naïveté or Old World

cynicism?—that is the question. Should we choose one or the other, selecting the better of two evils; or are we at liberty, with Mercutio in
Shakespeare's *Romeo and Juliet*, to call down a plague on both their houses?

And what of Graham Greene himself? Is it fair to associate him too
closely with his fictional anti-hero, Thomas Fowler? It is true that, like
Fowler, he deserted his wife and children; and it is true that, like Fowler,
he settled into a number of adulterous ménages in the years after he left his
wife. It is also true that, as with Fowler, his Christian (Catholic) wife would
not contemplate a divorce (though Fowler's fictional wife eventually
relented). Yet these similarities, though certainly not superficial, serve only
to mask the very real differences that exist between the life and beliefs of
the author and those of his fictional creation. Unlike the doggedly godless
Fowler, Greene was, and remained (for the most part), a believing
Catholic, a fact that separates him not only from Fowler but from the dog-
matically godless leadership of Europe. Greene is, therefore, an enigma
that warrants further investigation.

Greene's conversion to Catholicism in 1926 was influenced, in the first
instance, by the fact that the woman whom he would later marry was herself a convert. It would, however, be a grave error to explain, or explain
away, Greene's Catholicism as little more than an effort to please the
woman he loved. Other Catholic influences were also at work, such as his
evident admiration for the works of Eliot and Chesterton. Greene's early
novels, such as *Stamboul Train* and *Brighton Rock*, were set in Eliotic
wastelands, inhabited by Eliot's hollow men, in which we nonetheless
detect, as with Eliot's poems, the hinted, haunting presence of an (almost)
invisible Christ. His second novel, *The Name of Action*, published in 1930,
employed several lines from Eliot's "The Hollow Men" as its epigraph.

Greene's admiration for Chesterton emerged in his review of Maisie
Ward's biography of Chesterton, in which he described Chesterton's
Orthodoxy, The Thing and *The Everlasting Man* as "among the great books
of the age," and in which he also praised several of Chesterton's other
books, including *The Ballad of the White Horse* and the novels, *The Man
Who was Thursday* and *The Napoleon of Notting Hill*. It is also significant
that Greene would always consider Newman's *Apologia pro Vita Sua*, a
classic of conversion literature, as one of his favourite books.

If, therefore, Greene's Catholicism can be seen to be genuine, it does-
n't alter the fact that his practice of the faith, and his expression of it in his
works, was, at best, enigmatic, and, at worst, downright disreputable and

heretical. Greene knew as much, declaring to Malcolm Muggeridge upon the latter's reception into the Church in 1982 that he hoped "that you will make a better Catholic than I have done." And yet, beguilingly and paradoxically, Greene's troubled faith, and his marital infidelity, provided the inherent tension in the labyrinthine morality plays which were his novels.

Greene deserted his family shortly after the end of the second world war, leaving his wife for another woman. Vivien Greene remembered vividly the day that her husband left: "It was very difficult with the children . . . We went upstairs into the drawing room and then he left. And I thought, well, I'll probably never see him again and looked out of the window that was facing the street, and he looked back for a minute, didn't wave, but looked back." This dramatic moment clearly haunted Greene as much as it haunted his wife because it emerges, ghost-like, in *The Quiet American* when Fowler turned random memories over in his mind: "a fox . . . seen by the light of an enemy flare . . . the body of a bayoneted Malay . . . my wife's face at a window when I came home to say good-bye for the last time."

Greene's contorted conscience twisted itself agonizingly through the plot of *The Heart of the Matter*, the novel he wrote shortly after his desertion of his family, in which the convoluted moral convulsions of Scobie left many critics squirming. Whereas some writers, including Evelyn Waugh, Edward Sackville-West and Raymond Mortimer, had suggested that Scobie was a sinful saint, others had seen only the sinner: "Scobie commits adultery, sacrilege, murder (indirectly), and suicide in quick succession," one correspondent wrote. "In three of these cases he is well aware of what he is doing . . . he takes communion in mortal sin because he can't bear to hurt his wife's feelings. This isn't the way a saint behaves." These views were reiterated in another review by a Father John Murphy:

> Scobie is a Catholic with a conscience of the highest sensitivity and insight whose weak will ultimately leads him to adultery, sacrilegious Holy Communions, responsibility for a murder . . . and for full measure, to a suicide . . . How can you account for the fact that a man commits suicide in order, among other things, to avoid making any more bad Communions? But the answer is obvious: Because he despaired where he should have repented.

Another member of the Catholic clergy, in this case a bishop, reminded the author of *The Heart of the Matter* that "adultery is adultery whatever attempts may be made to disguise it by not using the hard word." Equally ruthless in his criticism was George Orwell who opined that if Scobie "really felt that adultery is mortal sin he would stop committing it . . . If he believed in Hell, he would not risk going there merely to spare the feelings of a couple of neurotic women."

At the other end of the critical spectrum, the Jesuit, C. C. Martindale, described *The Heart of the Matter* as "a magnificent book," adding that its effect on one "hard-headed man to whom this book was given" had been to serve as "the last necessary stimulus" to his becoming a Catholic. Another correspondent wished it to be "put on record . . . that one great sinner was so moved by Mr. Greene's last book that he has completely changed his way of life and returned to the practice of the Faith."

Greene's own response to the critical reaction indicated that these repentant sinners, rather than the novel's detractors, had the deepest affinity with his own understanding of the novel: "I did not regard Scobie as a saint," he wrote to Waugh, "and his offering his damnation up was intended to show how muddled a mind of good will could become when once 'off the rails.'" Ironically these words would become prophetically autobiographical. The longer Greene remained "off the rails" the more muddled he became in his approach to Catholicism.

By the time that Greene wrote his play, *The Potting Shed*, in 1957, even old friends and allies, such as Evelyn Waugh, were losing patience with his heterodox dabblings. The play was "great nonsense theologically," Waugh complained, "and will puzzle people needlessly." Three years later, after Greene had written to Waugh of how his latest novel, *A Burnt Out Case*, was intended "to give expression to various states or moods of belief or unbelief" and that the characterization of the doctor had represented "a settled and easy atheism," Waugh had replied impatiently that many would see the novel "as a recantation of faith": "To my mind the expression 'settled and easy atheism' is meaningless, for an atheist denies his whole purpose as a man—to love and serve God. Only in the most superficial way can atheists appear 'settled and easy'."

As Waugh observed Greene's descent from the realm of Reason and Creed to that of mere "mood," one wonders whether he was reminded of the wit of his friend Ronald Knox who had written half a century earlier of the similar descent from faith to "feeling" of Anglican Modernists who:

> . . . temp'ring bigot Zeal,
> Corrected "I believe" to "One does feel . . ."

In his last years, Greene showed a few tentative signs of returning to a more orthodox practice of the Faith, though it would be an exaggeration to describe his Catholicism as "settled and easy." "I've betrayed a great number of things and people in the course of my life," he stated in 1979, "which probably explains this uncomfortable feeling I have about myself, this sense of having been cruel, unjust. It still torments me often enough before I go to sleep." It is in this tormented light that we must view Graham Greene's relationship with his faith, his life, and his work. He never felt comfortable with Catholicism but then he never felt comfortable with anything else either. Like St. Thomas the Apostle, whom Greene chose as his confirmation saint, he was a doubter. He doubted others, he doubted himself and he doubted God. And yet the profundity of his novels never resides in the doubt itself but in the ultimate doubt about the doubt. It was this doubt about doubt that kept him clinging desperately to the Catholic faith, so much so that his biographer, Norman Sherry, insisted that "he remained a strong Catholic until his death."

Greene was paradox personified. He was a pessimistic pessimist, in the positive sense in which he was always pessimistic about his own pessimism, and in the positive sense in which these two negatives, in combination, made a positive contribution to the true moral depth of his work.

If, however, we can finish our investigation of Greene's doubtful depths on a positive note, acquitting him of being associated too closely with the old-world cynicism of Thomas Fowler in *The Quiet American*, where does he stand with regard to the President's present policy in Iraq? Does Greene, or the ghost of Greene, have anything to say on the present situation in the middle east? Is he as relevant to the present situation as Bush, or his speechwriters, seem to think? Yes he is, but not perhaps in the way that Bush intended.

Back in 1987, Greene was one of the most vocal critics of the Israeli government following the abduction of Mordechai Vanunu from Italy by Israeli agents. Vanunu's "crime," in the eyes of the Israelis, was to have exposed the fact that Israel possessed nuclear weapons which, by any stretch of the imagination, can be described as "weapons of mass destruction." Why is it, one wonders, that some countries in the middle east can possess weapons of mass destruction, with Bush's blessing, while others cannot? Why did previous American governments arm the Taliban in the name of "freedom" and "democracy"? Why did previous American governments arm Saddam Hussein in the name of "freedom" and "democracy"? Why did Bush's own government declare war on the only secular government in the middle east capable of resisting the Islamo-fascism of Iran? These are questions that only George W. Bush or Alden Pyle could answer. The rest of us remain baffled.

In his speech to the Veterans, Bush quoted a character in *The Quiet American* who said of Alden Pyle that he had never known a man "who had better motives for all the trouble he caused." Like Pyle, Bush is well-intentioned; like Pyle, he is dangerously naïve; like Pyle, his noble motives have caused a lot of trouble. And, like Pyle, he needs reminding of the old adage that the road to hell is paved with good intentions.

71. THE DA VINCI CON

I would not snare even an orc with a falsehood.
— Faramir

Faramir, a noble warrior in *The Lord of the Rings*, would not tell a lie even to a servant of the devil. Dan Brown, the ignoble author of *The Da Vinci Code*, snares even the innocent with a plethora of falsehoods. With seductive sedition, his novel, masquerading as "truth," tells one lie after another. At its deceptive heart is the "ancient" secret society, the Priory of Sion, which is said to have kept the "secret" about Jesus's marriage to Mary Magdalene. In fact, this "fact," which forms the basis of Brown's book, was exposed as a hoax concocted only fifty years ago by a French anti-Semite, Pierre Plantard. With malicious ingenuity Brown turned Plantard's anti-Semitic fraud into anti-Catholic "fact."

Let's take a closer look at the fraudulent source of *The Da Vinci Code* by looking more closely at its original inspirer, Pierre Plantard.

Plantard was born in 1920 and from 1937 onwards began fantasizing about Jewish and Masonic conspiracies. On 16 December 1940 he wrote to Marshal Pétain about the "terrible Masonic and Jewish conspiracy" against France, warning Pétain that he should act swiftly to counter the threat. Ever the fantasist, Plantard offered "a hundred reliable men . . . who are devoted to the cause" to fight against the Masonic Jews. In spite of his impeccable anti-Semitic credentials, the German authorities did not look kindly on his plans to found political associations. A police report on Plantard, dated 9 May 1941, highlights the sort of man whom Dan Brown takes as being authoritative: "Plantard, who boasts of having links with numerous politicians, seems to be one of those dotty, pretentious young men who run more or less fictitious groups in an effort to look important . . ."

After the war, Plantard's conspiracy theories became ever more bizarre. In 1956 he founded the Priory of Sion, the organisation that is depicted as having "ancient secret knowledge" in *The Da Vinci Code*. In the early 1960s Plantard claimed to be the true heir to the throne of France, descended from the Merovingian king, Dagobert II, who reigned in the seventh century. Needless to say, Plantard, the son of a butler and a cook, has no recorded links to the Merovingians, his parents had never made such claims, and he appears to have got the whole idea from an article in a French magazine published in 1960.

In 1962, Plantard, "the True King of France," collaborated with Gerard de Sede to write *Les Templiers sont parmi nous*, which is the original source of the popular version of the Priory of Sion found in *The Da Vinci Code*. Needless to say, once again, that all the claims made in this book can be easily exposed as historical fiction. None of the claims in the so-called Priory Documents existed before the early 1960s, in any shape or form, and none of them can be substantiated by known historical records. If more proof were needed that Dan Brown's book is a house of cards built with a pack of lies, one need look no further than correspondence between Plantard and his fellow conspirators, dating from the 1960s. These letters, in the possession of French researcher Jean-Luc Chaumeil, confirm that Plantard and his partners in crime were engaging in a shameless confidence trick. Is Dan Brown as gullible as so many of his readers in swallowing such nonsense, or is he a shameless liar on the scale of Plantard? Is he a conman or has he been conned?

In the late 1980s Plantard changed his story once again, admitting that the Priory of Sion had nothing to do with the Knights Templar, and that most of his "secrets" had been written under the influence of LSD. In 1993 Plantard admitted under oath that he had fabricated everything. He died in obscurity on 3 February 2000, only three years before Dan Brown would resurrect him, or rather his lies, from the dead.

Post Script

Following the success of *The Da Vinci Code*, Dan Brown is said to be working on a follow-up which he claims is as "true" and as "full of historical facts about the Catholic conspiracy against humanity." Thanks to my own connections, an Opus Dei nun posing as a reader at Doubleday, I can reveal the plot to the world before it is published. The new book will be called *The Van Gogh Virus* and it will tell of the efforts of the Pope, aided and abetted by the Learned Elders of Zion, Al Qaeda and a group of undercover aliens from the Planet Zog, to contaminate the world through a virus implanted in prints of Van Gogh's *Self Portrait*. Order your copy now and beat the rush.

72. HOMAGE TO A CIVILIZED MAN

I first met Henry Zeiter in 2004 at Thomas Aquinas College in Santa Paula, California. I had flown from my home in Florida to give a talk and he, as a long-serving member of the College's board of governors, was a guest of honour at the subsequent dinner. I had the great pleasure of sitting next to him and was struck immediately by the magnanimity of the man and by the magnitude of his knowledge. He waxed lyrical on art, literature, music, history, politics and philosophy. Had he not been constrained by my own woeful ineptitude he might have switched effortlessly in his lyrical loquaciousness to one or other of the several languages in which he is fluent, including French, Arabic and Spanish. Nonetheless we spoke, in English, of our many shared interests. Having confessed, almost apologetically, my great admiration for the music of Wagner, and particularly my enduring love for the masterful Tannhauser Overture, I was heartened to discover that he was that rarest of oddities, a Catholic Wagnerian. Our conversational perambulations continued and I learned that his catholicity of taste extended to Brahms, Beethoven, Bach and a host of other giants of the western musical tradition.

As we worked our way through the courses on the menu we simultaneously worked our way through the corpus of western literature, discussing Dante and discoursing on Dostoyevsky. We lingered on the literature of the French Decadence and I was again heartened to discover a kindred spirit who shared my passion for the lurid lucidity of Baudelaire and Huysmans. Moving onto the dessert and into the desert of the twentieth century I was deeply impressed by the breadth and depth of his knowledge of the key figures of the Catholic literary revival. He reminded me, in fact, of Maurice Baring, another Catholic Wagnerian and one of the unsung giants of the very revival we were discussing, whose work is awash with high culture beyond the reach of our cultureless age. If Baring is largely forgotten today it is not because he is not worth reading but because the modern age cannot read on the level at which he wrote. Modernity is culturally illiterate; it is not worthy of him or the culture in which he was steeped. As I read through the manuscript of Dr. Zeiter's autobiography[138] it reminded me very much, in spite of the many and obvious differences, of Baring's wonderful autobiography, *The Puppet Show of Memory*. Maurice Baring and Henry Zeiter have much in common, and we, who are common, have much that we can learn from them if we wish to ascend the heights of the civilization of which they and we are co-inheritors. Such were my first impressions of Henry Zeiter, and such was the deep impression he made upon me. As the meal ended a valuable friendship began.

Incidentally, and to allow myself the indulgence of a superfluous tangent, I cannot resist the comparison between my edifying cultural and culinary sojourn with Dr. Zeiter and the very different sort of culinary experience endured by the controversial poet, Roy Campbell, recounted graphically in his satirical poem, *The Georgiad*. May it suffice to say that my literary dinner with Henry Zeiter had nothing whatever in common with Roy Campbell's experience with the pretentious bores of Bloomsbury:

> Dinner, most ancient of the Georgian rites,
> The noisy prelude of loquacious nights,
> At the mere sound of whose unholy gong
> The wagging tongue feels resolute and strong,
> Senate of bores and parliament of fools,
> Where gossip in her native empire rules;
> What doleful memories the word suggests—
> When I have sat like Job among the guests,
> Sandwiched between two bores, a hapless prey,
> Chained to my chair, and cannot get away . . .
> O Dinners! take my curse upon you all,
> But literary dinners most of all . . .

Roy Campbell also wrote disparagingly about what he termed the "Peter Panic," the modern fear of growing old and the modern mania for staying young. There is in our myopic and meretricious age no interest in growing old with dignity, still less in treating the elderly with any dignity. Euthanasia is the logical product of youthanausea, the sickness of youth that sacrifices the dignity of the old on the altar of its own narcissistic self-worship. Youthful folly with its fallacious fancies has usurped the wisdom of the ages, and the wisdom of the aged. We no longer listen to our elders, believing that adolescents know best. "One's children want independence after being told what to do for the first eighteen years of their lives," writes Dr. Zeiter. "Their children are even further removed from our injunctions.

Nowadays the young actually distance themselves from the old and the wise, as if only their peers (who know nothing!) can teach them about life." This, of course, is the height of inanity from which, as a culture, we fall into the depths of insanity. It is tragic. It is comic. Dr. Zeiter's book, which is so much more than a mere autobiography, is an antidote to all such nonsense. As we turn the pages of this life we find ourselves in the presence of a learned elder from whom we can learn so much about our world, our culture, our heritage, our destiny, ourselves. We are also in the presence of a gifted storyteller who punctuates his narrative with sagacious anecdotes. The journey takes us from Lebanon to Latin America, and thence to Canada and, finally, to California; but it also takes us on a journey into the faith and philosophy of western civilization, and hence into an understanding of the meaning of life and consequently an understanding of ourselves. It is a journey beyond ourselves so that we can come to fully know ourselves.

I repeat and reiterate that this is so much more than a mere autobiography. In this edifying and efficacious life we meet not only Dr. Zeiter's family—his ancestors, his parents, his siblings, his wife, his children—we meet a host of his friends, many of whom he knows intimately, such as Aristotle and St. Thomas Aquinas; St. John of the Cross and Dante; Brahms, Beethoven and Bach; Eliot, Joyce and Hemingway. We discover also, perhaps to our surprise, that many of these people knew each other. Thus we discover that it was James Joyce who introduced Dr. Zeiter to St. Thomas Aquinas: "Ironically, it may have been the unhappy arch-heretic— as he called himself—James Joyce who deepened my love of Thomas Aquinas."

Like my own father, from whom I learned more than from any other learned elder, Dr. Zeiter can recite Thomas Gray's Elegy by heart. He courted a girl named Penelope by reciting impassioned lines from Pope's translation of the *Odyssey*. (One can't help but wish that he had also met a girl named Beatrice!) He also courted, more successfully, his future wife by taking her, on their first date, to a performance of Verdi's *Requiem*, after which they discussed metaphysics in general and Thomistic metaphysics in particular. Perhaps Dr. Zeiter's next book should be entitled *Aristotle and the Art of Seduction* or *Thomism for Lovers* or *Use the Muse to Improve your Love Life* or *Homer Sexual*! It is indeed typical of Dr. Zeiter's culture-saturated soul that he begins a refreshingly candid discussion of his and his wife's "mid-life crisis," which almost destroyed their marriage, by reciting the opening lines of Dante's *Inferno*:

Midway upon the journey of our life
I found myself within a forest dark,
For the straightforward pathway had been lost . . .

T. S. Eliot once wrote that he was so much in awe of Dante that all he could do in his presence was to point in the inimitable Florentine's direction and remain silent. At times I find myself so much in awe at Dr. Zeiter's mode of expressing profound thoughts that I can only imitate Eliot's silent reverence by pointing at the inimitable doctor and remaining silent. Thus, for instance, this is Dr. Zeiter on civilisation and culture:

The civilization that Greece bequeathed its testimony to the fact that the deepest currents of history are spiritual and cultural rather than economic. History is driven over the centuries by culture—by the ideas that men and women honor, cherish, and worship—by what a culture deems to be true and beautiful—and by the disciplines used to propagate these beliefs such as language, literature, religion, and the arts. A secular society, like the one ours is becoming attempts to build a culture devoid of its origin. That proves to be impossible. Christopher Dawson wrote around 1950, "We are in no man's land; this secular society being attempted since the First World War, has no end beyond its own satisfaction; it is a monstrosity—a cancerous growth on our traditions which will ultimately destroy itself." And that was said over fifty years ago; the traditions that have propped up our culture have deteriorated considerably since then.

And here's Dr. Zeiter extolling the praises of classical music:

I have always proselytized on behalf of classical music, just as a religious missionary would preach the good news, because I firmly believe that great and sublime music are joyful and spiritually uplifting. For this reason, I find great satisfaction in sharing artistic and musical experiences. They lead to the love of Beauty and, as a consequence, to the love of God.

And how's this for putting Eliot, Joyce and Hemingway in a nutshell?

T. S. Eliot progressed from being an agnostic American author to belief in the traditional tenets of Anglo-Catholicism, and he became a prophetic poet, the most celebrated of the first half of the twentieth century. Joyce left his traditional country and faith for a life of restless wandering in continental Europe. He was a linguist of the first order and established a new style of writing, but he lost his bearings and his soul in the process. Hemingway never had a faith to start with, and after several adventures he turned morose and ended up committing a skeptic's suicide.

And here's what Dr Zeiter has to say about the crass reductionism of modern democracy, a reductionism that was condemned by Chesterton as "the Coming Peril" of "the standardization by a low standard":

> The world has bit by bit lost the sense of the sacred. There is a tendency in democracies to bring down to a common level whatever is noble and elevated. Even God is now brought down to the level of friend and brother in exclusion of his awe-inspiring fatherhood as the mighty Creator of everything. Joseph Pieper has written a book on the new Church architecture in which he describes how shallow and sterile it has become compared to the Gothic and Renaissance temples of worship. He thought that modern church construction had lost the sense of the sacred. Just look at the tattered or immodest way people dress for Sunday Mass. There is an atrophied sense of respect left for the holy or the sacred.

It is clear that Dr. Zeiter shares Chesterton's disdain for the vulgarizing tendencies of the secular fundamentalist version of democracy. It is equally clear, as the whole *raison d'etre* of this present volume testifies, that he would agree with Chesterton's counter-vision of tradition-oriented democracy as espoused in his seminal *Orthodoxy*, in which Chesterton describes tradition as the extension of democracy through time, the proxy of the dead and the enfranchisement of the unborn.

Dr. Zeiter is steeped in Tradition and passes this tradition to us as he learned it from his own father, the "wise philosopher" who counseled him against arguing obvious points with obtuse people: "Son, remember the old Lebanese proverb, 'I argued with a wise philosopher and won, but when I argued with a donkey, I lost.'"

Although we live in an age of donkeys, the proverbial truths of tradition remain as perennial reminders of the permanent things. Again, we cannot do better than to quote Dr. Zeiter quoting his own father, on this occasion his father's "favorite four verses":

He who doesn't know, and knows he doesn't know is ignorant: teach him.
He who knows, but doesn't know that he knows is asleep; wake him.
He who knows, and knows that he knows is wise: follow him.
But he who doesn't know and thinks that he knows is a fool: shun him.

I reiterate and repeat: this book is so much more than a mere autobiography. It can teach those who know they don't know; it can awaken those who don't know that they know; and it can lead those who know that they know. It will only be shunned by the fool who knows no better.

For those who may never have the opportunity of long and enlightening dinners with Henry Zeiter, this book is the next best thing. You will enjoy the inimitable company of the author and will grow in the wisdom he offers. What is more, you will be truly blessed.

73. NEW SAINTS WE SHOULD KNOW

On May 16, 2004, I had the honour and privilege to be at St. Peter's in Rome, along with my wife, Susannah, our two-year-old son, Leo, and our unborn daughter, Gianna, for the canonization of Saint Gianna Beretta Molla and five others by John Paul II. What a joy to be present at such a glorious event! I felt that if our own Gianna had been big enough (she was only a few weeks old at the time) she would have emulated St. John the Baptist by leaping for joy in her mother's womb at the sheer wonder of being in the presence of Christ on such a holy occasion. As she was not yet able to do so, her parents expressed her joy vicariously as we witnessed the mystical birth of a saint who is an icon of modern motherhood and the culture of life.

Saint Gianna Beretta Molla is but one of a heavenly host of holy men and women, all of whom were canonized or beatified by John Paul II, who are brought together in this one volume by Brian O'Neel.[139] This is a book filled to the brim, filled to bursting, with sanctity and with shining examples of the nobility of virtue. In an age that shuns nobility and vilifies virtue the men and women who emerge from these pages are countercultural heroes and heroines, showing us the way through the darkness of the culture of death in the presence of the Source of all Life.

As a means of introducing some of the Saints and Blesseds who bless these pages, I'm going to indulge myself, and beg the reader's indulgence, with a personal selection of some of my own favourites amongst them. In doing so, I must begin by confessing the sins of omission that accompany such self-indulgence, and invite the reader to discover the other holy men and women within these pages for themselves.

Apart from obvious favourites, such as Mother Teresa and Padre Pio (to give them their less grandiose, non-canonised names), I have a particular devotion to Pope (now Blessed) Pius IX. What a defiant opponent of regressive "progress," and what an indefatigably courageous defender of the Church against the rise of secular fundamentalism! Along with St. Pius X and Popes Pius XI and XII, Blessed Pius IX is one of the four "pious" pillars upon which (under grace) the Church's resistance to communism, modernism, Nazism and liberal eugenicism rest securely.

I'm delighted that the Emperor Karl I has been beatified. His example of true Christian kingship, i.e., kingship as service, kingship that subjects itself in humility to the needs of its subjects, is an image of the Kingship of Christ and is worthy, therefore, of its place among the Blessed at His right hand. It is also gratifying to see the beatification of those martyred at the hands of communism. Blessed Vicente David Vilar, one of thousands of Christians killed at the hands of the communist and anarchist Republicans in the Spanish Civil War, kept the most difficult of Our Lord's commandments, loving his enemies even as they were about to shoot him in cold blood. "I forgive you," were his last immortal words. Blessed Miguel Pro's last words, uttered with his arms stretched out like Christ on the Cross as he faced his Mexican Marxist executioners, were "Viva Cristo Rey!" Long live Christ the King! These were also the last words the fourteen-year-old, José Luis Sánchez del Río, exclaimed as he was being repeatedly stabbed by his communist executioners.

Another martyr, though of a somewhat different sort, is Blessed Laura Vicuña, described by Brian O'Neel as "the 'other' Maria Goretti," who suffered sexual and physical abuse, eventually dying of her injuries. And, last but not least, how can we fail to mention Louis and Zélie Martin, the now beatified parents of St. Thérèse of Lisieux, who have rightly become icons of marital love and the self-sacrificial Christian parenthood that puts Planned Parenthood to shame.

This is but a sprinkling of the sparkling firmament of holiness that Brian O'Neel presents to us. In turning the pages that follow, you will be entering into an adventure that offers a new hero or heroine on almost every page. You will have your imagination baptized by their blood, your faith fortified by their courage, your hope heartened by their deeds, and your love enflamed by their passion. And, most importantly, as confirmed by their beatification or canonisation by the Church, you will know that they are able to intercede for you at God's right hand. *Deo gratias! Viva Cristo Rey!*

PART V
SELF-PORTRAITS

74. HOME THOUGHTS FROM ABROAD

O to be in England
Now that April's there,
And whoever wakes in England
Sees, some morning, unaware,
That the lowest boughs and the brushwood sheaf
Round the elm-tree bole are in tiny leaf,
While the chaffinch sings on the orchard bough
In England—now!
— Robert Browning (Home-thoughts, from Abroad)

O to be in England . . .

Sometimes, when Time permits moments of quiet recollection amidst the breathlessly frenetic flow of daily life, I find myself sharing Robert Browning's sentimental yearning for his native land. I, too, am an Englishman, and I, too, am in exile. A happy exile, perhaps, but an exile nonetheless. And although America has been good to me, and my American friends a veritable delight, the heart still, occasionally, leaps across the Atlantic to the familiar things of home.

Browning, of course, wrote of England from the warmth of Florence in Italy, whereas I write from the heat of Naples, Florida. Needless to say, the gulf between Naples, FL and its Italian namesake is immense, wider than the Atlantic itself, and I will confess, as a European, that my preference is decidedly in favour of the aging Italian original rather than its youthfully usurping US counterpart. In making the comparison I am tempted to descend to the level of Browningesque pastiche, verging on pitiful parody, by employing the sort of convoluted rhyme and verbal frivolity for which Browning was famous, or perhaps infamous:

The poet in exile writes wistfully, though happily,
From a place called Naples that will never be Napoli.

Browning was not, however, merely writing from a very different place than the present author but also from a very different time. Much has changed in England in the century and a half since his wistful words were written. The elm trees, once such a facet of the English countryside, have been decimated by Dutch elm disease, and the orchards, which caused the English landscape to blush with blossom, have been obliterated by the European Union and its disastrous agricultural policy. Much has changed but much remains. The chaffinch still sings and is the most beautiful of birds. Its subtle half-toned hue, highlighted with flecks of primary splendour, shows the master-stroke of its Creator's genius. The very sight of such a bird causes the heart to leap with unexpected joy and, as such, the creature is a channel of the Creator's grace. Of American birds, the cardinal has this effect upon me, but this resplendent rose fades beside the more homely beauty of the chaffinch. The former causes us to gaze in awed wonder at its magnificence while the more modest beauty of the latter overcomes such pomp with the power of pure simplicity. The former takes our breath away, the latter enables us to catch our breath. The former reminds us of exotic faraway places, the latter brings to mind the comfortable and the familiar. Great beauty takes us to great places but only the homely leads us home. Thus the magnificent bows before the magnanimous, much as Heaven bows before the Magnificat.

These thoughts of home have taken me on a flight of fancy beyond myself, and I find myself waxing more eloquently than I had intended. I have quite literally got carried away. I trust the reader will forgive me. The foregoing, for all its effusiveness, was meant merely to serve as an evocation of the desire for Home. Such desire is, of course, as close to home for Americans as it is to this Englishman abroad. And speaking of "broads" . . . my wife, who is American though with an Irish mother, quipped that as a woman and as a homebuilder she is better qualified to write an essay entitled "Home Thoughts from a Broad" than am I. Perhaps so. She certainly enjoys, or is afflicted by, the same penchant for puns as is her husband.

Enough digression. These 'Home Thoughts from Abroad' come from the mind and heart of an Englishman who loves his native land and is distressed at the way in which his homeland is sinking in the swamp of secular fundamentalism. He is equally distressed by the prospect that the swamp of secularism might itself be sinking beneath the rising tide of Islamic fundamentalism that has penetrated to England's darkened heart. His own heart is broken by these evils, echoing the words of Mercutio in

Romeo and Juliet: "A plague a' both houses!" My England is not the England of the Modern or the Muslim; it is the England of Shakespeare, Chaucer and St. Thomas More. Its spirit is encapsulated by William Blake, in the immortal lines of his poem "Jerusalem," a poem which, set to rousing music, has been justly adopted as the unofficial English national anthem. It serves as a fitting conclusion to my musings on Home, a knell of defiance against the massed hordes of modernity.

> *Bring me my bow of burning gold!*
> *Bring me my arrows of desire!*
> *Bring me my spear! O clouds, unfold!*
> *Bring me my chariot of fire!*
>
> *I will not cease from mental fight,*
> *Nor shall my sword sleep in my hand,*
> *Till we have built Jerusalem*
> *In England's green and pleasant land.*

75. RACE WITH THE DEVIL:
A JOURNEY FROM THE HELL OF
HATRED TO THE WELL OF MERCY

"A sound atheist cannot be too careful of the books that he reads." So said C. S. Lewis in his autobiographical apologia, *Surprised by Joy*. These words continue to resonate across the abyss of years that separates me from the abysmal bitterness of my past.

What is true of the atheist is as true of the racist. Looking back into the piteous pits of the hell of hatred that consumed my youth, I can see the role that great Christian writers played in lighting my path out of the darkened depths. Eventually, with their light to guide me, I stumbled out into the dazzling brilliance of Christian day. Looking back along that path, I can see, in my memory's eye, the literary candles that lit the way. There are dozens of candles bearing the name of G. K. Chesterton, of which *Orthodoxy*, *The Everlasting Man*, *The Well and the Shallows* and *The Outline of Sanity* shine forth particularly brightly. Almost as many candles bear the name of Chesterton's great friend, Hilaire Belloc, and several bear the name of John Henry Newman. And, of course, there is the flickering presence of Lewis and Tolkien. These and countless others light the path by which I've traveled.

Long before any of these candles were lit, I found myself groping in the unlit tunnel of racial hatred, the angst and anger of which had all but obliterated the blissful memories of a relatively carefree childhood. Guilty of ignorance, I left my innocence behind and advanced into adolescence with the arrogance of pride and prejudice—boyhood bliss blistered by bitterness.

I grew up in a relatively poor neighbourhood in London's East End at a time when large-scale immigration was causing major demographic changes. The influx of large numbers of Indians and Pakistanis was quite literally changing the face of England, darkening the complexion and adding to the complexity of English life. Perhaps inevitably, the arrival of these immigrants caused a great deal of resentment amongst the indigenous population. Racial tensions were high and violence between white and Asian youths was becoming commonplace. It was in this highly charged atmosphere that I emerged into angry adolescence.

At the age of fifteen I joined the National Front, a new force in British politics which demanded the compulsory repatriation of all non-white immigrants. As a political activist my life revolved around street demonstrations, many of which became violent. I filled my empty head and inflamed my impassioned heart with racist ideology and elitist philosophy. It was at this time that I made what I now consider to be my Faustian pact, i.e., my pact with the Devil; not that I had heard of Faust nor, as an agnostic, did I have any particular belief in the Devil. Nonetheless, I recall making a conscious "wish" that I would give everything if I could work full-time for the National Front. My "wish" was granted and I abandoned my education to devote myself wholeheartedly to becoming a full-time "racial revolutionary."

I never looked back. At the age of sixteen I became editor of *Bulldog*, the newspaper of the Young National Front, and, three years later, became editor of *Nationalism Today*, a "higher brow" ideological journal. At eighteen I became the youngest member of the party's governing body. Whether I believed in him or not, the Devil had certainly been diligent in answering my "wish."

Apart from the racism, the sphere of my bitterness also included a disdain for Catholicism, partly because the terrorists of the IRA were Catholics and partly because I had imbibed the anti-Catholic prejudice of many Englishmen that Catholicism is a "foreign" religion. Such prejudice is deeply rooted in the national psyche, stretching back to the anti-Catholicism of Henry VIII and his English Reformation, to Elizabeth I and the Spanish Armada, to James I and the Gunpowder Plot, and to William of Orange and the so-called "Glorious" Revolution. I knew enough of English history—or, at least, enough of the prejudiced Protestant view of it that I had imbibed in my ignorance—to see Catholicism as an enemy to the Nationhood which, as a racial nationalist, I now espoused with a quasi-religious fervour.

It was, however, in the context of "the Troubles" in Northern Ireland that my anti-Catholicism would reveal itself in its full ugliness. The IRA's bombing campaign was at its height during the 1970s and my hatred of Republican terrorism led to my becoming involved in the volatile politics of Ulster. I joined the Orange Order, a pseudo-masonic secret society whose sole purpose of existence is to oppose "popery," i.e., Catholicism. Technically, although only "Protestants" were allowed to join the Orange Order, any actual belief in God did not appear necessary. As a "Protestant" agnostic I was allowed to join and a friend of mine, an avowed atheist, was also accepted without qualms. Ultimately the only qualification was not a love for Christ but a hatred of the Church.

In October 1978, still only seventeen, I flew to Derry in Northern Ireland to assist in the organization of a National Front march. Tensions were high in the city and, towards the end of the day, riots broke out between the Protestant demonstrators and the police. For the duration of the evening and well into the night, petrol bombs were thrown at the police, Catholic homes were attacked and Catholic-owned shops were looted and destroyed. I had experienced political violence on the streets of England but nothing on the sheer scale of the anger and violence that I experienced in Northern Ireland.

My appetite whetted, I became further embroiled in the politics of Ulster, forging friendships and political alliances with the leaders of the Protestant paramilitary groups, the Ulster Volunteer Force (UVF) and the Ulster Defence Association (UDA). During a secret meeting with the army council of the UVF it was suggested that I use my connections with extremist groups in other parts of the world to open channels for arms smuggling. On another occasion an "active service unit" of the UVF, i.e., a terrorist cell, offered their "services" to me, assuring me of their willingness to assassinate any "targets" that I would like "taken out" and expressing their eagerness to show me their arsenal of weaponry as a mark of their "good faith." I declined their offer, as politely as possible—one does not wish to offend "friends" such as these! They were dangerous times. Within a few years, two of my friends in Northern Ireland had been murdered by the IRA.

Back in England violence continued to erupt at National Front demonstrations. Outside an election meeting in an Indian area of London in 1979, at which I was one of the speakers, a riot ensued in which one demonstrator was killed. A few years later a friend of mine, an elderly man, was killed at another election meeting, though on that occasion I was not present.

Predictably perhaps, it was only a matter of time before my extremist politics brought me into conflict with the law. In 1982, as editor of *Bulldog*, I was convicted under the Race Relations Act for publishing material "likely to incite racial hatred" and was sentenced to six months in prison. The trial made national headlines with the result that I spent much of my sentence in isolation and in solitary confinement because the prison authorities were fearful that my presence might provoke trouble between black and white inmates. Ironically one of the other prisoners in the top security wing was an IRA sympathizer who had been imprisoned for slashing a portrait of Princess Diana with a knife. He and I saw ourselves as "political prisoners," not as mere "common criminals," like the murderers, serving life sentences, who constituted the majority of the other prisoners on the top security wing.

Unrepentant, I continued to edit *Bulldog* following my release and was duly charged once again with offences under the Race Relations Act. On the second occasion I was sentenced to twelve months imprisonment. Thus I spent both my twenty-first and twenty-fifth birthdays behind bars.

During the first of my prison sentences, Auberon Waugh, a well-known writer and son of the great Catholic novelist, Evelyn Waugh, had referred to me as a "wretched youth." How right he was! Wretched and wrecked upon the rock of my own hardness of heart. Years later, when asked by the priest who was instructing me in the Catholic faith to write an essay on my conversion, I began it with the opening lines of John Newton's famous hymn extolling the "amazing grace . . . that saved a wretch like me." Even today, when forced to look candidly into the blackness of my past, I am utterly astonished at the truly amazing grace that somehow managed to take root in the desert of my soul.

How then did the cactus of grace, growing at first unheeded in the desert of my just deserts, become the cataract of life-giving waters washing my sins away in the sacramental grace of confession? How, to put the matter more bluntly and blandly, was I freed from the prison of my sinful convictions? How was I brought from the locked door of my prison cell to the open arms of Mother Church?

With the wisdom of hindsight, I perceive that the seeds of my future conversion were planted as early as 1980 when I was still only nineteen years old. In what barren soil they were planted! At the time I was at the very height, or depth, of my political fanaticism and was indulging the worst excesses of my anti-Catholic prejudices in the dirty waters of Ulster Protestantism. Few could have been further from Holy Mother Church than I.

The seeds were planted in the genuine desire to seek a political and economic alternative to the sins of communism and the cynicism of consumerism. During the confrontations on the streets with my Marxist opponents I was incensed by their suggestion that, as an anti-communist, I was, *ipso facto*, a "storm-trooper of capitalism." I refused to believe that the only alternative to Mammon was Marx. I was convinced that communism was a red herring and that it was possible to have a socially just society without socialism. In my quest to discover such an alternative someone suggested that I read more about the distributist ideas of Belloc and Chesterton. At this juncture one hears echoes once again of Lewis's stricture that "a sound atheist cannot be too careful of the books that he reads," not least because the book to which he was specifically referring was Chesterton's *The Everlasting Man*, a book which would precipitate Lewis's first tentative steps to conversion. In this, at least, I can claim a real parallel between C. S. Lewis and myself. For me, as for him, a book by Chesterton would lead towards conversion. In my case, however, the book which was destined to have such a profound influence was a lesser known book of Chesterton's.

The friend who suggested that I study the distributist ideas of Chesterton informed me that I should buy Chesterton's book, *The Outline of Sanity*, but also that I should read an invaluable essay on the subject, entitled "Reflections on a Rotten Apple," which was to be found in a collection of his essays entitled *The Well and the Shallows*. As he suggested, I purchased these two books and sat down expectantly to read the volume of essays. Imagine my surprise, and my consternation, to discover that *The Well and the Shallows* was, for the most part, a defence of the Catholic faith against various modern attacks upon it. And imagine my confusion when I discovered that I could not fault Chesterton's logic.

The wit and wisdom of Chesterton had pulled the rug out from under my smug prejudices against the Catholic Church. From that moment I began to discover Her as She is, and not as She is alleged to be by Her enemies. I began the journey from the rumour that She was the Whore of Babylon to the realization that She was in fact the Bride of Christ.

It was, however, destined to be a long journey. I was lost in Dante's dark wood, so deeply lost that I had perhaps already strayed into the Inferno. It is a long and arduous climb from there to the foot of Mount Purgatory. I was, however, in good company. If Dante had Virgil, I had Chesterton. He would accompany me faithfully every inch of the way, present always through the pages of his books. I began to devour everything by Chesterton that I could get my hands on, consuming his words with ravenous delight. Through Chesterton I came to know Belloc; then

Lewis; then Newman. During the second prison sentence I first read *The Lord of the Rings* and, though I did not at that time fathom the full mystical depths of the Catholicism in Tolkien's myth, I was aware of its goodness, its objective morality and the well of virtue from which it drew. And, of course, I was aware that Tolkien, like Chesterton, Belloc and Newman, was a Catholic. Why was it that most of my favourite writers were Catholics?

It was during the second prison sentence that I first started to consider myself a Catholic. When, as is standard procedure, I was asked my religion by the prison authorities at the beginning of my sentence, I announced that I was a Catholic. I wasn't of course, at least not technically, but it was my first affirmation of faith, even to myself. A significant landmark had been reached. Another significant landmark during the second prison sentence was my first fumbling efforts at prayer. I am not aware of ever having prayed prior to my arrival at Wormwood Scrubs prison in December 1985, at least not if one discounts the schoolboy prayers recited parrot-fashion to an unknown and unlooked-for God many years earlier during drab and lukewarm school services. Now, in the desolation of my cell, I fumbled my fingers over the beads of a Rosary that someone had sent me. I had no idea how to say it. I did not know the *Hail Mary* or the *Glory Be* and I could not remember the *Lord's Prayer*. Nonetheless, I ad-libbed my way from bead to bead uttering prayers of my own devising, pleading from the depths of my piteous predicament for the faith, hope and love that my mind and heart desired. It was a start, small but significant . . .

My release from prison in 1986 heralded the beginning of the end of my life as a political extremist. Increasingly disillusioned, I extricated myself from the organisation which had been my life, and which had delineated my very *raison d'etre*, for more than a decade. As a fifteen-year-old I had "wished" to give my life to the "cause"; now, in my mid-twenties, I desired only to give my life to Christ. If the Devil had taken my earlier "wish" and had granted it infernally, Christ would take my new-found desire and grant it purgatorially. Having spent the whole of the 1980s in a spiritual arm-wrestle, fought within my heart and my head between the hell of hatred within myself and the well of love promised and poured out by Christ, I finally "came home" to the loving embrace of Holy Mother Church on the Feast of St. Joseph, 1989. Today, I still find myself utterly amazed at the grace that could save a wretch like me.

76. HOPE IS THE SWEETNESS
OF OUR LIFE

Hail Holy Queen, Mother of Mercy,
Our Life, Our Sweetness and Our Hope;
To thee do we cry, poor banished children of Eve;
To thee do we send up our sighs,
Mourning and weeping in this vale of tears . . .

On first appearance it might seem that hope is the least important of the theological virtues. Love, it seems, is far greater. St. Paul tells us that love is the greatest of virtues, and that those who "have not love" are nothing but "a resounding gong or a clanging cymbal," and that those who "have a faith that can move mountains, but have not love" are "nothing." Faith also seems to be greater than hope. Even faith as small as a mustard seed can move mighty mountains. Hope, it seems, is destined to live in the shadow of its more illustrious brethren. It does so in humility, not merely in its willingness to be the servant of the servants of God but in its knowledge that "the last will be first, and the first last."

Like the Trinity at the heart of reality, the theological virtues are One even as they are Three. Like their source, of which they are a reflection and a type, they exhibit the Divine egalitarianism. If, therefore, hope is the least of the virtues it is, paradoxically, the least among equals. This convoluted paradox is exemplified by the fact that hope, as the "least" of the virtues, is the antidote to the poison of pride, the greatest of sins. Hope, as the humblest of the virtues, overthrows pride with humility. Where hope prevails, pride fails. Conversely, where hope is absent, pride prevails. Hopelessness is despair, and despair is the triumph of pride. Hope, the humble David of the virtues, slays the mighty Goliath of the sins.

Hope also has a special place in Pagan mythology, a place reserved for it in Pandora's Box. In point of fact, the box was not Pandora's at all. It belonged to the gods and she had no right to open it. As with Eve's plucking of the forbidden fruit, Pandora, the pagan Eve, opens the forbidden box. The curse of this original sin plagues humanity as, like a cloud of licentious locusts, vice and disease pour forth from the opened casket. Only hope remains in the box, the silver lining in the cloud that overshadows fallen humanity.

There is so much truth to be discovered in the myth of Pandora's Box that it's a shame that "myth" is so often used as a synonym for "lie." A lie is always a lie, but a myth is often true. I happen to believe in Pandora's Box, not merely because of the metaphors and allegories to be found in it, but because I once found myself actually living in it. Many years ago, or once upon a time, I found myself alone in a prison cell. It was during my own dark ages, before I was received into the Catholic Church. I was a leading member of a white supremacist organisation, an angry young man, who had been sentenced to twelve months in prison for "publishing material likely to incite racial hatred." It was during the first days of my sentence. I was in solitary confinement. I was alone; utterly, unspeakably alone. Or so I imagined. I was in fact surrounded by my own vices, my own sins, my own bitterness, my own hates. A plethora of plague-ridden doubts besieged me. My prison cell *was* Pandora's Box.

I had no faith, so I thought. I had no love, except for that love for family and friends that even the publicans and sinners have. And yet, hidden somewhere in the corner of my Pandora's Box was the barest flicker of hope. Someone had sent me a rosary. I had no idea what to do with it. I was not a Catholic, though the reading of Chesterton and Belloc had led me closer to the arms of Mother Church than I realized. I didn't know the *Hail Mary* or the *Apostles' Creed* or the *Glory Be*. I had been taught the *Our Father* many years earlier, at school, but had long since forgotten it. I had never prayed before in my life. What was I to do with this string of beads? It was then, in the midst of "the earthquake, wind and fire" of my sinful passions, that I heard that whispering hope, the "still, small voice of calm" that would exorcise the demons and still the waters of my heart. It was hope that guided my fingers from bead to bead; it was hope that formed the mumbled, barely articulate prayers onto the lips of my mind. It was hope that brought me the first inklings of the peace to be found in Christ. It was hope that taught me humility. It was with this thinnest thread of hope that I climbed downwards to my knees.

That was a long time ago. I have long since learned to say the rosary. I have long since learned to honour the Mother of God with the many anthems sung in her honour. I have come to understand that she is the one who allowed God Himself to repair the damage done by Eve (and Pandora). She is truly "our life, our sweetness, and our hope." And I have learned that hope is the very sweetness of our life.

Turn then, most gracious advocate,
Thine eyes of mercy towards us,
And after this our exile,
Show unto us the blessed fruit of thy womb, Jesus.

ENDNOTES

1   Strictly speaking, this definition of history only considers those things recorded in the past that have survived into the present. Things recorded in the past that have been lost to posterity are not part of "history" according to this definition.

2   It should be noted that everyone's judgment is informed by philosophy and theology. Even atheism is theological, in the sense that the presumption that God does not exist informs the way that the atheist perceives everything else. The "Real Absence" of God is as crucial to the atheist as is His Real Presence to the believer.

3   Humphrey Carpenter (ed.), *The Letters of J. R. R. Tolkien*, London:George Allen & Unwin, 1981, 60.

4   "The Hollow Men.'"

5   From *The Waste Land*. The purist will note that I have subjected the quote to the demands of my own syntax. If this sin taxes his academic sensibilities, I humbly beg his forgiveness!

6   I owe this metaphor to C. S. Lewis.

7   And I owe this one to Belloc.

8   Clare Kirchberger, ed., *The Coasts of the Country: A Treasury of Medieval English Devotional Literature* (Harrison, NY: Roman Catholic Books, undated). This essay was originally published as the preface to a new edition of this title.

9   I am using *eucatastrophe* in a more etymologically defined and refined way than the way in which Tolkien employs and defines it.

10   Since an author's philosophy and theology informs his work, we need to endeavour to understand the author's deepest held beliefs in order to see as he does.

11   Dorothy L. Sayers, *Introductory Papers on Dante*, London, 1954, 114.

12   E. F. Schumacher, *A Guide for the Perplexed*, London, 1977, 158.

13   Hilaire Belloc to Hoffman Nickerson, 13 September 1923, Belloc Collection, Boston College; quoted in Joseph Pearce, *Old Thunder: A Life of Hilaire Belloc*, San Francisco: Ignatius Press, 2002, 230.

14   John Beaumont, *Roads to Rome*, South Bend, Indiana: St. Augustine's Press, 2010.

15   Hilaire Belloc to E. S. P. Haynes, November 8, 1923; quoted in Robert Speaight, *The Life of Hilaire Belloc*, Freeport, New York: Books for Libraries Press, 1970, 377. This particular letter was also quoted by Siegfried Sassoon in a letter to a friend on 29 March 1960, in which he ascribed it erroneously as being written by Belloc to Katherine Asquith. Sassoon, one of the converts documented in the present volume, selected this self-same letter by Belloc as the epigraph to *The Path to Peace: Selected Poems by Siegfried Sassoon*, Worcester: Stanbrook Abbey Press,

1960, and it was also subsequently reproduced in D. Felicitas Corrigan (ed.), *Siegfried Sassoon: Poet's Pilgrimage*, London: Victor Gollancz, 1973, 181–82.

16   G. K. Chesterton, *Charles Dickens*, London: Methuen & Co. Ltd., 15th edn., 1925, 212.

17   These words were actually written by Holbrook Jackson in his *Platitudes in the Making* (1911); Father Brown's reply to the whisky priest is actually Chesterton's riposte to Jackson. See Joseph Pearce, *Wisdom and Innocence: A Life of G. K. Chesterton*, London: Hodder & Stoughton, 1996, 173.

18   John Milton, *Paradise Lost*, 4.75.

19   Maurice Baring, *Have You Anything to Declare?*, London, 1936, 147.

20   G. K. Chesterton, *The Man Who was Thursday*, London: Penguin, 1986 edn., 24.

21   Cardinal Wiseman, *Fabiola: A Tale of the Catacombs*, London: Burns and Oates, 1962 edn., 172.

22   Kurt Weinberg, *Kafkas Dichtungen: Die Travestien des Mythos*, Bern-Munich: Franke, 1963, 257–58.

23   All citations are taken from the Stanley Corngold translation (Bantam edn., 1972).

24   Grimm's *Deutsches Wörterbuch*; Kluge's *Etymologisches Wörterbuch der deutschen Sprache*; both cited in Franz Kafka, *Metamorphosis*, New York: Bantam Classic edn., 1986, 62.

25   James Joyce, *A Portrait of the Artist as a Young Man*, New York: Signet Classic edn., 1991, 23.

26   *Ibid.*, 163.

27   *Ibid.*, 248.

28   *Ibid.*, 223.

29   J. K. Huysmans, *Against the Grain*, New York: Dover Publications, 1971, 126.

30   *Ibid.*, 331.

31   J. K. Huysmans, *Là Bas (Down There)*, New York: Dover Publications, 1972, 222.

32   *Ibid.*, 286.

33   Oscar Wilde, *The Picture of Dorian Gray*, New York: Signet Classic, 1995 edn., 146.

34   Quoted in Maurice Baring, *The Puppet Show of Memory*, London: William Heinemann Ltd., 1930, 260. Baring quotes the epitaph in a French translation from the original Latin.

35   T. S. Eliot, *Selected Prose of T. S. Eliot*, New York: Farrar, Strauss and Giroux, 1988, 99.

36   *Ibid.*, 47–49.

37   *Ibid.*, 64.

38   *Ibid.*

39   Walter Pater, *Studies in the History of the Renaissance*, London: Macmillan, 1873, 210.

40   Eliot, *Selected Prose*, 99.

41   *Ibid.*, 64.

42   *Ibid.*

43   *Ibid.*, 65.

44   *Ibid.*

45   *Ibid.*, 66.

Endnotes

46 Helen Gardner, ed., *The Metaphysical Poets*, London: Penguin Classics, 1957, 19.
47 *Ibid.*
48 Eliot, *Selected Prose*, 100.
49 Gardner, *Metaphysical Poets*, 21.
50 For the textual evidence of Shakespeare's apparent indebtedness to Southwell, see Joseph Pearce's two critical studies, *The Quest for Shakespeare* (San Francisco, Ignatius Press, 2008), and *Through Shakespeare's Eyes* (San Francisco, Ignatius Press, 2010).
51 Gardner, *Metaphysical Poets*, 23–24.
52 *Ibid.*, 27.
53 Biography written by hacks with the purpose of hacking to pieces the reputation of its subject/victim.
54 This essay was written in 2008.
55 Hilaire Belloc, *A Shorter History of England*, London: George G. Harrap & Co., 1934, 7.
56 Hilaire Belloc, *A Conversation with an Angel and Other Essays*, London: Jonathan Cape, 1928, 166–67.
57 Robert Speaight (ed.), *Letters from Hilaire Belloc*, London: Hollis & Carter, 1958, 75.
58 Although I am not including a discussion of his significant contribution to the study of European military history or his work on the French Revolution it should not be assumed that the omission of such discussion signifies a lack of appreciation of his importance in these areas.
59 The finest riposte to Wells's discussion of man's so-called primitive beginnings in the caves was given by G. K. Chesterton in *The Everlasting Man* which was Chesterton's own inimitable response to Wells's *Outline of History*.
60 Quoted in Michael Coren, *The Invisible Man: The Life and Liberties of H. G. Wells*, London: Jonathan Cape, 1993, 32.
61 Roy Campbell, "Books in Britain," *Enquiry*, London, Vol. 2, No. 3 (September 1949); quoted in Joseph Pearce, *Bloomsbury and Beyond: The Friends and Enemies of Roy Campbell*, London: HarperCollins, 2001, 292.
62 Hilaire Belloc, Preface to Dom Hugh G. Bevenot, OSB, *Pagan and Christian Rule*, London: Longmans, Green & Co, 1924, ix.
63 Hilaire Belloc, *A Shorter History of England*, 8.
64 Hilaire Belloc, *Characters of the Reformation*, 13.
65 *Ibid.*, 7.
66 Hilaire Belloc— Elizabeth Belloc Correspondence, Special Collection, Georgetown University, Washington, DC; quoted in Joseph Pearce, *Old Thunder: A Life of Hilaire Belloc*, San Francisco: Ignatius Press, 2002, 229.
67 Hilaire Belloc to Hoffman Nickerson, 13 September 1923, Belloc Collection, Boston College; quoted in Pearce *op. cit.*, 230.
68 Hilaire Belloc, *The Great Heresies*, London: Sheed & Ward, 1938, 85.
69 *Ibid.*, 87.
70 Hilaire Belloc, *Europe and the Faith*, London: Constable & Co, 1920, 192.
71 Hilaire Belloc to Maurice Baring, 4 December 1909; quoted in Robert Speaight, *The Life of Hilaire Belloc*, New York: Books for Libraries Press, 1970, 325.

72 From Belloc's Preface to *The Four Men.*

73 To the pedant we will concede that *The Path to Rome* does not have a preface that is named as such but the prefatory section preceding the text, entitled "Praise of this Book," is indubitably a preface in all but name.

74 It seems that Belloc considered his novel *Belinda* his "best" work after *The Path to Rome,* declaring in a letter to Carl Schmidt that it was "certainly the book of mine which I like best since I wrote *The Path to Rome*"; see Joseph Pearce, *Old Thunder: A Life of Hilaire Belloc,* San Francisco: Ignatius Press, 2002, 234.

75 The words are uttered, of course, by someone impersonating the real professor de Worms, adding to the fun and confusion.

76 *Dial,* November 1924.

77 Roy Campbell, "Mithraic Emblems: Mithras Speaks 2."

78 Roy Campbell, "To the Sun."

79 Quoted in Matthew Hoehn, OSB, ed., *Catholic Authors: Contemporary Biographical Sketches 1930–1947* (Newark, NJ: Saint Mary's Abbey Press, 1947), 104.

80 Evelyn Waugh, *Brideshead Revisited,* New York: Alfred A. Knopf, Everyman's Library edn., 1993.

81 William Shakespeare, *The Merchant of Venice,* 5.1.58–65.

82 *Ibid.,* 5.1. 83–88.

83 For full details of these polls see Joseph Pearce, *Tolkien: Man and Myth* (San Francisco: Ignatius Press / London: HarperCollins, 1998), 1–10.

84 C. S. Lewis, *Surprised by Joy* (repr. London: HarperCollins, 1998), 168.

85 Lewis, *All My Roads Before Me: The Diary of C. S. Lewis, 1922–1927* (New York: Harcourt Brace, 1991), 392.

86 Humphrey Carpenter, *The Inklings* (London: George Allen and Unwin, 1978), 28.

87 *Ibid.,* 30.

88 Walter Hooper, *C. S. Lewis: A Companion and Guide* (London: HarperCollins, 1996), 425.

89 C. S. Lewis, *The Allegory of Love,* cited in Hooper, 424.

90 *Ibid.*

91 Dante, in a letter to his patron, Can Grande della Scala, cited in Dorothy L. Sayers's Introduction to Dante, *The Divine Comedy: Hell* (London: Penguin, 1949), 14–15.

92 J. R. R. Tolkien, Foreword to the second edition of *The Lord of the Rings.*

93 Hooper, *Lewis: Companion and Guide,* 426.

94 Humphrey Carpenter (ed.), *The Letters of J. R. R. Tolkien* (London: George Allen and Unwin, 1981), 172.

95 Humphrey Carpenter, *J. R. R. Tolkien: A Biography* (London: George Allen and Unwin, 1977), 151.

96 This summary is a paraphrased composite of Tolkien's exposition of the nature of myth from a variety of sources, including his essay "On Fairy Stories," his short allegory "Leaf by Niggle," his poem "Mythopoeia," his published letters, his creation myth in *The Silmarillion,* and the accounts given in a number of biographical studies.

97 Carpenter, *The Inklings,* 45.

98 Walter Hooper (ed.), *They Stand Together: The Letters of C. S. Lewis to Arthur Greeves (1914–1963)* (New York: Macmillan, 1979), 427–28.
99 Carpenter, *The Inklings*, 32.
100 Letter from Tolkien to Clyde Kilby, 18 December 1965; Wade Collection, Wheaton College, Wheaton, Illinois. Cited in Pearce, *C. S. Lewis and the Catholic Church*, 36.
101 Carpenter, *J. R. R. Tolkien: A Biography*, 207.
102 *Ibid.*, 204.
103 Carpenter (ed.), *The Letters of J. R. R. Tolkien*, 352.
104 For various quotes from Lewis expressing his opinion that *Till We Have Faces* is his "best book" and the "favourite of all my books," see Hooper, *op. cit.*, 243.
105 Visual Corporation Ltd, *A Film Portrait of J. R. R. Tolkien*, 1992; cited in Pearce, *Tolkien: Man and Myth*, 80.
106 *Ibid.*
107 Humphrey Carpenter, ed., *The Letters of J. R. R. Tolkien* (London: George Allen and Unwin, 1981), pp. 53–54.
108 Lewis, *Surprised by Joy*, London, Fount edn., 1998, 49.
109 Walter Hooper, ed., *C. S. Lewis: Collected Letters, Volume One*, London, 2000, 230–31.
110 Roger Lancelyn Green & Walter Hooper, *C. S. Lewis: A Biography*, London, 2002, 205.
111 Victoria Glendinning, *Edith Sitwell: A Unicorn Among Lions*, London, 1981, 260.
112 Lewis, *Surprised by Joy*, 147–48.
113 *Ibid.*, 166.
114 *Ibid.*, 173.
115 Humphrey Carpenter, *J. R. R. Tolkien: A Biography*, London, 1977, 173.
116 In a panel discussion broadcast by Süddeutscher Rundfunk on 19 September 1983, Causley made the following declaration: "I don't consider myself a Christian. I was brought up in the Christian tradition and I absorbed the Christian culture . . . and I am grateful for that great gift of the Bible to my imaginative process. I wouldn't be without that for anything. But organized religion has always made my blood run cold." Cited in Michael Hanke's essay on Causley's "I am the Great Sun," published in Michael Hanke (ed.), *Fourteen English Sonnets: Critical Essays*, Trier, Germany: Wissenschaftlicher Verlag Trier, 2007, 159–167.
117 Further evidence of the influence of Campbell's poem on Causley's is provided by Causley's emulation of Campbell's hallowing of the boat's fuel. Compare Campbell's *Increase the horse-power of my engine,/ Hallow my petrol ere I go!* with Causley's *". . . The devil's a weasel and travels on diesel/ But I burn the Holy Ghost!"*
118 *The Concise Oxford Dictionary of Current English*, Fifth Edition, Oxford: Oxford University Press, 1964.
119 There is, of course, an irony implicit in this definition considering that empathy derives, via the German *Einfühlung*, from the Greek, *empatheia*, which literally means "passion" or even "partiality." Nonetheless, *empathy*, in its current usage, is distinguished from its near relation, *sympathy*, precisely in the sense that the

former is *dispassionate* and *impartial*. Empathy demands the absence of both sympathy and antipathy in the service of objectivity.

120 Dana Gioia, "The Most Unfashionable Poet Alive: Charles Causley," published in two parts in *Dark Horse* (No. 5/ Summer 1997 & No. 6/Spring 1998). The full article is available on-line: www.danagioia.net/essays/ecausley.htm.

121 The sonnet was originally inspired by a crucifix in Normandy upon which were written the words, "I am the great sun."

122 The same is true of the Christian poet writing non-Christian verse, in which case the poet will consciously objectify the non-Christian position, removing all traces of his own belief in order to play devil's advocate, so to speak.

123 It must be emphasized, however, that the vast majority of poets do not even endeavour to attain the conscious objectivity of which Causley is an undoubted master, in which case we ignore the poet's beliefs at our critical peril.

124 The sonnet also deserves a thorough critical exposition on the level of Biblical theology but the present writer leaves such a reading to the trained theologian.

125 Maurice Baring, *Darby and Joan*, Leipzig: Bernhard Tauchnitz, 1936, 156–5.

126 Quoted in D. M. Thomas, *Solzhenitsyn: A Century in His Life*, London: Little, Brown and Company, 1998, 194.

127 Natalya Reshetovskaya, *Sanya: My Life with Alexander Solzhenitsyn*, Indianapolis/ New York: Bobbs-Merrill Company, Inc., 1975, 115.

128 *The (London) Times*, 23 May, 1983.

129 Joseph Pearce, *Solzhenitsyn: A Soul in Exile*, London: Harper Collins, 1999, 118.

130 Quoted in D. M. Thomas, *Solzhenitsyn: A Century in His Life*, London: Little, Brown and Company, 1998, 194.

131 Pearce, *Solzhenitsyn: A Soul in Exile*, 308.

132 I'm linking these words etymologically in spite of the normal etymology for *crutch* connecting it to the Old English *crycc* which derives from the Old Norse *krykkja*, meaning bend, from which we get *crooked*. An alternative etymology connects *crutch* to the Middle English *crouch*, meaning *cross*, from the Latin *crux*. The Crutched Friars, for instance, were so named for the cross that they wore. They were "crutched" because they were "crossed," not because they were crooked and bent and required the use of a crutch!

133 Regis Martin, *Unmasking the Devil: Dramas of Sin and Grace in the World of Flannery O'Connor*, Ypsilanti, Michigan: Sapientia Press, 2002.

134 Flannery O'Connor, *Mystery and Manners: Occasional Prose*, New York: Farrar, Straus and Giroux, 1974, 118.

135 Fyodor Dostoyevsky, *The Brothers Karamazov*, Spark Educational Publishing (Barnes & Noble Classics), 2004, 107.

136 O'Connor, *Mystery and Manners*, 173.

137 *Ibid.*, 118.

138 Henry Zeiter, *From Lebanon to California: A Marriage of Two Cultures*, Xlibris, 2006.

139 Brian O'Neel, *39 New Saints You Should Know*, Cincinnati, Ohio: Servant Books/Saint Anthony Messenger Press, 2010.

INDEX

City of God, The (St. Augustine), 101
classicism, 49–51, 73, 79–80, 84–6, 143
Cold War, 93, 246
Coleridge, Samuel Taylor, 73, 80–82, 86, 137, 150, 211
Collected Works of G. K. Chesterton (Chesterton), 193
Come Rack! Come Rope! (Benson), 115, 178–80
Common Sense 101: Lessons from G. K. Chesterton (Ahlquist), 193
Companion to Mr. Wells's "Outline of History", A (Belloc), 183
Confessions (Augustine), 164, 169
Confessions of a Convert (Benson), 178
conscious objectification, 273
Consolation of Philosophy, The (Boethius), 102–3
Constable, John, 66
Constantinople, fall of, 55
consumerism, 42, 135, 265, 316
Copernicus, Nicolaus, 22
Cornish separatism, 36
Counter-Reformation, the, 22, 56, 68–70, 82, 151, 195
country music, 11–2
courtly love, 79, 105
Cranmer (Belloc), 185
Crashaw, Richard, 74, 149 et passim,
Creativity, Divine, 7, 28, 231
creativity, human, 7–9, 28–9, 223–4, 231–2
Cromwell, Oliver, 64
Crown of Ireland Act (1542), 112
Cruise of the Nona, The (Belloc), 188
"Crystal, The" (Chesterton), 203
culture of death, 31–4, 148, 187, 305
Cuthbert, St., 71

Da Vinci Code, The (Brown), 118, 297–8

Dagobert II, 298
Daniel, 21
Dante, 24–5, 27, 32–3, 49–51, 52–3, 57, 59, 76, 85, 103–6, 119, 122, 143–4, 158, 208, 217, 222, 253, 287, 291, 299, 301–2, 316
Darby and Joan (Baring), 276
Darwinism, 88, 121, 213
Davidman, Joy, 248
Dawson, Christopher, 137, 182, 195, 267–8, 302
Day-Lewis, Cecil, 214
De doctrina Christiana (Augustine), 221
de Sede, Gerard, 298
Death of a Pope (Read), 115
Decadence, English, 83, 109, 156, 170
Decadence, French, 83, 124, 156, 299
deconstructionism, 33, 73
Defense of the Seven Sacraments (Henry VIII), see *Assertio Septem Sacramentorum* (Henry VIII),
"Defense of Poetry, A" (Shelley), 7, 82
deism, 82
de Mello, Anthony, 258
Denbigh, Countess of (Susan Feilding), 161
Derrida, Jacques, 32
Descartes, René, 14
"Development in Christian Doctrine" (Newman), 164, 168
Devil, the, see Satan
"Diabolist, The" (Chesterton), 126
Diana, Princess, 315
Dickens, Charles, 10, 36, 73, 88, 114–5, 143, 204, 215
distributism, 109, 205
Divina Commedia (Dante), see *Divine Comedy*

Green, Roger Lancelyn, 225
Greene, Dana, 176, 259
Greene, Graham, 113, 114–5, 120,
125, 127, 137, 168, 195, 210,
256, 261, 290–5
Greene, Vivien, 293
Greeves, Arthur, 224
Gregory the Great, St., 71, 103
Grief Observed, A (Lewis), 255
Guide for the Perplexed, A
(Schumacher), 104, 264
Guinness, Alec, 113, 138, 197
Gulag Archipelago, 86, 95, 277, 286
Gulag Archipelago, The
(Solzhenitsyn), 283, 285, 288
Gulliver's Travels (Swift), 133, 135
Gunpowder Plot, 313

Haldane, J. B. S., 249
Hamlet (Shakespeare), 14, 146–7,
152–3
"Ha'nacker Mill" (Belloc), 35, 190
Harfleur, battle of, 35
"Harvard Address, The"
(Solzhenitsyn), 288
Haüy, René Just, 22
Have You Anything to Declare?
(Baring), 117
Hawker, Robert Stephen, 36
Hawthorne, Nathaniel, 43
Heart of the Matter, The (Greene),
293–4
Heaven, 14, 30, 31, 41, 43, 63–4, 66,
69, 76, 81, 85, 102–3, 105, 111,
123, 136, 168, 174, 190, 231–2,
234, 291, 305, 310
Hegelianism, 96, 283
Helbeck of Bannisdale (Ward), 117
Hemingway, Ernest, 301–3
Henrician Affirmation, the, 199
Henry II, 56
Henry V (Shakespeare), 35

Henry VIII, 19, 41, 56, 64, 71,
107–8, 111–2, 147, 199, 201, 313
Herbert, Edward, (Lord Herbert of
Cherbury), 153
Herbert, George, 21, 74, 150–2, 161
Herod, 96, 170
Hind and the Panther, The (Dryden),
158
Hiroshima, 95, 184, 246
*Historia Ecclesiastica Gentis
Anglorum* (Bede), 59
History of England, A (Belloc), 185
History of Middle-earth, The
(Tolkien), 234, 238
Hitler, Adolf, 49, 80, 93, 96, 184,
207
Hobbit, The (Tolkien), 132
"Hollow Men, The" (Eliot), 8, 97,
245, 286, 292
"Home Thoughts from Abroad"
(Browning), 309
Homer, 7, 32, 49–53, 143–4, 157–8
homo superbus, 275
Hooper, Walter, 192, 194, 260
Hopkins, Gerard Manley, 36, 65–6,
81–3, 89–90, 113, 116, 137–8,
150, 152, 165, 168, 210–11, 216,
256
Horace, 143
Houselander, Caryll, 259
Housman, A. E., 150
How the Reformation Happened
(Belloc), 185
Humanae vitae (Paul VI), 259, 263
humanism, 49, 73, 80, 105, 158, 208
Hunt, William Holman, 81
Hussein, Saddam, 295
Huxley, Aldous, 97, 135
Huysmans, Joris Karl, 83, 120,
124–5, 137, 156, 159, 299
"Hymn before Sunrise in the Vale of
Chamouni" (Coleridge), 81